The Iraq War and Democratic Politics

Invading Iraq in 2003 has proved the most deeply divisive political decision of recent times. Despite considerable domestic opposition, the strong reservations of some close allies and the United Nations, and the anger of much of the non-Western world, the United States and Britain still controversially decided that they should commit their forces to toppling Saddam Hussein.

The Iraq War and Democratic Politics contains the work of leading scholars concerned with the political implications of the Iraq War and its relationship to and significance for democracy. The book shuns simplistic analysis to provide a nuanced and critical overview of this key moment in global politics.

Subjects covered include:

- the underlying moral and political issues raised by the war;
- US foreign policy and the Middle East;
- the fundamental dilemmas and contradictions of democratic intervention;
- how the war was perceived in Britain, the EU, Turkey and the United States;
- the immense challenges of creating democracy inside Iraq;
- the influential role of NGOs such as the Iraq Body Count website;
- the legitimacy of the war within international law;
- the relationship between democratic government and intelligence.

Drawing on specialists in the fields of political theory, international relations, international law and the politics of Iraq, this book is essential reading for all those concerned with the future of democracy.

Alex Danchev is Professor of International Relations at the University of Nottingham.

John MacMillan is Senior Lecturer in International Relations at Brunel University.

The Iraq War and Democratic Politics

**Edited by Alex Danchev
and John MacMillan**

LONDON AND NEW YORK

First published 2005
by Routledge
2 Park Square, Milton Park, Abingdon, Oxon OX14 4RN

Simultaneously published in the USA and Canada
by Routledge
270 Madison Ave., New York NY 10016

Routledge is an imprint of the Taylor & Francis Group

Selection and editorial matter © 2005 Alex Danchev and John MacMillan
Individual chapters © 2005 contributors

Typeset in Baskerville by Taylor & Francis Books Ltd
Printed and bound in Great Britain by Antony Rowe Ltd, Chippenham,
Wiltshire.

British Library Cataloguing in Publication Data
A catalogue record for this book is available from the British Library

Library of Congress Cataloging in Publication Data
A catalog record for this book has been requested

ISBN 0–415–35147–2 (hbk)
ISBN 0–415–35148–0 (pbk)

Contents

Contributors

Christopher Brewin is Senior Lecturer in International Relations at Keele University. He is the author of *The European Union and Cyprus* and has a Leverhulme Fellowship to work on Turkey and the European Union.

Alex Danchev is Professor of International Relations at the University of Nottingham. His latest work is a biography of Georges Braque (forthcoming).

Hamit Dardagan is Principal Researcher and Co-founder of Iraq Body Count.

John Dumbrell is Professor of Politics at the University of Leicester. He is the author of several books on US foreign relations, the most recent of which is *President Lyndon Johnson and Soviet Communism* (2004).

Richard Falk was Albert G. Milbank Professor of International Law and Practice at Princeton University from 1961 to 2001, and since 2002 has been Visiting Distinguished Professor, Global Studies, at the University of California–Santa Barbara. His most recent book is *The Great Terror War* (2003).

John Horton is Professor of Political Philosophy at Keele University. He is the author of *Political Obligation*, and has published extensively on contemporary political theory.

Dan Keohane is an Honorary Research Fellow at Keele University. His latest book is *Security in British Politics, 1945–99* (2000).

Yoke-Lian Lee is a research student at Keele University. She is currently completing her thesis on the relationship between sovereignty, gender and human rights.

John MacMillan is Senior Lecturer in International Relations at Brunel University. He writes on the relationship between democracies, peace and war and international theory.

Iftikhar H. Malik is a Professor of History at Bath Spa University College. His two most recent books are *Islam and Modernity* (2004), and *Islam, Globalisation and Modernity: The Tragedy of Bosnia* (2004).

Dan Plesch is a research fellow at the Universities of Keele and London. His latest book is *The Beauty Queens' Guide to World Peace* (2004).

Glen Rangwala is Lecturer in International Politics at the Department of Politics, Cambridge University.

John Sloboda is Professor of Psychology at Keele University, Executive Director of Oxford Research Group, and Co-founder of Iraq Body Count.

Gareth Stansfield is Lecturer in Middle East Politics at the Institute of Arab and Islamic Studies at the University of Exeter, and Associate Fellow of the Middle East Programme at the Royal Institute of International Affairs (Chatham House), London. His latest book (co-authored with Liam Anderson) is *The Future of Iraq: Dictatorship, Democracy or Division?* (2004).

Patrick Thornberry is Professor of International Law at Keele University. His latest books are *Indigenous Peoples and Human Rights* (2002) and (with M. A. Martin Estebanez) *Minority Rights in Europe: A review of the work and standards of Europe* (2004).

John Vogler is Professor of International Relations at Keele University. He has published a number of works on the European Union's external policy, notably *The EU as a Global Actor* (1999), with Charlotte Bretherton.

1 Introduction

The Iraq War and democratic politics[1]

John MacMillan

The Iraq War of 2003 was one of the most controversial wars fought by the United States and the United Kingdom in the post-1945 period and arguably the most radical.

The drive to war generated unprecedented levels of public protest and caused major and often very public diplomatic and political divisions between states, including those within the 'club' of Western democracies. Whilst the war itself was a brief affair, a year after George W. Bush declared the cessation of hostilities there remained a high level of military insurgency, political disorder and uncertainty over the future. The war continues to cast a long shadow over domestic politics and to command high-profile media attention. Yet from the national political institutions that bestowed or withheld their authority for the war, as a value system through which the legitimacy of the war has been contested, to the political model for a post-Saddam Iraq, democracy has been intimately intertwined with the war. It is this relationship, between democracy, democratic politics and the war, that forms the subject matter of this book.

Whilst democracies have used substantial military force with some frequency in recent years – witness for example Somalia, Bosnia, Kosovo, Sierra Leone, East Timor, Afghanistan – Iraq stands out: it disturbs more deeply. The reason for this, ultimately, is the question of the war's 'meaning', for it has brought into much sharper focus a range of existential concerns over the character of democratic politics and foreign policy and the role of democracies in the world at large, concerns which are at root those over the political identity and moral constitution of contemporary democratic states. From the general trend towards 'exceptionalism' in relation to questions of world order and foreign policy and the specific principle of preventive war, through the disregard for a set of international and democratic norms intended to restrain the overwhelming military power of democracies, to the false premises upon which the war was justified and the dehumanization and abuse of 'liberated' Iraqis, the war has severely challenged the authority of the West's claims to moral and political leadership.

During the 1990s foreign policy debate in Western democracies, particularly the United States, could be understood through the paradigm of an embedded if embattled (neo-)liberal internationalism. Sure, the Republican Right maintained a vociferous criticism of Clinton's foreign policy during this period, but it was dissatisfaction with the norms and polices of the liberal internationalist paradigm that provided its common thread. These norms included a greater presumption in favour of multilateralism, which included a recognition in principle (if not necessarily in practice) of the moral authority of the United Nations, and acceptance of certain restraints on the use of force. With Iraq, however, one can clearly see the erosion of this paradigm as a framework for understanding the conduct of democratic state foreign policy. The Rightward turn and radical contestation of the aims and means of US foreign policy provide the ideological context of this shift. A series of new security exigencies most clearly evident in the pervasive fears of 'terror' and the spread of weapons of mass destruction provide a dynamic and fluid political environment in which the limits of the politically possible and morally acceptable have been challenged and pushed back. The long-term repercussions of Western involvement in the Middle East and Islamic worlds, particularly of support for conservative and repressive regimes, are apparent in the rise of violent and committed transnational sub-state revolutionary networks, at the same time as the conceptual and political limitations of Western influence in the region are becoming more apparent. Iraq, then, proffers an abundance of meaning, but of inchoate, disorientating, *twenty-first-century* meaning.

That the world's most powerful democracy, the United States, with the support of a small number of democratic allies including in particular the United Kingdom, chose war as the response most fitting its existential condition and the pursuit of its interests at this juncture forms the central concern of this book. Accordingly, *The Iraq War and Democratic Politics* seeks to understand and interpret this dangerous turn in world politics. Whilst some chapters address the national debates in a number of states including the United States, the United Kingdom, Turkey and the 'European dimension' and offer insights into the evolving nature of the democratic process, others offer analyses and commentaries on the implications of contemporary trends in democratic politics from a number of perspectives.

Democracy and the war

Since the end of the Cold War it is 'democracy' that has provided reaffirmation of the West's political authority through serving as the principal political and ideological rationale for the leadership and hegemony of the world's most powerful group of states, of which the United States is clearly pre-eminent. For many in the West at least, 'democracy' and 'democratic values' are not only key indicators of political legitimacy but also primary mediators of meaning. That is to say, the values, principles and experience of democracy profoundly shape both the perception and judgement of action in the political world. In the case of Iraq, the relationship between democracy and the war is complex, for the war marks both the crisis and the continuation of democracy, the contravention and the extension of democratic politics.

Central to the widespread concern over the Iraq War have been questions of its morality, purpose and motives. Yet whilst Iraq presents these in exceptionally stark terms, these are questions that have beleaguered democracies whenever they have used – or in some instances failed to use – force in the post-Cold-War period. Indeed, a residual lack of consensus on the question of the use of force, apparent in a trail of democratic dilemmas and experimentation, has been costly in both human and political terms. In part, this problem is in the nature of the beast, for underlying democratic discourses of just war, humanitarian intervention and collective security rests the basic truth that war is a brutalizing and dehumanizing activity, whoever undertakes it and for whatever purpose. Yet it is the efforts by democratic states to exercise and/or justify the use of force in terms of higher values – the pursuit of higher goods – than the pursuit of state interests alone that add layers of politically significant complexity and create tensions and dissonance between the proclaimed ends of foreign policy and the means through which these are pursued. Indeed, a review of the use of force by democracies in the post-Cold-War period illustrates the difficulty democracies have faced in using force in a morally and politically satisfactory manner. One repeatedly finds democracies struggling to know how to act and to do so in a way that is in keeping with the values and sensibilities of their societies, which may themselves be deeply divided. That the period has for the most part been marked by an incomparably favourable geo-strategic environment strongly suggests that the reasons for this are internal and conceptual.

One important factor here is cultural: the widely promoted belief in the invincibility and precision of hi-tech weaponry has led to a gross overestimation within certain democratic societies of what war and force can achieve. The promises of swift, clean and decisive military action found in the language of *Top Gun*, surgical strikes and the 'Revolution in Military Affairs' stutter, however, when faced with high-level aerial bombing, unexploded cluster bombs and the realities of street-to-street fighting and house searches. But there has also been a conceptual shift in the use of force that has not been fully appreciated. In the post-Cold-War period, as Charles William Maynes has noted, deterrence – the use of force to prevent states doing bad things outside their borders – has largely been replaced by compellence – the use of force to persuade states to do good things inside their borders. Given the mixed or hybrid nature of the Iraq War, the point that exercised Western politicians throughout the 1990s remains pertinent: are democratic citizenries 'prepared to see their young men and women make the supreme sacrifice in the name of controlling others rather than defending ourselves?'[2] This question is itself part of the long recognized point that hard democratic state structures and capabilities are in certain respects and to a certain extent counter-balanced by their softer societal core – or underbelly – which limits the ability of democratic states to take full advantage of their military superiority.

This is significant, for fundamental to the strategic use of force is that the military instrument be part of a credible political process which, in the case of democracies, is a political process that should properly be concordant with democratic values and principles. That the coupling was poorly made in Iraq is clear from the levels of domestic dissent and from the naive and ethnocentric assumptions about the post-war bases of order in Iraq, readily apparent in the spiral of insurgency and repression under the occupation.

But it is not only Iraq where democracies have failed either to appreciate the political implications of the use of force or to mobilize sufficient political resources to address the post-combat stage. March 2004 witnessed the earlier victims of ethnic cleansing in the UN-administered province of Kosovo become the perpetrators. As one recent analysis has argued, an important contributory factor to this violence has been the policies of the administering authority: the management of the question of Kosovo's final status and the increasing disengagement from the elemental task of socio-economic reconstruction.[3] This seeming inability to match the willingness to intervene with a full commitment to assume the ensuing responsibilities for reconstruction creates the paradoxical condition coined by Michael Ignatieff as *Empire Lite*.[4] Whilst any state, regardless of regime type, would face the problem of synchronizing the military and political momentums of conflict, a series of post-colonial value tensions and political and fiscal constraints create especial problems for democracies in this regard.

The Persian Gulf War of 1990–1 was in several respects as near a model of (liberal-internationalist) paradigmatic simplicity as one is likely to find, but even here costly complexities and dilemmas quickly emerged. The war was waged in response to a clear-cut violation of international law – Iraq's invasion of Kuwait – against which the United States was able to secure a wide-ranging international coalition for the limited political goal of reversing the invasion. Yet an irresponsible confusion of signals proved costly for Iraqis as many were emboldened by George H. W. Bush's statement that another way the fighting could stop would be 'for the Iraqi military and the Iraqi people to take matters into their own hands, to force Saddam Hussein the dictator to step aside'. In the post-war revolt, Saddam Hussein lost control of fourteen of Iraq's eighteen provinces, but the West's clear message to Saddam that it had no intention of assisting the uprising enabled him to brutally re-establish his rule.[5] Politically, behind the scenes in Washington there lurked the question of the US role in the world and the value of its multilateral approach, apparent in disquiet and anxieties that such international action did not benefit the United States in proportion to the role it played, including the sacrifice of American lives while many others paid only financially.[6]

Faced with the break-up of Yugoslavia, particularly following the secession of Bosnia-Herzegovina in February 1992, the West's dilemmas over the use of force became visible for all to see. George H. W. Bush's policies of economic sanctions against Serbia, humanitarian assistance to the Bosnian Muslims and an arms embargo against all parties were criticized by presidential candidate Bill Clinton on the grounds that the United States had a moral responsibility to punish Serb action and to respond more forcefully to reports of ethnic cleansing. In office, however, the Clinton administration's endless meetings on the topic were described by one participant as 'group therapy – an existential debate over what is the role of America'.[7] Protracted discussions were marked, among other things, by an inability to decide whether the administration was facing a civil war or aggression in Bosnia and an unwillingness to act alone or to exert pressure on NATO. Yet it is the episode of Srebrenica, in which the failure to defend a UN safe area led to the genocide of 7,000 Bosnian Muslims, that provides the most bitter testimony to the responsibilities that accompany intervention in foreign affairs and the failure of the democracies to meet them.

The UN-authorized US-led operation in Somalia from 1992 to 1995 clearly illustrated the difficulty of engaging in humanitarian and peace-keeping operations without getting drawn into the wider conflict and towards peace imposition: the 'mission-creep' phenomenon. Somalia also illustrated that in asymmetric warfare there are a number of political factors that may deny the militarily superior party the advantage that might be expected when faced with a determined local opposition. The greater tragedy of Somalia, however, was that it effectively foreclosed intervention in Rwanda in 1994 in what has been called the 'preventable genocide' of 800,000 Tutsis and moderate Hutus.[8]

The NATO air campaign against Serbia in 1999 was justified in terms of the need to demonstrate firm resolve in the face of ethnic cleansing in Kosovo, particularly given the indecision that surrounded Bosnia. Yet the political and military differences between alliance members led to considerable disagreement over how to prosecute the war and very real concerns for the collapse of collective political will. This, in turn, further fuelled unilateralist tendencies within a Pentagon that was displeased with being hamstrung by its European allies. Further, the war highlighted the moral contradictions of bombing civilians in Serbia for the protection of civilians in Kosovo, which was itself a consequence of the political requirements of avoiding US military casualties. For the purposes of the present discussion, however, the most significant feature of the Kosovo War was the willingness of many, particularly on the liberal left, to support a war they recognized as illegal (in terms of public international law) but not illegitimate (in terms of liberal values).[9]

This shift to *legitimacy* over *legality*, discussed by Patrick Thornberry, is indicative of the wider liberal transformative project that has gained momentum in the post-Cold War period and of which the Iraq War is one, albeit extreme, manifestation. Whilst liberals may differ over specific policies, there has been fairly widespread agreement upon the desirability of revising the norms of international society – particularly those pertaining to sovereignty and the use of force – in the light of new geopolitical realities and opportunities. Certainly, it is not only Tony Blair and George W. Bush that have called for the reformulation of democratic norms and practices in this period. At the root of this transformative project is the fundamental liberal dissatisfaction with the world as it is and the belief that the spread of liberal values would be beneficial for the people of the world, which is an assumption critically discussed in this book by John Horton and Yoke-Lian Lee. A core working assumption of this generic liberal position is that a state's domestic political system is the primary determinant of its international behaviour and that the spread of democracy is an important (if not necessarily sufficient) part of the progressive development of the international society of states.

Politically this project is clearly apparent in the pervasiveness of 'good governance' criteria attached to much of the foreign aid given by democratic states and donor agencies to developing and transitional states. It is apparent also in the rhetoric of the Democratic as well as the Republican administrations in the United States: the interest of the Bush administration in the spread of 'democracy' – or 'freedom' – echoes the Clinton's administration's pronouncements on 'democratic enlargement'.[10] Whilst the language of Bush's 'axis of evil' may be formulated for a different domestic political audience, the rhetoric plays to the same democratic antipathy towards dictators as did his predecessors' concern with 'outlaw' or 'backlash' states.[11]

It was the Secretary-General of the United Nations in his report, *An Agenda for Peace* (1992), who asserted that the 'time of absolute sovereignty … has passed',[12] which was a position subsequently endorsed by the Commission on Global Governance's report, *Our Global Neighbourhood* (1995). However, the willingness of many on the liberal left to override sovereignty, by force if necessary, in the name of the 'good' of human rights has established a permissive context within which it is more difficult to criticize others who override sovereignty in the name of other 'goods', such as disarmament or the promotion of democracy. Inevitably, once one departs from the standard of international law one is increasingly arguing between different notions of the good, which is a position that is inherently destabilizing of international order.

In terms of the use of force specifically, one finds little reassurance in the efforts of political leaders to specify the circumstances of its use in the post-Cold War period. President Clinton's PDD-225 dealing with humanitarian operations, along with other statements on the use of force such as the administration's 1995 and 1996 National Security Strategy documents, were based on the Weinberger–Powell doctrines and designed to assuage a Republican Congress in the wake of Somalia, Bosnia and Haiti. Key features of these statements are that political leaders should provide military commanders with clear political objectives that can be translated into clear and attainable military missions, and that there is a clear exit strategy.[13] That these were politically driven is apparent in the comments of many at the time that no war in American history had ever been fought under these conditions. As such, these criteria are best read as reflecting – not overcoming – the deep existential divisions within democracies over their role in the world, serving largely to fudge the issue of when it is politically appropriate and acceptable to commit US military forces.

More recently, Tony Blair's efforts to define the circumstances in which the United Kingdom might use force have become increasingly blurred and politically contingent, illustrating the difficulty of preventing standards of legitimacy and justification for the use of force from slippage once one looks to principles other than sovereignty and non-intervention. During the Kosovo War, Tony Blair delivered his Chicago speech on the 'Doctrine of International Community' in which he sought to establish criteria for deciding when the United Kingdom might intervene in other people's conflicts. The Chicago checklist included the questions: 'first, are we sure of our case?'; 'second, have we exhausted all diplomatic options?'; third, 'are there military operations we can sensibly and prudently undertake'; 'fourth, are we prepared for the long term?'; and fifth, 'do we have national interests involved?' In the case of Iraq, however, as the security and humanitarian rationales for intervention have blurred, the cautionary and graduated response of Chicago has seemingly been thrown to the wind.

In his speech on the threat of global terrorism, delivered in March 2004, Tony Blair looked to his Chicago speech as part of his defence of the Iraq War. Employing some deft rhetorical manoeuvres, Blair first holds out a connection between Iraq and humanitarianism and then puts the war in the context of the wider 'War on Terror'. In cases where states proliferate or acquire weapons of mass destruction 'we surely have a right to prevent the threat materialising; and we surely have a duty and a right to act when a nation's people are subjected to a regime such as Saddam's'. But in seeming contradiction of this latter claim, he also states that 'regime change alone could not be … our justification for war. [Indeed,] our primary purpose was to enforce UN resolutions over Iraq and WMD', which is itself a claim severely strained by the failure of the United Kingdom to deliver the second resolution explicitly authorizing the use of force. Blair's principle appeal in the speech, however, is to the importance of allowing politicians latitude for 'judgement' in cases of imperfect knowledge or moral and political ambivalence. Gone are the attempts to establish exogenous yardsticks for authorizing the use of force, replaced by prophetic warnings that 'this is not a time to err on the side of caution'[14] and the need for the United Nations and international law to change to represent '21st century reality'!

The first of four specific difficulties with this reliance upon political judgement is that in claiming exceptional policing rights the approach risks undermining the international stability that democracy itself requires. In relying upon a preponderance of power relative to the rest of the world to maintain such rights the approach is a provocation to others to counter-balance or supersede the power of the West. The second is that it leads to the over-centralization of power in the executive which is itself corrosive of confidence in the value of the wider democratic process. The third is that it repeats the errors of the Cold War in which one meta-conflict – this time the war on terror rather than anti-communism – is permitted to obscure the specific characteristics of local conflicts, leading to conceptual misperceptions and policy misjudgements. The fourth is the sheer fantasy that one can base the most serious decisions a democracy will take upon the political judgement of the prime minister. Even if one were to accept that the experience of 9/11 authorized a greater degree of executive discretion, the experience of Iraq must surely curtail this on both sides of the Atlantic. In short, this is another doctrine that fails to make the connection between the use of force in foreign policy and the values and principles of democratic politics. In truth, it is not a doctrine but the refusal of doctrine. Some might argue that this is the point, the shrewd manoeuvres of state to maintain a political–strategic latitude and ambiguity over when and where to act. But, sophisticated democratic realists have properly appreciated the need for the state to carry society with it if it is to act effectively in the international arena, even if this requires negotiating an accommodation with the values and principles of liberalism.[15]

Further, the problem of defining the circumstances in which it might be right and proper to resort to force is not helped by the indeterminacy of liberal norms on the use of force. In the case of Iraq, for example, both opponents and supporters of the war were able to marshal the values and symbols of liberal democracy in order to advance their respective cases. In this mêlée, opponents could point to the lack of evidence of weapons of mass destruction (WMD) and the unnecessary and seemingly wilful abandonment of the UN inspection process, whilst supporters pointed to Saddam's track record of WMD development and earlier patterns of behaviour to argue that the only message he would understand would be the clear demonstration of the willingness and capability to use large-scale force. Claims that more time was available for the weapons inspectors to finish their job were countered by the alleged urgency of the threat – manifest for example in the '45 minutes' claim. As opponents appealed to the illegality of the war, supporters disputed this and appealed moreover to the fundamental illegitimacy of a regime that had used chemical weapons against its own people and which ruled through fear and brutality. The neo-imperial characterization of the war was countered with a narrative of 'liberation' and the prospect of democracy and democratization, not only in Iraq but also more widely in the Middle East. Concerns over unilateralism and militarism were countered with the need for new – proactive and preventive – approaches to security in the post 9/11 age. Indeed, that Iraq policy was already a moral and conceptual failure was exploited by those who argued in favour of the use of force to provide a decisive 'solution' to the Iraq question as a way out of the existing UN sanctions regime, with its malign effects on the civilian population and in particular children.

The inability of democratic norms to offer moral clarity is mirrored in the flimsiness of the key procedural and consequentialist arguments of the war's critics, effectively hostages to the political fortunes of US and UK diplomacy and the wildcard of Saddam's armaments programmes. For those opponents of the war who stressed the importance of legality and due process, a second UN resolution specifically authorizing the use of force in Iraq would have severely undermined their position, no matter that such a resolution would have been the product of international power differentials rather than a reflection of any genuine international consensus. That the United States and United Kingdom were unable to secure support for such a resolution is actually rather astonishing, particularly given that they had been set to declare a majority in the Security Council as a moral victory, disregarding any vetoes cast. For those opponents who base their judgements on the outcomes of action, the discovery of chemical or biological weapons in Iraq would have proved awkward, if not completely disabling. Such a discovery would have stolen the force of arguments about the accuracy and manipulation of intelligence and would have strengthened the hand of those advocating further robust 'preventive' action. Again, however, that Saddam did not appear to have resumed his WMD programmes has been cause for surprise well beyond the White House and Downing Street.

Yet despite the continuities and cross-cutting tensions surrounding the use of force in Iraq, the war nevertheless produced an exceptional reaction among the states and citizens of the democratic world, not to mention those beyond. The war as the contravention of democracy is apparent in the determination of Washington to pursue a war of choice in the face of widespread opposition and at the expense of diplomatic and multilateral alternatives. The war was clearly in keeping with the new militarism in US foreign policy heralded in the 2002 National Security Strategy that sanctioned preventive war and its ideological arrogance apparent in its emblematic nature as a statement of intent for Washington's wider reconfiguration of the Middle East. For after Iraq the heat was to be turned on Iran and Syria.

Indeed, the Bush administration had taken the trend for democratic exceptionalism in the post-Cold-War period, that is the willingness of many on the centre–left to exempt themselves from the norms of the society of sovereign states in the service of the norms and values of the liberal community of states, one significant step further. For the most part the liberal left tended to stress that force should be used as a last resort; the importance of multilateral authorization as a check against states acting as judge and jury in their own right; and that the use of force should credibly, in the eyes of (at least democratic) public opinion, serve some higher good.[16] The policies and statements of the Bush administration, however, mark a 'double exceptionalism' in that it has also been willing to disregard the norms and customs of the community of liberal states in the service of US national interests and the ideological objectives of a collection of conservative groups on the political right of US politics (discussed by John Dumbrell, Dan Plesch, Iftikhar Malik and others).

Several chapters in this book discuss the US turn to war. Richard Falk puts the war into the wider historical context and identifies the war as part of a fundamental shift in US geopolitical priorities. Falk probes both the limitations and contradictions of US claims to be bringing democracy to the region and identifies a 'triumphalist litany of normative distortion' in the Bush administration's manipulation of the symbols and language of democracy. Falk also takes issue with the US advocacy of democracy promotion from a policy perspective, arguing that until there is greater national and regional *post-colonial* self-determination, 'including control of indigenous resources, limitation of foreign influence, and the ending of the Palestine struggle with a viable sovereign Palestine', democratization risks strategic defeat through the prospect of fostering greater nationalism or Islamicization. Accordingly, a policy that encouraged greater respect for human rights might be more appropriate for developing moderate politics in the region. One implication of a human rights policy in the region, however, would be the dismantling of what has recently been referred to as the United States' own 'torture archipelago' comprising a series of extraterritorial sites including air bases, floating naval vessels and agreements with third states in the region. In the words of one former CIA agent, 'if you want a serious interrogation, you send a prisoner to Jordan. If you want them to be tortured, you send them to Syria. If you want someone to disappear – never to see them again – you send them to Egypt'.[17] Democracy, then, still has important domestic implications.

John Dumbrell examines the politics of the war in the United States, focusing upon the institutional context and public opinion. In his discussion of the political landscape, the difficulty of appearing unpatriotic in the post-9/11 environment, the influence of neo-conservatism and the widespread perception that Saddam Hussein did present a threat to US security are offset by a 'certain brittleness of support [for the war], evident in a range of areas: worries about going it alone; strong partisan splits; and concerns about dangers in the aftermath of war' that point towards the limited purchase of neo-conservative thinking in American politics and society. Dan Plesch tackles the neo-cons head-on, scrutinizing their arguments about the war both in their own terms and against principles of counter-insurgency developed by the British for the purposes of maintaining order in the empire. Besides showing that the overly ideological arguments of the neo-conservatives actually endanger American interests, he also demonstrates that for some in this group support for democracy is instrumental – a 'weapon of US policy' – rather than a fundamental end in itself.

Dan Keohane's focus is on the British debate for War. Keohane's is a nuanced account of British government policy that sets its support for the war in terms of wider developments within the Labour Party, particularly the centralization of leadership under Tony Blair, and the tensions that afflict the United Kingdom's perception of its international role. Foremost here are those between the Labour Party's pacificist internationalism, Blair's own 'crusading sense of moral righteousness' and the wish to maintain the United Kingdom's reputation both for being a close ally of the United States and for holding influence in Washington.

However, that democratic political systems have also proved effective platforms from which to oppose or refuse participation in the war should not be overlooked. John Vogler considers the European dimension and draws attention to the importance of an anti-war platform in Gerhard Schroeder's re-election campaign and the ability of France to deny the United States and the United Kingdom the veil of legitimacy they sought through a UN second resolution. He notes also the strength of anti-war public opinion across Europe, both East and West, and highlights the division that existed between those governments that supported the war and their citizenries. Perhaps the most dramatic and in certain respects courageous democratic expression of an anti-war stand came from Turkey, in which the parliament denied the United States a second front in the war against Iraq. Christopher Brewin discusses this episode, providing rich contextualization in terms of five different dimensions of democratic legitimacy in Turkey.

This first section of this introduction has itself sought to contextualize the Iraq War in terms of certain wider trends in the development of democratic internationalism and the use of force in the post-Cold-War period. Whilst undoubtedly radical, the war nevertheless marks certain continuities within democratic politics characterized by the residual difficulties democracies face in matching and reconciling the use of force with the moral and political values of democracy, and of recognizing and tackling the complexity and multi-dimensional nature of the problems this presents. Indeed, it is the trend, not the exception, for democracies to pursue value-based or ideological goals through high-profile military action whilst at the same time being underprepared for the political complexities such action generates and failing to assume the post-military political, social and economic responsibilities that such interventions incur.

In this view, Bosnia, Somalia, Rwanda, Kosovo, Iraq represent democratic path-dependencies and conceptual and political failures that are hard to escape. Reluctant and divided publics that may also demand rapid action and quick solutions, opposition parties ready to make political capital out of too much or too little interventionism, a deep-seated post-colonial uncertainty over whether and how to act, a characteristic liberal ethnocentrism, the malign influence of special interest and value-based groups on foreign policy and the sheer conceptual and political complexities of the operating environment all confound the prospects for successfully using force for democratic ends. This unpropitious set of considerations points in two directions. The first is for democracies to be much more sparing in the use of force for the defence of and pursuit of their values abroad. Underlying the political and conceptual problems such action presents is the deeper point that until contemporary liberal democracies have themselves developed a clearer notion of the political and policy implications of their own values and identity in relation to the rest of the world it is necessarily going to be problematic to project or defend them abroad. That this point has not yet been reached is clear in the contested nature of democratic foreign policy in the post-Cold-War period.

Secondly, however, the analysis points to the need for democracies to consider more seriously an extra tier of international institutions that are properly charged and equipped to tackle questions of international security and, in particular, the *causes* of insecurity in the wider world. Indeed, besides analysing the politics of the war in Europe, John Vogler holds out the prospect that the EU is well placed to contribute to this approach, in conjunction with other international agencies. Given the political as well as the economic cost of operations such as Iraq and the damage this adventure has done to the standing of the United States and United Kingdom in the wider world, such an investment in the future ought to be considered good value, as well as holding out the prospect of lessening the dissonance between the use of force and the higher aims and claims of liberal democratic political communities.

Patrick Thornberry, as well as offering an analysis of the legal arguments for war that offers little comfort to the US and British governments, stresses the importance of maintaining respect for international law for two principal reasons. The first is that in embodying the collective will of the society of states it contributes to the reigning in of any exceptionalist tendencies among the

Powers: 'international law may be a mesh with holes in it but it is capable of entrapping the hardiest gladiator'. The second is the more progressive reason that international law actually offers the soundest authority for the liberal trans-formative project that is part and parcel of liberal democracy's political nature. The gradualist, cautious and essentially multilateralist development of interna-tional law provides a much sounder basis for the articulation and expression of the evolving standards of international society than do claims by the powerful to speak on behalf of the world community.

Democratization in Iraq ... and on the home front

The ideological character of the Iraq War was apparent in the claims by the US and British administrations to pursue the democratization of Iraq following the removal of Saddam's regime. Sceptics will, however, protest that the war had little to do with democracy and everything to do with US geo-economic interests in oil and national security interests in establishing a new bridgehead in the region and dealing with the perceived – if seemingly mistaken – threat posed by a hostile regime in possession of WMD. Ideology and interests are, however, interconnected, and whilst a democratic Iraq may not necessarily be essential for US interests, there were several reasons why the United States thought it might be beneficial.

For one thing, an influential body of liberal scholarship maintains that there is a positive correlation between democracy and such political goods as peace and development, thereby offering social scientific underpinning to the general liberal transformative project discussed above.[18] The purported link between democracy and peace has been interpreted rather differently by American neo-conservatives (see Dan Plesch) who argue that the spread of democracy, by force if necessary, is essential for preventing a new generation of 'terrorists' emerging in the region. In the case of Iraq, neo-conservatives believed a friendly demo-cratic regime, particularly one led by an actual friend, in this case Ahmed Chalabi,[19] would be more likely to pursue moderate policies in the region and be better disposed towards accepting the right-wing Israeli and US position that resolution of the Palestinian question requires the prior satisfaction of Israeli security concerns. Further, a democratic Iraq would, the United States believes, become fully integrated in the world capitalist system and provide lucrative opportunities for American business. Finally, 'democracy' serves the wider ideo-logical function of providing both meaning and legitimacy to the war through providing what for domestic and certain international audiences may be thought a laudable goal.

'Democracy', however, is a complex force, and as an instrument of ideology and interests one that is difficult to control. Conceptually it is open to different interpretations – famously, its meaning and political implications are 'essen-tially contested' – and raises difficult questions of 'ownership'. That is to say, whilst some might claim to be masters in the art of democracy and democratic practice their right to impose this is inherently qualified by the nature of the concept, in which political authority ultimately rests locally with a specific people or 'demos'. It is this paradox that sets the defining political tension of the post-war occupation: US desire to control Iraq is both enabled and restricted by its public commitment to a set of political practices and institutions that rely for their credibility upon the relinquishing of authority to the people of Iraq themselves. This is a point that both publics in the democratic West and nationalists in Iraq may well agree upon. Accordingly, whilst the US commitment to a democratic Iraq could change, the public discourse of democracy creates exogenously set standards and expectations that are costly to disappoint.

Gareth Stansfield in this volume draws attention to 'the sheer scale of the task confronting the democracy-builders of the new Iraq', which is a conclusion supported from a number of different theoretical positions and analytical perspectives. Stansfield's discussion of recent literature on 'democratization' provides little comfort to the American nation-builders and his own analysis points to the irreconcilability of the various 'primordial' ethnic identities in the artificial – British – creation that is the Iraqi state. By contrast, Glen Rangwala stresses that the strength of local forces in post-war Iraq is at least in part a function of the politics of the occupation. This has created the troubling situation in which 'the institutions of the state remain weak and the governing power has sought to disperse authority in order to maintain its unchallenged position'. The (over-)centralization of power in the Coalition Provisional Authority has, then, pushed 'real politics' to the locality which has in turn had the effect of providing little incentive for an Iraqi-wide discourse on possible 'national' futures. One set of actors that might be expected to embark on such a discussion are political parties but as Rangwala shows, in the 'New Iraq' these actors 'operate largely as clientelistic networks, rather than as promoters of political programmes'. Nevertheless, Stansfield is surely right when he writes that the costs for Iraqis of failing to find a political solution that is based upon consensus, compromise and a normative understanding not to resort to violent means will be high.

The US democratization of Iraq, then, is from the start compromised by the objective of maintaining influence if not control over the new order. Indeed, a number of authors in this book including Richard Falk, Dan Plesch and Iftikhar Malik point to the historical record of US double standards and realpolitik to cast doubt on present claims of a commitment to democracy in the region. But there is also the question of what form of democracy might be appropriate in an Iraqi context. Of the contemporary Western model,

> to the extent that there is agreement about the definition of democracy, it is generally seen as a combination of institutions (free elections, political rights, independent judiciary), political values (accountability, toleration, participation), and a propitious political context (a wide availability of alternative sources of information, an ability to meet the basic needs of individuals, an educated population).[20]

Conceptually, however, it is worth remembering that historically there have been many models of democracy and that these have developed differently according to context.[21] As such there is no prima facie reason to assume that the form currently prevalent and promoted by the West is either the end point of democratic development or the form most suited to other regions of the world.

John Horton and Yoke Lian-Lee criticize the notion that liberal theory – that is to say, the concern of philosophers such as Brian Barry, John Rawls and Will Kymlicka to formulate idealized theories of justice – has anything to offer the project of political reconstruction in Iraq. They stress instead that political theorists would be better employed in seeking to understand Islamic political ideas and practices and to seek to engage with them, entertaining at least the possibility that 'we' might ourselves have something to learn. Iftikhar Malik also engages with the question of the West's credentials to export democracy, as seen from the standpoint of political Islam. Malik argues that powerful elements within the West disregard at their peril the popular appeal of political Islam in the region as an ideology that resonates against the legacy of exploitation, double standards and orientalism by traditional and neo-colonial powers. The chapter points to the need for Western countries to reform their own anti-democratic practices in the region and to develop greater sensitivity to the local and regional implications of their actions.

Indeed, these points have hardly been lost on Iraqis themselves. As one Iraqi, whose name I shall not repeat owing to the shame he feels, said of his abuse by the US military in the notorious Abu Ghraib Prison, 'The Americans got rid of Saddam Hussein. They told us about democracy and freedom. We are happy about that. Then [the soldiers] did this to … us. I am asking "Is that democracy, is that freedom?" '[22] One prominent Iraqi women's group, whilst not lamenting the collapse of Saddam Hussein's regime, has recorded the rise of violence under the occupation. According to Houzan Mahmoud, from the start abduction, rape, 'honour killings' and domestic violence have become daily occurrences and women cannot now go out alone but must be accompanied by an armed male relative. The Iraqi Governing Council, comprising religious and tribal leaders and nationalists, is said to take little interest in the question of women's rights, the Kurdish nationalist parties too have tried to suppress progressive women's organizations, and the possibility of Sharia law also promises the further subordination of women.[23]

Indeed, that a certain ambivalence marks many discussions of the democratization of Iraq lends itself to a Foucauldian interpretation in which democracy is the discipliner as well the enabler of 'freedom', politics and political participation. This duality is apparent in the way in which democracy sanctions whilst at the same time restricts the reach of formal politics. In this vein, theorists of 'low-intensity democracy', for example, have stressed that the contemporary conceptualization of democracy rests upon the prior separation of economics from politics, apparent in the entrenchment of property rights, which sets parameters for the reach of contemporary democratic politics through excluding the economic realm from democratic control.[24] For many, especially but not only in those states relatively low in the global capitalist hierarchy, this greatly restricts the 'meaning' or relevance of democracy as key spheres of social and political activity are effectively fenced off from the democratic process, particularly under conditions of neo-liberal globalization. This insight, in turn, feeds into the need for post-colonial self-determination as identified by Richard Falk in this volume. Furthermore, this condition tends to produce a certain form of conservative or reactionary democracy marked by the predominance of indigenous conservative groups that typically reach an accommodation with local and foreign business interests and the military, and which receive the support of the middle classes who are themselves fearful of the political claims of the working or agricultural classes. Under these conditions democracy may be void of meaningful content and unable to deliver on the hopes and aspirations that are often attached to it.

Whilst it is too early to know whether and how democracy in Iraq will develop, early indications are that in design at least democracy has been conceived to fit within a prescribed conceptual space. Plans for economic liberalization, for example, appear further developed than those for political liberalization and feature a four-year privatization programme that includes the opening of a large number of Iraq's economic sectors to foreign investment on equal terms with Iraqi investors. Iraq's prospective future membership of the World Trade Organization will confirm this trend. Further, early Iraqi enthusiasm for democracy, manifest in efforts by some staff in state-run institutions to hold elections for managerial posts in the public services, was rebuffed by the Coalition Provisional Authority (CPA). Indeed, this was itself part of the broader US concern over the power of democracy to establish alternative bases of legitimacy as the CPA also cancelled the scheduled local elections at about this time (see Rangwala).

Yet democracy remains a difficult force to control and this vulnerability of the US position as an occupying power in Iraq is itself part of the wider dialectic of empire through democratization. Whilst at the institutional level the United States may indeed be seeking to hold the ring through creating a set of weak central institutions and introducing a form of low-intensity democracy, at the societal level quite the converse is apparent: high-intensity expressions of political consciousness in which groups have recourse to the emancipatory rhetoric of democracy and its thicker-skinned comrade in arms, nationalism, as legitimate discourses for resisting foreign intervention. The degree of commitment that nationalist and religious groups might develop to national democratic structures remains as yet unknown, but it is regrettable that those who have sought to pursue a democratic politics within Iraq – over women's rights or in the workplace – and who were thereby actively engaged in the creation of meaning for democracy in Iraq have not received greater support. After all, democracy needs democrats, people at the grassroots level who can demonstrate that democracy is more than empty rhetoric and can satisfy the real needs and aspirations of real people. Developing the political and moral content of democracy is, of course, by no means only a problem for Iraq.

One civil society actor that has sought to redress what is increasingly recognized as a moral and political failing of the United States and United Kingdom to record the numbers and details of Iraqi civilians killed in the war and the occupation is the Iraq Body Count Project (IBC).[25] Whilst the British and US governments have been concerned with their own losses and have drawn attention to the deaths of Iraqi combatants and insurgents in battle, they have neglected the question of Iraqi civilian deaths. Yet as John Sloboda and Hamit Dardagan, the co-founders of IBC, show here, there is a crying need and enormous demand for this information, reflecting the profound moral point that 'what is now being made manifest at many levels of civil society is a determined refusal to place *any* human being in the category of "the other" '. In practical terms, moreover, if the occupying governments held any intention to assist those families left without a breadwinner, then this information is clearly essential.

Alex Danchev further probes the extent to which democracy in fact characterizes the practices of government, in this case through examining the phenomenon of the *post factum* 'inquiry', specifically the two parliamentary inquiries of the Foreign Affairs Committee and the Intelligence and Security Committee and the quasi-judicial inquiry led by Lord Hutton. Central to the chapter is the relationship between parliamentary government and intelligence, for not only has intelligence been placed centre stage by the war on terror, but also Iraq was a war that appears to have been firmly based on untruth: intelligence and the representation of intelligence about Saddam Hussein's possession of WMD. The portrayal of Blair's inner circle desperately engaged in a political struggle with its parliament, population and media offers rare insight into the nature of government and the character and reflexes of the national security state. The Hutton Inquiry in particular was a major political event in its own right. Its proceedings held up a mirror to the condition of democracy in the United Kingdom. The reflection was unflattering. The evidence it generated will be an important resource in debates on these questions for years to come.

Of democratic politics and the war, then, one finds in certain major respects that democracy has been sold short, most clearly in Iraq but also on the home front. If an authentic democracy does emerge in Iraq then it increasingly appears that this will be despite the occupation, not because of it. But within the belligerents too, the war's immediate origins in the triumph of exceptionalism and the prevalence of fear over reason have weighed the anchor of democracy. Symbolically as well as politically the war has brought into sharp relief the simmering political tensions that have characterized US foreign policy in the post-Cold War period that themselves reflect deeper uncertainties regarding the nation's identity and role in the world.

In reproducing these divisions in the foreign policy realm, not least in instances of the use of force, democracies have effectively engaged in an expensive indulgence, paid for principally by those outside the relatively secure and wealthy democratic zone. Yet whilst the authors of this volume have tended to be highly sceptical about the credentials of democracies to use force or to transplant democracy, democratic values remain central to the development of a more just and humane world. And there is the rub. Democracy is part problem, part answer, but until democracies are better able to recognize and appreciate this then there is little reason to think that they will not continue to squander the moral authority of the ideal. Indeed, it is highly doubtful that democracies will ever be able to deliver upon the aspirations of democracy or higher world order values – or to reconcile their domestic tensions between politics and morality – so long as the politics of democratic internationalism are conducted principally at the national level.

Finally, it is worth reflecting on the expectations put upon democracy in the post-Cold War period. Democracy has been vaunted as a political standard, encapsulation of the political good life, and culmination of humanity's polit-ical–historical evolution. This is quite a burden to carry and democracy has suffered for it. Whilst democracy's standing as a universal meta-concept is a source of genuine as well as hegemonic strength, in embracing so many goods it is, however, prone to lose resonance given the diversity of oppressions and grievances faced by peoples in real political situations, inviting disillusionment and cynicism. Accordingly, there is a need to expand the lexicon of progressive and emancipatory concepts and sentiments in order to avoid the subjectivity and parochialism of available political futures that is the inevitable consequence of pinning one's hopes on democracy alone. To meet this, there is a need for a rebalancing of the predominant moral language of the West, so that democracy sits alongside (rather than subsumes) the claims of cognate goods, namely rich notions of post-colonial self-determination, law, human rights, development and equal respect for peoples.

The war, if it achieves anything, ought at least to chasten the more rampant expressions of democracy. That the war was unpopular with most electorates and that the occupation has continued to disturb the democratic conscience and frustrate the democratic political imagination clearly signal the need for a deeper re-evaluation of the credentials and course of democracy in the first years of the new century. But let us not leave politicians with the responsibility to rise to this challenge, for the answers one is led to may be answers that they cannot reason-ably be expected to give.

Notes and references

1 The editors would like to thank the contributors to this volume for their enthusiasm for the project and Eric Herring, Hidemi Suganami and Rob Walker for their contri-butions to a workshop held at Keele University on 22 October 2003. The author of this introduction would also like to thank Alex Danchev for his very helpful comments on an earlier draft.

2 C.W. Maynes, 'Squandering Triumph: The West Botched the Post-Cold War World', *Foreign Affairs*, 78: 1, 1999, p. 21.

3 See International Crisis Group, *Collapse in Kosovo*, Europe Report No. 155, Pristina, 22 April 2004.

4 M. Ignatieff, *Empire Lite: Nation-Building in Bosnia, Kosovo and Afghanistan*, London: Vintage, 2003.

5 See L. Freedman and E. Karsh, *The Gulf Conflict 1990–1991*, London: Faber and Faber, 1994, pp. 410–27.

6 See D.H. Dunn, 'Anti-Internationalism and the New American Foreign Policy Debate', *Contemporary Security Policy*, 1996: 240–1.

7 See E. Drew, *On the Edge: Inside the Clinton White House*, New York: Simon and Schuster, 1994, p. 147, quoted in R.A. Melanson, *American Foreign Policy Since the Vietnam War: The Search for Consensus from Nixon to Clinton*, 2nd edn, New York: M.E. Sharpe, 1996, p. 257; see also S. Blumenthal, *The Clinton Wars*, London: Viking, 2003, p. 62.

8 See the report commissioned by the Organization for African Unity and undertaken by an International Panel of Eminent Personalities, *Rwanda: The Preventable Genocide*, published on 7 July 2000, available at: <http://www.visiontv.ca/RememberRwanda/Report.pdf> (accessed 15 May 2004).

9 Whilst the war in Kosovo lacked explicit UN authorization, supporters of the campaign argued that the perceived moral stakes, multilateral character of the operation and the fact that the UN Security Council voted by twelve to three against a Russian motion condemning NATO's action accorded authority to the operation. See D. Keohane, 'The Debate on British Policy in Kosovo', *Contemporary Security Policy*, 21: 3, December 2000, p. 89.

10 See D. Brinkley, 'Democratic Enlargement: The Clinton Doctrine', *Foreign Policy*, 106: Spring, 1997; T. Smith, *America's Mission: The United States and the Worldwide Struggle for Democracy in the Twentieth Century*, Princeton, NJ: Princeton University Press, 1994; but see also S. Smith, 'US Democracy Promotion: Critical Questions', in M. Cox, G.J. Ikenberry and T. Inoguchi (eds), *American Democracy Promotion: Impulses, Strategies and Impacts*, Oxford: Oxford University Press, 2000.

11 A. Lake, 'Confronting Backlash States', *Foreign Affairs*, 73: 2, March/April, 1994.

12 But note here the Secretary-General's 'Supplement to An Agenda for Peace' (1995) which observed that the UN possessed very limited capabilities for pursuit of military operations and was generally required to work in partnership with other organizations or states.

13 See E.O. Goldman and L. Berman, 'Engaging the World: First Impressions of the Clinton Foreign Policy Legacy', in C. Campbell and B.A. Rockman (eds), *The Clinton Legacy*, New York: Chatham House, 2000.

14 For a (realist) argument that the policy of containment would have continued to constrain Saddam, see J.J. Mearsheimer and S.M. Walt, 'An Unnecessary War', *Foreign Policy*, 134, January/February, 2004.

15 See, for example, J.H. Rosenthal, *Righteous Realists: Political Realism, Responsible Power, and American Culture in the Nuclear Age*, Baton Rouge, LA: Louisiana State University Press, 1991.

16 For discussion of liberal norms on the use of force see Dan Keohane in this volume and J. MacMillan, 'Liberalism and the Democratic Peace', *Review of International Studies*, 30: 2, 2004.

17 See S. Grey, 'America's Gulag', *New Statesman*, 17 May 2004, p. 24.

18 See, for example, B. Russett and J. Oneal, *Triangulating Peace: Democracy, Interdependence, and International Organizations*, New York: Norton, 2001.

19 Although at the time of writing this relationship has become somewhat more strained.

20 K. Fierlbeck, *Globalizing Democracy*, Manchester: Manchester University Press, 1998, pp. 30–1.

21 See D. Held, *Models of Democracy*, 2nd edn, Cambridge: Cambridge University Press, 1996.

22 See A. Buncombe and J. Huggler, 'The Torture Victim', *Independent*, 6 May 2004, p. 1.

23 See H. Mahmoud, 'An Empty Sort of Freedom', *Guardian*, 8 March 2004.
24 B. Gills, J. Rocamora and R. Wilson (eds), *Low Intensity Democracy: Political Power in the New World Order*, London: Pluto, 1993.
25 Besides the sources cited by Sloboda and Dardagan in this volume, see, for example, 'Iraq: Counting the Cost', *Guardian*, 19 May 2004, p. 23.

2 The global setting

US foreign policy and the
future of the Middle East[1]

Richard Falk

A glimpse of the past reveals the roots of present difficulties and opportunities for political and economic development in the Middle East and North Africa. The region suffers, more than elsewhere except possibly sub-Saharan Africa, from the dilemmas and disruptions of decolonization and the post-colonial geopolitical sequel, this latter being divided into the Cold War phase of super-power rivalry and the subsequent phase of American regional ambitions. Oil, and to a lesser extent the defense of Israel, have prompted the intrusive pursuit of hegemonic ambitions in the region by the United States in recent decades. Africa has suffered from the opposite geopolitical experience: virtual neglect during a period where the post-colonial and post-Cold War dynamics have generated severe civil strife and collapsed states. Unlike oil, the vast mineral resources and the geographic location of Africa do not touch nearly so directly the strategic interests of the dominant states, at least not yet. Furthermore, the combination of severe corruption and the absence of secure governing structures has made Africa less attractive to investors and foreign interveners than the Middle East.

Some observations on historical background and geopolitical foreground

The role of the Middle East

Many of the present difficulties of the Middle East can be traced to the region's colonization in the aftermath of World War I, which included constituting artificial states in the absence of a pre-existing unified national tradition. The collapse of the Ottoman Empire created a vacuum filled by Britain and France in a callous manner epitomized by the betrayal of regional nationalist, ethnic, and tribal leaders, many of whom had sided with the victorious European powers after being led to believe in the prospect of political independence at the end of combat. These historically rooted difficulties include the Balfour Declaration's cynical promise of an ill-defined Jewish homeland in the territory of Palestine that became a British mandate, supposedly 'a sacred trust' for the benefit of the inhabitants as embodied in a set of societal circumstances that existed in 1917.

In the period between the two world wars various degrees of nominal independence were achieved by the states in the Middle East, but the hegemonic role of the European colonial powers persisted.

World War II set in motion a collection of political forces, associated with anti-colonialism and nationalism, that eroded, and then gradually superseded, the European colonial roles in the region, creating a geopolitical vacuum that was immediately filled by the United States, producing a new set of political realities that were somewhat contested later on by Soviet diplomacy. Before quitting Palestine in 1947, Britain left the future of the increasingly tormented Israel/Palestine relationship dangerously unresolved. The Zionist drive for a homeland in Palestine was greatly accelerated by the Holocaust, leading many surviving Jews in Europe to seek safety in Israel, and inducing especially liberal democratic governments in Europe and North America, guilt-ridden by their own tepid responses to the Nazi persecution of the Jews, to support the establishment of an Israeli state in historic Palestine. Leaving aside the controversies surrounding this pivotal moment, the establishment of Israel in 1948 has fueled continuous difficulties for the Arab world, tragedy for the Palestinian people, and an abiding resentment against Europe and North America for seeking to solve 'the Jewish problem' in this imperialist manner.

Additionally, at least since the end of World War II the Middle East has been conceived by the United States as a region of vital strategic and symbolic interests, centering on oil and trade routes, but also connected with geographical considerations, the linkage of Europe, Asia, and Africa, and an overriding commitment to minimize the influence of rival external actors. These developments were reinforced by the weakening and later collapse of the British and French colonial presence in the region, highlighted by such events as the overthrow of the Mossadegh government in 1953 (restoring the Shah, re-privatizing the oil industry, and restructuring foreign ownership of the oil industry in favor of US companies), the diplomatic repudiation by the United States of the 1956 Suez Operation (emphasizing the unwillingness of the US government to defer to France and Britain within a region that had been earlier regarded as their domain), and the defeat of France in the Algeria War in 1962 (pronouncing the end of formal colonial rule at the point of deepest penetration, a dynamic of withdrawal that shook the foundations of the metropolitan state in an unprecedented manner).[2] After these developments the United States became the undisputed hegemonic presence in the region, although Cold War rivalries led to a rise of Soviet influence as a partial balancing force in the Middle East.

Of particular importance in this period was the 1967 Six Day War, disclosing Israel's military prowess, as well as resulting in the occupation of the West Bank and Gaza. From that moment on, Israel's role as a strategic partner for the United States in the region was solidified, which was much more secure with its Pentagon backing than it had been when depending on domestic ethnic and electoral politics in the United States to overcome the concerns of 'realists' in the US foreign policy bureaucracy who had previously argued that US regional interests were being dangerously jeopardized by alienating the Arab elites, especially in the oil-producing countries, as a result of supporting Israel. The risks of alienation and the strategic stakes were dramatized by the events associated with the 1973 Middle East War, especially the worldwide nuclear alert accompanying an announcement of Soviet plans in the midst of the war to send its troops to Egypt to rescue its beleaguered Third Army, and the subsequent OPEC oil embargo producing huge gas lines in the United States, and dramatically higher oil prices. American responses to such a challenge to the economic prosperity of the North were alarmist, even in the public domain. Prominent commentators such as Henry Kissinger and Robert W. Tucker described OPEC pressures at the time as 'economic strangulation' and as providing the West with a *casus belli*, an argument curiously reproducing the much more factually persuasive Japanese economisitic rationale for waging war in 1941 against the United States.

Further reminders of the region's strategic significance, second only to Europe, and perhaps equal to that associated with the defense of Japan, occurred during the late 1970s and 1980s. The Soviet intervention in Afghanistan in late 1979 prompted a hardening of foreign policy by the Carter presidency, including the issuance of Presidential Directive 59, which not only threatened war if the Soviet Union attempted to move militarily westwards from Afghanistan, but was widely understood as conveying the intention of relying on nuclear weapons if that should prove necessary in meeting a Soviet military challenge. These events coincided with the Iranian Revolution, toppling the United States' regional deputy, a leader that Kissinger in his memoirs called that rarest of things, an unconditional ally. This unexpectedly fierce challenge to US regional hegemony in 1979 brought to power a hostile Islamic leadership that depicted the United States as 'the Great Satan,' allegedly responsible for the worst ills of the region. As it turned out, political Islam, with its deep cultural roots, turned out to be a much more formidable and aggressive challenger to US regional ambitions and policies than either the Soviet Union or the oil weapon as wielded by OPEC. The United States tried to regain its position. In 1980 Washington sought to restore a favorable geopolitical situation in the region by encouraging Iraq to attack Iran, which at the time was thought (wrongly) to be a ripe fruit ready to fall, given the revolutionary turmoil that was convulsing the country. This embrace of Saddam Hussein's dictatorial tyranny and expansionist ambitions, besides being a serious tactical failure, has cast a long dark shadow over US efforts to legitimate its hegemonic role in the region, although it has not been nearly as responsible for anti-Americanism as has the unwavering support given to Israel and its expansionism.

Despite the ebb and flow of developments in the Middle East, the continuities of US hegemonic goals in the region have been surprisingly clear and consistent: oil, the security of Israel, and intense opposition to the emergence of any strong state in the region that might be expected to oppose the US role and worldview. Revealingly, American hostility to political Islam does not quite fit this pattern of historical continuity, but represents a shift of attitude following the outcome and ramifications of the Iranian Revolution, and above all the hostage crisis of 1979–81 during which period militants held the US embassy and its staff before the eyes of the world. As everyone now knows, prior to the revolutionary developments in Iran, the CIA had backed Islamic radical groups in Iran and around the world as a counter to feared leftist challenges to the Pahlavi dynasty, a well-documented early instance of blowback.[3] But even in the face of such a major geopolitical setback, the United States persisted with its efforts to enlist the support of political Islam in accordance with the anti-Soviet policy priorities of the Cold War era, and welcomed the formation of a brigade of Islamic volunteers recruited mainly from Arab countries under the leadership of Osama Bin Laden to stiffen the Afghan resistance to Soviet intervention in the 1980s. To this day US relations with Saudi Arabia exhibit an opportunistic willingness to align US business and government interests with the most extreme Islamic regime in the world, a willing-ness admittedly tested somewhat since 9/11 by the Saudi identity of a majority of the attacking hijackers and by a spreading appreciation of the anti-modern and anti-Western zeal of Wahabbism. Despite this background, the US relationship with Saudi Arabia has yet to be seriously questioned except in the most extreme neo-conservative circles.[4] What distinguishes the Middle East from the other regions of the world (compared to Africa, Latin America, Asia) is the unwillingness of the United States to soften, much less renounce, its hegemonic role; or, even more significantly, to act so contrary to world public opinion with respect to a fair resolution of the Israel/Palestine conflict.

This depth of geopolitical engagement, even in the face of a rising tide of anti-American hostility among the peoples of the region, is one manifestation of why the Middle East has been so consistently and bipartisanly treated as 'a strategic vital interest' of the United States, that is, worth fighting and dying for even in 'wars of choice.' At the core of the difficulties that have surfaced recently has been the opportunistic willingness of the United States to prop up authori-tarian and repressive governments that align with the West rather than pursue the goals favored by the overwhelming majority of the citizenry. The refusal to find a satisfactory solution for the Palestinian issue underscores the problem, as the American partisan alignment with Sharon's Israel can only be reconciled with other strategic regional interests if the pro-Western governments in the region are prepared to repress their own people and abandon their priorities. The Islamic movements have resonance because they expose this contradiction, blaming their own elites as corrupt, and the West, especially the United States, as a cruel and unjust enforcer.

This dismal set of realities makes a mockery of the US declared advocacy of democracy for the Arab world. To the extent that democratizing tendencies were institutionalized in the governing structures of the region, the official postures of de facto detachment from the Palestinian struggle would certainly end acquies-cence in the US role in the Middle East. The unsavory political conclusion is this: the US hegemonic role in the Middle East is only tenable so long as the important governments in the region do not reflect the popular will of their peoples, that is, so long as the leadership does not reflect democratic sentiments and embody in governmental policies the spirit behind the right of self-determination. In effect, US regional hegemony presupposes authoritarian states, and collides with the ideological insistence that democracy for the region is the highest US priority.[5]

The end of the Cold War

There were positive and negative consequences of the end of the Cold War for the region. The main positive consequence was to remove the pressure of rival superpower interventions associated with vital strategic stakes, with the consequent dangers of regional conflicts spiraling out of control, generating World War III. Put differently, superpower rivalry is most dangerous in contexts where tactical defeat is unacceptable to either or both sides. This was certainly the case in Europe throughout the Cold War, but mutual restraint was exercised to respect the status quo at moments of crisis. The Middle East was more fluid, without stable governments and lacking sharp boundaries separating East and West, and so could have easily produced an unintended cycle of escalation.

The most immediate negative effect of the end of the Cold War was the relaxation of geopolitical discipline, enabling Saddam Hussein to mount attacks, first, on Iran, and later on neighboring Kuwait, the latter undertaken without gaining clear prior approval from Washington and Moscow, which would almost certainly have been refused due to fears of escalation. The Gulf War of 1991 set the stage for current difficulties, involving the United States as the lead coalition partner in a major regional war, under nominal UN auspices, greatly increasing the US military and diplomatic presence in a manner unacceptable to large segments of Muslim public opinion. These new developments added to strong pre-existing anti-US resentments associated with its support for Israel and its efforts to override the oil policies of OPEC. There is little doubt that this deployment of large numbers of US troops in the vicinity of Islamic holy sites gave rise to the *jihadist* struggle of Osama Bin Laden that initially seemed mainly a reaction to the US presence and accusations of Saudi decadence as expressed by the acquiescence of the royalist leadership to the humiliating posture of subordination to the dictates of Washington. As the Cold War faded, the tide of political Islam rose, initiated by the extraordinary impact of the Iranian Revolution and its aftermath on the entire Islamic world.

The United States emerged from the Cold War with a status of unquestioned global pre-eminence.[6] In the aftermath of the Gulf War, which displayed the US military prowess in relation to hyper-modern wars of choice (recalling the elder Bush's victorious exclamation at the end of the Gulf War—'Thank God, we have finally kicked "the Vietnam Syndrome".'). What was the Vietnam Syndrome except a reluctance, because of an unwillingness to accept American casualties in non-defensive wars associated with strategic interests? The Gulf War, as reinforced by the Kosovo War toward the end of the 1990s, built up a counter-image to the legacy of Vietnam of 'casualty-free wars' (that is, non-defensive, but strategically worthwhile and winnable wars) that could be waged successfully, quickly, and with minimal casualties because of the supposed 'revolution' in US military doctrine and associated technological mastery.

Of course, the Iraq War was presented to the world as if it was a defensive war of necessity, but was correctly understood to be an illegal and imprudent war of choice by most governments and certainly by an overwhelming anti-war mobilization of world public opinion. This line of thinking about the Iraq War was confirmed for all except super-hawks when the alleged Iraqi stockpiles of weapons of mass destruction proved to be non-existent.[7] What became evident in this period of American pre-eminence was the quest for a framework of global security based on what the Pentagon throughout the 1990s described as 'full-spectrum dominance,' a degree of superiority that made *statist* resistance or rivalry futile.[8] By and large governments in the Middle East and North Africa accepted this new arrangement of power relations, resigning themselves to passive and deferential responses to the American geopolitical juggernaut. The extent of this passivity was somewhat disguised for some years by the Oslo Peace Process initiated in 1993, which gave rise to some optimism among Arab leaders that the Palestinian issue could be defused, with resulting economic benefits for the region and a reduced sense of populist frustration on their home fronts. Such a mildly favorable climate of opinion was more than offset by imposing a 'punitive peace' on Iraq in 1991 that maintained sanctions for more than a decade in a manner that caused several hundred thousand deaths among the civilian population, and disclosed both regional impotence in the face of hegemonic policies promoted by Washington along with US insensitivity to the values of life in the Muslim world and to attitudes of deep resentment prevailing on the Arab street. It was in this period that attention began to shift from traditional patterns of conflict among states to the new 'asymmetric' threats posed by non-state actors, starting with bombings in an apartment complex for US troops in Riyadh, the embassy attacks of 1998 in Kenya and Tanzania, and the attack on the USS *Cole* in 2000, and, most of all, the first attempt to destroy the World Trade Center in 1993.[9] But the 1990s were most notable for the emergence of an economistic geopolitics known generally as globalization. Washington sponsored the view that only a rigorous adherence to market logic could produce a vibrant world economy, contending that socialism had been permanently discredited by the Soviet collapse, and that its emphasis on social justice was no longer relevant. The countries of the Middle East and North Africa, unlike Asia and parts of Latin America, were unable to constitute themselves to gain materially from this approach to world economic development. And so the peoples of the region did not enjoy the sorts of gains in living standards being experienced in other parts of the world, which in turn led the governments not only to rely on repression to maintain domestic order, but also to find themselves further discredited as impotent when it came to problem-solving associated with eradicating poverty, promoting development, and sustaining the realities of political independence.[10]

There were other forces at work shaping the background of US political life in the 1990s. Despite global pre-eminence, there were disturbing signs of decay and fragmentation within American society that would play out overseas in later years. The rise of multiculturalism, the absence of the sort of unifying enemy provided by Soviet communism, the frantic capitalist expansionism producing a huge bubble, to the evidence of social disintegration climaxing in the rash of Columbine shootings in prosperous teenage high schools, strains on family structure, and the growing permissiveness of public mores, were among the indications that the United States was at risk of falling apart at home just as it

the mobilization of American patriotism; an insistence on defining the struggle as against 'terrorism' in general, including anti-state movements of self-determination; the enunciation of a vague and self-serving doctrine of pre-emptive war; and the insistence that all governments either join with the United States or be regarded as aligned with 'the enemy.'

The response to the 9/11 attacks was also the occasion for attention given to the *pre-existing* neo-con agenda with greater openness and acknowledgment: above all, launching a high-profile policy of regime change for Iraq, which was followed by recourse to the Iraq War despite the opposition of many traditional allies, in defiance of world public opinion, and without any mandate from the United Nations. The Bush anti-terrorist geopolitics took the unprecedented step of identifying a series of sovereign states as belonging to an 'axis of evil,' implicitly claiming for itself a unilateral right to intervene to prevent these designated countries from acquiring weaponry of mass destruction, promoting the dissemination of 'American values' as the only legitimate basis for governance for *every* country on the planet, and insisting on implementing openly the ideological shift from neo-liberalism to neo-conservatism with respect to relationships between global economic policy and the use of force as an instrument of foreign policy.

In actuality, *globally*, neo-conservatism amounts to the adoption of a more militarist version of neo-liberalism, which includes a renewed avowal of the security role of the United States as global hegemon, or what David Harvey has called 'the new imperialism.'[12] It also involved an abandonment of realism abroad (power tempered by considerations of prudence and a disciplined sense of national interests) and its replacement by a fantastic and ideological presentation of international conflict as an encounter between the forces of good and evil, prompting Tariq Ali to entitle his book on the world conflict as *The Clash of Fundamentalisms*. The neo-conservative turn also meant, despite its own secularity, giving the religious right an influential voice in the shaping of domestic social policy that was without precedent, as well as providing encouragement of a moralistic and paternalist tone in internal debates on such matters as gay marriage, immigration, government support for religious education, tolerance of prayer, and the invocation of the divine in the course of public discourse. President George W. Bush has been such an effective leader for this approach because he so clearly combines the politics of neo-conservatism with the metaphysics of religious conviction.

An important feature of the neo-conservative agenda has been to shift the main geopolitical attention from Europe to the Middle East as the fundamental adjustment called for by the collapse of the Soviet Union. The Middle East is viewed by neo-cons as the main arena of history-making for decades to come. The Iraq War, as initially conceived, should be understood in this light, rather than as a misguided extension of the 'war' against Al Qaeda and global terrorism. US strategic objectives in Iraq were above all to secure a base area that could dominate the region, including the oil reserves and supply lines of the nearby Gulf. The region is also the frontline of the encounter with political Islam, as well as the locus of the Israeli presence. It is by now widely reported that such neo-con stalwarts as Perle, Wolfowitz, Feith, and Kristol have close and deep ties with the far right of the Likud, even leading some interpreters to claim that US policy in the region is driven by the priorities of Israel's own expansionist ambitions in the region. It has been long established that Israel's well-being at the expense of Palestinian rights is a strategic part of the US worldview, turning a blind eye toward Israeli state terrorism and Sharon's aggressive policies associated with the construction of the so-called security wall (seizing an additional 14 percent of the remaining Palestinian territory, which was no more than 22 percent of the original Palestine mandate), unilateral policy of partial disengagement, inflammatory continued expansion of the settlements, and repudiation of all rights of Palestinian refugees.

The differences between neo-liberalism and neo-conservatism should be neither ignored nor exaggerated when it comes to understanding the bearing on the Arab world of this shift.[13] After all, it is possible that neo-liberalism will be revived sooner rather than later, and it should be recalled that the 1990s were notable partly as a soft power approach to global empire, which stimulated a mounting non-violent grassroots resistance to 'globalization' in the Arab world and elsewhere.[14] The Middle East would probably get a bit more breathing room for indigenous political development, but not necessarily, if the Bush leadership is removed. The main vectors of US policy toward the region would not change. These vectors are ultra-stable because US global leadership, whether based on soft or hard power, depends on regionally controlling the oil reserves, pricing, and supply routes, as well as a domestic power base that joins Wall Street and the Pentagon. At the same time, the distribution of domestic political power and influence in the United States inhibits all but the most trivial efforts at Israeli arm-twisting. If the Palestinian struggle is ever to be resolved in a sustainable manner, it will depend on radical changes in the Israeli political climate, undoubtedly encouraged by mounting regional and European pressures for a just solution and a deepening Israeli economic and psycho-political crisis.

Evaluating early twenty-first-century geopolitics in the Middle East

The contradictory impacts of recent ideological, political, and economic developments on the future of the Arab world are difficult to assess, especially given the uncertainties surrounding the intentions and capabilities of the transnational network of political extremists that perpetrated 9/11 and related incidents before and after.[15] At the same time, especially in the aftermath of the Iraq War, it seems more evident than ever that the Middle East, not Europe or Asia, will determine the outcome of this next phase of world politics, specifically the configuring of the violent interplay between US ambitions to establish a system of global security under its control and for its economic and political benefit, and the multiple forms of resistance generated in reaction.

The Iraqi failure

From the perspective of allowing regional forces to enjoy the benefits of political independence, especially with respect to self-determination on a national and regional level, it is important to anchor analysis in the still unresolved experience of the Iraq War. It seems reasonable to conclude that the only outcome in Iraq worse than 'failure' would have been 'success,' as measured and expected by the Bush leadership in Washington. That is to say, a political sequel to the ease of the battlefield victory involving a welcoming population, minimal resistance, and a smooth transition to a pro-Western functioning 'democratic' showcase that fully subscribes to a free market approach to development and adopts an accommodationist approach to the Israeli challenge. Such an outcome would have undoubtedly meant huge construction and development contracts for American companies with clout in Washington, privatization of the oil industry, and the establishment of large US military bases on a permanent basis. It would also have meant the exertion of pressures on Iran, Syria, Yemen, Sudan, Somalia, and Saudi Arabia to move toward 'regime change' resembling the Iraqi outcome, or face the prospect of a more overt US military intervention. It would have proved a vindication of the neo-con prescription to the overwhelming majority of the American electorate, and probably led to a reluctant acquiescence in the Bush approach to world order by most world leaders, although it might have triggered a renewal of geopolitical rivalry either by a greater military buildup by China or through an alliance between major states to contain the United States.

The neo-con hopes were inscribed most authoritatively in the White House document, National Security Strategy of the USA, released in September 2002 during the stage when a new US grand strategy was being formulated. The opening paragraphs of this important statement express, also, a missionary approach to the spread of the American model of governance. President Bush's covering letter presenting the document begins as follows: 'The great struggles of the twentieth century between liberty and totalitarianism ended with a decisive victory for the forces of freedom—*a single sustainable model for national success: freedom, democracy, and free enterprise.*' He went on to say, 'in the twenty-first century, only nations that share a commitment to protecting basic human rights and guaranteeing political and economic freedom will be able to unleash the potential of their people and assure their future prosperity.' At present, no government in the region, with the exception of Israel, and to some extent Turkey, comes close to approximating this exclusive, made-in-Washington, formula for *legitimacy* and *development* from which, it should be emphasized, there are no acceptable alternatives. Significantly, even China is reminded that if it wants success in this American-dominated global setting, then it must sooner or later abandon its current form of state socialism, and is explicitly instructed to forgo the buildup of military capabilities that might be threatening to neighbors and to abandon all plans of geopolitical rivalry with the United States even within its own region.

That kind of arrogant message is reinforced by affirming a US duty and opportunity to use its influence on the global stage to help the peoples of the world to benefit from this model. The report also links this affirmation of

American values with an assertion of 'unparalleled military strength' and a declared intention to sustain indefinitely a posture of dominance that is so commanding as to make challenges futile. While acknowledging the dangers that confront the United States due to the rise of non-state political actors relying on extremist violence, the report also sees the world situation as providing a historic opportunity that allows the United States 'to translate this moment of influence into decades of peace, prosperity, and liberty.' An additional element in this grand strategy is to replace the sort of realist assessment of interests, long the staple of great power foreign policy and the source of moderation in world politics, with an ideological adoption of a moralistic outlook that views the promotion of the US agenda as a vehicle of 'the good' while viewing resistance whether by states or non-states as 'evil.' On this basis, whole countries are denominated as partners in 'the axis of evil' and political movements struggling against oppressive states for elemental rights are criminalized because their armed struggles are automatically classified as 'terrorism.'

Two contradictions are immediately apparent: to the extent that terrorism involves violence against civilian innocents, the far greater cause of civilian death and societal destruction, 'state terrorism,' is exempted from scrutiny; and to the extent that a state fights against an internal adversary beneath the banner of anti-terrorism it has a green light to commit crimes against humanity and to oppress entire populations. It is such a triumphalist litany of normative distortion that might almost certainly have been followed by further wars had a *political* victory in Iraq been achieved.

But what of Iraq failure?[16] Here an assessment cannot but be preliminary. The situation is likely to remain fluid in the extreme for the foreseeable future. The chief architects of the policy in the Pentagon and White House, recalling similar deceptive reassurances year after year during the Vietnam era, are continuing to proclaim success in Iraq, lauding the opening of schools, hospitals, businesses, and treating the resistance as 'terminal,' at worst producing a victory after what Rumsfeld in his famous leaked internal memo of October 2003 called 'a long, hard slog.'[17] Disarmingly, as well, the memo admits in this internal channel exactly the opposite of the official insistence that the overall struggle against Al Qaeda is going well. Rumsfeld in the inimitable jargon of the Beltway writes 'today we lack metrics to know if we are winning or losing the global war on terror.' What is clear at this stage, given the daily number of hostile incidents, increasingly spread around the country, the steady flow of US casualties, and the non-acceptance by the most respected Iraqi leaders of an imposed constitution and managed electoral process, is that a political victory in the Iraq War is far from being achieved, and stands in stark contrast with the ease of the battlefield victory, which was almost the 'cake walk' the proponents of war promised.[18] These developments increasingly make Bush's orchestrated landing to speak in a flight jacket on the American aircraft carrier USS *Abraham Lincoln*, on May 1, 2003, with a banner unfurled behind the presidential rostrum reading 'Mission Accomplished,' seem like a cruel joke.

What does all this mean for the region? For one thing, the difficulties of the occupation tie American hands, especially with regard to any coercive approach to regime change elsewhere in the region. It is possible, however, that if the occupation deteriorates further, and seems to imperil Bush's position, a diversion of some sort will be staged, probably directed at either Syria or Iran in the months ahead. Rumsfeld for one is supposed to believe that the way to handle the failure to solve a problem is to enlarge the matrix so that the problem is redefined against a broader background of options. But more likely, the Iraqi resistance will persist and spread, creating a spectrum of unacceptable outcomes, as well as continuing US casualties: genuine democratizing leading to an Islamic republic under Shi'ia leadership; an imposed democracy resembling the regime change model inducing civil war and/or oppression; allowing the country to split into three parts;[19] a disguised return of Baathist rule; prolonged US occupation, possibly with some shift of formal authority to the United Nations, but resembling the Israeli role in the West Bank and Gaza. Any of these outcomes is likely to reinvigorate 'the Vietnam syndrome,' perhaps renamed 'the Iraq syndrome.' Such a climate of opinion would produce much greater mainstream opposition to any advocacy in the future of wars of choice that required US military occupation of potentially hostile populations.[20] The current policy dilemma for Washington appears to be this: an early US exit from Iraq will end the flow of blood and dollars, but it will highlight the failure of regime change making the effort appear futile or worse, whereas a continuing occupation will keep the issue on the front pages and will involve a continuing pattern of a demoralizing loss of American lives and an expensive diversion of resources and energies. Either precedent would seem likely to inhibit future reliance on 'regime change' as a geopolitical tool.

The impact on the internal politics of the Arab world is hard to gauge, and may be quite variegated from country to country. In the short run, the Iraqi failure lessens the prospects for a wider arc of US interventionary politics in the region, allowing governments to continue with their oppressive means of containing oppositional forces while making nominal gestures of accommodation to the democratization imperative. What is now evident in the Middle East is a heightening of caution, especially a reluctance of leaders to identify too closely with the American project for Iraq, although there are some contrary effects, most notably a willingness of Qaddafi's Libya to re-enter the world community by accepting the terms set by the American gatekeeper.

Overall, however, there is a reluctance by countries in the region to get directly involved in the occupation of Iraq. This attitude was undoubtedly reinforced by the Iraqi refusal in 2003, a posture surprisingly taken even by the Iraqi Governing Council in opposition to its Washington minders, to accept the Turkish offer to send 10,000 soldiers to bolster the coalition's occupying force, an offer that had been extended by Ankara partly to please Washington and partly to improve the prospects that Turkey could avoid an adverse outcome in the Kurdish region of Iraq.

Promoting democracy

What is meant by democracy? The Bush White House, as was the case with the Clinton presidency, verbally associates democracy with a combination of constitutional processes, mainly elections, and market-driven economics. Turkey is portrayed as a democracy even though the Turkish Army is never far removed from ultimate authority, the Kurdish movement for autonomy remains stifled by coercive means, and prison conditions fall far below minimum international standards. Wolfowitz indicated on Turkish TV after the combat phase of the Iraq War ended that he was 'disappointed' that the government in Ankara had not been able to circumvent the rejection by the Turkish parliament of a Washington request that US troops invade Iraq from the north as part of the invasion in March 2003. As in Iraq, the American advocacy of democracy is problematic from a policy perspective. Washington, while cheerleading for democracy in such key countries as Saudi Arabia and Egypt, realizes that implementing the call is almost certain to increase the influence of Islamic forces, and make it rather likely that the governing process will be Islamicized, or will generate the sort of backlash by established secular forces that produced the bloody Algerian Civil War.[21] Unless clarified, it may be quite inappropriate to press for democratization in the Arab world at this time, although it may be constructive to encourage greater respect for human rights as measured by international standards.

Here again the recent swing of US policy bears analysis. With the backgrounding of a regional approach resting on coercive regime change, the White House may be changing course, contenting itself for the present with a rhetorical campaign designed to produce regime reform, not change. In his speech to the National Endowment for Democracy on 6 November 2003, President Bush declared that 'our commitment to democracy is also being tested in the Middle East [as also in China],' which 'must be a focus of American policy for decades to come.' The speech goes on to say that in 'many nations of the Middle East— countries of great strategic importance—democracy has not yet taken root,' but to dismiss as misleading notions that the political culture of the region or the outlook of Islam are 'inhospitable to representative government.' Bush is even explicit in arguing that Middle East governments are beginning to understand 'that military dictatorship and theocratic rule are a straight, smooth highway to nowhere.' Several specific countries are then evaluated from the yardstick of democracy, and there is a welcome acknowledgment that democracy takes time and that it can assume different forms: 'Democratic nations may be constitutional monarchies, federal republics, or parliamentary systems. And working democracies always need time to develop.' But the fanciful idea underlying this vision is of moderate social and political forces contending peacefully, and with a shared commitment to the sort of secular and free market orientation that has taken hold in the West. As Andrew Bacevich has written of the democratization project as applied to the Arab world: 'this effort will encounter protracted, determined and bitter resistance. ... One thing is sure, the effort promises to be a bloody one.'[22]

Earlier experience and present reckonings suggest that the region cannot embrace political moderation of this sort until it achieves *post-colonial* self-determination (nationally and regionally), including control of indigenous resources, limitation of foreign influence, and the ending of the Palestine struggle with a viable sovereign Palestine. Until that time, US advocacy of democratization would likely induce strategic defeat to the extent that its stated aims were realized. There is even less reason to think that the US government would tolerate the sort of nationalism that had been manifest some decades ago in Mossadegh's Iran or the sort of political independence pursued by Nasser's Egypt. Regime change by ideological persuasion and diplomatic pressure is no more coherent as policy, or likely to succeed in practice, than if pursued by wars of choice. Yet such a shift from militarism to diplomacy might be a welcome move. After all, imperial rhetoric is much less harmful in most instances than imperial weapons.

Notes and references

1 This chapter is a greatly revised version of a paper initially presented at a conference 'Struggle and Hope for the Middle East: A future with repetition?' of Princeton University's Transregional Institute for the Study of the Contemporary Middle East, North Africa, and Central Asia, held at Versailles, France, 11–14 December 2003.

2 On the historical context, useful books include S. Kinzer, *All The Shah's Men: An American Coup and the Roots of Middle East Terror*, New York: Wiley, 2003; N. M. Ahmed, *Behind the War on Terror: Western Secret Strategy and the Struggle for Iraq*, Gabriola Island, BC, Canada: New Society, 2003.

3 See Kinzer. For the authoritative account of blowback see C. Johnson, *Blowback: The Costs and Consequences of American Empire*, New York: Metropolitan Books, 2000.

4 See D. Frum and R. Perle, *An End to Evil: How to Win the War on Terror*, New York: Random House, 2003.

5 Such a priority has been emphasized as the main justification for the Iraq War in the light of the failures to find WMD. It was also the centerpiece of President Bush's featured speech to the National Endowment for Democracy on 6 November 2003.

6 Depicted in G. J. Ikenberry (ed.), *America Unrivaled: The Future of the Balance of Power*, Ithaca, NY: Cornell University Press, 2002; A. J. Bacevich, *American Empire: The Realities & Consequences of U.S. Diplomacy*, Cambridge, MA: Harvard University Press, 2002.

7 For telling critiques see Christopher Scheer, Robert Scheer and Lakshmi Chaudry, *The Five Biggest Lies Bush Told Us about Iraq*, New York: Seven Stories Press, 2003; also Ahmed, *Behind the War*, pp. 150–242.

8 See F. Carlucci, R. Hunter and Z. Khalilzad, *Taking Charge: A Bipartisan Report to the President-Elect on Foreign Policy and National Security*, Santa Monica, CA: RAND, 2001; R. Mahajan, *Full Spectrum Dominance: U.S. Power in Iraq and Beyond*, New York: Seven Stories Press, 2003.

9 For one assessment of this background see R. Falk, *The Great Terror War*, Northampton, MA: Olive Branch, 2003; for a wide range of perspectives, M. L. Sifry and C. Cerf (eds.), *The Iraq War Reader: History, Documents, Opinions*, New York: Touchstone, 2003.

10 A world order analysis of globalization is the theme of R. Falk, *Predatory Globalization: A Critique*, Cambridge: Polity Press, 2000.

11 The neo-con agenda and worldview was authoritatively anticipated and most clearly set forth in the report of The New American Century Project entitled 'Rebuilding America's Defenses,' released just prior to the 2000 presidential elections.

12 D. Harvey, *The New Imperialism*, Oxford: Oxford University Press, 2003.

13 For establishment thinking on the range of approaches to global security see the Council on Foreign Policy report, *A New National Security Strategy in an Age of Terrorists*,

Tyrants, and Weapons of Mass Destruction: Three Options Presented as Presidential Speeches, New York: Council on Foreign Relations, 2003.

14 See M. Hardt and A. Negri, *Empire*, Cambridge, MA: Harvard University Press, 2000; S. Aronomwitz and H. Gautney (eds.), *Implicating Empire: Globalization & Resistance in the 21st Century World Order*, New York: Basic Books, 2003.

15 For broad perspectives on the wider implications see N. Chomsky, *Hegemony or Survival: America's Quest for Global Dominance*, New York: Metropolitan, 2003; G. Borradori, *Philosophy in a Time of Terror: Dialogues with Jurgen Habermas and Jacques Derrida*, Chicago: University of Chicago Press, 2003.

16 After adopting a posture of calculated ambiguity, the *New York Times* finally acknowledged 'failure' in a long editorial, 'Iraq Goes Sour,' *New York Times*, 16 November 2003.

17 Dated 16 October 2003.

18 See Scheer, *Five Lies*, pp. 117–45.

19 See L. Gelb, 'A Three-State Solution,' *New York Times*, 25 November 2003.

20 The first Gulf War was notable for limiting war aims so as to avoid such an occupation; the Kosovo intervention, and to some extent the Afghanistan War, were instances where it was reasonable to anticipate a relatively friendly occupation experience, but in both settings the post-conflict reconstruction has been costly in blood and treasure.

21 For an important assessment along these lines, A. J. Rubin, 'US Resistance to Direct Vote Galvanizes Iraq's Shiite Clerics,' *Los Angeles Times*, 3 December 2003.

22 A. J. Bacevich, 'American Dream, Super-Sized,' *Los Angeles Times*, 3 December 2003.

3 Bush's war

The Iraq conflict and American democracy

John Dumbrell

The Iraq War involved major, and profoundly controversial, assertions of unilateral presidential authority. Most Americans supported President George W. Bush's decision to invade a country that had not attacked the United States. Opposition to the war encompassed neither Cabinet resignations nor mass demonstrations on the scale seen in the capital of the United States' fellow-invader, the United Kingdom. American opposition to, and ambivalence about, the war was reflected in public opinion polling; but there was no parallel to some of the extraordinary poll results found in Western Europe. (In February 2003, Saddam Hussein and President George W. Bush were competing for the title of 'greatest threat to world peace'.)[1]

The early years of the twenty-first century saw an apparent widening of the Atlantic Ocean. Nevertheless, contrary to widespread European perceptions, Americans did not spend these years in a state of uninformed, blinkered and super-patriotic sentiment. Bush, after all, was a controversial leader, whose authority stemmed from the most disputed election in modern presidential history. (His 2000 electoral opponent, Al Gore, was one of the first leading Democrats to criticize the administration's line on Iraq in 2002. He described Saddam and his regime as a 'serious threat' to the Middle East, not an 'imminent threat' requiring an American invasion.)[2] Timidity and self-censorship are natural characteristics of times of (real or imagined) national crisis. However, the American political process is sufficiently fragmented and multi-centred to weather such dangers. Congressional debates and actions on the war were disappointing to those participants who sought to limit the president's discretionary authority. For Senator Robert C. Byrd, the West Virginia Democrat who emerged as the leading proponent of legislative war powers, Congress was irresponsibly allowing the executive to attack 'any nation that the President, and the President alone, determines to be a threat'.[3] Yet, the democratic process did at least allow the airing of a variety of views. According to Marcy Katpur (Democrat, Ohio) in the House of Representatives' war debate of September 2002, 'the driving force of this potential war on Iraq is oil'.[4] Similar points apply to the American media. Americans were bombarded with debates on military action – many of them generating little more than earnestness and emotion. William Powers wrote in late March 2003: 'Turn on CNN one recent Sunday, and you could catch Bianca Jagger earnestly debating actor Ron Silver on the merits of war.'[5]

From 9/11 to the gates of Baghdad

Despite the administration's best efforts, it proved difficult, indeed impossible, to establish a clear link between the dictator in Baghdad and the terrorist attacks of 11 September 2001. Bob Woodward reports the Secretary of Defense, Donald Rumsfeld, and his deputy, Paul Wolfowitz, as advocating a strike on Iraq as an immediate response to the 9/11 attacks.[6] Various attempts were made to implicate Saddam, notably via a putative meeting in Prague between Iraqi intelligence personnel and Al Qaeda leaders. As the connection failed to be established, the criticism grew that the administration's fixation on Iraq was harmfully diverting attention from the war on terrorism – primarily, from the war on Al Qaeda, whose religiously inspired leaders were actually fanatical opponents of the secularist regime in Baghdad. President Bush responded by invoking the danger of Saddam's 'terror weapons' being transferred to Al Qaeda – on the basis of any enemy of my enemy being a friend – or possibly of Islamic militants acquiring the weapons by some process of stealth. On 7 October 2002, Bush asked himself the rhetorical question, 'Why be concerned now' (about Iraq)? His answer was that the terror weapons could not be ignored – 'the longer we went, the stronger and bolder Saddam Hussein will become'.[7] There were reports of Al Qaeda activists operating within Iraq. (On 10 March 2003, Christopher Hitchens pointed out that a recent edition of the *New York Times*, containing an article by former President Jimmy Carter declaring that 'efforts to tie Iraq to the 9/11 terrorist attacks have been unconvincing', also carried a report on 'bin Ladenists' in Iraq.)[8] On 6 March, Bush made an explicit connection: 'September the 11th should say to the American people that we are now a battlefield, that weapons of mass destruction in the hands of a terrorist organization could be deployed here at home.' A Gallup poll, published in mid-March, revealed 88 per cent of respondents as believing that Baghdad supported terrorist organizations with plans to attack the United States; 51 per cent averred that Saddam Hussein was implicated personally in the September 2001 attacks.[9]

Direct Baghdad–9/11 connections were tenuous at best. The real significance of 9/11 for the war lay rather in the impact of the attacks on the trajectory of US foreign policy. The Bush administration's pre-9/11 approach was described by its defenders as 'Americanist'. It combined a strong tendency towards unilateralism with a willingness to disengage (notably in the Middle East) from apparently intractable regional conflicts. Unilateralism – the rejection of the Kyoto Protocol on climate change was, of course, the most celebrated example – derived to some degree from the later Clinton years. President Clinton's post-1994 compromises with the Republican Congress had pointed his administration in a unilateralist direction. (It is sometimes forgotten that US actions in Bosnia and Kosovo in the 1990s had no more UN backing than did the 2003 US invasion of Iraq.) Unilateralism also reflected the strongly nationalist mood of Republican foreign policy in the Clinton era. George W. Bush's pre-9/11 policy was also characterized by a preoccupation with rising Chinese power and by a commitment to continuing the military expansion, particularly in relation to National Missile Defense, inherited from the later Clinton era. (Continuities with the Clinton years were obscured by the extreme anti-Clinton partisan rhetoric of the Bushites, with their denigration of their predecessor's supposed penchant for 'foreign policy as social work', and the mantra of ABC – Anything But Clinton.) George W.'s foreign policy was also notable for the very early emergence of high-level splits, notably between Secretary of State Colin Powell's defence of multilateralism and the pugnacious 'Americanism' of Donald Rumsfeld and the Vice-President Richard Cheney. Bush himself appeared committed to a fairly narrow nationalist approach, but also prepared on occasion to speak the language of values and democracy-promotion. The National Security Adviser, Condoleezza Rice, inclined to the Right, certainly over issues like National Missile Defense, but was able also to support pragmatic and compromise positions.[10]

Against this background there emerged the carnage and crimes of 11 September 2001. Many of the features of the 'post-Cold War era' – Vietnam syndrome inhibitions on the use of US military power; apparently galloping economic and cultural globalization; the growing global importance of the Sino-American rivalry – were immediately called into question. In certain respects, 9/11 strengthened the hand of multilateralists within the administration. After all, as the president repeatedly emphasized, international cooperation, especially in intelligence issues, would be a vital ingredient in a successful war on terror. And post-9/11 US policy did involve some moves away from unilateralist-oriented nationalism. Partners were sought in 2002 – surrogates in the case of the Afghanistan Northern Alliance – despite the marginalisation of NATO, and sought again for the war of 2003. On 12 September 2002, contrary to widespread European expectations, Bush began the process of trying to secure UN support for his Iraq policy. The US rejoined UNESCO, while the president promised substantial aid to Africa.

Yet 9/11 also pulled in a different direction, one with important implications for Iraq. The 2001 terrorist attacks effectively destroyed the quasi-isolationist, disengaging tendencies of the early George W. Bush foreign policy. They strengthened the view that US national security could be at risk even in appar-ently remote, irrelevant regions and conflicts. And 9/11 also bolstered the neo-Reaganite agenda of US values and military power projection. Paradoxically, it tended to widen the breach with Europe. Large swathes of European opinion came rather too swiftly to the view that the United States, a country which had been spared the horrors of twentieth-century history, at least on its own soil, was overreacting to the attacks. To much of official Washington, European hesitancy seemed to reflect nothing more than a self-deluding confi-dence that terrorist attacks would be confined to the American side of the Atlantic. In those various ways, 9/11 bolstered the neo-conservative agenda, which clearly included military action, sooner rather than later, in Iraq.

Why exactly was it that the United States invaded Iraq? One very persuasive answer emerges from the foregoing discussion: 9/11 enormously boosted the perception that US national security – not just regional security, Israel's security or general economic security, but American life and limb – was at risk in faraway places. Iraq was not a will-o'-the-wisp like Al Qaeda, but a rogue state which was implicated in destructive weapons programmes and openly supporting terrorist groups in Palestine. Compared with Iran and North Korea, the two other countries on Bush's 2002 'axis of evil' list, Iraq was a relatively manageable target in military terms. The Iraqi regime also stood in a particularly vulnerable position as the violator of the terms of the 1991 Gulf War peace agreement.

Beyond this 'national security' explanation of the invasion, regime change in Baghdad also served other US interests and goals. These included the elimination of a vile abuser of human rights; the possibility of constructing a viable democracy in the region (with, of course, positive implications for the security of Israel); and the enhancement, in secure conditions, of Iraqi oil production. On this last point, the European populist line that the invasion was a simple US oil-grab, was little more than an expression of vapid anti-Americanism. Some British journalists made the deeper point about oil more coherently. According to Anatole Kaletsky, for example, Americans (even the oilmen like Bush and Cheney) were not primarily concerned to deny oil to Total and to pump it in the direction of Exxon. Rather, a boosting of Iraqi oil output, possibly to 10 million barrels a day, would assist Western interests, even if falling oil prices damaged some oil company profits. 'Iraqi production in the hands of a stable pro-Western regime could neutralize the power of Opec and protect the world economy from the oil shocks that have triggered each of the past four recessions.'[11] Such a goal is plausible, though it would be very long term. Iraqi oil reserves are abundant; indeed, they are the second largest proven oil reserves in the world. However, as Evan Davis has underlined, 'Iraq's oil is a long way from being developed.' By some estimates, production, even under optimum conditions, will reach 6 million barrels a day only after 2010. According to Davis, 'the easiest way to secure large supplies of oil from Iraq, and lower prices, would always have been to ignore Saddam's misdeeds, lift sanctions and let the oil flow freely again'.[12] This, essentially, was US policy before 1991, when Saddam was also seen as a valuable lever against fundamentalist Iran.[13]

The 2003 invasion may also plausibly be seen in terms of the US administration's desire, in post-9/11 conditions, to push for a regional solution in the Middle East. General Wesley Clark, a leading Democrat as well as head of NATO forces in Kosovo in 1999, identified a new US regional strategy: the achievement of an anti-terrorist government in Baghdad; the sending of signals to Syria and Iran; the reduction of US forces in Saudi Arabia in order to 'free the Saudis to take stiff measures against their own extremists'; and the Israeli–Palestinian 'road map', with Israeli concessions flowing from the reduced terrorist threat.[14] And the willingness to use military power, allied to a belief in the salutary demonstrative effect of such use, was an important aspect of the neo-conservative agenda.

Pre-emption, neo-conservatism and imperialism

The status of 9/11 as a nodal point in recent international history is not in question. However, massive shifts in the configuration of global power, pointing to sustained US military and economic dominance, were well in train before 2001.[15] Perceptions of the possibilities engendered by American primacy underpinned important aspects of Clinton's later foreign policy.[16] These perceptions were subsequently redirected: firstly after George W. Bush's election victory, and then again after 9/11. Of course, the terrorist attacks provoked a new sense of national vulnerability, and a new concentration on the potency of 'asymmetric' threats. However, the awareness of sheer US power, operating in a unipolar international context, also shaped post-2001 US policy. Nowhere was this awareness more evident than in the emergence of the Bush doctrine of pre-emption. Expressed most clearly in Bush's West Point address of June and in the National Security Strategy of September 2002, this doctrine had huge implications for the international order and for democratic politics in the United States. At West Point, the president argued that, in a world of terrorist threats, Cold War doctrines of containment and deterrence were outmoded. The United States must maintain overwhelming military superiority and must 'confront the worst threats before they emerge'.[17] The National Security Strategy promised to combat 'emerging threats' with 'anticipatory action'.[18] Thus, in June and September 2002, the administration committed itself to the possibility of presidentially adjudicated pre-emptive action against 'emerging' – not imminent – state terrorism.

In both statements of doctrine, the administration emphasized its lack of imperial ambition. 'America has no empire to extend or utopia to establish', Bush declared at West Point. Yet numerous commentators seized on the pre-emption doctrine as an instance of a new imperialist impulse and as an expression of undemocratic presidential high-handedness. Many linked it to the January 2002 Nuclear Posture Review, which had addressed the possibility of a first nuclear strike by the United States against a terrorist 'emerging threat' but possibly non-nuclear state. As former Secretary of State Madeleine Albright observed, Cold War presidents had 'quietly held in reserve' the 'tool' of 'anticipatory self-defense'. Especially in the Western hemisphere, anticipatory self-defence had actually been a stated rationale for military intervention. According to Albright, however, the Bush administration was converting pre-emption into 'the centerpiece of its national security policy'.[19] The undisguised and unapologetic advertising of a discretionary presidential right to pre-empt emerging dangers was novel. The new doctrine also conflated pre-emption (action taken against imminent, proven threats) and prevention (anticipatory attacks on remoter, potential dangers).

To some degree, Bush's doctrine built upon the legal erosions of national sovereignty which had occurred in connection with post-Cold War humanitarian interventions. Richard Haass, Director of Policy Planning at the State Department and certainly not a natural ally of administration unilateralists, went further. Sovereignty, he declared, 'entails obligations'. One is 'not to massacre your own people'. Another is 'not to support terrorism in any way'. If these obligations are not met, others, 'including the US, gain the right to intervene. In the case of terrorism this can even lead to a right of preventive, or peremptory, self-defense.'[20]

Set within the commitment to maintain US military primacy, pre-emption is a central characteristic of the neo-conservative strand in recent US foreign policy. Surrounded as it is by talk of cabals and conspiracies, neo-conservatism deserves a word or two of explication. Originally applied to various former leftists who drifted to the strongly anti-communist, pro-Vietnam War wing of the Democratic Party in the 1960s, the term 'neo-conservatism' became associated with opposition to détente and to President Jimmy Carter's human rights policy in the 1970s, and with the anti-Sovietism of the first Reagan administration. By the 1990s, key neo-conservative institutions included the *Weekly Standard* journal and the Project for the New American Century, founded in 1997. From the mid-1980s, the pages of *The New Republic*, historically a journal of left liberalism, witnessed the incursions and eventual ascendancy of neo-conservative ideas. In the 1990s, neo-conservatives like Michael Ledeen and William Kristol sought to recapture the Republican Party for what they saw as Reaganite authenticity: for an internationalist foreign policy, rooted in the commitment to spread American values and to sustain US military primacy. The movement's views were reflected in the Pentagon's leaked 1992 'no rivals' plan, authored by Paul Wolfowitz and Lewis Libby, under the direction of Richard Cheney, then Defense Secretary. The plan outlined a programme for US hegemony, conceived largely in realist terms, and including a commitment to pre-emption.[21] In 1996, Ledeen announced that 'our foreign policy must be ideological – must be designed to advance freedom'. He continued: 'It is unfashionable to state openly what the rest of the world takes for granted: the superiority of American civilization.'[22] Wolfowitz used the *Weekly Standard* to argue the case for pre-emptive regime change in Iraq in 1997. A year later, an open letter to President Clinton, signed by Wolfowitz and various other neo-conservative figures, called for Saddam's overthrow as a major US priority, as part of a regional solution for the Middle East.[23] In February 2002, William Kristol, testifying to the Senate Foreign Relations Committee, addressed the question, 'What's next in the war on terrorism?' His response was clear: 'The short answer is that Iraq is next.'[24]

Signatories to the 1997 letter to Clinton included Rumsfeld, John Bolton (an Undersecretary in Colin Powell's State Department), and Douglas Feith (Undersecretary of Defense for Policy from 2001). Various other neo-conservatives – such as Lewis Libby, Assistant to Vice-President Cheney – also found their way into influential positions under George W. Bush's administration. The new team, of course, was anything but monolithic. The Rumsfeld–Powell (unilateralist–multilateralist) tensions have already been noted. There are also, however, tensions *within* neo-conservatism: between 'offensive realism' (championed by Bolton) and 'offensive idealism' (the values-promotion defended by Wolfowitz). References to conspiracy are inappropriate; Bush's own position is also difficult to pinpoint.[25] What is undeniable, however, is that – especially after 9/11 – the administration's foreign policy came noticeably to bear the imprint of the neo-conservative approach. And this approach certainly included a values-promoting call for regime change in Iraq, as part of a 'solution' to the troubles of the Middle East.

For many critics of the Iraq policy, the events of early 2003 confirmed a view that Bush's approach *was* the neo-conservative approach, and that the United States was now more or less openly committed to a new imperialism.[26] The administration itself was eager to disavow any imperialist intent. Neo-conservatives outside or on the fringes of the administration were less circumspect. Writers like Charles Krauthammer, Max Boot and Michael Ledeen made approving use of the term '*Pax Americana*', if not 'empire' itself. The Project for the New American Century's report, 'Rebuilding America's Defenses', published shortly before the 2000 presidential elections, identified the main US strategic goal as to 'preserve *Pax Americana*'. Discussing the elder Bush's failure to remove the Baghdad dictator in 1991, the report concluded: 'While the unresolved conflict with Iraq provides the immediate justification, the need for a substantial American force presence in the Gulf transcends the issue of the regime of Saddam Hussein.'[27]

Congress and the war

Congressional debate on the war was concentrated into two phases of intense consideration of White House policy towards Iraq. The first, September to October 2002, culminated in the approval, on 10 October, of the executive's request for legislative authorization to use force. The request was approved 296–133 in the House of Representatives and 77–23 in the Senate. Republicans overwhelmingly backed Bush (48–1 in the Senate and 215–6 in the House); Democrats were fairly neatly divided (29–22 for the resolution in the Senate, 81–127 in the House). The second phase of concentrated congressional attention on the war began in February 2003. Following Bush's 19 March announcement that troops had been engaged, the Senate (unanimously) and the House (392–11) passed resolutions, expressing support for the commander-in-chief. (The unanimous Senate vote was achieved only by dropping President Bush's actual name from the citation.)[28]

Surveying the whole period from September 2002 to March 2003, it is easy to find jeremiads, woeful complaints about Congress neglecting its democratic duties and rolling over before the all-powerful executive. Senator Robert Byrd lamented the post-9/11 'power shift to the executive branch': 'Without a Congress willing to stand up for its prerogatives, and without a public that understands the importance of equal branches of government and separation of powers, that shift will gain the speed of a downhill truck.'[29] As war loomed, Members found it difficult to run the risk of appearing unpatriotic. The early 2003 phase of legislative debate was profoundly affected by a sense of patriotic closure. Congressman Robert Menendez (Democrat, New Jersey): 'Today, there are no Democrats and no Republicans. There are only patriots.' As war was announced, Democratic Senator Richard Rubin of Illinois said: 'Congress leaves the field. We're not even on the side-lines. We're in the stands watching from this point forward.'[30] In the earlier debate the patriotic effect worked a little differently. Members were considering the use of force resolution only one month before the midterm elections. (Senator Byrd mounted an unsuccessful effort to have the vote put back in order to free Members from immediate electoral pressures.) The links between patriotism and self-interest were expressed in a strangely naive fashion by Evan Bayh, Democratic Congressman from Indiana: 'The majority of the American people tend to trust the Republican Party more on issues that involve national security. ... We need to work to improve our image on that score by taking a more aggressive posture with regard to Iraq.'[31]

In many respects, the jeremiads were correct. The war on Iraq was yet another undeclared war, mounted contrary to the spirit if not the letter of the 1973 War Powers Resolution. On 21 March 2003, Bush reported his commitment of forces, 'consistent with the War Powers Resolutions'.[32] The October 2002 authorization was achieved only after incorporation of a reference to legislative war powers, and the need for an explicit presidential report to the effect that all diplomatic channels had been exhausted. However, the final authorization was still exceedingly broad in its scope. It gave the president authority to use military force 'as he determines to be necessary and appropriate' to defend the United States against 'the continuing threat posed by Iraq' and to enforce relevant UN resolutions. As in previous conflicts, references to legislative war powers embodied the requirement to report rather than to 'consult' in any substantive sense. As Joe Biden, Democratic Chairman of the Senate Foreign Relations Committee in 2002 (and ranking Democrat in 2003) put it immediately prior to war, not even Congress's financial powers – much less the 1973 War Powers Resolution or the constitutional power to declare war – were going to have much of an impact. 'The truth of the matter is that the theoretical notion of the check and balance on the administration through the purse strings in war is ephemeral; it doesn't exist.' Once the president decided to go to war – and many Democrats assumed the decision to invade had been made by the end of the Summer of 2002, if not sooner – Congress was 'not going to [deny] the military whatever they need'.[33]

The thrust of Democratic (and some limited Republican) opposition to the war dynamic involved various efforts to advance the case for prioritizing diplomatic and multilateral solutions. Congressional pressure certainly contributed to the administration's September 2002 decision to seek international support for its policies, and also to President Bush's February 2003 undertaking to attempt to secure a second, precipitating, resolution. Legislative willingness to persevere with the weapons inspection process was evidenced in late January 2003, when the Senate Judiciary Committee approved measures to allow former Iraqi scientists to become permanently resident in the United States. In February, six liberal Democratic Members filed a lawsuit in Massachusetts, challenging the White House's legal and constitutional authority to invade Iraq. Republican opposition emerged in the person of Senator Lincoln Chafee, the sole Republican to vote against the use of force authorization in the Senate. In the House, Republican anti-war feeling coalesced around a small group of conservative, libertarian Members, notably Ron Paul of Texas and J. J. Duncan of Tennessee. For Duncan, President George W. Bush, no less than Clinton, was effectively transforming the US military into 'international social workers': 'I am going to oppose spending billions of dollars overseas in Iraq when we've got so many needs here at home.'[34]

As the drums of war beat louder, the overwhelmingly Democratic legion of congressional doubters urged measures at least to keep Iraq as 'the world's problem, not ours', in Joe Biden's words.[35] Demands were made to require a second authorizing, or even war declaration, vote in Congress. Criticisms mounted over the economic consequences of war, and over the administration's reluctance, or inability, to give estimates of likely supplemental appropriations requests. (Congressman Bob Filner, Democrat from California, noted: 'This is the first time in history that we're going to go to war and have a tax cut.')[36] A few anti-war diehards, notably the Democratic Representative from Ohio, Dennis Kucinich, pressed on with resolutions to condemn the administration for taking the United States into war illegally and on the basis of false information.

The congressional die was cast in October 2002, when the Senate (then with a narrow Democratic majority) voted to authorize force. Many Senators and Representatives no doubt supported Bush in the use of force vote as a way of pressuring the UN. However, a vote to authorize war amounted to a vote of trust in presidential discretion. The White House also showed considerable skill in timing its request for force authorization to coincide with the run-up to the November elections. Following the midterm polls, with Republicans controlling both houses, the slide into war proved irresistible.

Public opinion

In the six months or so leading up to the outbreak of war, the American public was consistently interrogated by pollsters on the subject of Iraq. Foreign policy also occupied an unusually high profile in the November 2002 midterm election campaigning. In general, Americans supported the commander-in-chief. The midterms saw impressive Republican gains. For the first time since 1934, the president's party gained House seats in a first presidential term. A 51–49 Democratic majority in the Senate (achieved by the switching of allegiance in 2001 by Senator Jeffords of Vermont) was converted into a 51–49 Republican majority. A majority of GOP state legislators was returned for the first time since President Eisenhower's first term.[37] Polls consistently showed public backing for Bush's foreign policy: 90 per cent of Americans in a February 2003 Gallup poll saw Iraq as a threat to the United States; 66 per cent favoured military action in a CBS poll.[38] Closer examination of public attitudes, however, indicated a certain brittleness of support, evident in a range of areas: worries about going it alone; strong partisan splits; and concerns about dangers in the aftermath of war.

One consistent poll finding was that Americans agreed with Joe Biden's view about Iraq being a world, not just a US, problem. A December 2002 Gallup poll demonstrated that a majority of Americans would support an invasion of Iraq only if the UN gave its backing. Typically, fewer than one-third of poll respondents in early 2003 saw Iraq as an immediate threat to the United States. Among top US foreign policy personnel, Colin Powell, the perceived champion of multilateralism, achieved consistently the highest ratings. Harris polling in late 2002, for example, put public approval of Powell (75 per cent positive) well above that of George W. Bush himself (65 per cent positive). A January 2003 Gallup survey had 60 per cent indicating that they felt that the White House might conceal evidence that contradicted Bush's preferred position. As William Schneider pointed out in March 2003, however, there was no question that Americans saw the Iraq issue in terms of 9/11 and the war on terrorism. Doubts about the imminence of the threat, however, moved the public to an important degree away from the 'with-us-or-against-us' stance of the Bushites.[39]

Polling also revealed stark partisan divisions. At one level, 9/11 operated as a potent national unifying force. As Michael Barone put it in February 2003, on 'September 11, 2001, the United States changed from a nation that believed it was safe to a nation that knew it was in peril.'[40] That President Bush was able to enjoy a post-9/11 'rally round the flag' effect is not in question. However, the 2002 midterm results, though they bucked important historical precedents, saw only an aggregatively narrow, if operationally crucial, shift in the structure of partisan alignment. Virtually all post-election polling showed low levels of support among Democrats for Bush's Iraq policy. In February 2003, for example, 29 per cent of Democratic respondents to Gallup opposed an invasion under any circumstances. Schneider drew attention to the contrast between the partisanship attending the onset of war in March 2003 with George H. W. Bush's experience in 1991. A *New York Times*/CBS poll taken on the first day of the 2003 conflict showed 93 per cent of Republicans, and only 50 per cent of Democrats, expressing approval of George W.'s handling of the issue; the equivalent figures for 1991 were 94 and 81.[41]

The immediate aftermath of the conflict saw confidence in and approval of the administration decline markedly, albeit not catastrophically. A *Newsweek* poll in June 2003 had 38 per cent asserting that the administration had 'purposely misled' the public over weapons of mass destruction. Criticism of the war and its aims increased, again very much in line with partisan ties, as US casualties multiplied.[42]

Just as the structure of US public attitudes was more complex than often perceived in Europe, so it was with the media coverage. The impact, not only of 9/11, but also of the rise of Rupert Murdoch's Fox News Channel to top-rated cable network status needs to be taken into account. Fox offered embarrassing, ultra-right coverage of post-9/11 foreign policy, with Bill O'Reilly berating the 'liberal weanies' who opposed unilateral invasion of Iraq.[43] More generally, however, it was simply not the case that anti-war views were ignored or ridiculed in either the visual or print media. A survey in *Editor and Publisher* magazine found eighteen major newspapers in mid-March 2003 supporting more or less immediate war, and twenty-four still promoting diplomacy and weapons inspections. High-profile opponents of war – the Pope was the highest – had their views widely reported.

The onset of actual combat saw a swift, if not complete, shutting off of varied debate. During the short conflict itself, comment on the quality of war coverage focused on the innovation of having reporters 'embedded' in military units. Some 'embeds' themselves certainly felt that the innovation was dangerous and destructive of journalistic independence.[44]

Conclusion

The main purpose here has been to discuss and question some of the common stereotypes held in Europe of the US political and governmental process as the United States went to war in 2003. The events of 2002–3 set transatlantic allies apart to an extent that was potentially destructive of mature mutual understanding. In its doctrine of pre-emption (presidentially adjudicated and, if need be, unilateral), the Bush administration challenged not only the prerogatives of the US Congress but also the norms and conventions of international law and society. For largely understandable reasons, Congress did not defend its powers with any great efficacy or enthusiasm. Even after 9/11, however, US politics and society remained resiliently complex and pluralistic. Neo-conservatism remained an influential force within the administration, rather than a new and dominant consensus.

Notes and references

1 See *Sunday Times*, 16 February 2003.
2 Quoted in E. Drew, 'War Games in the Senate', *New York Review of Books*, 5 December 2002.
3 *New York Times*, 10 October 2002.
4 *Congressional Quarterly Weekly Report*, 28 September 2002.
5 W. Powers, 'Darkness and Light', *National Journal*, 22 March 2003.
6 B. Woodward, *Bush at War*, New York: Simon and Schuster, 2002, p. 49.
7 Quoted in A. Lewis, 'Bush and Iraq', *New York Review of Books*, 7 November 2002.
8 C. Hitchens, *Regime Change*, London: Penguin, 2003, p. 79.
9 Quoted in W. Schneider, 'War Has Its Reasons', *National Journal*, 22 March 2003.
10 See J. Dumbrell, 'Unilateralism and "America First"? George W. Bush's Foreign Policy', *Political Quarterly*, 73, 2002, pp. 279–87; T. Carothers, 'Promoting Democracy and Fighting Terror', *Foreign Affairs*, 82, 2003, pp. 84–97.
11 *The Times*, 20 March 2003.
12 S. Beck and M. Downing (eds), *The Battle for Iraq*, London: BBC, 2003, p. 176. See also J. Maggs, 'The Matter of Oil', *National Journal*, 15 March 2003.
13 The best study of pre-1991 US policy towards Iraq is B. W. Jentleson, *With Friends Like These: Reagan, Bush and Saddam, 1982–1990*, New York: Norton, 1994.
14 'Military Briefing', *The Times*, 1 May 2003.
15 See M. Cox, 'American Power, before and after 11 September: Dizzy with Success?', *International Affairs*, 78, 2002, pp. 261–76.

16 See J. Dumbrell, 'Was there a Clinton Doctrine? President Clinton's Foreign Policy Reconsidered', *Diplomacy and Statecraft*, 13, 2002, pp. 43–56.

17 The address can be consulted online. Available HTTP: <www.whitehouse.gov/news/releases/2002/06/2002061–3.html> (accessed 1 December 2003).

18 Online. Available HTTP: <www.whitehouse.gov/nssall.html> (accessed 1 December 2003).

19 M. K. Albright, 'Bridges, Bombs or Bluster?', *Foreign Affairs*, 82, 2003, pp. 2–19.

20 Quoted in H. Young, 'A New Imperialism Cooked up over a Texan Barbecue', *Guardian*, 2 April 2002.

21 See J. Petras and M. Morley, *Empire or Republic? American Global Power and Domestic Decay*, New York: Routledge, 1995, pp. 14–21.

22 M. Ledeen, 'A Republican Contract with the World', *The Weekly Standard*, 13 May 1996.

23 J. Kosterlitz, 'The Neoconservative Moment', *National Journal*, 17 May 2003.

24 Online. Available HTTP: <www.newamericancentury.org/foreignrelations-020702.htm> (accessed 1 December 2003).

25 See M. J. Mazarr, 'George W. Bush, Idealist', *International Affairs*, 79, 2003, pp. 503–22; M. Lind, 'The Texas nexus', *Prospect*, April 2003.

26 For various perspectives, see G. J. Ikenberry, 'America's Imperial Ambition', *Foreign Affairs*, 81, 2002, pp. 44–60; N. Mailer, 'Only in America', *New York Review of Books*, 27 March 2003; J. B. Foster, 'The New Age of Imperialism', *Monthly Review*, 55, 2003, pp. 1–14.

27 Quoted in Foster, 'New Age', pp. 10–11.

28 See *Congressional Quarterly Weekly Report*, 22 March 2003.

29 Quoted in K. Victor, 'Congress in Eclipse', *National Journal*, 5 April 2003 (Byrd's remarks were made in February 2003).

30 *Congressional Quarterly Weekly Report*, 22 March 2003.

31 Quoted in Drew, 'War Games'.

32 See R. F. Grimmett, 'War Powers Resolution: Presidential Compliance', Issue brief for Congress, Congressional Research Service, 24 March 2003.

33 *Congressional Quarterly Weekly Report*, 1 March 2003.

34 Ibid., 22 March 2003.

35 Ibid., 1 February 2003.

36 Ibid., 15 March 2003.

37 See M. Barone, 'Life, Liberty and Property', *National Journal*, 15 February 2003. Technically, Jeffords switched to independent status.

38 See W. Schneider, 'Still Asking, Why Now?', *National Journal*, 8 February 2003; *Congressional Quarterly Weekly Report*, 1 March 2003.

39 See Schneider, 'Still Asking'; 'Unilateralism Wins Few Friends', *National Journal*, 4 January 2003; 'The Cowboy and the Diplomat', *National Journal*, 15 February 2003; 'From Yes But to We Told You So', *National Journal*, 22 February 2003; 'A Worldwide Tide of Anti-Bush Feeling', *National Journal*, 15 March 2003; 'War Has Its Reasons', *National Journal*, 22 March 2003.

40 Barone, 'Life, Liberty'.

41 Schneider, 'War Has Its Reasons'; 'This is Bush's War', *National Journal*, 29 March 2003; 'The Wide Partisan Divide', *National Journal*, 26 April 2003.

42 W. Schneider, 'On Second Thought', *National Journal*, 19 July 2003.

43 *New York Times*, 7 April 2003. See also R. W. McChesney and J. B. Foster, 'The "Left-Wing" Media?', *Monthly Review*, 55, 2003, pp. 1–10.

44 See W. Powers, 'The Poodle Speaks', *National Journal*, 15 February 2003; G. C. Wilson, 'Iraqi Hope Shines through Smoke of War', *National Journal*, 12 April 2003, and 'Iraq is not Vietnam', *National Journal*, 12 April 2003.

4 The neo-cons

Neo-conservative thinking since the onset of the Iraq War

Dan Plesch

The rapid collapse of the regime of Saddam Hussein marked a defining moment for advocates of regime change. Operation Iraqi Freedom and its aftermath produced a number of challenging problems for Iraqis, their neighbours, the international community and, not least, the supporters of the invasion. For the last, these problems included the unexpected difficulty of the first phase of the campaign; the failure to find weapons of mass destruction; the lack of effective planning for the aftermath; and the continuing violent opposition to the new regime. This chapter examines key features of neo-conservative thinking in retrospect and prospect after the collapse of Saddam Hussein's regime.

Neo-conservatives had long argued for, and presumably prepared for, the forcible removal of Saddam Hussein from power and his replacement with a peaceful and democratic Iraq. Under the auspices of the Project for a New American Century, Elliot Abrams, William J. Bennett, Jeffrey Bergner, John R. Bolton, Paula Dobriansky, Francis Fukuyama, Robert Kagan, Zalmay Khalilzad, William Kristol, Richard Perle, Peter Rodman, Donald Rumsfeld, William Schneider, Jr, Vin Weber, Paul Wolfowitz, R. James Woolsey and Robert B. Zoellick wrote to the leaders of the US House of Representatives and Senate to that effect in May 1998.[1] The analysis here, however, will focus on key texts by Irving Kristol, Charles Krauthammer, and David Frum and Richard Perle, written since May 2003.[2] The first is a brief summary of the neo-conservative approach to foreign policy.[3] This provides an overview, written in August 2003 at a time when the Iraq insurgency was beginning to intensify. The second is a lecture given to the American Enterprise Institute in which the *Washington Post* columnist Charles Krauthammer outlined a new strategy for the United States called 'Democratic Realism'. Not only is Krauthammer a leading neo-conservative and opinion-former, but his lecture at the AEI was the annual Irving Kristol Lecture, introduced by Vice-President Dick Cheney. The third is *An End to Evil* by David Frum and Richard Perle, published in late 2003, describing how the war on terror can be won. Frum was a speechwriter for President George W. Bush. (His biography *The Right Man* describes in glowing terms Bush's suitability for the presidency.) He is credited with the phrase 'Axis of Hatred' that evolved into the notorious 'Axis of Evil' in the President's 2002 State of the Union Address. Richard Perle, the sometime 'Prince of Darkness', served President Ronald

Reagan in the Department of Defense and George W. Bush on the Defense Policy Advisory Board. He has long been a leading member of the neo-conservative community and was a passionate advocate of the liberation of Iraq. Their book is a detailed design of a 'war-winning' plan.

The analysis will also draw on other appropriate statements by leading neo-conservatives including the paper 'Rebuilding America's Defenses', written for the Project for the New American Century[4] in September 2000 by a group of neo-conservatives led by Irving Kristol and including Robert Kagan and John Bolton (the latter appointed to a senior position in the State Department by George W. Bush).

These ideas are tested against what has occurred as a result of their application in Iraq, and also against a set of criteria developed by the British Army for the conduct of successful counter-insurgency operations. British thinking on counter-insurgency evolved during centuries of imperial expansion and contraction. In its modern form it was codified by General Sir Frank Kitson in *Bunch of Five* (1977), who drew on the ideas of Major General Sir Charles Gwynn in *Imperial Policing* (1939).[5] Kitson wrote:

> The first thing that must be apparent ... is that there can be no such thing as a purely military activity, because insurgency is not primarily a military activity. At the same time there can be no such thing as a purely political solution.

He identified five key principles:

1   'It is no good having an overall plan composed of various measures unless they can be co-ordinated in such a way that measures of one kind do not cut across measures of another kind.'
2   Establish a favourable political atmosphere, particularly with respect to redressing grievances.
3   Have good intelligence.
4   'No country which relies on the law of the land to regulate the lives of its citizens can afford to see the law flouted by its own government, even in an emergency. ... In other words everything done by a government and its agents in countering insurgency must be legal.'
5   Secure your own base and deny the enemy a base of operations.

It is easy to be cynical about such principles. People on the receiving end of British imperial policy may have a less than generous view of British willingness to address grievances over the centuries. Their advocates claim that their implementation permitted the British Empire to function with minimal force, outside of Ireland, and then through the period of withdrawal from Empire after 1945, and that even in Northern Ireland these principles have proved effective in the latter part of the twentieth century. The point, they argue, is to concentrate on the system rather than argue over the history. For the purposes of this analysis,

British Army counter-insurgency doctrine can be considered to be a useful, if not definitive, test of the realism of neo-conservative thinking.

Irving Kristol is the founder of neo-conservatism. This status is proclaimed in his own book, *Neoconservatism: The Autobiography of an Idea* (1999). In a paper for the AEI, 'The Neoconservative Persuasion' (2003), he summarized neo-conservative thinking on foreign policy as having four basic 'attitudes'. These are to encourage patriotism as a natural and healthy sentiment; to regard international institutions 'pointing to world government with the deepest suspicion' for fear of the tyranny that world government may bring; to cultivate the ability to distinguish friends from enemies; and to recognize that the national interests of great powers such as the United States spread far beyond its borders and encompass material and ideological interests. That is why, 'barring extraordinary events, the United States will always feel obliged to defend, if possible, a democratic nation under attack from non-democratic forces, external or internal'. This policy, he argues, found expression in the Second World War and again today in the defence of Israel. For Kristol, the emergence of 'incredible military superiority' produces a requirement to use that power to implement the attitudes of neo-conservatism. The administration of George W. Bush, he observes, is comfortable both with the neo-conservative outlook and with the forceful expression of US power.

Kristol's first idea, patriotism, is in theory a flexible concept. Many opponents of the Iraq War regard themselves as deeply patriotic. John Kerry regarded himself as patriotic when fighting with the US Navy in Vietnam, and also when, on his return home, he helped lead the campaign to stop the war. However, as John Dumbrell indicates in Chapter 3 of this book, the expression of the call for war with Iraq in strongly patriotic terms limited the extent of political debate about the desirability and necessity of it, and also of the manner in which it was to be conducted. Vilification of opponents of the war in Iraq was widespread – even of principled sceptics, as Alex Danchev demonstrates – and led by neo-conservatives. It was in this climate of opinion that little attention was paid at the time to the advice of the US Army Chief of Staff that

> something on the order of several hundred thousand soldiers are probably, you know, a figure that would be required. ... We're talking about post-hostilities control over a piece of geography that's fairly significant, with the kinds of ethnic tensions that could lead to other problems. It takes a significant ground force presence to maintain a safe and secure environment, to ensure that people are fed, that water is distributed, all the normal responsibilities that go along with administering a situation like this.[6]

His views were reported, in a low-key manner, but not heeded.

The exemplar of neo-conservative patriotism in the aftermath of 9/11 was the Patriot Act, signed into law on 26 October 2001. Put forward as a measure to protect the United States, there was widespread concern in the United States that it was an attack on freedom. Richard Clarke, the then White House counter-terrorism chief, wrote in early 2004 that 'the Attorney General, rather than bringing us together, managed to persuade much of the country that the needed reforms of the Patriot Act were actually the beginning of fascism'.[7]

One issue that concerns the strongly assertive patriotism favoured by the neo-conservatives is the idea that the United States need not be concerned why people hate it and that even to raise the question is unpatriotic – such is the stuff of conservative talk radio. In this context it is interesting that even within the US Army there is a debate, purely as a means of maintaining operational effectiveness. The US Army's own research shows that anti-American feeling is rife among the armies of its closest allies and this requires the army and the United States as a whole to look at the causes of this hostility. Zita Simutis, Chief Psychologist of the US Army and Director of its Research Institute in Alexandria, Virginia, described a situation of 'anti-American sentiment expressed by and within partnering countries, both implicit and explicit'. 'Increased resentment and ill-feelings' presented the high command with the challenge of having to work with 'allies that harbor some measure of anti-Americanism'.[8]

This statement was an unprecedented admission from inside the US military that hostility to the United States was widespread among the coalition armies. The recognition of a systemic problem went far beyond previous information concerning discontent among the allies. Anti-American sentiment was normally attributed to US enemies and to uncooperative allies such as France. Concerns over tensions between the US and the coalition forces in Afghanistan and Iraq had centred on anecdotal claims that US forces were trigger-happy and heavy-handed. Simutis described a situation where anti-American sentiment was prevalent at the heart of the coalition. She also directly contradicted the line that it is unnecessary for the United States to try to understand why it was so hated. Her conclusion was not simply that understanding is essential to success but that action must be taken to find solutions. 'If the Army is to be successful … it is essential that it understand the sources of the anti-Americanism as well as what can be done to ameliorate those sentiments.'

There are, therefore, indications that a climate of fervent patriotism stifled open debate, prevented proper consideration of operational issues that affected the lives of millions of Iraqis and thousands of US troops, and served to divide rather than unify the United States itself. In terms of Kitson's criteria for success in counter-insurgency operations, an excess of patriotism can be seen to weaken the home base, harm the political climate, reduce confidence in the application of the rule of law, and impair coordination. By defining patriotism in terms of his own policy agenda, Kristol turns it into a divisive, even sectarian, notion far from the 'natural' or near-universal concept that is his starting point. His unqualified and effusive support for natural patriotism harms the security that his patriotic attitude purports to defend.

Kristol's second core attitude is a deep hostility towards any institution pointing towards world government. This attitude was certainly evident in the Bush administration's policies in the run-up to the invasion of Iraq. As is well known, the invasion took place without the sanction of the United Nations. The legal implications of this are explored in detail by Patrick Thornberry. The operational consequences for the United States were severe. Both Saudi Arabia and Turkey denied the use of their bases for air and land operations; US warplanes were only permitted overflight of Turkish airspace on a case-by-case basis. As a result, the US 4th Infantry Division and the 101st Air Assault Division had to enter Iraq from the south, with the former only arriving after the fall of Baghdad. The invasion force was considerably smaller even than the planned levels, which were themselves well below those the US Army believed would be needed to provide a prompt transition to a stable and peaceful society. Furthermore, there was no support from Arab nations, or from the leading continental European powers France and Germany. In 1991, by contrast, major units of the French, Syrian and Egyptian Armies took part in the liberation of Kuwait.

Thus the lack of international legal authority had a clear impact on the ability of US forces to conduct the invasion and to usher into being the new Iraq apparently so dear to the hearts of neo-conservatives. Moreover, Washington failed to take adequate compensating measures. The escalating insurgency came as a surprise to the administration, which promptly turned to the United Nations for assistance by seeking authority for the occupation. UN Security Council Resolution 1483 states:

> *Noting* the letter of 8 May 2003 from the Permanent Representatives of the United States of America and the United Kingdom of Great Britain and Northern Ireland to the President of the Security Council and recognizing the specific authorities, responsibilities, and obligations under applicable international law of these states as occupying powers under unified command (the 'Authority'),
> *Noting further* that other States that are not occupying powers are working now or in the future may work under the Authority ....

It was with this authority in hand that a number of US allies, including Ukraine, Poland, Japan and South Korea, began to provide troops to add to the coalition forces in Iraq.

Resolution 1483 neither met the requirement of full UN authority – which would have meant UN command and control – nor did it signal a change of heart amongst neo-conservatives. What it does show is that in the real world a US administration at the height of its powers found it necessary to obtain the authority of a body long derided as the epitome of the world government that is anathema to neo-conservatives.

The invasion of Iraq without UN authority was strongly supported by the neo-conservatives. In practice the decision to act in this manner did not work well. The absence of authority may well have played into the hands of Al Qaeda. Once again, Richard Clarke was the harshest critic: 'we invaded Iraq and gave Al Qaeda exactly the kind of propaganda victory it needed'.[9] Jeffrey

Record of the US Army's Strategic Studies Institute has described the invasion as a strategic error of the first magnitude:

> Of particular concern has been the conflation of al-Qaeda and Saddam Hussein's Iraq as a single, undifferentiated terrorist threat. This was a strategic error of the first order because it ignored critical differences between the two in character, threat level, and susceptibility to US deterrence and military action. The result has been an unnecessary preventive war of choice against a deterred Iraq that has created a new front in the Middle East for Islamic terrorism and diverted attention and resources away from securing the American homeland against further assault by an undeterrable al-Qaeda.[10]

Kristol's third precept is to remember one's friends, and his fourth that the United States will naturally support democracy. It is unclear whether the set of friends is a group that includes all democrats. Frum and Perle characterize France, for example, as a strategic adversary of the United States. It is equally unclear whether Kristol favours friends over democrats on certain occasions. During the Cold War the United States is known to have intervened against 'unfriendly' democrats, as for example in Chile. Given that an intellectual of Kristol's standing is unlikely to be engaged in careless tautology, some clarification might be helpful. The idea of friendship in this context is not easily compatible with the hard-headed realism on which neo-conservatives pride themselves (no permanent friends, only permanent interests). Perhaps it is consonant with the 'democratic realism' propounded by Charles Krauthammer?

Krauthammer argues that democratic realism combines the best features of two other US traditions: internationalism and realism. He believes that the internationalists, in the tradition of Woodrow Wilson, will stop at nothing to reduce US power and introduce global government based on the common values of freedom and democracy. On the other hand the realists, with whom Krauthammer naturally sides, propose an unabashed pursuit of US global domination. The problem, he argues, is that realists are just a bit too soulless, and with soullessness comes a certain lack of vision: absolute values like freedom and democracy can also be useful for US interests.

> The spread of democracy is not just an end but a means, an indispensable means for securing American interests. Realists are right that to protect your interests you often have to go around the world bashing bad guys over the head. But that technique, no matter how satisfying, has its limits. At some point, you have to implant something, something organic and self-developing. And that something is democracy.

Force should only be used where it matters to the United States. And it matters in the Islamic world. There, the mission is 'to bring a modicum of freedom as an antidote to nihilism'. Nihilism is Krauthammer's term for jihadists and suicide bombers.

Krauthammer has turned democracy into a weapon of US policy. He explicitly rejects the idea of committing substantial resources to supporting democracy for its own sake; democracy will only be supported when it is a US priority. Cynics may argue that this has always been the American way, but Krauthammer makes it policy, and makes it explicit. Yet such advocacy undermines the very cause he professes to support. The expression of democracy as a tool of US policy effectively labels pro-democracy activists as witting or unwitting tools of US policy. Moreover, Krauthammer's talk of 'implanting' democracy describes it as something foreign, to be imported, rather than an organic growth; this is not simply clearing the weeds of repression in order to allow democracy to flower.

The case of Iraq since the beginning of Operation Iraqi Freedom is enough to demonstrate that Krauthammer's democratic realism is somewhat short of both democracy and realism, while the implementation of policy elsewhere is not reassuring about the neo-conservative pursuit of democracy. In particular in the Caribbean and South America there is substantial evidence that the Bush administration has attempted to overthrow democratically elected governments in both Haiti and Venezuela. With respect to Haiti, following the departure of that country's first elected president, Bush announced:

> President Aristide resigned. He has left his country. The Constitution of Haiti is working. There is an interim President, as per the Constitution, in place. I have ordered the deployment of Marines, as the leading element of an interim international force, to help bring order and stability to Haiti. I have done so in working with the international community. This government believes it essential that Haiti have a hopeful future. This is the beginning of a new chapter in the country's history. I would urge the people of Haiti to reject violence, to give this break from the past a chance to work. And the United States is prepared to help. Thank you.

Aristide for his part said that he was evicted at gunpoint. The former US President Jimmy Carter confirmed that by underlining that 'the US Ambassador announced in advance that Aristide would either leave in a Gulfstream aeroplane or a body bag'.[11] There is a long history of antipathy within the US Republican Party towards Mr Aristide, from before he was elected. What is noteworthy is that no voice from within neo-conservative publications and organizations can be found in his defence. There are some voices to be found welcoming his departure, but they might not be representative. The absence of any voice in his support raises a question for future study. Is it possible that friends might be anti-democratic?

When one looks at events in Venezuela the question becomes rather sharper. Here, a coup failed, and so too have attempts to cut short President Chavez's period of elected office. Again, some neo-conservatives can be found calling for his departure, but it is difficult to find any in support. Rumours and allegations of US involvement abound; in the nature of covert operations, they are hard to substantiate. Interestingly enough, the *New York Times* reported telegraphically as follows:

> Pentagon orders review of its actions during 48-hour ouster of President Hugo Chavez of Venezuela to ensure that American military officials did not encourage coup; senior Defense Department official stresses that Pentagon has no evidence, nor even suspicion, of American involvement in Chavez's brief removal from office; Rear Admiral Carlos Molina, one of anti-Chavez leaders of failed coup, has said he believed he was acting with American support.[12]

There appears to be at least a prima facie case that, under the tutelage of the neo-conservatives, the Bush administration has placed its friends ahead of its commitment to democracy in both Haiti and Venezuela.

Moving from Kristol's philosophy through Krauthammer's framework we come to Frum and Perle's strategy for victory in the war on terror. The summary of their book ends with the resounding declaration that 'David Frum and Richard Perle make a convincing argument for why the toughest line is the safest line.' Their book, *An End to Evil*, is studded with quotations and references chosen to make their point from a variety of authors whose overall views are anathema to them. It opens with Thomas Paine, whose atheism is one of the despicable attributes of communist North Korea. It ends with a reference to the left-wing cartoonist, David Low. In between, it embraces the likes of Thomas Jefferson and John Maynard Keynes.

With respect to Iraq, they claim that, 'by toppling Saddam Hussein, we achieved at least seven great objectives'. They also make mention of some mistakes and lessons learned in the operation and conclude that the operation continues to be a huge success. The seven objectives are as follows:

Claim 1: The threat of Saddam's actual and potential weapons of mass destruction was ended. However, had such weapons existed their threat could continue by their transference to third parties including terrorists and the Syrian government. Thus the invasion could have spread any weapons in an unpredictable manner. As to future weapons, the clear apparent success of the UN inspections regime in preventing any weapons could presumably have continued to prevent any new weapons. As Hans Blix has pointed out, the cost of inspections was under 100 million dollars – one-thousandth of the cost of the war. The invasion need not have ended any actual threat and might have increased it. The adoption of that strategy to end future production was, even in cash terms, a highly costly venture.

Claim 2: A regime that sponsored terrorism for over thirty years was eliminated. This claim raises the issue of who is a terrorist. Some Zionists, African National Congress leaders and even American patriots have been terrorists in their day. But let us take this claim at face value. One of the key terrorist groups claimed by the US-led coalition to be operating in Iraq since the invasion has comprised Saddam loyalists and other Baathist operatives. In these terms the threat from the regime has not been eliminated. According to countless statements of US Central Command and the Coalition Provisional Authority these elements joined forces with criminals and foreign fighters. In April 2004 a senior official of US Central Command provided this analysis of the situation in Fallujah:

> You know, I am not absolutely certain yet. We'll find more out as we get into the operations that are ongoing. But it is more likely in my view that it revolves around the former regime element, but that's not to say that there couldn't have been some cooperation with the Zarqawi folks. I mean, he has got cells in Fallujah or a cell in Fallujah, and he's got influence in Fallujah, and we've seen more and more cooperation between former regime elements and some of the extremist groups like AIA and Ansar al-Islam and Zarqawi's networks. So I wouldn't – I don't think I could categorically say that they did or did not involve one or the other. It's possible that there was cooperation, but we think this was primarily former regime elements.[13]

The importance of the case of Fallujah is that is illustrates that a year after the supposed victory, the US military were stating clearly that both Baathists and external terrorists were active in killing US citizens in the country. A Baathist–Islamist guerrilla alliance was prospering a year after Frum and Perle assert it had been ended. These forces were killing and maiming Americans at a faster rate than at any time in the previous thirty years.

Claim 3: America's enemies would have had a 'huge victory' had Saddam been able to claim that he had survived. This claim takes no more than a sentence to make in the book. It presumes that it would have been impossible to gather an international coalition backed by the UN in support of the Genocide Conventions. Moreover the authors do not affect to notice the international discussion of intervention at a later stage. Perhaps more importantly, any 'victory' for Saddam would have been given to him by the very people who lobbied for a war that the world as a whole, and in this hypothesis, the US too, had rejected.

Claim 4: 'We have learned valuable lessons about how to fight wars in the region and how to rebuild afterwards.' Leaving aside the issue of just how much has been learned, we are left with the claim that a 'great objective' has been to learn how to fight and reconstruct – how to do what is going to be done more often. Learning lessons forms part of any organized activity, but they are not mission objectives, let alone 'great' ones, any more than a business launches a product line with the objective of learning how to make and sell things.

Claim 5: 'We gave other potential enemies a vivid and compelling demonstration of America's ability to win swift and total victory over significant enemy forces with minimal US casualties.' General John Abizaid and other US commanders have made it known that they believe that the Baath Party had always prepared to wage a guerrilla war from its heartland north and west of Baghdad. The notion that destroying the conventional armed forces of Iraq would be just the start of a long-drawn-out war was one of the main reasons why so many experts were concerned about the invasion. In April 2004 an open letter to Tony Blair from fifty former British diplomats provided a forcible reminder that 'all those with experience of the area predicted that the occupation of Iraq by the Coalition forces would meet serious and stubborn resistance, as had proved to be the case'.[14] The continuing and intensifying war a year after the end of 'major combat operations' saw US casualties rising to the levels seen during the first phase of the fighting, a phase that Frum and Perle regard as having been one of total victory. More Americans were killed in April 2004 than in April 2003. Frum's and Perle's assessment of victory as swift and total does not accord with the facts as they can be established. Had they chosen to claim a partial or considerable victory then the argument would be more complex, though given the US strength in conventional arms such an outcome would be scarcely surprising. But Frum and Perle go further. They claim that the victory stamped a powerful impression on the governments of Iran and North Korea. Both states offer a larger and more difficult military challenge than did Saddam's Iraq. Since the bulk of US combat power is tied up in Iraq both governments may consider the future with rather more equanimity than before the invasion. The North Koreans may note that the US infantry division based partly in South Korea and partly in the United States has had its US-based element diverted from the mission of reinforcing the army in South Korea to operating in Iraq. The Iranians can with some reason claim to have the US Army surrounded, since as an army of occupation it relies heavily on the consent of the larger Shia community which has strong ties to Iran.

Claim 6: 'We aided the forces of democracy throughout the region by demonstrating that even the most fearsome local dictatorships are far more fragile than they look.' There appears to be little evidence that people in the Arab world look at the invasion of Iraq in this way, especially in the absence of democratic elections.

Claim 7: 'We eliminated the Arab world's cruellest and most tyrannical ruler.' This objective was achieved. It is somewhat strange that this is the last of the great objectives. The achievement is somewhat marred by the track record on the six other issues just discussed and the flouting of international law in order to achieve it. Frum and Perle have sought Saddam's removal since the time of the first Gulf War. They do make significant points concerning failures of US policy in Iraq and they remind their readers that all wars involve risks and mistakes. They mention that a plan was made to handle starving refugees; fortunately there were none. They mention that the plan envisaged that surrendering Iraqi soldiers would form the new Iraqi security forces and the lack of prisoners prevented the creation of such a force. However, the major mistake that they identify is the failure to install Ahmed Chalabi as head of a provisional government in the same way that Charles de Gaulle was assisted to liberate Paris. This failure they blame on obstruction from the CIA and the State Department and they explore it at some length. They have no time for those who criticize Chalabi's suitability or acceptability to Iraqis. A year after he arrived in Baghdad and despite or because of major assistance from the coalition his approval rating with the Iraqi people was extremely poor. In answer to the opinion poll question: 'Which national leader in Iraq, if any, do you trust the most?', Chalabi scored 0.2 per cent – below Saddam Hussein on 3.3 per cent and Ayatollah Sistani on 4.7 per cent. In answer to the question: 'And, if any, which one do you not trust at all?', Chalabi led the poll on 10.3 per cent, a clear seven percentage points ahead of the next most distrusted figure, Saddam Hussein.[15] Frum and Perle argue that US forces are not trained to act as police and so, without Chalabi, disorder was inevitable. They make no recommendation for a change in training of US forces, not even in treatment of prisoners.

Saddam Hussein has indeed been removed, but all the other objectives claimed by Frum and Perle are illusory. The Baath Party fights on; the celebrated 'weapons of mass destruction programme-related activities' were not prevented by the invasion as that had already been achieved; terrorism is rife; other states see the United States humbled rather than triumphant; and it is hard to find any lessons that have been learned.

Finally, Frum and Perle mount a vigorous defence of the doctrine of pre-emptive war on Iraq. They argue that it does not matter that Saddam's threat was not imminent because, as the case of Osama Bin Laden shows, action should be taken as soon as possible. Yet assessed against the objectives claimed by Frum and Perle, the intention to implant the democracy espoused by Krauthammer and the attitudes recommended by Kristol has been an almost complete failure. The United States looks weaker than it was before the invasion. The idea of all-powerful, all-conquering force has been shattered by images of all-too-human US troops.

But how does the Iraq campaign fare when assessed against Kitson's five principles of counter-insurgency? First of all, there was no unity of planning: the US political command of the Coalition Provisional Authority ran to the White House and was replaced by an ambassador responsible to the State Department. Under a separate command chain, the US military reports through Central Command in Qatar and Florida to the Pentagon. The lack of unified command and coordinated policy breaks both a fundamental rule of command and Kitson's principle of coordinated policy. Next, the political atmosphere in and around the war in Iraq was and remains extremely negative. Iraqi perceptions of the US presence were in continuous decline throughout 2004. The occupation continued to provide encouragement for anti-American sentiment in the Arab world and more widely. In these circumstances acquiring and applying good intelligence to conduct operations in Iraq became ever more difficult. The rejection of international law weakened the United States militarily and politically during the campaign and after. Finally, the insurgent forces in Iraq were able to target the political and military bases of the US forces almost at will, while the insurgents' own base amongst the population was, if anything, consolidated.

Neo-conservative policies as applied to Iraq have been self-contradictory and self-defeating for the United States and deeply destructive for Iraqi society. Outside the neo-con cocoon, a policy of toughness resembles nothing more than naivety.

Notes and references

1　Online. Available HTTP: <http://www.newamericancentury.org/iraqclintonletter.htm> (accessed 8 July 2004).
2　I. Kristol, *The Neoconservative Persuasion*, American Enterprise Institute online, aei.org, August 2003; C. Krauthammer, *Democratic Realism*, Lecture to the American Enterprise Institute, 2003; D. Frum and R. Perle, *An End to Evil: How to Win the War on Terror*, New York: Random House, 2003.
3　Kristol, *Neoconservative Persuasion*; *Neoconservatism, the Autobiography of an Idea*, Chicago: Dee, 1999.
4　Online. Available HTTP: <http://www.newamericancentury.org/RebuildingAmericas Defenses.pdf> (accessed 8 July 2004).
5　General Sir F. Kitson, *Bunch of Five*, London: Faber, 1977, pp. 283ff.; Major General Sir C. Gwynn, *Imperial Policing*, London: Macmillan, 1939.
6　*New York Times*, 26 February 2003.
7　R. Clarke, *Against All Enemies*, New York: Free Press, 2004, p. 286.
8　E. Simutis, foreword to C. Moskos, 'International Military Education and Multinational Military Cooperation', US Army Research Institute Research Note 20004–03.
9　Clarke, *Enemies*, p. 273.
10　J. Record, 'Bounding the global war on terrorism', US Army Strategic Studies Institute, Carlisle Barracks, PA, December 2003.
11　*Independent*, 22 March 2004.
12　*New York Times*, 23 April 2002.
13　Senior CENTCOM Official, Background Briefing, 5 April 2004, Centcom.mil.
14　Letter from former British ambassadors, high commissioners, governors and senior international officials, *Independent*, 27 April 2004.
15　Oxford Research International for ABC/BBC, February 2004.

5 The United Kingdom*

Dan Keohane

In the decades since the Suez conflict of 1956, no major external war involving the United Kingdom has generated more turmoil within the governing party and doubts about the judgement of the prime minister, nor more anti-war protest throughout the country, than the Iraq War of 2003. In the same period no major conflict has aroused so much contention about the legitimacy of the war, the United Kingdom's international reputation and relations with the United States and other countries. In sharp contrast with major conflicts like the Falklands and the Gulf, Iraq had not triggered a Western military response by a sudden, grave and clearly illegal act. The war was not preceded by an Iraqi attack on another state nor by the emergence of an urgent threat to international order. Rather in the period from 1999 until 2003, Iraq's domestic and international behaviour, however disdainful of the United Nations, had not altered significantly. Thus in the lead-up to the war, the Blair administration had to make strenuous efforts to persuade the Labour Party, Parliament, the public and media that going to war was a necessity not a choice. The government faced the immense handicap of a widespread perception that after the attack on the United States of 2001 an influential section of the Bush administration used that traumatic event to attack Iraq, irrespective of Baghdad's behaviour.

This chapter deals with four aspects of the topic. First it sets out how from 1997 the Blair leadership managed the process of government, perceived the United Kingdom's international role, and handled the issues of Kosovo and the attack on the United States. It then reviews British policy for the containment of Iraq focusing particularly on Operation Desert Fox in 1998, going on to explore major aspects of the British debate preceding the war by using two concepts long espoused by the Labour Party. These illuminate the issues that divided most sharply the advocates of force (principally the Labour government and the Conservative opposition) from the assorted coalition of politicians that opposed the war, drawn from the Labour Party, Liberal Democrats, Conservatives and the Scottish and Welsh Nationalists. The concepts are the presumption against the use of force enshrined in the UN Charter and in Just War theory, and the insistence that the United Kingdom should not be the sole judge of its own decision for war but should instead seek to act in full conformity with international norms and opinion.

Finally the chapter examines how the debate casts light on the legitimacy of the war and assesses how it came about that a Labour government acted in a way quite contrary to the expectation of many British citizens. It also considers how the consequences have affected the standing and role of the Blair government's foreign policy.

Context

Labour from opposition to government

As Labour leader from 1994 to 1997, Tony Blair established himself as the most dominant politician ever to head the party. Unlike previous leaders, he is not deeply rooted in the culture and traditions of the party and has little regard, let alone reverence, for the tribal instincts or the ideas of the party. His progressive inspiration, which is offset by a deep respect for successful entrepreneurs, institutions and countries, derives equally from Liberals like Gladstone and Asquith and Labour figures such as Attlee and Bevin. His perspective on politics is influenced by Christian socialism and by a strong concern to promote understanding between Christians and Muslims.

Blair's leadership of Labour, first in opposition and later in government, manifests an impatience with what he perceives as the inertia and attachment to old ways of a range of institutions, British and international. This is coupled with a fierce concentration on achieving results, even involving very high risks, and with a ruthless pragmatism about the means thereto.[1] As leader of the official opposition from 1994 to 1997, Blair sought to contrast Prime Minister John Major's perceived weakness in managing his government and party with his own rigid control of the Labour Party. To this end Blair ensured that Labour's leadership further diminished the role of activists and trade unions in the counsels of the party and secured an overwhelming voice in making all important decisions.

Except for a stark lack of governmental experience, Blair's administration started in 1997 with remarkably propitious domestic and international conditions. He had a relatively strong economy, an overwhelming parliamentary majority, a demoralized Conservative opposition, the goodwill of Liberal Democrats, public opinion and much of the media, close ties with the Clinton administration and a welcome from Britain's European partners. Thus with a popular and strong government, the United Kingdom aspired to play a very prominent part on the international stage.

Blair exalted his role as leader of the country. He gave particular attention to ensuring that the media depicted his government's policies in the most attractive terms and assessed its performance favourably. Compared with his predecessor, the new prime minister marginalized his Cabinet, and diminished the status of Parliament and the Labour Party.[2] The significance of the full cabinet as the primary collective decision-making body was much reduced. Blair increased his direct control over its members, by making them individually responsible to him for achieving agreed targets. Concurrently he gave senior members of his enlarged non-elected staff of advisers strong powers to coordinate and control the activities of ministers and civil servants. Thus Cabinet members are valued more for their managerial skills in delivering outcomes than as national politicians shaping the big decisions of government. In consequence of these shifts of role and power, key advisers to the prime minister are deemed to enjoy greater influence than most Cabinet members in the 'court' of Tony Blair.[3]

The primary vision of the United Kingdom's international role articulated by the first Blair government (1997–2001) was not especially distinctive from the broadly realist approach of its predecessors. It emphasized the United Kingdom's global interests and leadership role in the UN Security Council, NATO, the European Union, the G7, and the Commonwealth, and its core concern to maximize the country's international status and influence.[4] In the Strategic Defence Review (1998) the government denied that it aspired to be a world policeman, but undertook tasks implied by that role. It insisted the United Kingdom would remain the closest ally of the United States, an aim facilitated by the practice of consulting Washington on security issues before any other ally and in 1997–2001 by the parallel outlooks of Blair and Clinton. The United Kingdom also claimed to be at 'the centre of Europe' and repeatedly made the presumptuous assertion it was the bridge between Europe and the United States, a contention that strongly implies it is not wholeheartedly committed to a European future.

A second strand of the government's foreign policy reflected liberal internationalist ideas long espoused by Labour and Liberals or Liberal Democrats. It acknowledged that the United Kingdom had a moral responsibility to individuals and communities abroad and that sovereignty is much less relevant in a globalized world. Labour's general election manifesto (1997) and the Strategic Defence Review declared the United Kingdom would use its assets and influence to be 'a force for good' in the world. This concept meant the United Kingdom would take certain measures that would benefit the world collectively in attaining more security and stability, even if it did not necessarily advantage the United Kingdom.[5] Thus it would use a variety of instruments (diplomatic, economic, military, legal) to promote human rights, reduce international poverty, assist conflict prevention, support arms control and deal with climate change. In line with this approach Blair argued that sovereignty should offer no protection to regimes guilty of ethnic cleansing. His Chicago speech during the Kosovo War of 1999 on 'The Doctrine of the International Community' proposed that the core principle of non-intervention should be modified to permit intervention in cases like genocide and massive flows of refugees that unsettle neighbouring countries, issues pursued by Patrick Thornberry elsewhere in this volume.

In the Kosovo conflict, like Margaret Thatcher over the Falklands, Blair revelled in the role of war leader, and emerged as the most morally driven leader of the United Kingdom for many decades, who sees some issues in stark terms of right and wrong, a trait he shares with George W. Bush. He demonstrated a crusading sense of moral righteousness and while other countries, such as the United States, hesitated to risk the lives and reputation of their armed forces, demanded that NATO use whatever means might be necessary. His keen admiration for the British armed forces, a service he has used a number of times to implement foreign policy (in Kosovo, Sierra Leone, Afghanistan and Iraq), contrasts with his criticism of other British public services. The latter question his methods of achieving results; he has depicted them as 'forces of conservatism'. He was determined not to repeat what he came to regard as the shameful refusal by the Conservative government, in the mid-1990s, to accept any moral obligation to protect the Bosnian Muslim victims of ethnic cleansing.[6] That refusal was supported by the Labour frontbench which included Tony Blair.

The readiness of a Labour Cabinet to use force over Kosovo, without UN approval, was remarkable (albeit with Foreign Secretary Robin Cook being quite reluctant).[7] On that occasion it enjoyed the consensual legitimacy deriving from the express approval of all EU and NATO governments, the states neighbouring Kosovo and most Muslim countries; it had the implicit support of the majority in the UN Security Council, and British public opinion was favourable. Domestically only about 3 per cent of Labour MPs opposed the action and some prominent Conservatives expressed keen reservations. Labour and Liberal Democrat MPs were quite willing to support military intervention and the use of force for apparently compelling humanitarian reasons.

Within an hour or so of the 11 September 2001 attack on the United States – involving the largest ever British loss of life from terrorism – Blair positioned the United Kingdom as the closest ally and supporter of the United States, marking the multiple ties between the two countries. In the previous eight months, the British government rapidly adapted to the major shift from the engaged internationalist perspective of the Clinton administration to the unilateral approach of the Bush presidency. It did so by publicly minimizing serious differences on security issues, while underlining its aspiration to maintain a supposed role as the bridge between Europe and the United States. More than other British politicians, the prime minister gained a deep understanding that 11 September was a 'defining moment in international relations'[8] and would have a profound psychological and political impact on the US sense of vulnerability, on US strategy across the world, and thus on the United Kingdom's role as its junior partner. The attack on the United States also revealed to Blair that groups like al-Qaida might acquire WMD from rogue states, groups or individuals and use them to 'bring about Armageddon'.[9] Calculating that 'only the most voluble expressions of solidarity with the United States would purchase any influence over the White House',[10] the prime minister responded with a three–part strategy. From the start the United Kingdom stood 'shoulder to shoulder' with the United States in time of need, accepting the risks involved, with Blair attending memorial services for the victims of the attack in both countries and instituting a counter-terrorism programme in the United Kingdom. Secondly, in the three months after the attack, he became a missionary for the international coalition against al-Qaida and associated groups, undertaking more than sixty flights to persuade governments in Russia, Pakistan and elsewhere to join the US-led group. The

United Kingdom also provided a diplomatic bridge between the United States on the one side and countries that Washington deemed to be supporters of terrorism, such as Iran and Syria, on the other. Blair's solidarity with the US people and his leading role in and commitment to defeating al-Qaida were recognized by President Bush, the US Congress and public, in a manner that may have affected his own subsequent perception of Anglo-American relations, with British and American media designating him 'US ambassador to the world'. Third, British military forces played a significant part in the UN-mandated war in Afghanistan that followed the attack on the United States, although many British Muslims and some Labour MPs opposed the military action. From the start of the campaign Blair advised the Bush administration to concentrate on al-Qaida and Afghanistan and leave issues like Iraq for later.[11]

The Blair government and Iraq

The containment of Iraq

In May 1997, the Blair administration inherited a controversial and complex strategy to contain and deter the Iraqi regime that was not well known to or understood by the British people. At the end of the Gulf War in March 1991, the victorious international coalition led by the United States and United Kingdom, aware that the International Atomic Energy Agency (IAEA) inspection system had failed to discover Iraq's nuclear weapon programmes before the Gulf War, sought much more than restoring the *status quo ante*. Fearing further aggression, including the use or threat to use WMD by the Ba'athist regime that claimed it had 'won' the war, the international community sought to deprive it of current and future WMD capability, along with related means of delivery.[12] Washington and London hoped that the imposition of draconian terms would encourage Iraqis to overthrow what they saw as a uniquely treacherous and menacing ruling Ba'athist group, without destabilizing the country.

UN Resolution 687 of April 1991, the so-called 'mother of all resolutions', and its successors set out most of the key provisions of the containment strategy, including retaining mandatory economic sanctions, making the UN Special Commission (UNSCOM) and the IAEA responsible for divesting Iraq unconditionally and indefinitely of all WMD and ballistic missile delivery systems over 150 kilometres. A third leg of the containment and deterrence strategy, one that lacked express Security Council authorization, consisted in the no-fly zones in the north and south of Iraq, patrolled by the United States, the United Kingdom and France (until the French ceased this function in 1998). Taken together the enforcement of economic sanctions, the highly intrusive monitoring of UNSCOM and IAEA, and the air exclusion zones, meant that Iraq was subjected to a deeply humiliating and coercive system. It also signified that, unless Iraq adhered to the UN resolutions, the Gulf War ceasefire of late February 1991 had only changed the terms of the engagement from full-scale war to limited war and other means of coercion. For the United States and

United Kingdom, Baghdad's obstruction, defiance and delay of UN inspectors and concealment of data provided persuasive evidence that Iraq remained a potent threat to security and stability, as did the terrorizing of its own people.

From 1992 to 1998, there was limited public debate in the United Kingdom on the containment of Iraq and until the mid- to late 1990s only a handful of MPs and prominent journalists objected vehemently to the deaths, disease and malnutrition and the forbidding ethical difficulties associated with the application of UN economic sanctions. In 1998 the resignation of the UN humanitarian coordinator in Iraq, Denis Halliday, in protest against sanctions, generated much impetus against them in the United Kingdom, a development welcomed by Baghdad.

In November 1997, Tony Blair insisted Iraq must be 'forced to back down' from developing WMD because otherwise 'we will face this problem, perhaps in a different and far worse form, in a few years' time'.[13] Some months later, Robin Cook warned that 'the UN inspectors are our only guarantee that Saddam will not fulfil his ambition to acquire the weapons that could wipe out whole cities'.[14] Thus the Blair government claimed Iraq's threat was increasing and would become even more serious if UN inspection was ended or rendered ineffective.

The British response to the obstruction of UNSCOM by the Iraqi regime in February 1998 confirmed that Blair would maintain the US–UK approach on Iraq going back to August 1990. In early 1998, the United Kingdom, which held the Presidency of the EU, was unable to secure a common European response to Iraq's violation of Resolution 687, in the face of strong French opposition. Instead it worked closely with the United States on backing diplomacy with a threat of air attack. During the February confrontation, the government asked for specific House of Commons authorization for the use of force against Iraq and secured an overwhelmingly favourable vote, with about 6 per cent of Labour MPs opposed.

Ten months later, after further crises between UNSCOM and Baghdad, Iraq's obstruction led the United Kingdom to join the United States in a four-day campaign of air strikes against Iraqi military targets called Operation Desert Fox. The campaign in mid-December, preceded by the publication of a brief government dossier, *Iraq's Weapons of Mass Destruction*, was supported by MPs from across the main parties, with a small minority of critical Labour MPs. In the Commons debate on Operation Desert Fox, MPs questioned whether the US response was conditioned by President Clinton's weakness as he faced threats of imminent impeachment and in October 1998 the Iraqi Liberation Act was passed by Congress (at the prompting of the neo-conservative group, Project for the New American Century) that provided assistance to opposition groups to overthrow the Iraqi regime. Blair defined his objective for Desert Fox to be the diminution of the threat from Iraq to neighbouring states. Subsequently he noted that it inflicted some damage, not decisive, on Iraq's WMD infrastructure.[15]

Operation Desert Fox, the first major external military action in decades mandated by a Labour government supposedly to uphold UN authority, was implemented by two permanent members of the Security Council in the face of clear hostility from three other permanent members, France, Russia and China. It also lacked strong support from European allies or countries in the Middle East. This isolated stance left the UK government at risk of 'being perceived as the deputy sheriff of the world, with the United States as the sheriff'.[16] The readiness of the government to use force without explicit UN authorization was at odds with Robin Cook's earlier statement that, though the government thought existing UN resolutions authorized military action, there 'should be a further Security Council resolution to demonstrate to Saddam ... the United States and the United Kingdom has the support of an international consensus',[17] an opinion shared by the Liberal Democrats but not by the Conservatives.[18]

Operation Desert Fox enabled the Blair government to show the UK elec- torate and the US administration that Labour would use force if necessary to defend British interests. Thus he could 'exorcise the demon of unilateralism',[19] and of anti-militarism, and prevent his Conservative rivals from resurrecting an issue that greatly benefited them previously.[20] In the event, the operation meant Iraq ended all cooperation with UNSCOM, partly on the basis that the commis- sion was excessively influenced by the United States. In this way, Iraq was not monitored on its WMD capabilities for nearly four years and the containment strategy relied on the increasingly porous instrument of economic sanctions, involving US and British naval forces in the Gulf, and the patrolling of the no-fly zones that included air attacks by the United States and United Kingdom.

Two main concepts in the UK debate on war with Iraq

In the British debate preceding the war in Iraq, political leaders and media commentators often focused on two concepts. First, they enquired whether the case for war was sufficiently compelling to overcome the strong presumption in international law, the UN Charter and in Just War theory against the use of force.[21] This presumption declares that the norm of conducting orderly relations in international society by prohibiting the resort to war can be waived only in cases of individual or collective self-defence. Secondly, the debate examined how far the British decision about waging war in coalition with the United States and Australia respected agreed international processes and international opinion; that is, any one state, however powerful, does not take upon itself the right to ignore existing norms and create new rules, which it then applies to another country. Instead, it must secure consensus in the international community to legitimize a resort to war. In 2002 the Bush administration enunciated a doctrine of pre-emptive use of force and regime change against 'Axis of Evil' states and terrorist groups, including Iraq. This major shift in the US approach to interna- tional security, together with a strong British perception that a section of the US leadership was committed to attacking Iraq, permeated the entire British debate in the months before the war. The pre-emptive doctrine purports to remove the major constraints placed by international law and the UN Charter on the use of force and instead permits the initiator to decide when, where and how to do so. Thus it has seriously destabilizing implications in offering precedents for other countries to do likewise. In addition, the US administration declared a commitment to maintaining primacy in the international arena, especially in the military sphere.

From September 2002 to March 2003, Blair made the case for the early disarmament of Iraq's WMD, preferably by Baghdad disclosing its full capability to UN inspections; failing that, by force. He built an argument that it would be a war of necessity on the basis of three interrelated contentions: that Iraq had repeatedly used chemical weapons, thereby violating fundamental international norms and obligations; that the Iraqi regime was deeply committed, in the face of intense demands and pressures by the United Nations over 11–12 years, to protect and enhance WMD capability for purposes of internal repression and external aggression; and that the coercive containment system, resting mainly on a brutal sanctions policy and the no-fly zones, had collapsed in 1998.[22] In consequence he argued this created two separate but related grave risks from Iraq. One concerned the possibility it might use its supposed WMD to further long-standing ambitions against neighbouring states, thereby entangling the United Kingdom in the conflict. Another more wide-ranging threat stressed by Blair, echoing Bush, was of a real and growing danger to the United Kingdom's national security from Iraq, other rogue states, and groups or even individuals within states, that were already conducting an illegal trade in nuclear weapons technology. Whether for financial, ideological or other reasons, these actors might well supply WMD to terrorist groups that sought to kill not 3,000 as on 11 September 2001 but 30,000 or 300,000.[23] In the 1980s the United Kingdom learned to its cost that a rogue state, Libya, had supplied large quantities of explosives and weapons to the Provisional IRA.

In September 2002, the US president, entreated by Blair to take the UN route to disarming Iraq, warned the world body that if it failed to enforce its resolutions against Iraq, it would become like the 'failed' League of Nations, and the United States would act unilaterally against that country as part of the 'war' on terrorism. Over the previous four years the United Nations permitted Iraq to deny entry to its weapon inspectors and to dilute the impact of sanctions leading to the near collapse of containment. Intense pressure, by the United States, keenly supported by the United Kingdom, persuaded the Security Council to pass Resolution 1441 unanimously. This declared Iraq in material breach of its obligations under successive UN resolutions and transformed the UN strategy from containment and deterrence, albeit declining in efficacy, to active disarmament backed 'by a credible threat of force' that meant war if the threat failed.[24] Resolution 1441 gave Iraq 'a final opportunity to comply with its disarmament obligations', requiring it to provide a 'currently accurate, full and complete declaration of all aspects' of its WMD programmes and the 'precise location of such weapons' and it warned of the serious consequences of non-compliance. The demand that Iraq fully disclose its WMD was informed by the knowledge that in 1995 the regime admitted to possessing programmes of biological and nuclear weapons and delivery systems only after an Iraqi defector disclosed the fact. Thus UN inspectors had not been able to overcome Iraq's concealment measures by their own efforts.

The prime minister asserted that formally the principal *casus belli* for the United Kingdom was Iraq's failure to comply with Resolution 1441 that in turn embraced Baghdad's WMD. British public opinion would be unlikely to support a policy that could cost a sizeable number of the armed forces their lives to enforce a UN resolution, unless that declaration was strongly linked with the protection of British security and interests. However, the credibility of the British rationale for war was later undermined by the admission of Paul Wolfowitz, US Deputy Secretary for Defense, that 'for bureaucratic reasons we settled on one issue, weapons of mass destruction, because it was the one reason everyone could agree on'.[25] Likewise, the fact that during the war, some British forces lacked protective suits against nuclear, biological and chemical attack and chemical agent detection systems did not match Blair's rhetoric before the conflict.

According to the Blair government, which had the strong support of the Conservative opposition, Resolution 1441 provided a Janus-type mechanism whereby, as Robin Cook argued in 1998, the clearer the demonstrated willingness to use force, 'the better the chance' of securing a diplomatic solution.[26] In November 2002, the US deployment of military force to the region was probably the reason Iraq permitted the return of UN weapons inspectors to resume their work. For the British and US governments, this event offered further confirmation that the threat or the use of force was the only way to ensure Iraq's disarmament, a stance that was not fully consistent with Blair's assurance to British opinion that war would be a last resort. The prime minister noted that if Baghdad cooperated fully and genuinely with the inspectors to prove it was not guilty of the charge of possessing and planning to use its WMD, then it would be allowed adequate time to disarm, as with South Africa in the 1990s. However, given that after 11–12 years of persistent and well-documented deception and obstruction of UN inspectors, Iraq had failed to disclose all relevant information, account for all WMD material and permit unfettered access to its nuclear scientists, it was essential in Blair's view to disarm it by force, because it would not do so peacefully. In this perspective, if the United States and United Kingdom failed to act, it would almost guarantee further obstruction by Iraq and by other rogue regimes, undermine the shaky authority of the Security Council and further weaken the international non-proliferation regime. In March 2003, the Security Council did not vote on a draft resolution promoted by the United Kingdom, United States and Spain that would have set a number of benchmarks to test if Iraq was willing to cooperate fully with the UN inspectors, failing which force would be used against Iraq.

Because the Conservative opposition strongly supported the alignment of the Blair government with US policy, Parliament did not fully reflect the division of British opinion on Iraq and British government policy was not subjected to as rigorous a scrutiny as would often obtain on a controversial domestic policy. While the party leader Iain Duncan Smith agreed with the US pre-emptive strategy, most of the Conservative leadership did not articulate a definite perspective on the issue.[27] The underpinning by the Conservatives meant that the prime minister, who was anxious they would exploit any divergence between him and the Bush administration,[28] enjoyed a buffer of about 20–25 per cent support for his Iraq policy in the House of Commons.

In Parliament, opposition to government policy was articulated by a large number of Labour members, the Liberal Democrats, prominent Conservatives, the Scottish National Party, Plaid Cymru and retired senior officials on the Lords crossbenches, and outside Parliament by the Green Party, leading figures in the Anglican, Roman Catholic and other Christian Churches, prominent Muslim spokespersons and a wide array of groups in the Stop the War Coalition.

Within and beyond Parliament, opposition to the war was based on a range of perspectives, with all opponents agreeing that major hurdles should be overcome before it would be legitimate to initiate war in March 2003. For a British resort to war that was consistent with international law and a Just War approach, the government needed to identify a grave and pressing threat and to exhaust diplomatic means if it was to offer a credible *casus belli*.

British opponents of government policy on the war were acutely aware that US strategy towards Iraq sharply contradicted the presumption against the use of force. They focused on clarifying to what extent the British approach was shaped by the United States which was committed to a pre-emptive doctrine. Critics of the war also concentrated on clarifying why Iraq's threat required a prompt military response, and on the timing of war in relation to the work of the UN weapons inspectors.

In elucidating the tension between the Blair government policy and the presumption against force, two issues come together, namely the timing of the war and the role of the UN weapons inspectors. A senior Conservative, ex-Cabinet minister, John Gummer, observed: 'There is no Member of Parliament who does not know that this is war by timetable, and the timetable was laid down long before the United States had any intention of going to the United Nations.'[29] This deep unease about US dictation of an imprudent and dangerous undertaking was shared not only by Cabinet ministers Robin Cook and Clare Short, but also by other prominent politicians and retired officials, not noted for anti-American attitudes. These included on the Conservative side ex–Chancellor of the Exchequer Kenneth Clarke,[30] ex-Foreign Secretary Sir Malcolm Rifkind,[31] ex-Foreign Secretary Lord Hurd,[32] Liberal Democrat leader in the House of Lords Baroness Williams of Crosby,[33] and Sir Michael Quinlan, a former Permanent Under-Secretary at the Ministry of Defence.[34]

Anti-war politicians across the parties rejected the alleged nexus between Iraq and al-Qaida identified by Bush and Blair as a grave threat, and on the contrary argued that a war on Iraq might greatly exacerbate the dangers from terrorism (as President Mubarak of Egypt had warned). However, in March 2003 the core point of contention focused on whether to choose war, and if so on whose authority, or allow more time for the UN Monitoring and Inspection Commission (UNMOVIC), backed by the threat of force. Critics of the British policy argued that with containment and deterrence restored and now reinforced by the presence of large US and British forces, there was little immediate risk of Iraq endangering others with its WMD. On 14 February 2003 the Executive Chairman of UNMOVIC, Hans Blix,[35] told the Security Council that Iraq was cooperating with the commission and that the inspectors needed more time (assumed to be a matter of months) to demonstrate to the maximum extent whether the regime would comply fully with its obligations under UN resolutions.[36] Thus Labour, Liberal Democrat and Conservative opponents of war judged it quite unreasonable for the US and British governments to refuse the request of the UN inspectors. Most of British public and parliamentary opinion trusted UNMOVIC personnel to act as well-qualified and impartial agents for the international community. Unlike the British and US governments, the anti-war politicians assumed that it was unreasonable to expect Iraq to prove its innocence as required by Resolution 1441 and they saw no reason to believe that Iraq was planning an immediate and catastrophic action. In the circumstances obtaining in Iraq in early 2003, the US and British refusal to give more time to weapons inspectors was perceived as confirmation that all peaceful options of dealing with Iraq had not been exhausted.

For British critics of the war, a second major issue concerned the extent to which the US and British resort to war was properly motivated and supported by an international consensus. The entrenched perception that the Bush administration harboured self-interested strategic, economic or political objectives made the need for international approval all the greater in the eyes of British critics. The importance of explicit UN approval was highlighted by Blair's conduct of one of the most sustained and exhaustive diplomatic campaigns by any British government to secure a second UN resolution, albeit without success. Internationally, the attack on Iraq was not approved by the UN Security Council or the Secretary-General; nor was it supported by NATO and the EU. As John Vogler shows in Chapter 6 of this volume, in most European countries majority public opinion rejected the strategy and in the Middle East region, major actors well disposed towards the United States, like Turkey and Egypt, did not endorse it.

Domestically the widespread opposition to the war was manifest in public opinion polls and in probably the largest ever public demonstrations. The debate in the House of Commons on 18 March 2003 confirmed that it was not backed by a broad consensus. One key factor that accounts for the extensive opposition refers to the context set by the Bush administration from early in 2001. That administration assumed that what was beneficial for the United States must also be in the international interest. Accordingly it sought to minimize the constraint of international institutions and treaties on its behaviour, as illustrated by its withdrawal from the ABM Treaty, the rejection of the Kyoto Protocol and of the International Criminal Court (ICC), and it sought to persuade countries to sign a special waiver giving US citizens and forces immunity from prosecution by the ICC. Moreover, unlike the Clinton presidency, the Bush administration was reluctant to play a full role in promoting the peace process between Israel and the Palestinians. However, US lack of respect for international law and opinion was most clearly manifest in the holding of detainees in Camp Delta at Guantanamo Bay without access to legal process and outside the remit of the Geneva Conventions. Moreover, Defense Secretary Rumsfeld and Vice-President Cheney did not hide their contempt for the United Nations.

The attitude of the Bush administration to international obligations, norms and opinion, together with the adoption of a doctrine of pre-emptive war that promotes the use of force, is profoundly opposed to British perspectives on international politics that greatly value international legitimacy. They are especially hostile to the values, traditions and instincts of the Labour Party and the Liberal Democrats which subscribe to universalist assumptions, believe in a concept of an international community and judge that force can only be envisaged as a last resort. Likewise many Conservatives did not agree with the US approach. This incompatibility between the US approach and the British outlook meant the domestic and international efforts of the Blair government to build up support for the use of force were severely handicapped from the outset, a burden exacerbated by negative perceptions of President Bush in the United Kingdom. Thus in parliamentary debates, war opponents from all parties credited Blair with making exhaustive effort to induce the United States to take the UN route. Yet in March 2003, the prime minister decided to join with the United States in war and thus erode the United Kingdom's invaluable reputation as a law-abiding country. For a very sizeable section of opinion among Labour and Liberal Democrat MPs and the public, the judgements of the Security Council and of UN weapons inspectors carried much more weight and confidence than the perceived motivations of an ideologically driven US administration.

Assessing the British decision for war and its aftermath

From 1997, Prime Minister Blair sought to maximize British influence on international security issues. He reached the zenith of his leadership, firstly during the humanitarian military intervention in Kosovo and secondly in helping to organize a coalition against terrorism after the attack on the United States.

On Iraq and its WMD, Blair inherited a protracted limited war between the United States and United Kingdom on one side and the Saddam Hussein regime on the other. This bitter contest was conducted in the Security Council, UNSCOM and IAEA inspections on the ground and through the misuse by US intelligence agencies of data belonging to the commission. It also embraced the air patrols of the no-fly zones that regularly attacked Iraqi targets, the enforcement of sanctions by US and British naval forces in the Gulf and an assassination attempt on ex-President Bush in Kuwait. Blair's deep concerns about Iraq's WMD and the Saddam Hussein leadership meant he favoured a rigorous regime of containment and deterrence. Accordingly, in 1998 the United Kingdom joined the US-led Operation Desert Fox that lacked UN collective authorization. It was the only European country to do so, using the occasion to end any doubts about the willingness of the Labour government to use military force.

In 2002–3, Britain's intense and sustained diplomacy to give international legitimacy to Bush's disarmament plan bore fruit in the ambiguous UN Resolution 1441. But the issue of dealing with Iraq crystallized in February–March 2003 after Baghdad fractured the Security Council by partly complying with UN demands and the United States insisted it would not allow the inspectors more time to complete their task. Thus the United Kingdom had to choose whether to join with the United States in war, to stand aside militarily but give diplomatic support to the United States or to dissociate the United Kingdom from the war.

Given their common approach to Iraq since 1990, dissociation was not a serious possibility. The option of giving diplomatic but not military support to the US action, as Spain did and as the Foreign Secretary Jack Straw may have suggested, was unattractive for three reasons.[37] First, as the United States had involved the United Nations in the process as requested by the United Kingdom, and as Blair shared the views of the Bush administration on the special threats from fanatical violent groups and rogue states, he decided the United Kingdom must maintain a full commitment not only to disarming Iraq but to removing the regime, despite the onerous costs involved. Not to support the United States in a war seen in Washington as more about regime change than disarmament would be widely regarded as abandoning its partner in the twelve-year struggle with Iraq, in effect admitting that the approach of successive British governments, including his own, was mistaken. It might also encourage other rogue states and terrorist groups. This was in line with Blair's insistence that what he viewed as outdated processes and norms should not frustrate valued objectives. Secondly, with most British troops already in the region, to withdraw at the last moment would severely damage the forces' morale, the reputation of the British government and confidence between London and Washington. All were immensely important to Blair who had invested special effort in British–American ties and put up with the costs of being regarded as an apologist for an extreme US leadership. Thirdly, to step aside would give an opportunity to Blair's Conservative rivals and others, one they could be expected to fully exploit. The prime minister had not forgotten that in the 1980s, Labour's reputation suffered almost terminal damage from the electorate's perception that it could not be trusted to defend the country. That perception was nurtured by fierce attacks from the Conservatives, a section of the media, and leading US politicians and officials.[38]

The British decision for war derived mainly from the relations of the prime minister with his Cabinet, party, Parliament, MPs and public opinion, especially the latter two. Blair's immense electoral successes domestically and his achievements abroad consolidated his domination in the Cabinet, the Labour Party and Parliament. Robin Cook noted that Tony Blair 'does not regard the Cabinet as a place for decisions' and commented that in the many reports to cabinet on Iraq only himself and International Development Secretary Clare Short challenged the 'trajectory in which we were being driven'.[39] Subsequently both, who subscribe to Labour's anti-militarist tradition and have considerable international experience, resigned from the government.

From September 2002 Blair recognized that without an authoritative indication that war against Iraq was necessary, consistent with international law and had some semblance of international legitimacy, he could not justify it to Parliament, the people and especially to the armed forces. That in turn led the government to issue exaggerated, misleading and flimsy opinions about Iraq's WMD, and to make heroic but unavailing efforts to secure UN authorization for war. Shortly before the invasion, the attorney-general received a request from the chief of defence staff for written confirmation that the war was legal.[40] A few days prior to the war, the attorney-general published conclusions to that effect. A senior legal adviser at the Foreign Office resigned.

In Parliament, three features of the House of Commons debate of 18 March 2003 on the war merit particular note. First, more than one-third of Labour MPs voted against their government, although many owed their seats to Blair's leadership and they knew he would resign if he lost the vote overall and maybe if a majority of them voted against. Moreover, the largest ever parliamentary rebellion occurred although the government warned Labour MPs that a high negative Commons vote would damage the morale of British troops on the eve of war and raise the confidence of the Iraqi regime. Secondly, in the vote on an amendment that declared the case for war not yet established in the absence of specific UN consent, the prime minister secured the support of about 85 per cent of Conservatives compared with about 60 per cent of his own party, while 10 per cent of Conservatives voted against compared with about 34 per cent of Labour MPs. Thus he secured a margin of 75 per cent from the Conservatives, who had ties with neo-conservatives in the United States, and only 26 per cent from his own party. If the Conservatives had opposed Blair because they viewed British interests differently or for opportunistic reasons, he would probably have lost and resigned from office. The Labour MPs who opposed the war reflected the widespread hostility of members of the party and many in the British Muslim community, a feeling shared by Liberal Democrat MPs. However, on the main resolution authorizing all necessary means to disarm Iraq, over 60 per cent of MPs voted in favour, with less than 25 per cent opposed, giving a very decisive affirmative vote.

Thirdly, the consistent opposition to war by a majority of British opinion was reflected only marginally in the decisions of the Blair government. At the international level, the acute awareness that the public and the Labour Party would attribute much importance to UN sanction for military action gave impetus to the diplomatic efforts by the United Kingdom. Domestically, the government made a limited accommodation to the anti-war sentiment by recalling Parliament in September 2002 and arranging many debates on the issue. The key concession, instigated by the Leader of the House, Robin Cook, and the Foreign Secretary, Jack Straw, was the acceptance that the House of Commons would decide whether to mandate British troops to go to war after a full debate and before the event. This course, which was not supported initially by Tony Blair,[41] meant that power shifted from the prime minister, using the Royal Prerogative, to Parliament. But the quality of the Commons deliberations[42] and decision of 18 March was distorted by two major constraints, namely that British troops had been sent to the Gulf well before the vote, and that the prime minister appears to have committed the United Kingdom to support US military action long before Parliament voted.

In the wider public arena, the Hutton Inquiry into the circumstances surrounding the death of Dr David Kelly, analysed in Chapter 14 of this volume by Alex Danchev, illuminated many aspects of official conduct before and during the war. Blair gave evidence on Iraq to the Liaison Committee of the Chairmen of the Commons Select Committees, and to private hearings of the Intelligence and Security Committee, but the government refused to provide essential papers and witnesses for the Foreign Affairs Committee, and instead manipulated its hearings, as Alex Danchev shows. Blair subjected himself to intensive questioning by sometimes hostile audiences on national television and held monthly press conferences for the national and international media. But despite his excess of confidence that he could persuade opinion to his outlook, all of these efforts failed to dispel a widespread perception that this was an untimely war, dictated by a US administration contemptuous of international law and opinion.

The refusal of the Blair leadership to remain loyal to party traditions and to long-established international norms on using force was a product of various pressures. It meant that except for the Polish socialists, Labour was the only European centre–left party whose leadership supported the war;[43] internationally Blair was associated with right-wing or centre–right governments on the issue. With the reinvention and repositioning of the party since 1989, Labour has become a much more top-down, leadership-dominated party, without a coherent ideology or a heavy anchor, and with the key institutions of the National Executive Committee and annual conference shorn of most power and significance. Thus a modernizing prime minister, who is inclined to resort to war more than any previous Labour leader and who displays a strong tendency to allow objectives to dictate the means of their achievement, was able to persuade or cajole a majority of his MPs to support his decisions. His priorities were shaped by his assessment of the probable net costs of not going to war. Blair was determined to seek influence on a war made in Washington (still numbed by the attack of 2001) and on US global strategy, by demonstrating again that the United Kingdom was the United States' best friend. This was buttressed by his fear that WMD and terrorism would eventually combine to produce catastrophic results, possibly occurring while he was leader of the United Kingdom, and by an anxiety that an often feeble United Nations could not be trusted to disarm threatening countries and groups in a timely fashion, however dangerous. Moreover Labour's 1980s traumas on security policy and his experience as prime minister may have prompted him not to alienate very powerful forces in the United States and in the British media, even at the price of dismaying a large section of British opinion, including many in the Labour and Liberal Democrat Parties, and in other countries.

The consequences of the Iraq War for the Blair administration, if not necessarily for the United Kingdom, were negative in the short term, with certain major exceptions. Despite fierce pressures, Blair ensured the United Kingdom remained the most loyal ally of the United States, thereby preventing a grave rupture in the United Kingdom's most fundamental foreign relationship extending over many decades while maintaining such diplomatic, political and security benefits as derive from ties with the only superpower. On the other side, the deep division manifest in the Security Council over the war diminished the authority of a key international organization and of international law, and inflicted the worst diplomatic defeat experienced by the United Kingdom since Suez by refusing to pass a second UN resolution. The United Kingdom's claimed pivotal role on the world stage, including the supposed bridge between Europe and the United States, was undermined by the war, which signalled that the United Kingdom had little confidence in acting collectively on security with some European partners. Moreover, Blair's vehement criticism of France in effect deprived him of a central role in EU decision-making and weakened his hand in the awkward threesome at its heart, the relationship between the United Kingdom, France and Germany.

In Iraq, the coalition, including the United Kingdom, failed to find WMD, but it claims the war fostered major gains for reversing and countering proliferation by encouraging more responsive behaviour from Libya, Iran, Pakistan and North Korea. The war removed the illegitimate and murderous Saddam Hussein regime, at a cost in lives of thousands of Iraqis, significant numbers of coalition forces and other personnel, thereby allowing terrorist groups to enter and use Iraq as a battleground. The invasion also had the immensely important effect of giving the people and communities of Iraq a potential opportunity to shape their fate, albeit in an intensely violent and insecure context. The reconstruction of Iraq also requires a large and sustained investment by the United Kingdom thus ensuring it remains a very important arena for British foreign policy for the foreseeable future.

Domestically, the end of the war did not mean the end of the divisions over the issue, nor did it conclude debates about the prudence, legitimacy, legality and impact of the conflict. Rather the continuing turbulence in Iraq and the political struggle to shape future British policy has generated a sustained dispute over whether to assess the war as a disastrous, destabilizing and dangerous aberration or a template for future security strategy. The intensity of the contention arises largely from the fact that, far from apologizing for the United Kingdom's participation in the war, Tony Blair continues to insist he does not resile from the decision. This is remarkable for an event that cost thousands of lives and casualties, was based on no reliable evidence, divided the Labour Party, public opinion, the EU, NATO and the UN Security Council, and undermined the United Kingdom's international standing. It also weakened the bond of trust between many British citizens and their government. Nevertheless, Blair has argued that new and uniquely menacing threats have to be destroyed before they inflict enormous suffering on countries like the United Kingdom, and contended that international law and UN responses ought to be changed to meet this expectation. Change is needed, but not at home.

Notes and references

* I am grateful for the comments of Alex Danchev, John MacMillan, Brian Doherty, Robert Ladrech, Thomas Poguntke, Rhiannon Vickers, and the participants in the Keele workshop on the volume on 22 October 2003.

1 P. Hennessy, *The Prime Minister: The Office and Its Holders since 1945*, London: Allen Lane/Penguin, 2000, comments that for Prime Minister Blair, 'There is a frustration in waiting for the pay-off and he doesn't have time', p. 518.

2 R. Rose, *The Prime Minister in a Shrinking World*, Oxford: Polity Press, 2001, ch. 1. Labour's policy on devolution was mostly inherited by the Blair leadership.

3 Hennessy, *Prime Minister*, pp. 494–502; K. Clark, *House of Commons, Official Report*, 21 January 2004, Col. 1337. Clare Short identified Alastair Campbell (Director of Communications and Strategy), Jonathan Powell (Chief of Staff), Baroness (Sally) Morgan (Domestic Policy Adviser) and Sir David Manning (Foreign Policy Adviser) as the key officials based at 10 Downing Street who shaped policy leading up to the Iraq War. See House of Commons Foreign Affairs Committee, *The Decision To Go To War in Iraq*, London: TSO, 2003, pp. 43–5.

4 Prime Minister's speech to Lord Mayor's Banquet, 10 November 1997. Online. Available HTTP: <http://www.number10.gov.uk/print/page1070.asp> (accessed 2 February 2004). See also *The Strategic Defence Review*, London: TSO, 1998.

5 See Tony Lloyd, Minister of State at the Foreign and Commonwealth Office, evidence to House of Commons, Session 1997–8, Defence Committee, Eight Report, *The Strategic Defence Review, vol. 111, Minutes of Evidence and Memoranda*, paper 138–111, question 2803.

6 Interview with Tony Blair, 'A New Generation Draws the Line', *Newsweek*, 19 April 1999.

7 J. P. Rubin, 'Countdown to a Very Personal War', *Financial Times*, 30 September 2000.

8 See S. McGuire, 'Onward Christian Soldier', *Newsweek*, 3 December 2001.

9 Prime minister's speech, 'PM warns of continuing global terror threat'. Online. Available HTTP: <http://www.number10.gov.uk/output/page5470.asp> (accessed 25 March 2004).

10 A. Rawnsley, 'His Greatest Gamble', *Observer*, 4 November 2001.

11 In September 2001, the Bush–Blair discussions failed to elucidate that, for the United States, military action against Iraq was a question of when, but for the United Kingdom it was if. See P. Riddell, *Hug Them Close: Blair, Clinton, Bush and the 'Special Relationship'*, London: Politico's, 2003, p. 160.

12 Before the Gulf War, the British government was worried about Iraq's battlefield biological and chemical weapons and warned Saddam Hussein not to use them. See J. Major, *John Major: the Autobiography*, London: Harper Collins, 1999, pp. 222–3.

13 See *House of Commons, Official Report*, November 1997, Col. 323. Blair told Paddy Ashdown, the Liberal Democrat leader, 'I have seen some of the stuff on this. It really is pretty scary. He is pretty close to some appalling weapons of mass destruction … it's deadly serious.' *The Ashdown Diaries, vol. II, 1997–1999*, London: Allen Lane/Penguin, 2001, entry for 15 November 1997, p. 127.

14 *House of Commons, Official Report*, 10 February 1998, Col. 143.

15 *House of Commons, Official Report*, 24 September 2002, Col. 2.

16 *House of Commons, Official Report*, 17 November 1998, Col. 1142.

17 *House of Commons, Official Report*, 17 February 1998, Col. 905.

18 Robin Cook considered military action without a UN resolution would be illegal but Tony Blair was advised that UN Resolution 687 was 'all the justification he needed'. J. Kampfner, *Blair's Wars*, London: Free Press, 2003, p. 30.

19 J. Rentoul, *Tony Blair Prime Minister*, p. 422. In the Commons debate on Iraq on 26 February 2003 Conservative ex-Cabinet minister John Gummer observed that he was a supporter of Cruise and Pershing missiles when Blair was a member of CND. *House of Commons, Official Report*, 26 February 2003, Col. 310.

20 In the early 1980s Cook was an eloquent advocate of the party's anti-nuclear strategy. In the 1991 Gulf War about 25 per cent of Labour MPs opposed force, with Clare Short resigning from the frontbench.

21 On Just War, consult 'Just War Revisited – Archbishop of Canterbury's Lecture to the Royal Institute of International Affairs', 14 October 2003.

22 *Transcript of Blair Interview, BBC2 Newsnight*, 7 February 2003. Online. Available HTTP: <http://news.bbc.co.uk/1/hi/programmes/newsnight/2732979.stm> (accessed 1 November 2003).

23 On the coming together of rogue states with WMD and terrorist groups, Blair noted, 'even if I'm the last person left saying it, I'm going to say it'. See *Newsnight*, Blair Interview, 7 February 2003.

24 See J. Straw, *House of Commons, Official Report*, 18 March 2003, Cols 901–2.

25 S. Tanenhaus, 'Bush's Brains Trust', *Vanity Fair*, 515, July 2003, p. 145.

26 *House of Commons, Official Report*, 17 February 1998, Col. 907.

27 For a cogent critique of the US doctrine on the pre-emptive use of force and regime change by Conservative MP Andrew Tyrie, see *Axis of Instability: America, Britain and the New World Order after Iraq*, London: Bow Group and Foreign Policy Centre, 2003.

28 R Cook, *The Point of Departure*, London: Simon and Schuster, 2003, p. 104. In September 2002, the Conservative leader Iain Duncan Smith noted that Saddam Hussein has had 'Ten years of second chances. Now, surely, is the time to act.' *House of Commons, Official Report*, 24 September 2002, Col. 9.

29 J. Gummer, *House of Commons, Official Report*, 26 February 2003, Col. 310.

30 K. Clarke, *House of Commons, Official Report*, 26 February 2003, Cols 293–5.

31 M. Rifkind, 'That's Enough Grovelling', *Spectator*, 10 May 2003.

32 Lord Hurd, 'Between Peace and War: Iraq in Perspective,' *RUSI Journal*, 148, 2003, pp. 8–10.

33 Baroness Williams, *House of Lords, Official Report*, 26 February, 2003, Cols 254–8.

34 M. Quinlan, 'A Test of Wisdom for President Bush', *The Tablet*, 26 October 2002.

35 Mohammed El-Baradei, Head of the IAEA, also reported on that date.

36 H. Blix, *Disarming Iraq: The Search for Weapons of Mass Destruction*, London: Bloomsbury, 2004.

37 On Straw see Kampfner, *Blair's Wars*, p. 303. In the 1960s, the Wilson government coupled diplomatic support for the US war in Vietnam with a refusal to send troops. This policy did not prevent severe damage to Labour unity and morale.

38 See D. Keohane, *Labour Party Defence Policy since 1945*, Leicester: Leicester University Press, 1993, ch. 4.

39 Cook, *Departure*, pp. 115–16. In 2004, Cabinet Secretary Sir Andrew Turnbull commented: 'Indeed, the way Cabinet is working now, there is probably more discussion than there was in the final years of Mrs Thatcher.' *House of Commons, Public Administration Committee*, Uncorrected Transcript of Oral Evidence, 4 March 2004. Online. Available HTTP: <http://www.publications.parliament.uk/pa/cm200304/cmselect/Cmpubadm/uc423-i/uc42> (accessed 18 March 2004).

40 See A. Barnett and M. Bright, 'War Chief Reveals Iraq Legal Crisis', *Observer*, 7 March 2004.

41 See Cook, *Departure*, pp. 187–90.

42 D. Beetham, 'Political Participation, Mass Protest and Representative Democracy', *Parliamentary Affairs*, 56, 2003, pp. 597–609.

43 Prime Minister, *House of Commons, Official Report*, 26 February 2003, Col. 258.

6 The European dimension

John Vogler

The US and coalition attack on Iraq came at a pivotal moment for the European Union. Already within sight of enlargement to twenty-five members, on 1 May 2004, it suffered the indignity of being divided into 'old' and 'new Europe' by the US Secretary of Defense. About to undertake the first missions of the long-planned European Security and Defence Policy it found the two existing Member States possessing significant military capability engaged in vitriolic public exchanges over Iraq. Having for years attempted to concert the foreign policies of Member States at the United Nations it was confronted with a situation where Britain and Spain on the one hand and France and Germany on the other squared up to each other at the Security Council. As millions of its citizens took to the streets in anti-war demonstrations, on a scale without precedent in the post-1945 period, it found itself incapable of responding either through an emergency meeting of the European Council or through the European Parliament. The experience has given rise to powerful and apparently contradictory reactions. On the one hand critics, including leading officials of the EU's Common Foreign and Security Policy (CFSP), have been moved to near despair by the division and impotence displayed by the EU during the early months of 2003. On the other, the brutal demonstration of US hegemony in the invasion of Iraq has led commentators to construct the EU as some form of counterbalancing or alternative force in world politics – a force wedded to a multilateral approach and peaceful forms of democracy promotion.

Certainly since 1992, and probably long before that, any discussion of foreign policy in Western European states has had to be informed by a European dimension. The interest of this book in the tensions between democratic principles and processes and political or national interests in foreign policy thus relates not only to the national level but to the external policy-making structures of the EU. This chapter investigates the EU response to the Iraq crisis and the ways in which popular and electoral factors bore upon the (in)ability of the EU to formulate a collective policy and to act in its own right on the world stage. It also attempts to evaluate the implications of these events for the EU in terms of its identity and capacity to be a significant actor in its own right. The obvious comparison here is with the United States and concerns the ability to use force and to promote democratic change or otherwise re-engineer the political systems of other members of the international system. There is also the question of whether the EU itself has sufficient popular legitimacy to play such a role.

EU external policy and Iraq

It was by no means immediately evident that the EU, as distinct from its Member States, should play any role in the gathering crisis over Iraq. To appreciate the situation it is necessary to consider the bases of the EU's external activities. From its inception the European Community has enjoyed exclusive competence for the conduct of external trade which has meant that the Commission conducts a single policy on behalf of all the Member States. Further external competences have developed over the years and include Community development and humanitarian assistance policies (the latter now administered by the European Community Humanitarian Office – ECHO). For many years the 'high politics' of foreign policy and defence remained untouched by such Europeanization despite a realization of the potential benefits of common action and attempts to provide some coordination between the positions of the Member States. Even since the creation of an intergovernmental CFSP under the 1992 Maastricht Treaty and now a nascent European Security and Defence Policy (ESDP), it is still the case that the EU's role in the world is overwhelmingly dependent upon its position as a trader and aid-giver. It is here too that the EU appears most like a single purposive actor led by the Commission and that the major non-military instruments of foreign policy, whether they be trade sanctions or the grant of access to the Single Market, reside. Over the years the Commission has established its own delegations in over 120 countries and now has a dedicated Delegation-General for Foreign Relations, RELEX, headed at the time of the Iraq war by Commissioner Chris Patten. Acting under its competences the Community has established a complex array of association agreements with most other members of the international system.[1] Thus it is with the trade and aid competences of the European Community that any serious consideration of the role of the EU with regard to individual countries or regions of the world must begin.[2]

What is striking about the EU and Iraq is that there have been few if any relations in those areas in which the EU has demonstrated its capacity as a single actor. There has been no EC delegation in Baghdad and no cooperation or association agreement with the previous regime. UN sanctions meant that up until 1996 there was effectively no trade upon which to build a relationship and the status of the Baathist regime as an international pariah would in any case have rendered this impossible. Since the initiation of the UN Oil for Food Programme the EU has imported Iraqi oil, comprising some 25 per cent of Iraq's export market, while the equivalent figure for the EU's share of Iraqi imports is 20 per cent. In 2001 the value of EU oil imports was 3,494 million euros while machinery and other exports to Iraq were valued at 1,931 million euros.[3] European Community action towards Iraq thus had and continues to have a mainly humanitarian character, currently through the operations of ECHO. Between 1991 and 2002 the Community spent the small sum of 157 million euros on relief projects but since the US and allied attack in March 2003 and the subsequent Madrid Donors Conference at the end of October, humanitarian funding has risen sharply. The EU budget contribution to Iraqi reconstruction allocated to the end of 2004 stands at 200 million euros.[4] When placed alongside the estimated costs of such reconstruction and the national contribution of Britain, this is a none too impressive sum.

While the EU has little existing basis for a role in Iraq through the activities of the Community, the implications of the Iraq War for the CFSP were unavoidable. The latter is an essentially intergovernmental process of foreign policy coordination which operates through the development of common positions and joint actions and which endeavours, not always successfully, to link these to the trade and financial instruments that are within the remit of the Community and the control of the Commission. In the unwieldy architecture created by the 1992 Treaty of Maastricht the Commission, although not formally part of intergovernmental decision-making, is nevertheless 'fully associated' with the CFSP. It is important to stress that the CFSP and ESDP were never designed as single policies subject to the disciplines of Community decision-making, qualified majority voting and parliamentary assent. Instead they rely upon collaboration between independent Member States governments. The decision-making bodies of the CFSP are, at the highest level, the European Council comprised of the heads of Member States governments and the more regular meetings of the Council of Ministers in its GAERC (General Affairs and External Relations Council) formation. Daily business is conducted at the level of national ambassadors known as Permanent Representatives and through a network of committees and working groups in Brussels staffed by national officials and organized by the Secretariat of the Council of Ministers. The diplomacy of the CFSP is carried out by the Presidency in Office of the Council (during the first part of 2003, Greece) assisted by the 'Troika' which includes the previous and next holders of the rotating six-month-long presidency. In an attempt to provide a focus for the CFSP and to respond to Henry Kissinger's celebrated jibe about the absence of a European phone number, the Amsterdam Treaty created the new office of High Representative and Secretary-General of the Council – occupied at the time of the Iraq War by its first incumbent, Xavier Solana.

The purposes and obligations of the CFSP, as a means of enabling the EU to play a part in international politics commensurate with its evident economic might, are encapsulated in the solemn undertaking that in the conduct of their foreign policies:

> The Member States shall work together to enhance and develop their mutual political solidarity. They shall refrain from any action which is contrary to the interests of the Union or likely to impair its effectiveness as a cohesive force in international relations.[5]

It would be something of an understatement to say that the Iraq crisis of 2002–3 demonstrated the limits of such solidarity.

The CFSP and Iraq – the EU as bystander

With four of the EU's principal Member States (France, Germany, Spain and Britain) locked in public dispute in the Security Council, the Iraq question was at best an acute embarrassment and at worst a resounding demonstration of the irrelevance of the CFSP. It had to cope not only with unfolding events in New York but also with the frequently devious diplomacy of Member States of which the presidency and the high representative were often unaware.

While the CFSP has been active in many areas notably in the Balkans and Mediterranean and in the Middle East, it studiously avoided the question of Iraq. In the words of one Brussels permanent representative:

> It was as if there was a tacit agreement not to discuss the country. Since France and Britain disagreed over the imposition of a no-fly zone for Iraq and especially the sanctions policy, we kept the issue of Iraq off any agenda. It was a mistake. Iraq was taboo. By failing to deal with the issue, we failed to build any common policy over Iraq.[6]

Thus when the events of late 2002 made the issue unavoidable the CFSP was engaged in a reactive exercise in papering over the cracks between its Member States. The situation was to be complicated by the imminent accession of ten East European states who were already routinely associated with CFSP positions but now became openly involved in taking sides over Iraq. The emerging divisions were enthusiastically exploited by US government spokespersons and notably by Secretary of Defense Rumsfeld.

It now seems clear that the British government, while making an early private commitment to participation in a US-led attack, persuaded a highly reluctant US administration into legitimizing such action through resort to the UN Security Council. This set in train a series of dramatic meetings in New York leading first to Resolution 1441 of 8 November 2002 and ultimately to the doomed search for a 'second resolution' that would explicitly authorize the invasion of Iraq. While there have been concerted efforts in the past to coordinate the positions of EU Member States at the United Nations, it was clearly impossible in this instance although the effort was made. There was, for example, an unprecedented 'concertation' meeting with the presidency, the Troika, Solana and the four UN Member States on the Security Council at the end of January 2003.[7] France was to lead the opposition to US policy in the Council and to demand that Resolution 1441 should not contain any element of 'automaticity' whereby adverse reports from weapons inspectors would provide an immediate UN authorization for US military action. In this it was joined by Germany as a rotating member of the Security Council. As the crisis mounted in the first two months of 2003, the French and British governments became involved in open and often acrimonious public diplomacy as they competed for votes in the Security Council.

In Brussels it was the role of the hapless Presidency (Greece in the first part of 2003) to attempt to arrive at a common stance acceptable to the divergent Member States on the Security Council. Subsequent to the adoption of SC Resolution 1441 the GAERC issued a carefully worded statement on 19 November 2002 welcoming the resolution, stressing the unity of the international community and stating that the 'clear objective' of EU policy was the disarmament of Iraq's WMD. Although Iraq was 'urged to grasp this final opportunity' the Council also stated that the 'role of the Security Council in maintaining international peace and security must be respected'.[8] An essentially similar declaration emerged from the European Council Meeting at Copenhagen on 12–13 December 2002.[9]

By January 2003 it became evident that Franco-British differences were unlikely to be reconciled. Privately the French government had concluded that Britain was irrevocably in the American camp.[10] French official statements made it clear that evidence from the UN Blix/El Baradei inspection in Iraq was unlikely to provide justification for the use of force demanded by the US government. Foreign Minister de Villepin thus indicated that 'nothing today justifies envisaging military action',[11] a sentiment in which Germany (which would assume the chair of the Security Council in February) joined. Franco-German unity in opposing US and British policy was emphasized by the celebrations reaffirming their forty-year-old Elysée Treaty of friendship on 22 January 2003. This was badly received in London where the developing problem between Britain and Germany was underlined by a public falling out between one of Blair's ministers and the German ambassador.[12]

Despite these public differences between Member States the Greek Presidency's attempt at maintaining some sort of common front in the CFSP continued. At the GAERC meeting of 27 January 2003, the Council registered its 'deep concern' and sent an 'unambiguous message' to Iraq that this was its 'final opportunity to resolve the crisis peacefully'.[13] Alongside this the primacy of the Security Council was reasserted. The Council was further marred by a dispute over Zimbabwe with the French government denying the spirit if not the letter of EU policy by the issue of an invitation to Robert Mugabe to attend a Franco-African summit. This was not best calculated to improve Franco-British relations.

Almost immediately the affair of the 'letter of eight' further undercut efforts to present a common front over Iraq. US Secretary of Defense Rumsfeld had earlier in the month made his celebrated observations on the distinctions between Franco-German 'old Europe' and the emergent 'new Europe' of Atlanticist Member States and accession countries. As if to amplify his point, *The Wall Street Journal* and *The Times* of London carried an open letter on 30 January 2003 pledging support to US policy and signed by the leaders of Spain, Britain, Italy, Portugal, Hungary, Poland, Denmark and the Czech Republic (subsequently to be joined by Slovakia). The provenance of this letter illustrates the point to which intra-European relations had descended. It was originally the idea of a *Wall Street Journal* writer but was taken up by Spanish Prime Minister Aznar 'angry that the French and Germans gave the impression at the UN and elsewhere that they represented the views of the EU'.[14] In great secrecy the other European leaders were 'signed up' without informing ambassadors. The only other party to be informed of the letter was the US government. The French Ambassador to London, who was involved in what were supposed to be 'fence-mending' discussions with Prime Minister Blair at the time, was specifically not informed of the letter leading to a further worsening of relations.[15] Within days further exacerbation resulted from the decision at NATO of France, Germany and Belgium to veto the provision of assistance to Turkey in the event of war in Iraq.

Inevitably the EU Presidency and the High Representative were excluded from all this secret diplomacy and 'point scoring' as they continued the hopeless struggle to provide some façade of unity for the CFSP. On 4 February 2003 the Greek Presidency, acting on behalf of the EU and its acceding and associated states, executed a *démarche* addressed to Iraqi missions which demanded immediate compliance with Resolution 1441 and full cooperation with the international inspectors, while making the point that Iraq would be responsible for 'all the consequences' of its inaction.[16]

By mid-February 2003 the dissension between Member States, anti-war demonstrations on a huge scale in most European capitals on Saturday 15 February and the pace of events in New York convinced the Greek government to convene an Extraordinary European Council on the following Monday. Held at heads of government level this really was a last-ditch effort to find some European unity. The resulting statement adopted familiar positions but with greater urgency: 'War is not inevitable ... force should be used only as a last resort.' It went on to 'recognise that the unity and firmness of the international community ... and the military build-up have been essential in obtaining the return of the inspectors'.[17] At the same time there was a need to invigorate the peace process in the Middle East and to implement the long promised 'road map'. Here, at least, was an area where the CFSP had been continuously active, where the EU itself was recognized as a key negotiating partner in the 'Quad' (with the United Nations, United States and Russia) and above all where there was substantial agreement between the Member States on their collective interest in a solution which, amongst other things, maintained Palestinian rights. It was also an area, unlike Iraq, where the EU already had a major investment in terms of funding for the Palestinian Authority and numerous economic and other links with both Israel and its neighbours. Finally it is worth mentioning that Britain was fully committed to using the political capital it had built up with the Bush administration to press it to move forward on publishing the 'road map'. The Conclusions of the European Council ended with an invocation, ironic in the circumstances, that 'The unity of the international community is vital in dealing with these problems. We are committed to working with all our partners, especially the United States, for the disarmament of Iraq and for peace and stability in the region.' It appears that the text could only survive because it lacked any reference to a deadline for Iraqi compliance and the likely consequences if this were not forthcoming.

The East European accession states had not been invited to the European Council but they were almost immediately involved again in the arguments over Iraq. The occasion was a follow-up to the 'letter of eight': the 'Vilnius declaration' of ten East European governments in support of US policy. In the aftermath of the Extraordinary Council, President Chirac responded with a series of incendiary remarks about East European countries. They were indulging in 'childish and irresponsible behaviour' and had prejudiced their chances of joining the EU.[18] From this point onwards attention focused on the Security Council and the doomed attempt, led by Britain, to obtain a new UN resolution which would serve to legitimize an inevitable US and coalition invasion of Iraq during March. Observers of European politics were treated to the unseemly spectacle of French and British representatives pursuing each other around Africa in a competitive attempt to influence votes in the UN Security Council. (From 24 February 2003 de Villepin made a tour of African states where he was followed by Baroness Amos of the FCO (Foreign and Commonwealth Office). The British prime minister also involved himself in hectic personal diplomacy to the same end.) From a British and Spanish point of view it was to no avail for it became clear that only the votes of Britain, the United States, Spain and Bulgaria would be forthcoming. There would be no 'second resolution' and the Franco-German line appeared to have triumphed. On 10 March, only days before the opening of hostilities, the French president stated:

> My position is that, whatever the circumstances, France will vote 'no' because she considers this evening that there are no grounds for war in order to achieve the goal we have set ourselves; that is to disarm Iraq.[19]

The British government's response was to interpret this to the press in such a way as to suggest that it was France that had destroyed the possibility of UN backing for what was now an unavoidable invasion of Iraq. It constitutes the nadir of recent Franco-British relations and very probably of the fortunes of the CFSP as well.

Popular and electoral issues

The ways in which the European governments oriented themselves towards the hegemonic power and the consequent divisions that plagued the CFSP derived from a complex set of historically conditioned interrelationships between domestic politics, electoral gain (or sacrifice) and conceptions of national interest both widely and narrowly conceived. Within the existing fifteen members, with the sole exception of Denmark, public opinion was to a greater or lesser extent opposed to the US-led operation while at the same time desirous that the EU itself should play a greater role in world politics. Many governments were prepared to adopt an unpopular stance because of their view either of the right-ness of the cause or of a fundamentally Atlanticist analysis of their own national interest. The latter category clearly includes the East European accession states but also Britain, Spain, the Netherlands and Portugal. The French and German governments, supported by Belgium and Luxembourg, provided the principal opposition to US action in the extended UN Security Council debates of late 2002 and early 2003. In this they rode a tide of domestic public opinion. For France there were no contradictions because the stance on Iraq represented a popular continuation of long-established independence and scepticism towards US leadership. The case of Germany is much more interesting and really does indicate the influence of popular and electoral concerns because the policy of the SPD–Green coalition was a dramatic reversal of traditional certainties about German national interests and the centrality of the US alliance. Working from a much more ambiguous position in terms of popular assent, the British Labour government provided stalwart support for US Iraq policy which finally descended into open antipathy towards its fellow European Permanent Member of the Security Council. One can interpret this at face value, in terms of the justice of the cause, or one can point out that it follows from a deeply rooted bipartisan and post-imperial view of British national interest to the effect that Britain must always remain the principal ally of the United States. This appears to have trumped not only popular and party disquiet over the war but also the assiduous efforts that had been made by the Blair government to establish Britain 'at the heart of Europe'. The Atlanticist position of supporting US action was also taken up by the governments of Denmark, the Netherlands, Italy, Spain and Portugal. Right-wing governments in the latter three countries were assailed by their political opponents on the Left for ignoring majority expressions of popular dissent over Iraq. In the case of Spain, electoral punishment was to come in the form of the defeat of the incumbent government almost a year after the invasion of Iraq. The circumstances of this defeat, in the immediate after-math of the appalling terrorist attacks in Madrid on 11 March 2004, are still controversial and unclear, but there can be little doubt that the opposition prof-ited from public antipathy to Spanish involvement in the United States' Iraq coalition. Also involved were the other countries of 'new Europe' amongst the accession states, most notably Poland, Hungary and the Czech Republic. While, as set out below, there is polling evidence to suggest that the war was also unpop-ular in Eastern Europe, the governments of the accession states maintained a strongly Atlanticist line consistent with their recent history and conceptions of national interest, even if it aggravated some of the founding members of the EU.

Uncertain and negative as the EU response was, it did not, like some Member State governments, contradict what the polling evidence described as a Europe-wide reluctance to become involved in an essentially American adventure. While many tests of public opinion were conducted both before and during the war in Iraq, the best comparative evidence available is derived from polling conducted for Eurobarometer within all the fifteen Member States in October 2003. This found that 68% of European Union citizens are of the opinion that the military intervention of the United States and her allies in Iraq was not justified. Of those 41% took a strong stance, confirming their belief that it was 'not justifiable at all'. Only 29% of respondents believe that this military intervention was justified, of which a mere 7% are totally convinced of this.[20] In only one EU country that supported military action, Denmark, did a majority (57 per cent) believe that such action was justified and there is some evidence that this represented an acquiescence in government policy after earlier scepticism.[21] In Britain, despite the commitment of large numbers of troops to the coalition cause, there was a slight majority, 51 per cent, against with only 15 per cent strongly in favour and 29 per cent strongly opposed. The comparable figures for other countries whose governments had been strong supporters of US policy and signatories of the 'letter of eight' are striking. In Spain 79 per cent were opposed to the war with 3 per cent describing themselves as strongly in favour and 61 per cent strongly opposed. Portugal registered 67 per cent against and Italy 60 per cent. Only 5 per cent and 3 per cent respectively were strongly in favour of their government's policy.[22]

The 'accession states' were not included in the Eurobarometer survey but such alternative evidence as exists would indicate that publics did not entirely follow the lead of their governments over the war. In early 2002, polling in the Czech Republic indicated only 12 per cent support for military intervention without UN cover.[23] In Poland, the staunchest of American allies, 63 per cent were against sending a Polish contingent (although 52 per cent would offer political backing to the United States) while Hungary, in a Gallup Poll of 27 January 2003, registered 82 per cent opposition to military action under any circumstances.[24] In contradiction to the expressions of Atlantic solidarity in the 'letter of eight' and Vilnius declaration, 'new Europe' does not appear to have enjoyed a secure popular base. In fact there is some evidence that in a number of East European states pro-American governments deliberately concealed the extent of their support for and participation in the war from largely sceptical publics.[25] On occasion there was no substance to that support anyway. At the outset of the war EU accession state Slovenia found itself involuntarily amongst the US-led 'coalition of the willing'. 'Slovenes are used to being mistaken for Slovaks but were outraged to hear that the US State Department had named their country as backing the war – even allotting a few million dollars for its support'.[26] Thus the stance of European protagonists of US policy can not be represented as following the views of their respective electorates in defiance of 'old Europe'. By contrast the opposing Member State governments went with the grain of their public opinion. In the same survey 72 per cent of the German population were opposed, 81 per cent of the French and a spectacular 96 per cent of the Greek. Recently freed from 'cohabitation' after the elections of May 2002, President Chirac of France was in no way constrained from pursuing what was easily recognizable as a traditional Gaullist policy towards the United States which clearly enjoyed widespread popularity in France and beyond and gave focus to the many anti-war demonstrations staged in European cities during February 2003.

The behaviour of the ruling SPD–Green coalition in Germany was much more of a departure. Historically the German Federal Republic has been both staunchly European and Atlanticist providing a reliable ally within NATO for US administrations faced with French waywardness and defection. Triggered by the prospects of war over Iraq something very untypical occurred in German policy which was to lead to perhaps the worst ever relations between a German federal chancellor and a US president. The explanation for Chancellor Schröder's robust opposition to war is rooted not apparently in any firm conviction or settled course but in German electoral politics. (An aide to Schröder is quoted as saying that 'he was agnostic about the war. With the economy in trouble and with other things going wrong, the only area where his ratings were consistently high was opposition to US military plans'.)[27] In the summer of 2002, the SPD, having presided over a period of economic stagnation, was by all accounts facing electoral defeat. Two factors appear to have influenced a revival of Chancellor Schröder's fortunes and a very narrow election victory for the SPD and their coalition partners the Greens on 22 September. The first was the Chancellor's prompt and decisive response to the flood emergency that affected much of Central Europe and southern and eastern Germany in the late summer of that year. The second, commentators agree, was his clearly enunciated opposition to the use of force against Iraq. Facing electoral defeat he appealed to that most resonant of post-1945 themes – peace: 'never again war he said and the swing votes of older women who remembered the horrors of war kept him in his job – just'.[28] This position had a certain irony for the chancellor because it was his government which had overturned the settled and indeed constitutional policy of the Federal Republic prohibiting military involvement in actions beyond Germany's borders. Thus German troops had recently been committed to US and allied operations in Kosovo, Macedonia and Afghanistan. Electoral necessity now propelled a policy that went far beyond a reluctance to be involved in an Iraq operation, but gave Germany a leading role, with France, in organizing international opposition. On occasion the electoral rhetoric verged on anti-Americanism and the chancellor was forced to sack the minister for justice (Herta Däubler-Gmelin) who made a *maladroit* comparison between Hitler and Bush. Essentially, however, the polling evidence shows that it did not represent a sudden rise in anti-American sentiment amongst the German public, rather a profound wish not to be involved in military operations. Thus in the Eurobarometer survey more British respondents (54 per cent) considered the United States to constitute a threat to the peace than German respondents (45 per cent).[29]

The policy of the re-elected chancellor had a number of immediate implications. It made possible a renaissance of the Franco-German axis that had for so long dominated the European Community. Since the arrival of the SPD–Green government and the election of a Labour government in Britain this had been replaced by a more complicated diplomatic *ménage à trois* between the three largest EU Member States. Britain in particular had begun to develop an important new military understanding with France sealed by the 1998 St Malo meeting which had given impetus to the development of a European defence identity in the ESDP. At the same time the SPD had been involved with the British Labour Party (and President Clinton) in a joint exploration of the 'Third Way' or 'Die Neue Mitte' in the development of the centre–left and a possible reconciliation of Anglo-Saxon ideas and those of continental social democracy. In the very changed circumstances of mid-2002 these alignments were already under threat but the events of the German election appear to have facilitated a reversion to the old Franco-German axis in EU affairs.

The first indication of this was revealed at a bad-tempered European Council meeting on 24 October 2002 at which there was unexpected Franco-German agreement to delay reform of the Common Agricultural Policy despite the exigencies of admitting ten new Member States. On defence issues the German government aligned itself with France in the continuing discussions on the ESDP, its relationship to NATO and the vexed question of the need for a new and separate European headquarters. In this they were joined by the Belgian government. Its Prime Minister Guy Verhofstadt, himself facing a difficult election, 'knew that hostility towards US military plans brought in votes'.[30] When Chirac and Schröder emphasized their common approach to international problems and their desire to 'adopt common positions' in international bodies this was not just a question of further intergovernmental cooperation but also a pledge explicitly based on the will of their respective peoples. As the German chancellor wrote in the *Berliner Zeitung*, 'In the crises involving terrorism, Iraq and North Korea, our peoples can count on the governments of Germany and France to join forces to preserve peace, avoid war and ensure people's security.'[31]

The European Parliament

The other dimension of potential democratic involvement is provided by the European Parliament and the extent to which it was capable of both articulating what was clearly a majority distaste for military action and influencing the course of the CFSP. The directly elected European Parliament serves as a source of democratic legitimacy for the EU project. However, the quip is often made that if the EU were to apply for membership of itself, in the same way as accession states must do, then its institutions would be found seriously wanting in terms of the EU's own 'Copenhagen Criteria' regarding democratic procedures and legitimacy. Arguably, however, the much maligned European Parliament is no more lacking in control over foreign policy than many of the national assemblies, although it signally failed to articulate a majority position on the war. In fact the EP has always enjoyed powers in respect of budgetary authority over the Community's 'own resources' and in respect of its right to eject the entire Commission – a right exercised for the first time against the Santer Commission during 1999. To this has been added a growing legislative competence described as 'co-decision' whereby in many policy areas the EP approves Commission proposals alongside the Council. In foreign policy it could hardly be expected that the EP could exercise control over the intergovernmental CFSP when in the Member States the conduct of foreign policy and decisions to use force usually remain an executive prerogative. Indeed the Blair government in Britain made much of the ground-breaking nature of its concession in allowing a House of Commons debate and vote on British participation in the military operation in Iraq. It would probably be true to say that most Western governments, while avoiding legislative involvement in the specifics, do in the end seek to gain endorsement for the use of force and the United States is also required to do so under the 1973 'War Powers' legislation passed as a consequence of executive military adventures in Indo-China. The EP can and does question the Presidency, Commission and High Representative on CFSP matters both in Plenary Session and has a right to be consulted by and make 'recommendations' to the Council (TEU Art. 21). It has a specialized Committee on Foreign Affairs, Human Rights Common Security and Defence Policy which is responsible for detailed parliamentary oversight of the CFSP and such matters as exercising the EP's rights (as with most legislatures) of assent to treaties and association agreements concluded by the Community (note that the EU, which does not have legal personality, cannot enter into such agreements).

The CFSP's difficulties with Iraq in early 2003 did not involve the exercise of the EP's powers, nor was there any question of voting for or against a specific course of action. Subsequent to a Plenary Session discussion of Iraq on 29 January 2003 the EP passed a resolution (of 30 January) which opposed, in general terms, tyrannical governments, weapons of mass destruction and the unilateral resort to force. It signally failed, however, at its sessions of 12 February, 12 March and 20 March even to consider a resolution that might express what was clearly the majority opinion of European publics in opposition to the war. The reasons are not difficult to fathom and are revealed by a reading of the transcript of the Emergency Plenary Session on Iraq held on 20 March.[32] The rather loose trans-European party groupings that operate in the EP divided along national as well as ideological lines, which meant that there was no possibility of reproducing the kind of broad consensus that appeared to exist in Europe-wide public opinion. The EP elections had resulted in a marked shift to the right with the EPP–EDD (European Peoples Party and European Democrats) which unites Christian Democrats holding the largest number of seats (232). Including both German Christian Democrats critical of Schröder's anti-American position and British Conservatives the EPP–EDD was generally in favour of military action, except of course for French members. The second largest group was the PES (Party of European Socialists) with 175 members. Although its spokesman opposed the war the group had to contend with the dissent of British Labour Party members. Robin Cook, who happened to chair the Presidium of the PES at the time, recounts the difficulties and his conclusion that at the meeting of 21 February 'there were just too many different national perspectives for us to agree a common European position'.[33] Elsewhere the Left (Cohn Bendit of the Greens) and the extreme right (Le Pen) found themselves in an unlikely alliance against the US-led coalition. One Iraq-related policy area over which the EP can exercise budgetary control is ECHO, a point emphasized by Commissioners Patten and Neilson. Herein lies a danger because as one Green MEP put it, 'The EU, Commissioner Patten, cannot be reduced to a humanitarian agency and Parliament cannot be reduced to a humanitarian agency advisory board.'[34] In fact this might be taken as a fairly accurate representation of the EU's substantive Iraq policy and the EP's part in it! Yet it should not provide the basis for a generalization on the inevitable insignificance of the EP in foreign relations. As far as the CFSP is concerned, the EP only has the right to be informed. However, the continuing basis of the EU's role in the world rests with the activities and budgets of the Community and here the EP has acquired real powers. Consider, for example, its critical position in relation to the funding and very survival of the Palestinian Authority. Its representative in Brussels was spending much of his time and energy in early 2003 on attempting to prevent the EP passing a motion to investigate EU funding on the grounds that it might be implicated in terrorist acts. Such a motion would have had the immediate effect of freezing EU financial assistance to the Authority [35]

Implications for the EU as an actor

It is far too soon to arrive at any definitive judgement on the implications of the Iraq crisis for the EU as an actor in world politics. The events of 2002–3 intruded upon an ongoing debate about the nature, capability and role of this peculiarly post-modern political entity. In terms of the democratic theme of this volume a number of preliminary conclusions are possible concerning the nature and credibility of the CFSP and the distinctive role of the EU in democracy promotion. Underlying them is the question of the very identity of the EU itself and its legitimacy for the diverse publics of twenty-five Member States.

In the words of a previous Director-General for External and Politico-Military Affairs at the Council of Ministers the crisis leading up to the war in Iraq seemed to 'epitomize everything that is wrong with the practice and even the concept of the CFSP'.[36] However, as we have seen, the events of late 2002 broke in upon what had been a long-running and rather successful attempt to keep Iraq off the agenda. This not only was because the EU had no formal position in Iraq, but also arose out of the awareness of Member State governments that this was a matter for the British and French given their permanent membership of the UN Security Council. However, as Crowe argues it was also born of a desire to protect the CFSP. Member State governments knew 'that any attempt to forge a common EU position on Iraq would be more damaging than helpful to a still fragile CFSP which was making real progress in other areas, notably the Balkans and even the Middle East'.[37]

The role of public and electoral pressure could be regarded negatively – as another restraining factor alongside the diverse national interests and external orientations of governments making it impossible for the EU to take decisive external action. However, the range of the CFSP's other activities, notably in the

Middle East and in its approach to Iran, indicate that Iraq provides the exception rather than the rule. In retrospect it is possible to evaluate the inability of the CFSP to support the opposition of France and Germany to US action as an opportunity foregone. A united European front at the Security Council might just have persuaded the US administration to wait for verified evidence of Iraqi weapons of mass destruction and to take military action only on the basis of a new mandate from that Council. Such a stance by the EU would have enjoyed overwhelming public support in Europe and whatever its effects upon the Bush administration would have enormously enhanced both the legitimacy and credibility of the CFSP. In the event, of course, US diplomacy was able to move aggressively to exploit the divisions between 'old' and 'new' Europe. It was not the dictates of public opinion or indeed electoral advantage that allowed this to happen, rather a contrary pursuit of the assumed primacy of US over European alignments by the British, Spanish, Italian and Portuguese governments.

Given the severity of the problems encountered by the CFSP over Iraq it might also have been expected that its extension, in the emergent ESDP, would sustain similar damage. The policy, agreed at the Cologne Council of June 1999, reflected the desire of Member States that the:

> Union must have the capacity for autonomous action, backed by credible military forces, the means to decide to use them, and a readiness to do so, in order to respond to international crises without prejudice to actions by NATO.[38]

The uses of force envisaged were limited to the 'Petersberg Tasks', relatively low-level rescue, humanitarian and peacekeeping missions and most definitely excluded significant war-fighting or intervention to procure regime change. The ESDP, however, did represent a major departure for the EU and one which, because of the implications for the primacy of NATO, caused difficulties for the United States, Turkey (which for a period vetoed the use of NATO assets) and for Britain and other Atlanticist Member States. At the beginning of 2003 arrangements were in place for the first operation of the ESDP, a very limited police operation in Bosnia-Herzegovina, and it was envisaged that the EU would later in the year take over the existing NATO military operation in the Former Yugoslav Republic of Macedonia. [39]

The emergence of the ESDP was the fruit of a new rapprochement between France and Britain, the EU's leading and in some respects only military powers, that had been achieved at the St Malo meeting at the end of 1998 and was given added point by European reliance on the United States to conduct the Kosovo operation of 1999. As relations between London and Paris deteriorated during the early months of 2003 it seemed that the new ESDP might become a casualty of the invasion of Iraq. In February 2003 France, Germany and Belgium cast an unprecedented veto at the NATO Council over preparations to assist Turkey in the event that the latter became involved in hostilities in Iraq. Also, the same three countries and Luxembourg emphasized their opposition to US policy and the possibility of action beyond NATO by holding, during April 2003, the so-called 'chocolate summit' in Brussels to discuss the creation of a dedicated non-NATO ESDP headquarters. Although this caused a diplomatic flurry at the time, the proposal was soon forgotten. More significantly the initial operations of the ESDP proceeded as planned. On 1 January 2003 the EU Police Mission in Bosnia-Herzegovina was launched replacing the existing UN operation and on 31 March an EU military operation in the Former Yugoslav Republic of Macedonia (Concordia) assumed the tasks that had previously been undertaken by a NATO force. Finally on 12 June and at the behest of the UN Security Council the EU launched a small operation (Artemis) in the Congo involving mainly French but also some British personnel. Whatever the Iraq crisis had demonstrated about the failings of the CFSP it was not allowed to impede the introduction of the ESDP.

Despite these initial forays into the use of force, the EU remains a highly distinctive and overwhelmingly non-military actor. Its strengths lie in its trade competences, its global network of association agreements and its leading role in environmental policy. In these areas it has challenged the United States directly at the WTO and over the Kyoto Protocol on climate change plus a string of other multilateral undertakings including the International Criminal Court.[40] It is possible to interpret the EU's role and identity in various ways and a lively transatlantic debate paralleled and drew sustenance from the Iraq crisis. For some such as George Monbiot the EU was required to exercise a counter-hegemonic role.[41] For others, notably Robert Kagan, the EU was simply incapable of exercising serious political and military power. In Kagan's view the EU came from Venus while the United States enjoyed the attributes of Mars. The United States continued to be a military giant fully appraised of the realities of the Hobbesian world that it bestrode, while Europe existed in a 'rule-governed' Kantian world of its own made possible only by virtue of a benign US hegemony.[42] Without entering into this controversy, it is clearly the case that the United States and EU constitute very different types of international actor. As German Foreign Minister Joschka Fischer said during the Iraq crisis, 'Europe does not do war'. One reason for this is the unwillingness of European publics either to countenance or fund a military effort in any way comparable to that of the United States even if this were to be technologically possible. Equally it is very difficult to envisage that the EU, as opposed to some of its more bellicose Member States, could ever be involved in the coercive introduction of 'democracy' in Iraq or elsewhere. This is not to say, however, that the EU has no role in the promotion of democratic values and good governance. It is just that its approach is necessarily very different from that of the United States.

Democracy and human rights promotion has indeed become a significant aspect of the EU's external policy. Although lumped together for funding purposes in the European Initiative for Human Rights and Democracy (EIDHR) they are really not synonymous. However objectionable US use of the death penalty or treatment of Guantanamo Bay prisoners may appear from a European human rights perspective, there is no suggestion that these practices in some way invalidate the United States' status as a democracy.[43] Both the United States and EU are engaged in external democracy promotion but the methods and their applicability to the Iraq situation differ markedly. One of the critical issues in the wake of the Iraq war is the extent to which the 'free West' of political rhetoric continues to exist and more precisely whether there can be any practical cooperation with the EU in the ambitious campaign, announced by President Bush in his Banqueting House speech of November 2003, to bring democracy to the Middle East.

Initially the Community's dealings with third countries had an overwhelmingly economic character and the standards required of others were those that would facilitate commerce. By contrast the United States was throughout the Cold War engaged in a highly selective campaign of democracy promotion. However, the circumstances of the ending of the Cold War provided the opportunity, even the necessity, for the EU to press ahead with a democracy and good governance agenda. This was recognized at Maastricht where developing and consolidating democracy and the rule of law was proclaimed as both a CFSP and development policy objective.[44] In pursuit of this objective democratic and good governance issues routinely form part of the institutionalized political dialogue that the EU conducts with third states. Good governance clauses have also been incorporated in the Lomé and Cotonou Conventions that provide the framework for EU relations with the African, Caribbean and Pacific countries, some of which have had their membership suspended for violations.

The EU approach is generally one of pragmatic engagement which only comes into play once some basis of democratization has been established in the target country.[45] It is not essentially concerned with direct institution building but by contrast with US practice focuses upon the encouragement of civil society through the indirect funding of NGOs.[46] Above all it relies upon an accession or trade and aid relationship. According to a recent study the outcome has been mixed – generally successful in relation to accession states, but much less so in cases such as the Ukraine and Morocco.[47]

Even if the political will existed amongst the Member States it is difficult to envisage a role for the EU in the democratic reconstitution of Iraq. The coercive construction of a new political system by outside influences is clearly beyond its experience and alien to the policy tradition that has been developed. Moreover the EU has a lack of status and weight in Iraq. Its activities elsewhere have been founded on contingency arising from extensive economic and or regional interconnections, which are manifestly absent. Given the high dependence of the EU upon Middle East oil the future stability of Iraq is clearly in the European interest, but the EU does not have the standing to exercise any major influence. However, the case of Iran provides an instructive parallel. Here the EU, faced with another founder member of President Bush's 'axis of evil', has been able to demonstrate an alternative approach to coercive democratization.

Ultimately the further development of the EU as an international actor, particularly one with an enhanced military dimension, will require popular support and democratic legitimation. It is hardly an original observation that the primary focus of popular allegiance remains with national Member States. As Jacques Delors once remarked, 'on ne tombe pas amoureux avec un grand marché!'[48] The Iraq War did not pose a test of allegiance for the EU and current policies, based as they are on intergovernmental consensus, are very unlikely to provoke citizens in ways comparable with what occurred at national level in a number of Member States. What is known from the polling evidence is that a majority across the fifteen existing Member States thought that the EU's performance over the Iraq conflict had either not diminished its role or actually reinforced it![49] This is, alas, rather more likely to indicate popular ignorance of the operations of the CFSP than a more subtle absence of expectations grounded upon an understanding of the inherent limitations of the policy. Nonetheless EU decision-makers can take heart that those policies that have been adopted enjoy public support across the EU. Multilateral action through UN agencies for the reconstruction of Iraq was endorsed (by 59 per cent) as was EU humanitarian assistance (by 82 per cent) and continued involvement in the search for a peaceful solution in the Middle East (by 81 per cent).[50] With a number of Member States involved in operations in Iraq there was still a strong majority opposition to the deployment of EU peacekeeping troops in Iraq. Despite the manifest imperfections of the CFSP and the supposed 'democratic deficit' in Brussels this provides some indication that the EU's external role was backed by its citizens, who would doubtless also have endorsed the adoption of the Franco-German position on the legitimacy of the invasion.

Notes and references

1 They are founded upon special trade relations but include much else. Association agreements typically have an aid dimension, some form of political dialogue and, increasingly, human rights, sustainable development and 'good governance' clauses. Despite the high profile given to the CFSP it is these relations and the ways in which they are exploited that provide the essential basis for the claim that the EU constitutes a significant international actor in its own right. Substantive decisions of the CFSP in Pillar II usually require active cooperation with the Commission in Pillar I because the latter controls the necessary policy instruments and budget lines. Thus in the case of Iraq CFSP decisions in accord with UN sanctions policies require implementation involving the Commission because trade competence is vested in the Community.

2 The use of the separate terms European Community and European Union is intentional even though it is now commonplace simply to refer to the European Union. The European Community has its own legal personality alongside the Member States and is based upon the original Treaty of Rome, now the much amended Treaty Establishing the European Community (TEC). The Commission and the European Parliament are extensively involved along with the Council of Ministers in policy-making across a wide range of issues within the competence of the Community. Subsequent to the 1992 Maastricht Treaty creating the European Union (TEU) the Community constitutes Pillar I of an overarching EU structure. The other pillars, of which Pillar II constitutes the CFSP, rely not upon Community decision-making methods but upon intergovernmental cooperation. All this is subject to extensive revision under the draft European Constitution.

3 European Commission, *The European Union's Relations with Iraq*, 2003.

4 C. Patten, 'Must we help re-construct Iraq?', 23 October 2003. Online. Available HTTP: <www.europa.int/external_relations> (accessed 25 November 2003).

5 TEU Art. 11(2).
6 J. Dempsey, 'Follow My Leaders', *Financial Times Magazine*, 12, 12 July 2003, pp. 14–23, 20.
7 Xavier Solana, Statement to the European Parliament, sitting of Wednesday 29 January 2003.
8 European Commission, *The EU's Relations with Iraq: General Affairs and External Relations Council (GAERC)*, 2003. Online. Available HTTP: <http://www.europa.eu.int/comm/external_relations/iraq/intro/gac.htm> (accessed 25 November 2003).
9 Council Conclusions, Copenhagen, 12–13 December 2002, Annex IV.
10 J. Kampfner, *Blair's Wars*, London: Free Press, 2003, p. 248.
11 UN Security Council Statement of 20 January 2003.
12 Kampfner, op. cit., p. 250.
13 European Commission, GAERC, op. cit.
14 Kampfner, op. cit., pp. 250–1.
15 Ibid., p. 253.
16 Presidency, 4 February 2003/5963/03 (Presidency 28).
17 Council of the European Union, *Extraordinary European Council, 17 February 2003*, 6466/03 POLGEN 7, Brussels 21 February 2003.
18 BBC News, 18 February 2003.
19 Quoted in Kampfner, op. cit., p. 287.
20 European Commission, *Flash Eurobarometer 151: Iraq and Peace in the World*, October 2003, p. 5.
21 Ibid., p. 7.
22 Ibid., p. 6.
23 Online. Available HTTP: <http://www.radio.cz/en/en/article/3857> (accessed 9 December 2003).
24 Online. Available HTTP: <http.//www.alternet.org/thenews/newsdesk/L30567527> (accessed 9 December 2003).
25 I. Traynor, 'The Last to Know', *Guardian*, 29 August 2003.
26 I. Black, 'Inside Europe', *Guardian*, 31 March 2003.
27 Kampfner, op. cit. p. 241.
28 T. Garton Ash, 'The Road to Zermatt', *Guardian*, 20 February 2003.
29 European Commission, *Flash Eurobarometer 151*, op. cit., p. 78.
30 Kampfner, op. cit., p. 270.
31 *Guardian*, 22 January 2003.
32 Online. Available HTTP: <http://www3.europarl.eu.int/omk/omnsapir.so/debats> (accessed 12 December 2003).
33 R. Cook, *Point of Departure*, London: Simon & Schuster, 2003, p. 300.
34 M. Frassoni (Verts/ALE), Session of 20 March 2003.
35 Interview with P. A. Representative, Brussels, 15 January 2003.
36 B. Crowe, 'A Common European Foreign Policy after Iraq?', *International Affairs*, 79, 2003, pp. 533–546, 534.
37 Ibid., p. 535.
38 Council Conclusions, Cologne 1999.
39 By 2003 agreement had been reached on the 'headline goal' of 60,000 troops to be committed to the ESDP, on the creation of a dedicated politico-military structure located within the Council of Ministers and on the sensitive question of the relationship with NATO and the use of alliance assets. There continued to be an outstanding question concerning the character of the ESDP headquarters (NATO or national for the Atlanticists as opposed to the French preference for a dedicated European HQ). The ESDP was declared operational at the Laeken Council of December 2001 and the first operation was planned (a police mission in Bosnia) for the beginning of 2003.
40 For an assessment of the EU as an international actor which places emphasis on these areas rather than upon the CFSP and which reflects external constructions of the

EU's identity, see C. Bretherton and J. Vogler, *The European Union as a Global Actor*, London: Routledge, 1999.

41 G. Monbiot, 'The Bottom Dollar', *Guardian*, 4 March 2003.

42 R. Kagan, *Paradise and Power: America and Europe in the New World Order*, London: Atlantic Books, 2003.

43 A worldwide campaign against the death penalty as a fundamental violation of human rights has been waged with some success by the EU and provides some basis for the claim that the EU is exercising normative power. See Ian Manners, 'Normative Power Europe: A Contradiction in Terms?', *Journal of Common Market Studies*, 40, 2002, pp. 235–58.

44 The most pressing requirement occurred in dealings with the accession states. Under the 1993 Copenhagen Criteria acceding states' membership of the EU would require 'stability of institutions guaranteeing democracy, the rule of law, human rights and respect for and protection minorities'. This was backed up by the promise of membership and by active funding of transnational civil society groups. Such a process is occurring to a greater or lesser extent with Turkey. The other significant arena of democracy promotion has been provided by the long-standing aid and trade relationship with the ACP (African, Caribbean and Pacific States). Under the last Lomé Convention IV, and now Cotonou, the maintenance of the benefits of a relationship with the EU are in part conditional upon observance of good governance and human rights criteria. The negotiations on this point were difficult and 'good governance' is described as a 'fundamental but not essential' element of the partnership with the ACP (K. E. Smith, *European Union Foreign Policy in a Changing World*, Cambridge: Polity Press, 2003, p. 129).

45 Ibid., pp. 126–7.

46 Ibid., pp. 136–7.

47 P. J. Kubicek, 'International Norms, the European Union and Democratization: Tentative Theory and Evidence', in P. J. Kubicek (ed.), *The European Union and Democratization*, London: Routledge, 2003, pp. 1–29.

48 Quoted in Bretherton and Vogler, 1999, op. cit., p. 233.

49 European Commission, *Flash Eurobarometer 151*, op. cit., p. 55; 42 per cent felt that the EU role had not been diminished and 12 per cent that it had actually been reinforced.

50 Ibid., pp. 23, 59.

7 Turkey

Democratic legitimacy

Christopher Brewin

On 1 March 2003 the Turkish Grand National Assembly defeated the Turkish government by three votes. By this narrow margin, the Turkish Parliament prevented the American and British governments from attacking Iraq from the north. This controversial vote has momentous implications for the future of Turkish democracy, itself intimately bound up with Turkey's relations with the democracies of the United States and the European Union. This chapter considers Turkey's involvement with the Iraq War from five very different angles of what constitutes democratic legitimacy.

Public opinion

In the first place, the Parliament's anti-war vote was in part driven by public opinion. In March 2003, an Ankara research centre reported that Turks were 94 per cent against the use of Turkish bases and troops by the American forces, and that 87 per cent opposed American intervention. However, elite opinion was deeply divided on the issue. Many senior officers in the army and officials in the Turkish Ministry of Foreign Affairs approved of the government decisions to comply with American requests to seek permission from Parliament in the spring of 2003 for the use of Turkish facilities and in the autumn of 2003 for Turkish peacekeeping forces to be made available to the Iraqi National Council.

National interest defined by elected government

However, it is legitimate for an elected government to go against public opinion in defining what constitutes the national interest. In the Turkish case, the government could point to the popular vote for the moderate Islamist AK (Justice and Development) Party in the recent election of November 2002. Having won nearly two-thirds of the seats in Parliament, the AK Party formed the government, ending two decades of rule by coalition. The Turkish government was therefore at least as entitled as the British, the Spanish and some East European governments and the Italian prime minister to support the American use of force in Iraq as being the better view of the Turkish national interest.

Foundation myths of secularism and territorial integrity

More controversially, what may be called the foundation myths of a republic may be invoked to justify opposition to either public opinion or to government actions. For example, some say that the Weimar Republic should not have allowed Hitler's party to come to power on an anti-democratic platform; this was held to justify Bonn's refusal to tolerate fascist or communist parties in post-1945 Germany. Others say that de Gaulle was justified in refusing to accept Vichy's cession of French territory, or that Michel Debré was justified in opposing de Gaulle's cession of Algeria. In Turkey's case in 2003 both kinds of foundation myth could have been invoked to undermine the elected government. As recently as 28 February 1998 the Turkish armed forces, with public support, had seen it as their duty to safeguard the secular republic by what was called a 'velvet coup' against Prime Minister Necmettin Erbakan, leader of an Islamic party that was then judicially dissolved as having aims incompatible with the secular Constitution. In March 2003 Recep Tayyip Erbakan, the leader of the AK Party, was engaged in returning to Parliament in a by-election in Siirt. As a consequence of reciting a famous poem about mosques being the helmets of Islam, and minarets being like swords, he had been banned from standing in the general election of 2002.

If the myth of secularism was a potential powder keg for all sides caught up in a war with a secular Iraqi state whose citizens were both Shia and Sunni, this has to be distinguished from a second salient foundation myth. The territorial integrity of Turkey is taught to every Turkish child by reference to the Treaty of Sèvres (1920). By this treaty, the victorious European powers sought to reduce Ottoman territory to an indefensible slice of Central Anatolia, envisaging Armenian independence and a referendum in which Kurds could choose secession. Between 1985 and 1998 Turkish opinion had been consistently hard line in supporting state repression of Abdullah Öcalan's Kurdish secessionists in a civil war costing 30,000 lives. There was widespread resentment in Turkey that Kurdish self-rule in northern Iraq after the first Gulf War, and the external supply of money and arms from Kurdish refugees in Western Europe, threatened the Turkish Republic's territorial integrity. Moreover, Kurdish cultural demands for Kurdish-language schools undermined the related foundation myth of one Turkish citizenship, at once civic and ethnic. American and European governments are perceived as ambivalent towards claims to self-determination on behalf of 23 million Kurds, seeing Kurdish nationalism as a possibly legitimate aspiration but unable to say where the borders of a Kurdish state might lie. The legitimacy of secularism in Turkey and secession from Turkey are separately the third and fourth issues raised for Turkey by the Iraq War.

Normative grounds of legitimacy

In Western Europe, many demonstrators and opinion-formers held that the legitimacy of the war depended on adherence to international law. The demand for a further resolution from the Security Council of the United Nations showed commendable hope that, after the end of the Cold War, that peculiarly ordered body could become an arbiter of those legal and political disputes most dangerous to humankind; it also provided pious cover for opposition to the war. In Turkey, President Necdet Sezer, a constitutional lawyer by training, powerfully represented this normative strain of democratic discourse. He consistently argued in March 2003 and again in the autumn that adequate UN authority was required before Turkey could openly send its troops outside Turkey.

For an Islamic country, moreover, there is another set of norms perceived as binding. Islamic rulers should respect the Islamic realm of peace, and not participate in Western crusades. Bülent Arınç, Speaker of the Parliament, articulated this external normative aspect of the internal issue of secularism. Arınç led the successful revolt within the AK Party on the grounds that Islamic deputies could not vote for war against their Islamic neighbours. A month later he also divided the governing party by allowing his wife to parade her headscarf at a state function. His principled stance endangered democracy, in that an intervention by army commanders alarmed by his Islamic priorities would have received American support, as Paul Wolfowitz was to make clear on Turkish television in May. Perhaps in March the waters were sufficiently muddied in that Arınç's support of Rauf Denktaş's opposition to the Annan plan for the reunification of Cyprus was in line on that issue of nationalism with the views of secularist enemies.

In the case of Turkey, therefore, these five grounds for claiming democratic legitimacy – public opinion, governmental authority, foundational myths of secularism and territorial integrity, and external normative requirements – form the criteria for analysing Turkey's policy with respect to the war in Iraq that began on 20 March 2003. The analysis begins with Turkey's policy on Iraq as a regional actor, and then considers the effects of the Iraq War on Turkey's relations with the United States and the European Union.

Turkey and Iraq

Public opinion

Turks see themselves as a model of democracy for the region[1] and do not see the repressive Baathist Parties of Iraq and Syria as similar to the pluralist Kemalist Parties of post-1945 Turkey. However, this does not mean that Turks have a duty or even an interest in establishing democracy by force in neighbouring Iraq or Syria, any more than Britain and the United States felt obliged after 1991 to democratize Kuwait. The Turkish threat to invade Syria in 1998, which led to the expulsion of Abdullah Öcalan, the leader of the Kurdistan Workers' Party (PKK), was not accompanied by any suggestion that the Baathist leadership in Syria should become democratic. While some forty Caucasian organizations have vociferously campaigned in Turkey on behalf of the human and democratic rights of Chechens, this has not changed the Turkish state's cautious and low-key relations with the Russian Federation. The short-lived Kurdish Parliament established in northern Iraq in 1992–4 was as unwelcome to Turkish opinion as the meetings of a Kurdish Parliament-in-exile in the Netherlands and Brussels.

Nor was a weakened Iraq perceived as threatening democracy in Turkey. Turkey differs from West European countries in that war with its neighbours is always a possibility. Turkey shares with Greece the dubious distinction of being the two NATO countries to increase military expenditure after the end of the Cold War. Yet when in 1995 Ambassador Sükrü Elekdağ expounded the doctrine of preparation for 'two and a half wars', he had in mind a civil (half) war against the PKK simultaneously with regional wars with two out of Greece, the Russian Federation, Iran and possibly Armenia, but not Iraq or Syria.[2] When the Turkish military mounted a large-scale incursion into Iraq in 1995,[3] or threatened to invade Syria, they were not expecting this to become a war. Nor were Turks after 1991 much worried by Saddam Hussein's weapons of mass destruction. Philip Robins claims that the Turkish public and elites did not take UNSCOM'S work on WMD seriously until 1995.[4] Even so, Iran was a much more dangerous rival. In so far as there was a threat from Iraq, Anglo-Saxon air attacks on surface-to-air missile sites in northern Iraq were thought to have removed the imminent threat to Turkish cities while cooperation with Israel on a version of ARROW anti-missile technology would reduce the future threat. It was not until war seemed imminent in 2002 that the Turkish press became concerned by the inability of a divided NATO Council to allocate to Turkey AWACS cover and Patriot missiles, on the model of the meagre provision during the Gulf War. It was not until February 2003 that NATO's Defence Planning Council persuaded the Netherlands and Germany to send these items together with protective clothing.[5]

If public opinion in Turkey was like the rest of Europe in not being persuaded by arguments on democracy and the dangers of WMD, what seems to have made Turkish opinion more hostile than others to adventurism was the general view that Turkey had been left after the Gulf War to bear the brunt of the ensuing economic and political costs of the blockade. The unemployment and economic crisis that had led to the electoral triumph of the AK Party was itself a reason for avoiding further disruption on Turkey's border with an oil-rich country. It has been well observed that, in voting for the AK Party, conservative Sunni Turkey showed itself profoundly in favour of compromise. What is more interesting is to explain the division of opinion on Iraq within the incorruptible Turkish military and foreign policy elites which, since the disappointment with the Luxembourg Council's refusal of Turkish candidature in 1997, had been strongly identified with American and Israeli perspectives on the Middle East.

Turkish national interests in Iraq

In going against public opinion, the government decision to put to the Turkish Parliament a resolution permitting 62,000 American troops to attack Iraq from Turkish soil was based on its view of the national interest. In this section the focus will be on the political and economic factors relating specifically to Turkish policy on Iraq.

Politically, Saddam Hussein's weakened regime suited Turkey. In 2003 all that was left of Saddam's bold plan to position himself as leader of the Arab world was a tariff of subsidies to Palestinian martyrs. Moreover, a unitary Iraq ruled by the secular Baathist Party also suited Turkish interests. The disintegration of Iraq would allow the Shia majority in the south to develop closer links with Iran, Turkey's fundamentalist rival for influence in the Caspian. Worse, disintegration might well enable Iraqi Kurds to develop the autonomy they had enjoyed in northern Iraq, becoming a pole of attraction and external source of support for Kurdish secessionists in Turkey, Syria and Iran.[6] As this issue, and the refugee issue, raises the question of Turkey's territorial integrity, it is reserved for a later section of this chapter.

For present purposes what are worth highlighting are the roles of the elected Parliament, the civilian prime minister, and the president in defining the national interest in the decade after the end of the Cold War. Thus in 1991 President Turgut Özal's decision to join the coalition to save Kuwait seemed such an adventurist reversal of Turkey's status quo policy that both the head of the Foreign Office and the chief of staff resigned. The resignation of General Necip Torumtay was all the more sensational in that the civilian prime minister had gone against the wishes of the armed forces in appointing him in 1987. Moreover, the Turkish Parliament had displayed what the *International Herald Tribune* called 'firm opposition'.[7] This opposition was strong enough to prevent the participation of any Turkish troops in the thirty-nation 1990–1 coalition that assembled in Saudi Arabia against Iraq. Both Islamic and ultra-nationalist circles took strong exception to Özal's imaginative scheme to return Kurdish refugees under the protection of a no-fly zone authorized by the United Nations. On 28 December 1994, for example, Necmettin Erbakan, leader of the Islamic Refah Party, denounced Operation Provide Comfort as 'an occupation force and a second Sèvres'. When he became prime minister a few months later he chose not to confront the army's wish to retain this cover for its own anti-PKK operations within Iraq. Three political parties, Mesut Yilmaz' right-of-centre Motherland Party (ANAP), Bülent Ecevit's left-of-centre DYP, and the Islamic Refah Party, all joined President Demirel in supporting in government what they had opposed in opposition. Every coalition government offloaded onto the Grand National Assembly responsibility for authorizing the attacks in their successive manifestations of Poised Hammer, Provide Comfort and Provide Comfort 2, and, after the French withdrawal in 1997, Northern Watch. Twice a year the Parliament renewed its mandate allowing American and British use of the Incirlik air base near Adana, American ground troops to base themselves in Silopi, and support elements to live in Batman. Nevertheless, Turkish willingness to treat Saddam Hussein's regime as the properly established authority was also evident. For example, in 1993 Turkey reopened its embassy in Baghdad. In 1996, Erbakan's Justice Minister, Sevket Kazan, went as far as to say in Baghdad that UN sanctions were unfair and that it was Turkey's 'duty to stand by its friend'.[8] In February 1998, Prime Minister Bülent Ecevit manoeuvred to make an American confrontation with Baghdad over weapons inspections unsustainable.[9]

Turkey's economic interests were more affected than any other major participant by war in Iraq. In 1984 Turkey had become Iraq's second most important trading partner, after Germany. It happily supplied both sides in the Iran–Iraq conflict in defiance of the American trade embargo imposed on Iran after the hostage crisis. Turkey has electricity links with the Iraqi grid, and has helped the Barzani faction of Iraqi Kurds (PUK) build power stations. Turkey controls oil exports to the Mediterranean coast through two pipelines and the huge fleets of tanker trucks that cross into southern Turkey. When Özal suddenly closed the pipelines in August 1990, that measure alone cost Turkey $250 million per annum in fees. Turks estimate that in 1990–4 their annual losses from sanctions against Iraq ran to some $5 billion. Although Turkey was to benefit from the provision in UNSC Resolution 986 of 14 April 1995 that the 'larger share' of petroleum exports should be via Yumurtalik, and despite Turkey's trade with Iraq's new northern enclave, Turks remain convinced that they bore the brunt of the economic costs of UN sanctions.

In the buildup to the war in 2003, the new Turkish government therefore put a high price on Turkish participation. The election victory of 2002 had been won primarily because of the unemployment and economic downturn caused by a banking crisis whose roots lay in the costs of a large army and the corruption of a clientelistic political system. The government's political credibility depended on being able to demonstrate simultaneously to its own people that it could restore the economy and to foreign investors that it could meet immediate demands for the scheduled repayment of external debt. The phasing out of American Cold War subsidies had to some extent been replaced by generous American subsidies to Turkish troops in Afghanistan. Newspapers reported that in December 2002 Paul Wolfowitz was prepared to offer $6 billion in cash. In addition, a figure of $20–24 billion in soft loans or forgiveness of past military debt was at least discussed.[10] Finally, the essential point for Turkey was that Washington should continue to use its political influence in persuading the IMF to continue its biggest ever support operation in Turkey.

Territorial integrity

The war in Iraq posed a double threat to the territorial integrity of Turkey to an extent that is difficult to appreciate in Western Europe. A foundational myth of the Turkish Republic is that its frontiers were established in January 1920 by the 'national promise' of the then Ottoman Parliament to defend the territory established by the Armistice of Modroos of 30 October 1918. Thereafter, Ataturk's slogan of 'peace at home' meant that all individuals living within those limits were to be citizens of the new republic. This civic conception could too easily become an ethnic conception, allowing in 1943 special taxes on Greeks and Armenians, and in 1955 and 1964 populist attacks on the Greek community in Istanbul stimulated by reports from Cyprus. The slogan 'peace abroad' meant that the republic took no responsibility for either Turkish-speakers or Muslims who lived outside the frontiers established at Modroos. This too became modified by the contrived incorporation of Hatay into Turkey in 1938–9, and by the Grand National Assembly's declaration in 1997 that the fate of Turkish Cypriots was a 'national question'. In March 2003, the Turkish Cypriot President Rauf Denktaş was able to exploit this moment of heightened nationalism to reject 'with the firm support of the Turkish general staff and the foreign ministry' the second version of the Annan plan for the reunification of Cyprus.[11]

Before and during the Iraq War, a similar Turkish identification with the Turcomen of Kirkuk became a distinct possibility. Turkish special forces in northern Iraq saw it as part of their mission to protect the Turcomen against the Kurds returning to replace the Arabs favoured by Saddam Hussein.[12] If Turkey had been a combatant force, it might well have trumpeted the self-determination of Turcomen linked to its own territorial claims established by the Armistice of Modroos. At the end of October 1918, British troops were 30 kilometres south of Mosul. In 1925 the League of Nations had recognized the claim of the then very weak Turkish Republic to the oil wells of Kirkuk by assigning it a tenth of petroleum revenues for twenty-five years.

However, in the negotiations with the Americans before the war, and after the war in the negotiations on a possible Turkish peacekeeping force, the dominant concern was not how to expand Turkish territory. It was how to prevent the loss of south-east Turkey to an eventual Kurdish federation claiming to bring democratic self-determination to 23 million Kurds. Turkey's territorial integrity was at stake for two separable but connected reasons, one relating to changed demography within Turkish borders, the other to the creation outside Turkey of external sources of legitimacy and material aid.

War in Iraq has in the recent past meant the destabilizing influx of refugees into Turkey itself. In 1987, 40–50,000 Kurds crossed from Iraq into Turkey, of whom 35,000 became permanent residents after Baghdad re-established control in 1988. In 1991, 400,000 Kurds fled to Turkey, of whom 250,000 arrived in the two months of March and April. For the next decade, Turkish newspapers proclaimed that Turkey had been unfairly saddled with the economic costs of this sudden strain on public resources in the poorest region of the country. During this period of a thriteen-year civil war, peaking in 1995, newspapers did not openly discuss Kurdish politics, making it difficult to gauge how many joined the Kurdish Workers' Party (PKK), how many returned to Iraq, how many went on to Istanbul and the major cities of Europe, and how many of the 850,000 Kurds in Western Europe contributed, willingly or not, funds to the PKK. What is clear is that Turkish opinion and the organs of the Turkish state took a hard line against the revolutionary secessionism of the PKK. Despite the loss of 30,000 lives, no legitimacy was accorded to Kurdish claims for self-determination. However, once Turkish armed threats had compelled the expulsion of Abdullah Öcalan from Syria, and Turkish forces had captured him in Nairobi in 1999, Turgut Özal's more flexible policies returned to the agenda. On the one hand, the PKK declared a unilateral ceasefire within Turkey, and reformed itself by 2002 as a non-violent organization, KADEK. On the other hand, Foreign Minister Ismail Cem and Mesut Yilmaz risked opprobrium by suggesting that cultural rights in broadcasting and education would preclude secessionist demands. In 1999, Ambassador Sükrü Elekdağ wrote three newspaper articles in *Milliyet* in which he advocated legalizing the reception of broadcasting in Kurdish, most of it coming from outside Turkey.[13]

In the Turkish view, a more serious danger than the arrival of refugees was the establishment in northern Iraq of an autonomous Kurdish area within a federation. In January 2004, the Turkish armed forces threatened 'a difficult and bloody future' for any Iraqi federalist state based on ethnicity.[14] Worse would be an independent self-determining Kurdish democracy that would encourage Kurdish separatism in Turkey. It would be interesting to know why the Kurdish deputies within the AK Party voted against their own government in opposing a war supported by Iraqi Kurds. It may be yet another sign of disunity among Kurds, or a sophisticated calculation that the presence of the Turkish Army in northern Iraq would be detrimental to Kurdish autonomy. The historic isolation of Kurdish nationalism had been its major weakness. In 1984, Turkey had signed a treaty with Iraq entitling both countries to pursue Kurdish guerrillas across each other's borders. The creation of external legitimation in the form of the Kurdish Parliament-in-exile allowed to meet in Brussels or the Netherlands was one aspect of the danger. Since 1991, Turkey had come to accept reluctantly the need to negotiate with some sort of entity, transcending the armed struggles between the KDP (Kurdistan Democratic Party) of Sheikh Massoud Barzani, generally favoured by Turkey, and the PUK (Patriotic Union of Kurdistan) led by Jalal Talabani and often influenced by Iran. On at least four occasions between 1992 and 1996, Turkey considered establishing a buffer zone similar to that set up by Israel in the Lebanon.[15] In 1995 Ankara supported American efforts to end the armed conflict between the Kurdish factions of Barzani and Talabani. Although the principal motive was to help Barzani concentrate his fire on the PKK, then at the height of its success, the effect was Turkish acceptance of a Kurdish entity in northern Iraq, which the United States was to call a federation after 1997. As the war drums became louder in 2002, the Kurdish Parliament, established ten years earlier, came together again. In 2002–3, somewhere between 1,000 and 10,000 Turkish special forces were deployed prophylactically up to 20 kilometres within the Iraqi side of the border to deter an influx of refugees and to support groups in Iraq favoured by Turkey. In July 2003 both the Turkish presence and its relative impotence were dramatized by the forty-eight-hour detention by American special forces of Turkish officers at their headquarters in the Iraqi town of Suleimaniye, allegedly for plotting the assassination of the Kurdish mayor of Kirkuk.[16]

Secularism

Members of the Turkish armed forces take seriously their oath to uphold democracy, by which they mean the secular institutions of a modern republic. For example, in 2003 the Land Commander, General Aytac Yalman, was completely serious in saying that 'the Turkish military is the guarantee of democracy, so far from being an obstacle to democratization'. The Iraq War, like the Cyprus issue, was an obvious lever for those who interpreted the national and democratic interest as requiring the overthrow or at least the subordination of the conservative Islamic government elected in 2002. As recently as 28 February 1997 the National Security Council had made impossible the continuance of the coalition government led by the Islamic militant, Necmettin Erbakan. That velvet coup had been occasioned by irritation at a local mayor's links with Iran, intended to reintroduce Sharia law. However, the coup was supported by the army, by Kemalists across the spectrum, and accepted without demur by the Turkish public. For secularists, Islam should be a subordinate state-funded instrument of Ataturk's secular state. The Islamists of the AK Party are more dangerous than Erbakan's followers precisely because they have adopted liberal ideas on the desirability of a new Constitution, civilian control of the military, and establishing contact with ordinary voters through efficient local government and charitable organizations.[17] Like socialist and conservative parties in Western Europe, Turkish secular parties have lost contact with the clubs and celebrations of urban workers. For secularists, the reluctance of AK deputies to support war against fellow-Sunnis in Iraq was seen as proof of their long-term vision of Islamic solidarity in a realm of Islamic Sharia law. According to Daniel Pipes, in mid-2003 the chief of staff was privately scolding the prime minister on this issue. Publicly, he spoke of military 'sensitivities' concerning the AK Party and warned it against engaging in 'anti-secular activities'.[18] General Tuncer Kilinc, the Euro-sceptical Secretary-General of the National Security Council, warned that 'there are those who seek Islamist rule in Turkey'. He was replaced in August 2003, as were the commanders of the navy and the air force.

International norms

In Turkish self-perception, Turkish diplomats have been loyal to the consensus on Iraq established throughout the 1990s at the United Nations, in spite of the disproportionately negative impact on Turkey of UN sanctions. In their view, this loyalty negates Greek propaganda that Turkey does not adhere to international law.

In the run-up to the war of 2003, the UN card was transformed from being a source of support for a US-led coalition into a means of preventing the United States from legitimately attacking Iraq. Throughout Western Europe, opposition to the war on normative grounds mostly took the form of arguing that an attack on a member of the United Nations could only be legitimate if specifically authorized by a resolution of the Security Council. The President of Turkey, Ahmed Sezer, is widely understood to have argued that Turkish forces could not legitimately be deployed in Iraq without a new resolution. He maintained this view before the war and in August 2003 insisted that a resolution would also be required before the despatch of Turkish peacekeeping forces. Although there was no such resolution, mainly because the United Nations withdrew from Iraq after its headquarters were bombed, in October 2003 the Grand National Assembly reluctantly agreed to permit Turkish troops to go to Iraq if requested. The question of whether the president would veto this resolution was by-passed as the Iraqi National Council itself decided it did not want Turks to defend the Turcomen or the pipelines from Kirkuk to Yumurtalik.

In Turkey, however, there was a much deeper moral source of opposition to the American war. Before the velvet coup of 28 February 1997, political Islam portrayed itself as an alternative capable of resisting the political domination, economic exploitation and cultural sickness of the secular West. When he became prime minister in 1996, Erbakan visited only Islamic capitals to promote Turkish leadership of an alternative Islamic security and economic system. The pragmatism of Erdoğan's AK Party is demonstrated by his decision to visit European capitals and Washington to reassure the West that his objective was membership of the European Union and economic recovery. The views of the Speaker were marginalized as those of a minority within the governing party.

Turkey and the United States

Public opinion

Although the Turkish diaspora in the United States is better educated and organized than its equivalent in Europe, the Turkish role in the Iraq War was not an issue for American public opinion comparable with the controversies over the Turkish role in Armenia or Cyprus. For one network of the foreign policy elite, however, the parliamentary decision of 1 March 2003 was a disaster and a betrayal. Philip Robins has pointed out how

> a small number of highly influential … officials and commentators have exercised a disproportionate influence on Turkey's behalf in Washington DC. Many of these, like Richard Perle and Paul Wolfowitz, are leading members of the US defence establishment. Partisans of Turkey have come from other agencies, notably Morton Abramowitz, Marc Grossman and Alan Makovsky from [the] State [Department] and Paul Henze from the CIA.[19]

It is noticeable that Secretary of State Colin Powell is not on this list, and that he did not visit Ankara before the war began.

Turkish public opinion, on the other hand, has been pro-American in much the same sense that opinion in Britain and Germany is generally convinced that their country has a special relationship with the power on which its security depends. During the Cold War, Turkish aspirations to 'Westernization' did not distinguish between Americanization and Europeanization. After the March vote, American Ambassador Mark Parris sought to excuse Turkish opposition by pointing to grounds for Turkish disillusionment with the American ally:

Economic and military assistance programmes zeroed out, and cash purchases were subject to congressional holds. Turks, still absorbing the security and economic aftershocks of the first Gulf War, and smarting from the failure of America and Gulf Arab Coalition partners to make good on promises of post-conflict assistance, were disillusioned with their senior NATO ally.[20]

It can more credibly be argued that Turkish opinion made a favourable comparison between solid American backing on IMF financial support packages and on the EU membership issue with European hesitation on whether Turkey should be an equal in Brussels decision-making on economic and military matters. No European politician could match President Clinton's skill in flattering the Grand National Assembly on 15 November 1999 by saying that 'Turkey's future will be critical to shaping the 21st Century.'

On whichever side the truth may lie, there is no doubt about the vitriolic reaction of pro-American elite opinion to the March vote. Two examples must suffice to convey the tone of the attack on the government. Cengiz Çandar, an adviser in 1991 to Turgut Özal, lamented that, 'in one fortnight, Turkey jeopardized its decades-old – if not centuries-old – Western vocation'.[21] A journalist with strong links to the establishment complained that

> the AK Party was totally indecisive and wavering, to say the least, in what was expected from a 'strategic partner'. … Promises, however general, … were not kept. Bilateral military negotiations ended with distrust and failure. … The price of Turkish support for the US war effort was branded as nothing but commercial.

Finally, there were divisions of opinion within the Turkish armed forces, not just in March 2003 on the war, but also in the autumn on the issue of sending Turkish troops to Iraq as peacekeepers. A deep rift developed between the internationalists who feared that Turkey would become a backwater if deserted by the United States, and the nationalists who argued that Turks might be used as cannon fodder on the ground for wars that were decided unilaterally by the dominant partner. On 21 August 2003, Mustafa Özyurek, the Deputy Chairman of the secular opposition party in the Parliament, the CHP, said publicly that some commanders question sending Turkish troops instead of Americans to die in Iraq.

National interests

Since 1999 Turkey, like Israel, had been designated a 'strategic partner' by President Clinton. Echoing President Bush in 1991, this designation has no treaty basis. In American eyes, it seems to imply a regional role for the partner in line with a strategic vision formulated in Washington. In Turkish eyes, it implied status, with the promise of military, financial and diplomatic support. Such support was essential to Turkey on a range of issues from containing Kurdish aspirations to independence, the rivalry with Iran, financing the pipeline from Central Asia to the Bay of Ceyhan, payments to Turkish troops in Afghanistan, support for IMF underpinning of Turkey's debts and for Turkey's candidacy for the EU and the UN Security Council. Turkish commentators were not alone in going along with the American revival of geopolitics.[22] No Turkish author reminds his readers that Japan and Germany became prosperous after they had been forced to abjure this power political doctrine; instead they are flattered that Turkey figures prominently as a 'pivotal' state in post-1989 American strategy.[23]

In planning for war in Iraq, negotiations to permit American use of Turkish facilities involved two separable sets of issues – compensatory finance and Turkey's political 'red lines'. Talks started in the autumn of 2002. General Hilmi Özkök visited Washington in November. It is impossible to be sure whether his reported comment (while accepting an offer of attack helicopters) that the United States should avoid war in Iraq was a negotiating ploy or an early indication of Turkish reluctance to get involved.[24] On 4 December 2002, Marc Grossman and Paul Wolfowitz let Turkish journalists report that, in return for Turkey's support, the United States would pay financial compensation of the order of $20–25 billion, of which $6 billion would be in cash. However, Turkey remained opposed to both a British sector in northern Iraq and the arming of the Kurdish peshmergas.[25] The clash of interests on northern Iraq may be illustrated by Turkish objections to an agreement signed in Washington in September 1998 for a federation between the two warring Kurdish groups. This 'critical step in the implementation of the new US policy of actively organising and supporting opposition forces against Saddam Hussein' aroused Turkish officials to assert their different interests by summoning Barzani and Talabani to Ankara to declare that federation did not mean undermining Iraqi territorial and political integrity.[26]

After the March 2003 vote, both the Turkish government and the Parliament signalled that they wanted to repair relations with the United States. In the afternoon of 20 March, the day the war began, the Turkish Parliament allowed the Americans to overfly Turkish airspace. The same day it authorized the Turkish government to send Turkish troops into northern Iraq. In August 2003, an American request for 10,000 Turkish peacekeeping troops was accompanied by a Congressional delegation led by the Chair of the Foreign Relations Committee, Richard Lugar. In October 2003, the Turkish Assembly by a majority of 2:1 allowed the government to send 10,000 peacekeeping troops, if requested. The foreign minister promised that these troops would go for only one year, and not as occupiers. In the event American negotiations to keep the Turks to the Euphrates Basin did not satisfy the Iraqi National Council. For their part, the Americans debated internally whether to withdraw completely from Incirlik, whether to cooperate with Turkish special forces inside Iraq, and whether to offer Turkish companies any reconstruction contracts. In November 2003, an American offer of up to $8.5 billion in loans was felt to be so much linked to the deployment of peacekeeping troops that the economy minister announced that it would not be taken up immediately. However, the main point was that the United States did not take revenge by destabilizing the lira, for example by interfering with the regular payment of IMF loan tranches.

Foundational myths

To its credit, Washington accepted the decision of the March vote, and chose to regard the redeployment of troopships from Mersin to Kuwait as an inconvenience rather than the disaster that would have ensued if Saddam Hussein really had been able to mount a biological attack on a single concentration of troops. Nevertheless after the war Paul Wolfowitz asked Mehmet Ali Birand to come to Washington. On the TV channel CNN Türk, Wolfowitz complained that the Turkish armed forces 'did not display the strong leadership role and attitude that we would have expected'. They should have replaced Turkey's parliamentary democracy with 'a democratic autocrat'.[27] The benign interpretation of this hollow-sounding understanding of democracy might be that 'democratic' modifies autocrat in the sense that armed forces should have chosen a civilian politician to front their rule.

A comparison with the Israeli understanding of the usefulness of the concept of democracy in dealings with Washington is helpful. On the one hand, just as Israel points up its status as the only democracy in the Arab world, so Turkey claims to be the only democracy in the Muslim world. For example, the previous head of the Turkish Ministry of Foreign Affairs was ambassador to Washington during the crisis. He gave two reasons for expecting that Turkish relations with Washington would be repaired:

> If concepts of 'stability, democracy and friendship' drive US policy in this vast geography from the Middle East to the Balkans and from the Caucasus to Central Asia, and if eradicating terrorism is an overriding objective for the US, then the US will need Turkey on its side.[28]

When Prime Minister Erdoğan visited the United States in January 2004, he chose democracy as his theme for a passionate and intelligent speech at Harvard, the university attended by his son. On the other hand, neither state has any strong commitment to fostering democracy in the region. The following quotation from a very senior Israeli diplomat appears in a recent journal article published by the Turkish Ministry of Foreign Affairs: 'Washington's self-confidence regarding the superiority of its democratic system, and the appropriateness of the free market concept as the economic model for the 21st century may prove to be exaggerated with respect to Iraq and the entire Arab world.'[29]

In any case, as a non-participant in the war, the Americans did not allow Turkey any say in the central constitutional question in Iraq, whether to promote Baghdad's authority by setting up nineteen small regions or whether to recognize the reality of Shia control of the south and Kurdish control of the north.

International norms

President Sezer consistently held that for Turkey legitimately to send troops abroad a UN resolution was required. His reason why the Parliament should postpone the decision on sending peacekeeping forces from August to October 2003 was to await an expected UN resolution. The August bombing of the UN headquarters in Baghdad put a temporary end to UN involvement on the ground so that one can only speculate that Turkey would have responded favourably to Sergio de Mello's request for Turkish help in training a police force, and that this would have been turned down by the Iraqi National Council.

Turkey and Europe

Public opinion

The Turkish Parliament's refusal to allow the American government to launch its attack on Iraq from Turkey did the image of Turkish democracy in Europe a power of good. Since the military coup in 1980 – the third such intervention – European states and European opinion have been sceptical about the realities of Turkish democracy. The privileged role of the army in the Turkish economy and in Turkish decision-making, the judicial repression of Kurdish and Islamic parties, the accusations of systematic torture, and the role of the Security Courts in the provinces under martial law were the main items listed as differentiating Turkey from other European democracies. The Luxembourg Conclusions of 1997 were deeply resented by Turkish opinion, 'reinforcing the anti-European tendency that became prevalent among the Turkish governing elites in the 1990s'.[30] Yet at the Helsinki Summit in 1999 EU leaders agreed to accord Turkey the status of a candidate country, and to open negotiations as soon as Turkey had implemented democratic reforms to be agreed with the European Commission. At the time this offer was made, it was much less positive than it now appears. Those opposed to Turkish membership as too big, too poor, or culturally too different did not expect that Prime Minister Ecevit could put through far-reaching democratic reforms, let alone change his mind on the legitimacy of Turkish Cypriot self-rule in northern Cyprus.

Interests

The EU and its Member States have no clear idea whether Turkey is for them a producer or a consumer of security. The fear of moving the EU security frontier to the borders of Iraq and Syria is weighed against the advantages of incorporating the second largest army in Europe. Historically, the main concern of West European states has been to distance themselves from any war between Greece and Turkey. Thus, when Greece refused to sign the Maastricht Treaty unless it was accorded full membership in the West European Union, the other signatories revised Article V so that they would not be obliged to support Greece against Turkey. In the debates on a European Rapid Reaction Force, the EU aggravated

Turkish concern about its status by insisting that, as a non-member, Turkey could not participate as of right in decision-making. Similarly, as the EU has not developed a concept for the Middle East, it is unable to see the advantages of including a state with good links to both Israel and Islamic states. The EU's non-involvement in the Iraq conflict is illustrated by the reputed failure of the Foreign Minister of the presidency country, Dominique de Villepin, to telephone Ankara in March 2003. After an unscheduled meeting on Iraq in mid-February, EU leaders met subsequently on 21 March and 20 June 2003.

In contrast, the government put its recently acquired enthusiasm for getting a date for the opening of accession negotiations at the top of its agenda. Some of the required reforms suited the AK Party. Greater legitimacy for religious political parties would preclude the indignity suffered by Erdoğan in not being able himself to be a candidate in an election in which his party triumphed. Demonstrating that, as during the Israeli wars of 1967 and 1973, Turkey was not an American Trojan horse reassured Islamic fundamentalists. Civilian rule precluded a repeat of the velvet coup of 1998. European membership would reassure secularists that Turkey was not about to introduce Sharia law and above all would bring the foreign investment, subsidies and protection against global competition which would bring jobs to Turks at home. While the Iraq War did entail allowing Denktaş to reject compromise on Cyprus, it did not prevent the government from carrying through the sixth and seventh reform packages and then returning to the Cyprus question with a demonstration of amazing flexibility. The government kept its 2002 election pledge to be flexible in foreign policy and accountable to the Grand National Assembly.

It may be worth recalling the distance travelled by Turkey towards the EU since the first Gulf War. Then the Turkish government had refused all publicity for the considerable and prolonged EU aid to Kurdish refugees. One reason for this cold-shouldering was the acceptance in Brussels of an application in September 1990 for membership from the Republic of Cyprus. Another was that Turkey remained an Associate Member of the Western European Union when Greece became a full member.

Foundational myths

The European Economic Communities were established by six Christian Democrat prime ministers as a community of merchants with a consultative assembly of parliamentarians seconded from the Member States. No map was attached to the Treaty of Rome because the territorial integrity of Germany was too much in question, and Algeria was then a part of France.

In 2003, the requirement that Turkey fulfil the political criteria laid down at Copenhagen shows how far the EU has come to be at least a society of states committed to human rights. The EU became the leading security actor in Central and Eastern Europe by using its application procedure to enforce respect for minorities and established frontiers from would-be members. In Turkey's case the European magnet was so strong that an Islamic party beset by real internal and external threats to its survival undertook reforms that were far more democratic than the adoption of a two-party system on the American model after the Second World War.

International norms

As most European states regarded the attack on Iraq as illegal, there are examples of states using their leverage to deter Turkey from itself going into Iraq. The German socialist government, elected on an anti-war platform, threatened that if Turkey went into Iraq, Germany would withdraw the AWACS planes seconded to it to give warning of missile attack from that quarter. Moreover, once it was clear that Saddam Hussein had no SCUD missiles and no weapons of mass destruction, the AWACS were withdrawn, thus depriving Turkey of surveillance capacity over northern Iraq. Similarly, on 3 April 2003, the Greek Foreign Minister, Georgios Papandreou, sent a blunt message in public: 'If Turkish troops enter northern Iraq, then NATO won't support Turkey anymore. Such an action would damage Turkey-EU relations and also jeopardize Turkey's EU membership bid.'[31] This concern for international law may also have been motivated in both Germany and Greece by popular sympathy for Kurdish claims denied for a century. In short, there is a cleavage between Western European assumptions that Kurds may legitimately claim cultural and possibly political freedoms, and Turkish fears that minority rights for Kurds in Iraq or in Turkey may advance instead of preclude Kurdish secession.

Conclusions

For Turks, the coalition invasion of Iraq raised critical questions for voters, governments, military officers, imams and lawyers. These questions were not just about policy but about the foundational meaning of republican democracy and the implications of a strategic partnership with an American suzerain and of membership of the EU.

The most important conclusion to be drawn is that Turkish public opinion was in line with that in the rest of Europe. Hitherto the absence of an active Europe-wide public opinion has been the biggest weakness of the democratic pretensions of the EU. From the Treaty of Rome to the Treaty of Maastricht, European unification has been a matter for elites, with public opinion as at best permissive rather than pro-active. Unlike demonstrations by farmers and miners in their sectoral interests, the Iraq issue unified opinion throughout Europe. Unlike the demonstrations during the Vietnam War, the objective was to prevent European governments from supporting a war that had not yet begun. If this is a turning point, then Turks can claim to have participated to the full.

Meanwhile, the strength of Turkish opposition to the war has made it impossible to argue that Turks are militaristic by nature, aggressive towards their neighbours, an American Trojan Horse, or necessarily subordinated to undemocratic state institutions. The acceptance by the government and by the Turkish armed forces of the consequences of the vote of 1 March 2003 convinced many doubters in Europe that Turkey was a parliamentary democracy. It has suddenly become possible that the European Commission and Member States will recognize that, by pushing through democratic reform packages without being distracted by the Iraq crisis, Turkey has met the democratic criterion for the opening of accession negotiations.

Nevertheless the Turkish government was in line with some other European governments in asserting that it had to support the American-led coalition in the national interest. The Turkish government did not excite fears of weapons of mass destruction as endangering the Turkish population, nor hopes that Iraq would become either a democratic neighbour or a rich market for Turkish agriculture. Its interest was in meeting its obligations as a strategic partner of the United States, and obtaining a veto on political developments in northern Iraq. For the Turkish government, unlike other governments, the Iraq lever could have been used by either the secularist establishment or by fundamentalist Islamic deputies to undermine its recent electoral triumph. It remains to be seen whether coded fears for Turkish territorial integrity will be quelled by the acceptance by Kurds in Iraq of a limited autonomy, and by Kurds in Turkey of cultural autonomy, ideally within a multicultural EU.

Notes and references

1   See Prime Minister Recep Tayyip's 'deep democracy' in an address at Harvard University on 'Democracy in the Middle East, Pluralism in Europe: Turkish view' on 30 January 2004. Online. Available HTTP: <http://www.mfa.gov.tr/Harvard.htm> (accessed 5 July 2004).

2   S. Elekdağ, '2.5 War Strategy', *Perceptions* (Ankara), 1, March–May 1996.

3   In March 1995, 35,000 Turkish troops were in Iraq for six weeks. See K. Kirişçi, 'The Kurdish Question', in L. G. Martin and D. Keridis, *The Future of Turkish Foreign Policy*, Cambridge, MA: MIT Press, 2004, p. 291.

4   P. Robins, *Suits and Uniforms: Turkish Foreign Policy since the Cold War*, London: Hurst, 2003, pp. 203–4.

5   J. Dempsey, 'NATO agrees to strengthen country's border defence', *Financial Times*, 20 February 2003.

6   Robins, *Suits and Uniforms*, p. 315.

7   *International Herald Tribune*, 11–13 August 1990.

8   Y. Bozdağlioğlu, *Turkish Foreign Policy and Turkish Identity: A Constructivist Approach*, London: Routledge, 2003, p. 135.

9   Robins, *Suits and Uniforms*, p. 68.

10 C. Çandar, 'Turkish Foreign Policy and the War in Iraq', in Martin and Keridis, *Turkish Foreign Policy*, p. 47.

11 Ibid., p. 48.

12 Kurds cite the 1957 census when Kurds were 48 per cent of the inhabitants of Kirkuk. In 1977 the Arabs were the largest group with 44 per cent and Turkmen 16.3 per cent. See N. Raphaeli, 'Iraq Reform', *Middle East Media Research Institute*, No. 168, 2004, p. 3.

13 On 21 June, 28 June and 10 September 1999. See Kirişçi, 'Kurdish Question', p. 288.

14 *Al Sharq Al-Awsat* (London), 17 January 2004.

15 Robins, *Suits and Uniforms*, p. 317, n. 7.

16 Çandar, 'Turkish Foreign Policy', p. 55.

17 S. Ayata, 'Changes in Domestic Politics and the Foreign Policy Orientation of the AK Party', in Martin and Keridis, *Turkish Foreign Policy*, pp. 253–4.

18 *New York Post*, 5 August 2003.

19 Robins, *Suits and Uniforms*, p. 18.

20 M. Parris, 'Starting Over: US-Turkish Relations in the Post-Iraq War Era', *Turkish Policy Quarterly*, 2, 2003, p. 48.

21 Çandar, 'Turkish Foreign Policy', p. 48.

22 See Z. Brzezinski, *The Grand Chessboard: American Primacy and its Geostrategic Imperatives*, New York: Basic Books, 1997.

23 See R. S. Chase, E. Hill and P. Kennedy, 'Pivotal States and US Strategy', *Foreign Affairs*, 75, 1996, pp. 33–51.

24 *Turkish Daily News*, 8 November 2002.

25 Ministry of Foreign Affairs, *Turkish Press Review*, 4 December 2002. Online. Available HTTP: <http://www.mfa.gov.tr> (accessed 4 December 2002). See also *Turkish Daily News*, 8 May 2003.

26 Kirisçi, 'Kurdish Question', pp. 307–8.

27 US Department of Defense News Briefing, Deputy Secretary of Defense Paul Wolfowitz, 5 May 2003; see also *Turkish Daily News*, 8 May 2003.

28 O. F. Loğoğlu, *Turkish Policy Quarterly*, 2003, p. 31.

29 A. Liel, 'The Middle East after Saddam and Arafat', *Turkish Policy Quarterly*, 2, 2003, pp. 41–52.

30 A. Eralp, 'Turkey and the European Union', in Martin and Keridis, *Turkish foreign policy*, p. 63.

31 *Turkish Daily News*, 4 April 2003.

8 'It seemed the best thing to be up and go'[1]

On the legal case for invading Iraq

Patrick Thornberry

We let ourselves be swept along by the tide of war and division.[2]

The invasion of Iraq by 'coalition' forces in 2003 was mounted in the face of enormous opposition in the countries composing the coalition and in those outside it. The political and moral arguments rumble on, even after the military defeat of Saddam Hussein and his capture. Civilian and military casualties continue to mount. Iraq has become a vacuum into which sundry 'terrorists' are drawn. As other contributors to this book make clear, peaceful transition to an engineered 'democracy' remains a problematic exercise. There are few signs of any diminution of resistance activity. The USA, the UK and other countries sending forces into the quagmire continue the work of occupation,[3] the work of the warriors, despite the deaths, despite the chaos, despite the lack of acceptance by many among the 'liberated' population, despite the partial retreat by some international organizations.[4] On the basis of sundry UN resolutions, there is at last a 'formal' endgame for the re-transfer of sovereignty to the Iraqis, but only a mist of possibilities beyond that.

On the international law front, it is hardly an exaggeration to claim that the great majority of international lawyers,[5] including those in the USA, have regarded the war as an illegal enterprise from its inception,[6] and that many governments take a similar view. On the other hand, the 'official' US and UK positions continue to assert the legality of their actions against Iraq, even if there are nuances of emphasis as to which legal norms best lend strength to the enterprise. Perhaps the UK has strained the harder of the two to find and describe underpinning principles consistent with the existing framework of international law. There is also a sense with the UK and the USA of 'shifting the goalposts' in search of justifications, or adopting the retrospective approach, lauding the end of a tyrant and the liberation of his people as justi-fication in itself. Some supporters of the invasion concede the point on illegality but claim it was 'legitimate', or suggest that insisting on 'formal' ille-gality is 'counterproductive' bearing in mind that the UN is a political institution as well as a legal one.[7] The illegality of the war has been more or less conceded by one of its architects, Richard Perle, even if his is not the offi-cial position. In Perle's view, international law 'stood in the way of doing the right thing'.[8] Others would simply dismiss international law and the UN as 'irrelevant', certainly if it impedes the pursuit of the national self-interest of the USA, an approach which has the potential to reach beyond the confines of the Iraq conflict to the wilder shores of international order and disorder. Against the US 'exceptionalists' and their acolytes, something approaching a *consensus gentium* refuses to concede that international law is irrelevant but that, on the contrary, and despite its various *lacunae*, it provides the only viable framework in which to situate and appraise the political decisions of states including those in the vital area of security.

The present chapter provides a reminder of the UN legal framework and the principal UN Security Council 'signposts' in the unfolding Iraq crisis, followed by a rehearsal of the main justifications in the context of the conflict – the self-defence and weapons of mass destruction arguments; the claims of Security Council authorization; and the subsidiary or default mode calling up of humanitarian intervention and regime change. The chapter does not separately investigate the dubious claims of linkages between the regime of Saddam Hussein and international terrorism, except when referred to in the justifications. The principal planks in the coalition argument are appraised in the light of the contemporary framework of international law, or at least 'international law as we understood it'. Partly because the writer is an under-labourer in the field of human rights, more elaborate attention is paid to the role of human rights in the whole scenario, especially through the mediating notion of 'humanitarian intervention'.[9] This concept flits like a bat around the primary justifications, even if it does not stand out consistently or stand alone. The NATO intervention in Kosovo was largely premised on addressing a humanitarian emergency and may have contributed to a lowering of the intervention threshold for Iraq and the future. While humanitarian intervention arguments have a certain antiquity in international relations, they may exert a particularly strong pull on a contemporary constituency schooled in sensitivity to human rights. Deploying human rights as a reason to violate sovereignty raises hard questions of international law, encouraging us to consider how to 'do' human rights, and the nature of the tasks for those who claim to further the cause of human rights as duty, vocation or career.

Relevant aspects of the UN Charter

Collective security and self-defence

> And I analyzed a thorough body of intelligence … that had led me to come to the conclusion that it was necessary to remove Saddam Hussein from power. We gave the world a chance to do it. Twelve times the United Nations Security Council passed resolutions on recognition of the threat that he posed. And the difference … is that some were not willing to act on those resolutions. We were … because he posed a threat.[10]

There is enough principle in the Charter to scrutinize the quality of the coalition justifications. Coalition partners and their critics draw on the Charter as a reservoir of legal principle. The Charter of the United Nations incorporates notions of collective security, and of self-defence, individual and collective.

The first expressed purpose of the UN is the maintenance of 'international peace and security'. Article 2(3) provides for the settlement of international disputes by peaceful means 'in such a manner that international peace and security, and justice, are not endangered'. Widely regarded as expressing a principle of customary international law,[11] and of *ius cogens*,[12] Article 2(4) of the UN Charter forbids the use or threat of force in international relations 'against the territorial integrity or political independence of any State, or in any other manner inconsistent with the purposes of the United Nations'.[13] The purposes of the UN are various, but combine security elements with elements on human rights. Article 2(7) of the UN Charter protects the state in its domestic jurisdiction from intervention by the UN, except in the case of enforcement measures under Chapter VII of the Charter. According to Article 24 of the Charter, the Security Council has primary responsibility for the maintenance of international peace and security, and can determine the existence of threats to the peace, etc. In dealing with such threats, the Security Council possesses the power to decide on measures up to and including the use of armed force. Enforcement action by regional 'arrangements or agencies' also requires authorization by the Security Council.

Article 51 furnishes an exception to the prohibition on the use of force, and reads in part:

> Nothing in the present Charter shall impair the inherent right of individual or collective self-defence if an armed attack occurs against a Member of the United Nations until the Security Council has taken the measures necessary to maintain international peace and security.

A key phrase is 'if an armed attack occurs', suggesting a restriction on the occasions when self-defence may be rightfully employed under Charter law. Self-defence should not be interpreted broadly. Article 51 is an exception to Article 2(4) and is caught by the principle that exceptions to a rule should be interpreted narrowly. Then exercise of self-defence must be proportionate and necessary.[14] Self-defence is a 'temporary measure' in the eye of the Charter; that is, it is permissible until the second limb of Article 51 operates, and the matter turned over to the Security Council. 'Anticipatory' self-defence against imminent attack is not specifically mentioned in the Charter, still less the notion of 'a preventive war', though it is broadly accepted that hostile events in motion or which are 'imminent' justify the use of force in self-defence. The logic of the Charter is compelling in its cautious and restricting approach to the unilateral use of force by states: the collective security elements predominate, to be orchestrated by the Security Council. What is particularly to be avoided is the 'remote sensing' of threats, leading to the taking of allegedly preventive action, though international law is not so much of a suicide club as to require that states wait for weapons of mass destruction to rain upon them before reacting to a threat with counter-force.[15]

Human rights and self-determination

> The hugely increased normative ambitions of international society are nowhere more visible than in the field of human rights and democracy – in the idea that the relationship between ruler and ruled, state and citizen, should be a subject of legitimate international concern; that the ill-treatment of citizens and the absence of democratic governance should trigger international action; and that the external legitimacy of a State should depend increasingly on how domestic societies are ordered politically.[16]

The Charter incorporates statist and Enlightenment elements. On the first of these, the Charter principles command respect for sovereign equality, territorial integrity and, as noted, non-intervention in domestic affairs.[17] On the second, the language of the rational, the secular, the democratic and the universal disseminated in key texts such as the French Declaration on the Rights of Man and the Citizen, and the American Declaration of Independence eventually found its way into the Charter of the United Nations and the Universal Declaration of Human Rights.[18] In the Charter, human rights figure in the Preamble, among the Purposes of the United Nations, and elsewhere – there are seven distinct references to human rights in all, scattered throughout the text.[19] The Charter also underpins the Enlightenment legacy of peoples' rights from its opening phrase: 'We the Peoples of the United Nations'. Some read the Charter to mean that governments and states derive authority from the peoples, and not the peoples from the states.[20] Articles 1(2) and 55 refer to self-determination, Chapters XI (declaration regarding non-self-governing territories) and XII (international trusteeship system) imply it.

The *Universal Declaration of Human Rights*[21] proclaimed by the General Assembly in 1948 exhibits a content and structure which has conditioned thinking on human rights to a significant degree. The Declaration was conceived by its authors as a new fact in the world, adopted by an assembly of the world community. In the process of drafting, its title was changed from the 'International' to the 'Universal' Declaration, drawing attention away from the authors of the document to its addressees, its readership.[22] The Declaration incorporates categories or 'generations' of rights, with civil and political rights granted only lexical priority, with economic, social and cultural rights fully recognized.[23] Solidarity rights of a universalistic kind are intimated in Article 28, which provides that everyone 'is entitled to a social and international order in which the rights and freedoms set forth in this Declaration can be fully realized'. The Universal Declaration of Human Rights was followed by the International covenants – on Civil and Political Rights and Economic, Social and Cultural Rights. While the Charter does not attempt to list or categorize potential holders of rights, the inclusion of the non-distinction/discrimination formula rendered it not improbable that bodies of law could be developed for racial groups and ethnic minorities, women, speakers of languages and adherents of religions. International organizations have also carried through that programme with a vengeance, adding rights of children, the disabled, migrant workers, refugees, etc. Besides categories of persons, international law has developed rules and principles about particular 'practices' and 'conditions' including apartheid, genocide, torture, slavery and statelessness. The *corpus* of instruments includes treaties and declarations, politically binding agreements, myriad varieties of 'soft' and 'hard' texts, customary law, *jus cogens* or fundamental principles of peremptory law. The texts inscribe, restate and supplement basic principles of State responsibility.

Human rights are regarded as a matter of legitimate international concern, a principle affirmed by the Vienna Declaration of the World Conference on Human Rights.[24] International organizations have chosen to develop programmes of implementation of human rights by softer methods than the use of force.[25] International standards are backed up by varying qualities of implementing mechanisms: mandatory reports of states to international supervisory bodies, systems for dealing with individual claims and accusations of rights violations, systems for interstate claims, procedures for mass violations of rights, courts and other types of tribunal, committees and commissions, working groups for monitoring states or practices and rapporteurs for the same. The courts, committees, etc., are assisted and complemented by complex rights bureaucracies of international organizations. 'Mechanisms' in a broad sense also include programmes of technical assistance, programmes of conflict prevention through solidifying human rights within states, preventive diplomacy and diplomacy in general. In sum, to cite the International Commission on Intervention and State Sovereignty (ICISS): 'What has been gradually emerging is a ... transition from a culture of sovereign impunity to a culture of national and international accountability.'[26]

The conflict in Iraq – UN 'signposts'

The invasion of Kuwait by Iraq in 1990 triggered a spate of UN Security Council resolutions designed to end the occupation of Kuwait by Iraq. The most notable are Resolution 678 (1990), sanctioning the use of force against Iraq; Resolution 687 (1991), setting out the terms for a ceasefire; and Resolution 1441 of November 2002. Resolution 678 authorized member states to use 'all necessary means' to uphold and implement the previous and subsequent relevant resolutions on Kuwait 'and to restore international peace and security in the area'; in the resolution, the Security Council decided to remain 'actively and permanently seized of the matter until Kuwait has regained its independence and peace has been restored'. Resolution 687, *inter alia*, addressed the issue of Iraq's weapons of mass destruction, demanding that Iraq accept, unconditionally, 'the destruction, removal, or rendering harmless, under international supervision', of chemical and biological weapons, and ballistic missiles with a range greater than 150 kilometres, as well as 'unconditionally agree not to acquire or develop nuclear weapons or nuclear-weapon-usable material', etc. The Iraq–Kuwait conflict was a 'classic' interstate conflict, not about human rights, though among the resolutions pertaining to the crisis of the early 1990s mention should be made of Resolution 688 which condemned 'the repression of the Iraqi civilian population in many parts of Iraq, including most recently in Kurdish-populated areas, the consequences of which threaten international peace and security'. Resolution 688 made reference to 'a massive flow of refugees towards and across international frontiers and to cross-border incursions' as justification for labelling the repression of the Kurds as a threat to *international* peace and security; it seems tolerably clear, however, that it further blurred the division between the international and the internal by treating the post-Kuwait violations of human rights by the Iraqi regime against the Kurds as an international rather than an internal question. [27]

Security Council Resolution 1441 recalled previous resolutions on Iraq and recognized 'the threat Iraq's non-compliance with Council resolutions and proliferation of weapons of mass destruction and long-range missiles poses to international peace and security'. Iraqi non-compliance with Resolutions 678 and 687 was specifically recalled, as well as non-compliance with Resolution 688 by failing 'to end repression of its civilian population'. The resolution decided that Iraq 'has been and remains in material breach' of its obligations under relevant resolutions, gave the Iraqi authorities thirty days to declare fully its weapons of mass destruction to international bodies including the Security Council, and underlined that false statements would constitute a further material breach. The resolution did not specifically threaten or authorize 'all necessary means' in the manner of Resolution 678, but instead recalled 'that the Council has repeatedly warned Iraq that it will face serious consequences as a result of its continued violations of its obligations'. In the final paragraph of the resolution, the Council decided 'to remain seized of the matter'. The matter of the 'occupation' of Iraq is addressed principally by Security Council Resolutions 1483, 1500 and 1511 referred to above. Resolution 1483 'Calls upon all concerned to comply fully with their obligations under international law including in particular the Geneva Conventions of 1949 and the Hague Regulations of 1907.'

Coalition justifications for the invasion of Iraq in 2003

Justifications for the armed action against Iraq have been delivered by the authorities of the USA, the UK and others with considerable regularity and emphasis, if not always with matching clarity and consistency. Consolidating statements of legal principle from intervening governments would help to set future benchmarks for action; for the time being we have a patchwork of justifications. The *topoi* of international approval, self-defence and humanitarian rescue have been presented not through neat schemes but through complex statements mixing various justifications, as if relying on only one ground might not provide sufficient 'cover' for the action. Legal reasoning, it is said, is not like the links of a chain, but like the legs of a chair – a set of mutually supporting arguments that produce a steady platform. The problem with the analogy is that three or four shaky arguments make neither a convincing case nor a steady chair.

The action had in effect been approved by the UN Security Council

In a written parliamentary answer on 17 March 2003, the attorney-general of the UK delivered a chain of justifications for the use of force against Iraq: Security Council Resolution 678 authorized force against Iraq to eject it from Kuwait and restore peace and security in the area; Security Council Resolution 687 imposed continuing conditions against Iraq to eliminate weapons of mass destruction; 687 merely suspended 678 but did not terminate the authority to use force; a material breach of 687 revives the authority to use force under 678; Security Council Resolution 1441 determined that Iraq was in material breach of 687; 1441 gave Iraq a final opportunity to comply with its disarmament obligations, warning of serious consequences if it did not; non-cooperation with 1441 would be a further material breach; Iraq is in material breach of its disarmament obligations; the authority of 678 continues; 1441 requires reporting of measures to the Security Council, but does not require a further express Security Council decision to use force. References to Iraq's breach of disarmament obligations leave the justification exposed to the results of factual investigations as to whether UN disarmament objectives had already been fulfilled through UN inspection of Iraq's weaponry. Critics of the war in the USA and the UK raised their decibel levels in the wake of statements by David Kay, Head of the Iraq Survey Group, and others, that such weapons may never be found. Coalition 'intelligence' is under critical scrutiny. It is difficult to know whether we should term the above approach as one of 'implicit' approval by the UN;[28] it looks more like a claim of 'continuing approval' or the 'fulfilment of a UN process set in motion by the invasion of Kuwait' – in colloquial terms, finishing the job.

A related claim, not quite UN approval but a UN-linked justification (also heard for the NATO intervention in Kosovo),[29] is that the coalition acted in some obscure manner to serve the higher purposes of international order and the UN – hence for example the observation in the Azores Declaration that 'Saddam's defiance of United Nations Security Council resolutions ... has undermined the authority of the UN', recalling that 'For 12 years, the international community has tried to persuade him to disarm and thereby avoid military conflict, most recently through the unanimous adoption of UN Security Council resolution 1441.' Here also Prime Minister Blair – 'The UN should be the focus both of diplomacy and of action. That is what 1441 said ... to will the ends but not the means ... would do more damage in the long term to the UN than any other course.'[30]

With respect to the authors of the advice to the UK government, there is clearly an element of artificiality in the above arguments. It seems fairly obvious that the earlier UN Resolutions – 678 and 687 – related to Kuwait and the immediate aftermath of the Iraq–Kuwait conflict. Like a criminal conviction, the resolutions were 'spent'; they related to a situation which had lost its relevance over time. Resolution 1441 was the product of frantic politicking, and part of the politics is that it did not provide authorization for the use of force, however much some parties might have wished that it had. Comments made by the USA and the UK on the adoption of 1441 were to the effect that it could not be read as a trigger for intervention; restrictive readings of 1441 were articulated by others. Resolution 1441 provided for further UN inspections; the UN Security Council remained 'seized of the matter'. It was not open to states to take it upon themselves to enforce UN law unilaterally.[31] To accept such a doctrine would ultimately eliminate the need for explicit collective authorization of the use of force in relation to specific crises. In factual terms there was and is little evidence for Iraq's *current* possession of weapons of mass destruction; on the balance of present evidence, the UN inspection process appears to have done a thorough job of locating and dismantling them.

In addition to the 'factual' doubts about the existence of these weapons, there has been a subtle shifting of the ground, a degree of backtracking, on what exactly was the issue: hence the remarks of the US Under-Secretary of State, John Bolton – whether Saddam Hussein actually possessed weapons of mass destruction is not really the issue but 'the capability that Iraq sought to have weapons of mass destruction programmes'.[32] The sense of 'weapons of mass destruction primed to act' has also been downgraded by President Bush in his State of the Union speech to 'weapons of mass destruction-related programme activities and significant amounts of equipment'.[33]

Self-defence and the begetters of chaos

> There was no corner of the known world where some interest was not alleged to be in danger or under actual attack. If the interests were not Roman, they were those of Rome's allies; and if Rome had no allies, the allies would be invented ... the fight was always invested with an aura of legality. Rome was always being attacked by evil-minded neighbours.[34]

We are less familiar with the wilder evocations of the rights of self-defence, preventive and pre-emptive wars. The coalition emphasis on weapons of mass destruction ties in with the UN approval claim, and we also hear a superimposed strain of justified self-defence in response to a threat. If this is so, we are entitled to ask questions in the light of the norms on self-defence. Was there an imminent threat? How imminent? To whom? Was there capability, and intention, to carry through a threat?

Tony Blair's speech of 18 March 2003 to the House of Commons was mostly devoted to the vindication of the UN Security Council line of argument. But there was an added element of sensing a menace or threat from the Iraqi regime, either alone or in conjunction with other, shadowy forces. As the prime minister saw it: 'The threat is chaos. And there are two begetters of chaos. Tyrannical regimes with WMD and extreme terrorist groups.' He continued: 'At the moment, I accept that association between them is loose. But it is hardening ... the possibility of the two coming together ... is ... a real and present danger.' The speech also refers to 'strategic anxiety', and to threat from dirty radiological bombs, and anthrax. The intention seems to be to link the post-11 September 2001 frame with the 'axis of evil' frame – the almost unidentifiable and the identifiable 'enemy' united in grand conspiracy; the non-sovereign Al-Qaida linking with the target sovereign state. The threat is merely a potential threat; the linkage not yet conclusively demonstrated, but 'hardening'. We are clearly some way from the 'if an armed attack occurs' formula in the UN Charter, even with the extra ingredient of the terrorist group. Of course, if a state sends a terrorist or other group on to the territory of another state, the right of self-defence may be properly invoked, and in the case of the post-11 September allied attack on Afghanistan, the accusation against the Taliban was even less than that, an allegation that the regime 'harboured' a terrorist group.[35] In cases where the Article 51 formula is stretched, the element of proof becomes even more critical, and thus far, there appears to be little evidence that Al-Qaida had links with the Iraqi regime; on the contrary, its ideology was violently opposed to secular Ba'athism, so that the movement and the regime were enemies rather than conspirators.[36] On the other hand, the UK has not, it seems, dispensed with the reading of Article 51 which requires an imminent threat to trigger the application of Article 51.[37] The rather remote justificatory discourse of the 'begetters of chaos' does not cohere well with claims in UK government literature on the 'imminence' of threat from Iraq's WMD. The notorious '45 minutes' claim, paraphrased in the UK tabloid press as '45 minutes from doom' – discussed in Chapter 14 of this volume by Alex Danchev – continues to haunt the UK prime minister in particular.

The self-defence concept articulated by the USA has sometimes relied on anticipatory self-defence, and is perhaps moving again in that direction, even to preventive war, prefaced by the identification or remote sensing of specific countries as an 'axis of evil', one of whom has now been invaded.[38] The rationale for enhanced preliminary action by the USA is set out in the National Security Strategy of the USA, which includes under the rubric of 'Prevent our enemies from threatening us, our allies, and our friends with weapons of mass destruction', the following:

> We must adapt the concept of imminent threat to the capabilities and objectives of today's adversaries. Rogue states and terrorists do not seek to attack us using conventional means. ... The United States has long maintained the option of pre-emptive actions to counter a sufficient threat to our national security. The greater the threat, the greater is the risk of inaction—and the more compelling the case for taking anticipatory action to defend ourselves, even if uncertainty remains as to the time and place of the enemy's attack.

To forestall or prevent such hostile acts by our adversaries, the United States will, if necessary, act pre-emptively ... in an age where the enemies of civilization openly and actively seek the world's most destructive technologies, the United States cannot remain idle while dangers gather. ... The purpose of our actions will always be to eliminate a specific threat to the United States or our allies and friends. The reasons for our actions will be clear, the force measured, and the cause just.[39]

It will be observed that the precise term used is 'pre-emption' rather than 'prevention', but the further explanation suggests that the strategy veers towards prevention and 'preventive wars', as in the included phrase 'to forestall or prevent'.[40] In this context, 'pre-emptive' and 'preventive' might just be a distinction without a difference. In terms of current international law, any argument for the legality of such a concept is untenable in terms of the UN Charter. Extending 'imminence' to future threats not yet crystallized is deeply problematic under existing law, and to any imaginable future revision of the UN Charter.

It is not entirely clear that there is a thoroughgoing exceptionalist case in the statement. It is also unclear what influence the current framework of international law exerts on the national security doctrine of the USA. There are elements in the doctrine to be interpreted in less than dramatic terms, notably the promise that pre-emptive action will not spill over into aggression. This brings into focus the international understanding of aggression, notably the 1974 consensus definition of aggression – UN General Assembly Resolution 3314 (XXIV).[41] One may presume that the USA does not intend to abandon the possibility of condemning aggression under international law, including bringing to account individuals who commit 'crimes against peace' in the sense of the Nuremberg Charter or even in terms of the crime of aggression under the Statute of the International Criminal Court. In the case of Iraq, the concept of 'imminence' of a threat appears to have been stretched to breaking point, and we have heard claims that the attack was part of a longer-term plan of action by the US administration against the 'evil' Saddam Hussein.[42]

Hijacking Iraq

> Iraq's talented people, rich culture, and tremendous potential have been hijacked by Saddam Hussein.[43]

The last assertion above takes us into the domain of 'regime change'. In the invasion of Iraq, the 'saving the people' argument has been, at most, a subsidiary or *sotto voce* accompaniment to the justifications of UN authorization and the extended rationale of self-defence. Regime change as such has been formally denied as a justification for the action, at least by the UK. Tony Blair asserted before the UK House of Commons on 18 March 2003 that 'I have never put the justification as regime change'.[44] But there is evidence of a conceptual movement which, while not validating forcible regime change per se whether linked or not to 'disarmament', deploys 'humanitarian' justifications for the coalition action. The removal of the regime of Saddam Hussein was 'simply the right thing to do'. Hence the prime minister at a press conference in September 2003:

> Let me say why I still believe Iraq was the right thing to do and why it is essential that we see it through. If we succeed in putting Iraq on its feet as a stable, prosperous and democratic country, then what a huge advertisement that is for the values of democracy and human rights, and what a huge defeat it is for these terrorists who want to establish extremist states.[45]

To similar effect, the more dramatic terms of President Bush's 2004 State of the Union message, which alloys the international to the 'humanitarian':

> Had we failed to act, Security Council resolutions on Iraq would have been revealed as empty threats, weakening the United Nations and encouraging defiance by dictators around the world. Iraq's torture chambers would still be filled with victims, terrified and innocent. The killing fields of Iraq, where hundreds of thousands of men, women, and children vanished into the sands, would still be known only to the killers. For all who love freedom and peace, the world without Saddam Hussein's regime is a better and safer place.

The UK was sceptical about the existence of any doctrine of 'humanitarian intervention' in the past, but has moved towards its acceptance in the light of the Iraqi repression of the Kurds and the NATO intervention in Kosovo. The invocation of human rights is important to the argument. Stated baldly, 'regime change' could imply the removal of regimes which threatened the national interests of great powers. This is not what is being hinted at by the UK prime minister whose statement approaches more closely the domain of 'humanitarian intervention' – to rectify a situation where an outside state or group of states 'intervenes' in a target state with the intention of rescuing the population of that state from their own oppressive government. Additionally, the UK appears to have taken on board the fashionable concept of 'responsibility to protect', with Blair reported as saying:

> Where a population is suffering serious harm, as a result of internal war, insurgency, repression or state failure, and the state in question is unwilling or unable to halt or avert it, the principle of non-intervention yields to the international responsibility to protect.[46]

The choice of terms ('the international responsibility to protect') is interesting – the present chapter has cited the work of the International Commission on Intervention and State Sovereignty, and this, it seems, is what the prime minister has also been reading. As other justifications for action lose their lustre under critical scrutiny, we sense that humanitarian intervention is on the rise in the pecking order of justifications.

How we 'do' human rights

Sovereignty and human rights

The defensive wall, the *catenaccio* of sovereignty, and the corollary principle of non-intervention strongly suggest that armed adventures in more interventionist directions, humanitarian or otherwise, require explicit and sustained justification. The non-intervention norm is not simply formalistic or structural: 'The non-interference rule not only protects states and governments: it also protects peoples and cultures, enabling societies to maintain the religious, ethnic, and civilizational differences which they cherish.'[47] From a different angle, the same is true of the principle of self-determination which, minimally, implies a state or political system in the 'ownership' of its people. Even bad governments 'belong' in a twisted sense to the people concerned, so that resistance in Iraq may continue against the occupation forces from patriotic or nationalist motives of resistance to outsiders, as well as for more nefarious reasons. This is a flaw in doctrines of humanitarian intervention: even the best-intentioned intervener will face opposition from forces loyal to the country if not the regime. There are likely to be few if any 'surgical strikes' or regime change by stealth of night. These 'cultural' and 'ownership' considerations are crucially important in an age replete with talk of the clash of civilizations or more optimistically a dialogue of civilizations.[48] Talk of a move back to empire is fanciful – in terms of international relations, self-determination has only begun to work its magic; nation-building has barely consolidated in many of the world's regions. National sovereignty is not a market opportunity. If Saddam Hussein 'hijacked' Iraq this does not entitle others to do likewise.

However, respect for diversity and ownership of political processes apart, interpretations of 'sovereignty' to the effect that it implies a government can do what it likes to its own people are not any longer seriously held. The growth of international human rights law has cut back the non-interference principle of Article 2.7 of the Charter; the 'erosion' of the domestic jurisdiction principle in the name of human rights has been a staple of commentary for decades. Human rights supply *criteria of judgement*. Human rights principles, though they incorporate nuances favouring cultural and political diversity as well as commonality, contribute to a contemporary standard of governmental legitimacy, conditioning our understanding of democracy, decency and tyranny.[49] The point is that human rights move us in the direction of shared understandings of where a political system or social practice stands in the spectrum of acceptability. The articulation of these shared understandings reaches beyond the understandings preferred by any particular state, however powerful, though it strives to include them. Human rights instruments provide the international community with a shared judgemental lexicon. The book of human rights and wrongs is more 'readable' than the simple expression of moral outrage or 'gut feeling' about the rebarbative practices of some governments and terrorist groups, even if the rights and wrongs are not precisely 'measurable' despite attempts at codifying sets of 'indicators'.

The totalizing effect of human rights principles is summed up by the UN secretary-general in terms of an 'emerging' *summum bonum* of principle: that is,

> an international norm against the violent repression of minorities that will and must take precedence over concerns of State sovereignty. It is a prin-ciple that protects minorities – and majorities – from gross violations. And let me ... be very clear: even though we are an organization of member States, the rights and ideals ... the United Nations exists to protect are those of peoples. ... No government has the right to hide behind national sovereignty in order to violate the human rights or fundamental freedoms of its peoples. ... This developing international norm will pose fundamental challenges to the United Nations.[50]

The language of the secretary-general is conservative and qualified. Apart from being couched in highly abstract terms, the principle is only 'emerging' and we may doubt if it has fully 'emerged' since his statement. The statement can only be the harbinger of discourse: the 'challenges' require elaboration; the modali-ties of intervention likewise. There is nothing in the statement that cuts across a concern for multilateral approaches in accordance with the international rule of law; on the contrary, the statement may be read as a refinement of this legal ideal, an anxiety directed towards its perfection in the light of evidence of continuing mass violations of rights.

The ICISS postulates the 'human rights effect' not as one of a clash between sovereignty and human rights, but as reappraisal of sovereignty itself:

> It is acknowledged that sovereignty implies a dual responsibility: externally to respect the sovereignty of other states, and internally to respect the dignity and basic rights of all the people within the state. In international human rights covenants, in UN practice, and in state practice itself, sovereignty is now understood as embracing this dual responsibility. Sovereignty as responsibility has become the minimum content of interna-tional citizenship.[51]

The duality of sovereignty implied in the statement retains the importance of the 'external' as well as the 'internal' sense; the issue is one of finding a balance, a synthesis not a sacrifice of principle.

Putting judgements into practice

The international community has adopted modalities for implementation of human rights. Few subjects have been more agonized over than improving the implementation of human rights; the UN and regional bodies, and NGOs, daily deliver ideas for improvement. The mantra of 'from standard-setting to implementation' drones on. All this may be utopian, but is none the worse for that – as Michael Ignatieff has observed, human rights are attractive to populations in all countries, a seed of hope for the future in the face of oppressive reality. The promise of an international regime of human rights may, however, be more than can be delivered, and the methodologies misunderstood by those whom it is designed to succour. The mechanisms of the international instruments are not designed for instant results. States are indeed expected to 'deliver' a range of human rights benefits to their citizenry and to others under their jurisdiction, though it is also true that the 'management' of human rights is still largely under state control, exercised by means of non-accession and reservations to human rights treaties, derogations from principle in times of emergency, restrictive interpretations of key treaty commitments, and even 'denunciations' of – withdrawing from – human rights instruments. There is constant backsliding, and many governments may give up on the international commitments, effectively infantilized by demands that cannot be met. The prevailing, necessary and pragmatic ethos is necessarily one of patience and continuing engagement, the slow inculcation of a human rights culture or processes within states, in constructive dialogue with governments so that the rights are seen as 'outgrowth' rather than outside imposition.

Present structures for the implementation of human rights are not set in stone, but they do have easily overlooked virtues. In their essence, human rights bodies of the UN are multinational in personnel: it is considered essential that they represent the main streams of civilization. They proceed from concern for the people and the government of states in dialogue. They work to interpret a common body of norms – the prescribed texts. They answer questions of interference with the response that the governments have consented to the relevance and operation of norms. They engage with national NGOs and human rights institutions, with concerned citizens; they engage with diverse communities within the parameters of their institutional practice. They strive ideally to keep a balance between the interests of different states, to avoid double standards. Their *métier* is legal, with sensitivity to the political and diplomatic. Their loyalty is formally to human rights, despite the diverse national origins of the personnel. They strive to make the standards work better, to bite into social and political life more deeply, to reach the most deprived human beings. Their basis is collective appraisal of the condition of rights.

The heart of standing …

Taking coalition justifications as they stand, and keeping in mind the degree of 'overlap' among them, we may provisionally conclude that the argument of UN 'authority' for the invasion is a weak argument. To put the matter bluntly, the level of 'implied' authority, or the level of 'agency in defence of' the UN, is bottom-rung. Engagement with UN legal discourse equals limitations on interpretative latitude as well as limitations on conduct. The majority of members of the UN Security Council were right not to be convinced of the case for war against Iraq. It does not behove the Security Council to 'consent' to exercises of lethal force which stretch the UN frame to breaking point, nor does it behove individual members. The Security Council is a creature of the UN and is bound by the Charter. Delegation by the Security Council of the right to use force to restore international peace and security should be as clear and explicit as possible and in conformity with Charter principles. The 'sign-posts' to force should be easily legible. These requirements were not met in the case of the 2003 invasion of Iraq.

But although the justification is flawed, it points up the centrality of collective as opposed to unilateralist approaches to international peace and security. The UN was never an irrelevance; on the contrary, the Charter approaches the status of *fons et origo* of international legitimacy, the UN membership pledged to observe its norms. While action in accordance with UN norms does not exhaust international legitimacy, the residue of legitimacy for actions outside this frame is likely to be meagre. Hence the strenuous efforts of the UK in particular to convince the main players that the Charter and the decisions of the Security Council were no impediment to action but on the contrary mandated it.

Secondly, the (mainly) US-inspired doctrine of pre-emptive force has been described by a former UK foreign secretary as follows:

> The ... doctrine of pre-emptive strike blows a hole through the principles on which the UN was founded. In revulsion at two world wars of aggression, the UN established the principle that no country had the unilateral right to invade the sovereign territory of another. The doctrine of pre-emptive strike resurrects just such a unilateral right. The world will be a safer place if we bury it fast.[52]

The general benefits of the existing principles regarding self-defence are widely recognized. It is not clear if the doctrine of pre-emptive strike will go the way of the dodo on account of the evident dangers it presents to international peace and security.[53] The appeal of the doctrine to one or more 'exceptionalist' powers may have only a limited, temporal dimension; Article 51 may have the staying power. While the temptations of exceptionalism may lure this or that governing class, it does not work as legal principle. All law is collective in the minimal sense that it addresses a class of actors; this is part of its architecture. In terms of legality, if one state exercises a power, others will be tempted to follow. In the absence of camp-followers, the exceptional is simply illegal. International law does have in-built mechanisms for change in the form of customary law, of amendments to charters and lesser treaties, or their abandonment. But there is little evidence that other states are ready to follow the pre-emptive path; on the contrary, the prevailing ethos is critical and oppositional. There are perils in the face of the law's condemnatory judgements. International law may be a mesh with holes in it but it is capable of entrapping the hardiest gladiator: the line between justified self-defence and international aggression is a fine one, crossed at legal and political cost even for a superpower. Even if the patient is not in the best of health, rumours of the death of Article 51 are greatly exaggerated. The UK at least has made statements about the 'imminence' of the danger from Iraq which demonstrate respect for limiting interpretations of Article 51. The present author would not favour the elaboration of any new project to 'supplement' Article 51 along the lines of extending its reach to encompass less-than-imminent threats.

Thirdly, the concept of humanitarian intervention deserves more serious consideration for the future, though its application is also fraught with dangers to international stability. One of the greatest challenges for the international community is to provide an instrumental framework to give substance to its glimpse of the essential oneness of humanity through the gauze of multiple sovereignties and cultural and national diversity. Human rights are strong on principle, strong on mechanisms for dialogue with governments, but relatively weak on 'emergencies' of a humanitarian nature. This imbalance has the potential to encourage adventures beyond the legal framework on the basis of claims that the system is irredeemably sclerotic. But unilateral rescue exercises raise issues of motive and authority; and scepticism as to motives is the almost inevitable order of the day – 'the rarer action is in virtue than in vengeance'.[54]

The imprimatur of the international community is critical in such cases. Principles or justifications for intervention should be more than those of the rescuing state or states but be shared and systemic. Cultural and civilizational differences may compound the difficulties surrounding humanitarian interventions. In particular, the USA and the UK should have been the very last powers to intervene in Iraq – they carry too much historical and religious baggage. Interventionist 'Western' powers articulating Manichean discourses weaken the cosmopolitan pull of human rights; the rights become implicated in clash of civilizations theses instead of an essential condition for intercivilizational dialogue, threatening to mutate into paradigms of orientalist discourse, demonstrations of the superior knowledge of the West, a taxonomy and denigration of the Other. All interventions are assimilated into historical narratives. This one is no different.

And yet, and yet – great violations of human rights engage the emotions and impel to action. Humanitarian intervention pushes fear of disorder against the relief of distress, the pluralist against the solidarist, the impulsive against the diligent. We do not mourn the passing of tyrants. In an era of explicit declarations of human rights and public knowledge of violations, the air is full of sweet noises for universal betterment. Human rights mechanisms require supplementing with proactive prevention, and the elaboration of mechanisms for urgent action. The ICISS has elaborated a set of key principles for humanitarian intervention as a last resort operation with just cause, right intention, proportional means and reasonable prospects of success. The principles look very much like the transposition of classic 'just war' requirements to a contemporary frame. A major element in their prospectus is 'right authority', primarily the UN Security Council but failing that, the UN General Assembly, or regional organizations subject to their seeking subsequent authorization from the Security Council. The ICISS warns that UN credibility is damaged where the Security Council declines to act in the face of conscience-shocking situations which cry out for action.[55] The ICISS is also strong on post-intervention responsibility to rebuild, 'addressing the causes of the harm the intervention was designed to halt or avert'. The proposals have appeal but movement towards them is likely to be cautious. Radical overhaul of systems is immediately unlikely. There is nothing in this to validate self-assessing unilateral interventions, and it may be doubted if the Iraq intervention approaches the parameters of last resort, proportional means, etc., let alone 'right authority', though the element of 'just cause' continues to commend itself to the intervening powers. Following the intervention in Iraq, governments may be less ready than before to engage unilaterally in the adventure of rescue; and collective approaches may benefit from strengthened appeal. This is reform, not revolution: 'The heart of standing is you cannot fly.'[56]

Notes and references

1 W. Empson, 'Aubade', in J. Wain (ed.), *The Oxford Library of English Poetry*, Vol. III, London: Guild Publishing, 1986, pp. 379–80.

2 UN Secretary-General, Message for the New Year, 2004. Online. Available HTTP: <http://www.un.org/News/Press/docs/2003/sgsm9095.doc.htm> (accessed 31 January 2004).

3 Regarding the legal framework for the occupation, see Security Council Resolutions 1483, 1500 and 1511 (2003): the last of these '*Reaffirms* the sovereignty and territorial integrity of Iraq, and *underscores*, in that context, the temporary nature of the exercise by the Coalition Provisional (Authority) of the specific responsibilities, authorities, and obligations under applicable international law recognized and set forth in resolution 1483 (2003), which will cease when an internationally recognized, representative government established by the people of Iraq is sworn in and assumes the responsibilities of the Authority' (emphasis in original). *Inter alia*, Resolution 1511 welcomed the establishment of 'the broadly representative Governing Council as an important step towards an internationally recognized representative government', and invited the Governing Council to provide by 15 December 2003 'a timetable and a programme for the drafting of a new constitution for Iraq and for the holding of democratic elections under that constitution'. For observations on the implementation of 1511 and other issues surrounding the situation in Iraq, see 'Report of the Secretary-General', UN Doc. S/2003/1149, 5 December 2003.

4 The attack on the UN Headquarters on 19 August 2003 in which, *inter alios*, the UN high commissioner for human rights was killed, precipitated a partial 'pullout' by the UN. The secretary-general has stated his conviction 'that the future of a nation of more than 26 million people and of a volatile region is at stake. The process of restoring peace and stability to Iraq cannot be allowed to fail' – S/2003/1149, para. 114.

5 Or, 'the consensus of legal opinion', according to Michael Mansfield. Letter to the *Independent on Sunday*, 1 February 2004.

6 'I think it was unlawful from the beginning, and they haven't found anything since to make one change one's mind' (Prof. J. Crawford), 'War on Iraq was Illegal, Say Top Lawyers', *Independent*, 25 May 2003.

7 A.-M. Slaughter, cited in J. Lobe, 'Law Groups Say US Invasion Illegal', *One World*, 21 March 2003.

8 O. Burkman and J. Borger, 'War critics astonished as US hawk admits invasion was illegal', *Guardian*, 20 November 2003. In a more sophisticated vein, Prime Minister Blair has made strong points on the need to reform the UN, and perhaps international law, adding that 'for me, before September 11th, I was already reaching for a different philosophy in international relations from a traditional one that has held sway since the Treaty of Westphalia in 1648; namely that a country's internal affairs are for it and you don't interfere unless it threatens you, or breaches a treaty or triggers an obligation of alliance' – Speech of 5 March 2004. Available online from: <http://www.number-10.gov.uk/output> (accessed 31 March 2004).

9 Apart from inherent legal and political difficulties, a certain caution is advisable in putting the 'humanitarian' into 'humanitarian intervention' – as a recent think-tank advised, the 'use of an inherently approving word like "humanitarian" tends to prejudge the very question at issue – that is, whether the intervention is in fact defensible'. *The Responsibility to Protect: Report of the International Commission on Intervention and State Sovereignty* (ICISS), Ottawa: International Development Research Centre, 2001, para. 1.40.

10 President Bush, 30 July 2003, cited in Stephen Zunes, 'Distortions of history'. Online. Available HTTP: <globalpolicy.org/security/issues/iraq> (accessed 30 September 2003).

11 Charter principles are often assumed to have a status beyond 'mere' treaty law. Reviewing international customary law on the use of force, the International Court of Justice in the case of *Nicaragua* v. *the United States* found that the customary law on the use of force corresponded in essentials to the principles of the UN Charter, a view accepted, according to the Court, by both the USA and Nicaragua (ICJ reports, 1986, para. 188). Further, Article 103 of the Charter provides for the supremacy of Charter obligations over obligations under any other international agreement.

12 Articles 53, 64 and 71 of the Vienna Convention on the Law of Treaties, 1969; *Nicaragua* v. *the United States*, para. 189.

13 'Certain portions of *ius cogens* are the subject of general agreement, including rules to the use of force by states': I. Brownlie, *Principles of Public International Law*, Oxford: Oxford University Press, 1990, p. 515.

14 *Nicaragua* v. *US*, International Court of Justice 1986, para. 176.

15 Discussed extensively in *Legality of the Threat or Use of Nuclear Weapons*, Advisory Opinion of the International Court of Justice, October 1996.

16 A. Hurrell, 'Power, Principles and Prudence: Protecting Human Rights in a Deeply Divided World', in T. Dunne and N. J. Wheeler (eds.), *Human Rights in Global Politics*, Cambridge: Cambridge University Press, 1999, p. 277.

17 Article 2, paras 1, 4 and 7.

18 There were of course other influences. J. Morsink, 'The Philosophy of the Universal Declaration', *Human Rights Quarterly*, 6, 1984, pp. 309–34.

19 The Preamble, Article 1.3, Article 13(c), Article 55(c), Article 62.2, Article 68 and Article 76(c).

20 R. Falk, 'The Rights of Peoples (In Particular Indigenous Peoples)', in J. Crawford (ed.), *The Rights of Peoples*, Oxford: Clarendon Press, 1988, pp. 17–37.

21 See generally J. Morsink, *The Universal Declaration of Human Rights: Origins, Drafting, and Intent*, Philadelphia: Pennsylvania University Press, 1999.

22 Morsink, *Universal Declaration*, p. 33.

23 'The organic unity of the document reflects on the part of the drafters a belief in the fundamental unity of all human rights': Morsink, *Universal Declaration*, p. 238.

24 Para. 4, which continues: 'The organs and specialized agencies related to human rights should … further enhance the coordination of their activities based on the consistent and objective application of international human rights instruments'.

25 A broad multifaceted review of UN systems is undertaken in P. Alston and J. Crawford, *The Future of UN Human Rights Treaty Monitoring*, Cambridge: Cambridge University Press, 2000.

26 *The Responsibility to Protect*, para. 2.18.

27 For comment on a similar approach by the Security Council in Somalia, and on the ECOWAS interventions in Liberia and Sierra Leone, see *The Responsibility to Protect*, ch. 2.

28 See C. Gray, 'From unity to polarization: international law and the use of force against Iraq', *European Journal of International Law*, 12, 2002, pp. 1–19, for a detailed account of the notion of 'implied authorization' in the Iraq and Kosovo contexts.

29 Discussed by the present author in 'Come, Friendly Bombs ...', in M. Waller, K. Drezov and B. Gokay (eds.), *Kosovo: the Politics of Delusion*, London: Cass, 2001, pp. 43–58.

30 Speech of Prime Minister Blair to the House of Commons, 18 March 2003, as released by 10 Downing Street.

31 'We had to force conformity with international obligations that for years had been breached with the world turning a blind eye': Blair speech of 5 March 2004.

32 A. McSmith, R. Whitaker and E. Lean, 'Britain and US will back down over WMDs', *Independent*, 7 September 2003.

33 State of the Union message, 20 January 2004.

34 Joseph Schumpeter, cited in G. Vidal, *Dreaming War: Blood for Oil and the Cheney-Bush Junta*, London: Clairview Books, 2003, pp. 44–5.

35 P. Thornberry, 'Invisible Cities', in B. Gokay and R. B. J. Walker (eds), *11 September 2001: War, Terror and Judgement*, London: Cass, 2003, pp. 13–29.

36 One of the deleterious consequences of the invasion has been the apparently large-scale infiltration of terrorist groups allied to the Al-Qaida ideology.

37 See the summary of events and claims in 'What We Were Told, What We Know Now and the Unresolved Issues', *Independent*, 6 February 2004.

38 Iran, Iraq and North Korea – President Bush's State of the Union message, 29 January 2002. In a speech, US Under-Secretary of State Bolton added Cuba, Libya and Syria – BBC News, 6 May 2003.

39 The document nonetheless warns that the USA will not use force in all cases to pre-empt emerging threats, nor should pre-emption be used 'as a pretext for aggression'. Online. Available HTTP: <http://www.whitehouse.gov/nsc> (accessed 31 January 2004).

40 According to H. Charlesworth, the US version of pre-emptive self-defence 'can be summarised as the right to use force to prevent a future attack by another state, even when there is no concrete evidence that an attack has been planned. The argument was ... that Iraq, a "rogue state", part of the "axis of evil", which held aggressive intentions towards the United States, held stocks of weapons of mass destruction, [and thus] constituted an ongoing threat to the United States.' 'Is international law relevant to the war in Iraq and its aftermath?', Telstra Address, National Press Club, Canberra, 19 October 2003.

41 Article 2 of which provides one more conceptually 'awkward' principle for those inclined to favour pre-emptive action: 'The First use of armed force by a State in contravention of the Charter shall constitute prima facie evidence of an act of aggression although the Security Council may, in conformity with the Charter, conclude that a determination that an act of aggression has been committed would not be justified in the light of other relevant circumstances, including the fact that the acts concerned or their consequences are not of sufficient gravity.'

42 R. Suskind, *The Price of Loyalty, George W. Bush, the White House and the Education of Paul O'Neill*, New York: Simon and Schuster, 2004.

43 Azores Summit Statement of the President of the USA, and the Prime Ministers of Spain and the UK, 16 March 2003.

44 Restated in his speech of 5 March 2004.
45 McSmith *et al.*, 'Britain and US'.
46 A. McSmith and J. Dillon, 'Blair Seeks New Powers to Attack Rogue States', *Independent*, 13 July 2003.
47 *The Responsibility to Protect*, para. 4.11.
48 The year 2001 was proclaimed by the UN General Assembly as the Year of Dialogue among Civilizations. See General Assembly Resolution 53/22 of 1998.
49 J. Rawls, *The Law of Peoples, with 'The Idea of Public Reason Revisited'*, London: Harvard University Press, 1999.
50 Speech of 7 April 1999.
51 *The Responsibility to Protect*, para. 1.35.
52 R. Cook, 'Gilligan's Glorious Diversion', *Independent on Sunday*, 1 February 2004.
53 While the main UK justification for the invasion of Iraq remains the enforcement of UN resolutions, perhaps we have a foretaste of a pre-emptive future in the prime minister's claim that the struggle against the begetters of chaos (above) leads to a new type of war, which 'will rest on intelligence to a greater degree than ever before'. Speech of 5 March 2004. From the viewpoint of international law, what remains to be demonstrated is the willingness of other states to follow this kind of thinking, a willingness that is scarcely in evidence at the time of writing.
54 Prospero, in Shakespeare's *The Tempest*.
55 Tony Blair shares this sentiment. Speech of 5 March 2004.
56 Empson, 'Aubade'.

9 The transition to democracy in Iraq
Historical legacies, resurgent identities and reactionary tendencies

Gareth Stansfield

Freedom is the non-negotiable demand of human dignity; the birthright of every person—in every civilization. Throughout history, freedom has been threatened by war and terror; it has been challenged by the clashing wills of powerful states and the evil designs of tyrants; and it has been tested by widespread poverty and disease. Today, humanity holds in its hands the opportunity to further freedom's triumph over all these foes. The United States welcomes our responsibility to lead in this great mission.

George W Bush, September 17, 2002[1]

The United States' strategy for regime change in Iraq was arguably one of the most ambitious programmes of political engineering witnessed since the immediate years following the Second World War. From being identified as a founder member of the 'axis of evil' in President Bush's State of the Union address of January 2002, Iraq was a primary influence behind the formulation of the National Security Strategy (NSS) and the 'Bush doctrine' of preventive war – of acting against emerging threats before they are fully formed.[2] The NSS, however, was not purely about defeating potential enemies. It also envisaged the promotion of American values throughout the world. Not only was Iraq going to undergo democratic transformation, it also marked the 'first phase in a grand design for the moral reconstruction of the Middle East'.[3] It was considered that Saddam's demise would herald a new era for Iraq, one in which its long-suffering peoples would live in harmony and peaceful coexistence, and the nurturing of democracy in Iraq would become an example to the rest of the region of the benefits of embracing American ideals. Indeed, it was envisaged that as a 'beacon of democracy' Iraq's example would penetrate like a search-light into the darkest despotic corners of the Middle East, vividly illustrating to the oppressed and marginalized what government should be like, albeit with US colouring. In the president's own words, 'a new regime in Iraq would serve as a dramatic and inspiring example of freedom for other nations in the region'.[4] What was rarely said, however, was the unwritten caveat that any new regime which emerged, including Iraq's, would need to be acceptable to US interests, if not actually designed by the US government itself. Two sets of 'freedoms' can therefore be identified. One is a freedom satisfying the demands of a nation newly liberated from the grotesque barbarities of a brutal dictatorship. The other is freedom as interpreted, portrayed, and accepted by the US administration and its electorate. As we shall see in Iraq, the two do not always coincide.

Whether this grand plan is considered to be a work of visionary genius or one of monumental folly remains to be seen. What is clear, however, is that if this plan is to have any chance of success, the political reconstruction of Iraq cannot be seen to fail.[5] Speaking in November 2003 at the National Endowment for Democracy in Washington DC, President Bush said, 'the establishment of a free Iraq at the heart of the Middle East will be a watershed event in the global democratic revolution'.[6] Indeed it may be, but the failure of this policy would be an even greater watershed as an already destabilized Middle East would be plunged into deeper instability. The US position in the region would be undermined; states neighbouring Iraq would be sensitized (Syria, Turkey) and potentially destabilized (Saudi Arabia); and there would be a ready supply of proxy forces in Iraq to take up arms for initiatives planned in other regional capitals.[7] Countries in the Middle East would become riddled by transnational forces, impervious to the constraints imposed by state boundaries. Shi'ism in the Gulf and Kurdish nationalism across the Zagros Mountains are but two distinct possibilities which could accompany the more widespread pernicious threat from Al-Qaeda-associated activities.

With so much seemingly at stake both for Iraq and for the United States, an obvious question to ask is: 'what would it take for this policy to work?' Yet it is a question that has rarely been seriously discussed as many analyses understandably become engrossed in the vivid day-to-day events of contemporary occupied/interim Iraq.[8] The answer to the question differs depending on where the question is asked. One would, at the very least, expect a successful policy to result in a stable, consolidated democracy, with a constitution enshrining the rights of individuals and recognizing the multi-ethnic nature of the state. Such requirements are easily stated, but they have rarely, if ever, appeared in Iraq's tortured eighty-year political history. Assuming that democracy will emerge as the natural state of being for the people of Iraq, the basic building blocks of democratic order will therefore have to be created from scratch rather than rediscovered in the wreckage of Iraqi political culture.[9] Andreas Wimmer ominously contends that 'the seeds of democracy may have difficulties to germinate in the sandy soils of Iraq', and Daniel Byman asks whether the ideal of a democratic Iraq is at all possible, noting that the question raises up grave concerns regarding whether Iraq has the necessary prerequisites for democracy. Developing this already bleak picture, Byman further asserts that deep divisions exist between Iraq's communities, and the role outsiders play in imposing a political order could potentially destabilize the situation further.[10]

These concerns are important to address. It was initially thought that the desires of the Iraqi people would ultimately match the plans of the United States dreamed up in the decision-making halls of Washington DC. Such plans obviously required a willingness for Iraqis to embrace a US-inspired and influenced system of government. Instead, the United States has been faced with a multitude of normative viewpoints as to what Iraq should 'be', and what democracy in Iraq should look like. With the removal of the sinister Ba'athist regime, previously subdued primordial identities are now flexing their political muscles. The Shi'a, mobilized by figures within the religious establishment (the Hawza al-Marja'iyya), including Grand Ayatollah Ali Sistani, or by popularist radicals such as Muqtada al-Sadr, recognize the benefits of elections in order to prove their majority. The Kurds, similarly, consider it their democratic right to express their desire for autonomy within Iraq. This expression of the rights of self-determination by a considerable proportion of Iraq's population (around a quarter) presents the United States, the non-Kurdish Iraqis and the region with a peculiarly difficult problem which could be the precursor to a potent manifestation of Kurdish nationalism across the Middle East. Sunni Arabs are associated with the growing insurgency against occupying forces,[11] and it would not be overly pessimistic to suggest that a Sunni Islamist-coloured rebellion could easily turn its attention to a government perceived to be dominated by Shi'i clerics in the future.[12] These positions are certainly polarized and may not reflect the huge swathe of moderate political sentiment which exists in Iraq, but these groups, through their own organizational abilities and the willingness of the United States to empower them in the ethnically and sectarian designed Iraqi Governing Council (IGC), are the current dominant political forces within Iraq. As such, they warrant close attention.[13]

Events in Iraq can now be classified according to the triumvirate of dissonance which has haunted the state since its inception: the traditional role of leadership for the Sunni has resulted in a Sunni-associated insurgency through fear of disempowerment; Kurdish nationalism is fuelling a drive for autonomy with hints of possible secessionist tendencies; and Shi'i marginalization under the Sunni is now forcing their leaders to attempt to impose their will over the institutions of the new Iraq. As these new manifestations of historical dissonance become apparent to the US public, the political need to avoid the appearance of failure has pushed the United States to undertake several sharp policy transformations.[14] Each transformation has had as much to do with consolidating US public opinion as with creating the necessary requirements for the introduction and consolidation of democracy in Iraq. From the targeted, limited, policies of General Jay Garner's Office of Reconstruction and Humanitarian Assistance (ORHA) in April 2003, through to the wide-ranging and comprehensive agenda of Ambassador L. Paul Bremer's Coalition Provisional Authority (CPA) in May 2003, and then the subsequent retreat by Bremer on issues relating to the transition of power in November 2003 and February 2004, it can be argued that with the November 2004 presidential election looming, US policy development stems more from satisfying US public perceptions that Iraq is, at least, better than it was under Saddam by doing whatever is necessary to react to immediate events on the ground – this is certainly not the same as making progress towards a consolidated democracy.[15] The price of this inconsistency is potentially devastating for Iraq as the transitional period is governed more by reaction to immediate events which are often characterized by the actions of extremists rather than by a planned agenda with the greater picture in mind. US policy modifications have witnessed a move towards either attempting to match, or dilute, certain Iraqi political realities such as Ayatollah Sistani's demand for elections, or ignoring other political realities which are of such magnitude that involvement would place US policy in an even more intractable position within Iraq and the region at large (such as Kurdish demands for autonomy).

This chapter addresses concerns about the transition to democracy in Iraq, and the possibilities of consolidating any such democracy in the 'post-transition' future. It does so by comparing US policy, as viewed through the matrix of the record of US actions in Iraq since the removal of Saddam, and the activities, actions and aspirations of the principal Iraqi political groups. I commence with an assessment of the 'raw materials' available to the builders of the new Iraqi state, assessing the legacy of decades of authoritarianism and particularly focusing upon resurgent national and sub-national identities. I will then elaborate upon the theoretical conditions deemed necessary to ensure that democracy can be established and consolidated, drawing particularly upon the work of Juan Linz and Alfred Stepan, and Francis Fukuyama.[16] With an assessment of the political characteristics of Iraq in place, and a theoretical understanding of what is needed to ensure democratic consolidation, I will then analyse the record of political development in Iraq since the removal of Saddam Hussein from power.

The historical legacy of state building, part I (1919–2003)

From its inception, Iraq was an artificial British creation. This statement presupposes that some states are inherently 'natural', but, if one were to construct the theoretical parameters of an ideal state, it is reasonable to assume that Iraq would be somewhat removed from them.[17] The most obvious fact of its artificiality is evident in the apparent allegiances of its citizens. While arguments can be constructed to support the notion that an 'Iraqi' identity was evident before the creation of the state in 1920, it is obvious that a sense of belonging to the Iraqi state was not an initial characteristic of its varied peoples in the formative years of the state.[18] In terms of absolute numbers, Hanna Batatu provides a rough estimate of Iraq's ethnic and religious composition in 1947 as follows: 51 per cent Shi'i Arab; 20 per cent Sunni Arab; 19 per cent Kurdish; Christians 3 per cent and Jews 2.5 per cent.[19] The figures suggest a diverse society, but does this necessarily mean that Iraqi national identity was weak? The first British-implanted monarch of Iraq, King Faisal I, certainly thought so. Reflecting on this mosaic of discord, he commented that 'there is still – no Iraqi people but unimaginable masses of human beings, devoid of any patriotic idea, imbued with religious traditions and absurdities, connected by no common tie ... prone to anarchy and perpetually ready to rise against any government whatever'.[20] Although referring to 1930s Iraq, King Faisal's lament may still be echoing in the halls of the CPA some seventy years later.

The sociologist Andreas Wimmer identifies two factors which encourage ethnic heterogeneity to promote competition and violence within nascent states. Firstly, no strong networks of civil society organizations develop prior to the introduction of the modern state, and, secondly, the incipient state is weak and cannot enforce equality before the law, democratic participation, protection from violence and access to services, for all the citizens of the state. Such conditions encourage elites to discriminate between groups and promote patron–client relationships, giving preference to members of their own socio-political group, with groups bridging these divides either too small or even non-existent. Political authority therefore becomes quickly divided according to communal solidarities.[21] For Wimmer, Iraq fills these conditions admirably, with identity in the year of independence (1932) commonly associated with ethnicity (and particularly Arab, Kurd and Turkmen) or religion (Sunni Muslim, Shi'i Muslim, Christian and Jewish). Wimmer develops this argument by noting that Iraq had an absence of civil society organizations with a trans-ethnic reach, and 'traditions of statehood' were hardly going to be strong in this ex-backwater of the Ottoman Empire.[22]

As a modern state, Iraq was encumbered with two attributes which together condemned its people to a painful future as 'the state' strove to control a fractured and violence-prone society.[23] The first of these was the continuation by the British of the previous Ottoman method of governing the region – through Iraq's minority Sunni Arabs. Indeed, the association of Sunni elites with the institutions of state led the Shi'i to protest that 'the taxes are on the Shi'i, death is on the Shi'i, and the posts are for the Sunni'.[24] The second, often overlooked, decision of the British was to attach the Kurdish-dominated province of Mosul to the Arab-dominated provinces of Baghdad and Basra. The British legacy to Iraq was therefore the formation of a weak state with a political system dominated by an inbuilt Sunni minority government (and associated disempowerment of the Shi'i majority), and a recalcitrant Kurdish nationalist movement which would fight stubbornly against any government in Baghdad in an attempt to gain autonomy. The Shi'i political problem was essentially of an internal nature – over who would control the state of Iraq. The Kurdish problem was the opposite and external – over how the Kurds could escape the authority of Baghdad.[25]

The history of the political development of the Iraqi state is one of a central government seeking to manage/manipulate the cleavages apparent within Iraqi society. It is also one of the institutions of state becoming wholly Arabized.[26] However, even though state institutions were the preserve of an increasingly select clique of Sunni Arabs, a sense of an Iraqi identity did develop, particularly from the 1950s onwards. Influenced greatly by the wave of pan-Arabism which swept over the region following the creation of Israel in 1948 and the rise of Nasser in Egypt, an Iraqi identity became prominent particularly among the Arab secular classes, if not among the Kurds, but the old loyalties were never far in the background and Iraqi governments remained 'minority' affairs, favouring particular sections of society over others. In such an environment of distrust, 'the state' sought detachment from society.[27] From 1958, this task of detachment was made considerably easier due to Iraq benefiting from the independent control of its oil resources. By the early 1970s, Iraq received an estimated average of US$ 600 million per annum. By 1980 this figure had reached US$ 26 billion. With the government financially independent from society and benefiting from immense amounts of revenue, it could embark upon a further method of controlling the fractious state – the now infamous use of carrot and stick, the carrot being the expansion of the public sector, the stick being the expansion of the security services. The historian of Iraq Toby Dodge notes that between 1958 and 1977, the number of state employees increased from 20,000 to 580,000, with a further 230,000 people employed in the armed forces and 200,000 people receiving a state pension. By 1990, 21 per cent of the workforce and 40 per cent of households were directly dependent upon the state for their well-being.[28]

For the development of representative government, the impact of this grandiose rentier system on Iraq was devastating. With the Ba'athist-controlled state assuming the position of benevolent supplier to the vast majority of Iraq's social groups, there was little incentive for individuals to subscribe to political groups pursuing an agenda attempting to change the status quo. While state patronage was undoubtedly effective in limiting political opposition, Saddam's regime also remained wholeheartedly committed to the more violent attributes of state control. A long-standing opponent of Saddam's regime, Kanan Makiya, meticulously breaks down the numbers of armed men relative to population in 1980, coming to the conservative conclusion that one-fifth of the economically active labour force of over 3 million were institutionally charged, during peacetime, with one form of violence or another. In such an environment, Makiya despondently notes, 'opposition can no longer arise except in people's mind, and then it is not really an opposition at all'.[29] Stories regarding the brutality of life under Saddam's pervasive security measures are well documented, and the ease by which the 'Butcher of Baghdad' could be demonized was eagerly seized upon by the spin doctors of London and Washington. What has rarely been addressed (owing to the near-impossibility of conducting meaningful research on political issues in Saddam's Iraq) is the legacy such oppressive measures have left behind.[30] In the introduction to his detailed analysis of Iraq's security and intelligence network, Ibrahim Marashi lists the five primary agencies that constituted the security apparatus: Jihaz al-Amn al-Khas (Special Security); al-Amn al-ʿAmm (General Security); al-Mukhabarat (General Intelligence); al-Istikhbarat (Military Intelligence); and al-Amn al-ʿAskari (Military Security). In addition to these principal, heavily overlapping groups, there also existed a plethora of party security agencies, police forces, paramilitaries and special units, all armed to protect the regime from any actual, perceived or threatened form of opposition.[31] These organizations formed an Orwellian web of mistrust, fear and coercion which comprehensively permeated every aspect of Iraqi life. Few formations of civil or political life could exist in such an environment, least of all the fragile institutions necessary for representative democracy to emerge.

To establish and consolidate democracy in post-Saddam Iraq, the traumatic psychological legacies of Iraq's history are major hurdles to overcome as the US and fledgling Iraqi institutions seek to identify, empower and, at times, create the building blocks of the new state. Indeed, 'create' is not too strong a word to use in this regard as Iraqi society has increasingly been 'atomized' by the effects of the Ba'athist regime's political and economic structures and actions. The Iraqi academic Isam al-Khafaji stresses that 'the success of Ba'athism in subjugating the Iraqi people to its rule for a relatively long period lies precisely in its ability to atomise the population and link each individual vertically to the patron-state.'[32] In such an individualistic environment dominated by one powerful party, other political identities were easily overshadowed and, sometimes, eradicated. Class-based political organizations in particular struggled to survive, as the very notion of horizontal linkages in society were targeted and weakened by the regime. Those that did manage to maintain some semblance of organizational structure, including communists and socialists, gained themselves the attention of the regime's omnipotent security services. It would seem that the institutions of civil society deemed necessary for the initial emergence of democracy rarely have existed in Iraq, and have struggled to emerge beyond anything but a superficial measure in a post-Saddam Iraqi society.[33]

If the basic structures of civil society are difficult (or perhaps impossible) to find in the immediate-aftermath environment, it is logical to ask what exactly does exist 'on the ground' and what raw materials have emerged from the wreckage of regime change that can be used to reconstruct the state. Such a question brings us around full circle in historical terms, and back to the creation of the Iraqi state in the aftermath of the First World War. From the perspectives of both Iraqis and their occupiers, the situation is a historical rerun. The American analyst Judith Yaphe cuttingly notes that 'when the Arabs of southern Iraq saw the American and coalition forces enter Iraq in March 2003, it must have been with a curious sense of historical *déja vu*'.[34] If the US and coalition forces also possessed an institutional memory spanning back to the 1920s, they too would have been hit by some striking similarities. Then, Iraq was clearly less than the sum of its three parts. The provinces (*vilayets*) of Mosul, Baghdad and Basra each had a distinct ethnic or sectarian identity. Further, each would develop differing positions as to what their own position should be in relation to the state and how the state itself should be constructed. Indeed, the failure of the Iraqi state has been that its 'state-builders' have been unable to develop an identity that was more than the sum of its three basic parts and that enjoyed any measure of longevity.

Throughout the twentieth century, groupings of 'primordial' movements have sporadically challenged the dominance of the Sunni-dominated state, starting with the Kurdish and Shi'i rebellions of 1919 and 1920, and continuing unabated throughout the decades.[35] Indeed, Saddam did not create this antipathy towards the centre – it was an inbuilt structural weakness of the state itself, given to the unfortunate Iraqis by the Ottomans and then the British. All Saddam did was manage these inherent weaknesses in a far more brutal (and bloodily effective) manner and use the weaknesses endemic within a fragmented society to strengthen the position of his Ba'athist regime as the one truly unified political entity. A palimpsest of interlinked identities therefore existed in Iraq, with sectarian, tribal and ethnic bonds overlaid with identities of modernity such as class, trans-regional (pan-Arab in particular), nationalist (Iraqi) and a range of different interests. With the removal of Saddam, the palimpsest has been scratched back, uncovering the raw, traumatized sectarian and ethnic identities with which the United States and its allies have to work. The task of the United States therefore remains the same as that which has confronted every Iraqi government – to weld together an entity greater than the sum of its disparate parts. Whether the United States can achieve this when all others have failed remains to be seen.

The building blocks of state building, part II (2003–?)

The initial US plan for governing Iraq after the removal of Saddam Hussein was quite simple – the man himself, along with his high-ranking colleagues in the Ba'ath Party and state institutions, would be replaced, allowing the long-established administrative structures of the state to continue operating, albeit with new leadership.[36] The plan was elegant in its simplicity, but, with hindsight, it is clear that is was fatally flawed. Ironically, by removing the Ba'ath Party, the United States effectively eliminated the one organization that could perhaps claim a national support base and had the means to project power (at least among the Arab population, if not with the Kurds). The demobilization of the national army, similarly, eradicated the most capable of organizations available to post-Saddam Iraq and allowed a security vacuum to develop which has proved impossible to fill. It also flooded the 'Iraqi street' with thousands of trained, armed and, most importantly, disgruntled ex-soldiers shamed by their failure to protect the state against the forces of imperialism, complete with the extensive arsenal of the military. Whether they supported Saddam or not (and many did not), it would be a reasonably straightforward progression to go from being a disgruntled ex-serviceman to be reborn as a freedom fighter against occupying forces, using stockpiles of ex-army weaponry. The liquidation of the 'Iraqi state' and its agents of control (whether of an administrative (government), political (the Ba'ath Party), security (e.g. the *mukhabarat*) or military (the army) nature) also released the patrimonial and coercive pressure which had successfully kept Iraq's fractious communal 'mosaic of discord' together. Without these consolidating and centripetal features of the Saddam era, political authority became localized overnight, facilitating the resurrection of socio-political forces previously subdued by the combined effects of state patronage and state coercion.[37]

Nearly a hundred years earlier, the British military entered Iraq in 1914, finding a society characterized by 'isolation, political disarray, tribal unrest, social chaos, and economic uncertainty'.[38] The comparison between the experience of the British in 1914 and the Americans in 2003 is an obvious one to draw. Iraqi society of 2003 exhibits many similarities to that of 1914 – it has been isolated both internationally by sanctions and internally by 'atomization'; it is in political disarray with the elimination of the Ba'athist regime and the trauma implicit with life under Saddam; the tribes are again powerful across the county after many were reinvigorated by Saddam; and uncertainty in all sectors of life appears to be the norm.[39] There are, however, two significant differences between 1914 and 2003. Firstly, oil has transformed Iraqi society. Secondly, the state of Iraq has existed for nearly a century and has created its own realities on the ground. Both of these two differences sharpen the problems already faced. Oil revenue can indeed be used to benefit the entire society if distributed correctly, but in the short term it is seen as little more than the reward for securing power. The existence of the Iraqi state also could be a seen in beneficial ways, if the experience of living in that state had been positive. On the whole, however, apart from isolated times of peace and prosperity, it was not and considerations of the state (particularly from those oppressed by it in the past) are commonly of a more negative hue. Because of these considerations, the US position is far more complex than that faced by the British. Furthermore, the United States no longer has the privacy of operation enjoyed by its imperial predecessor. In today's media-saturated world, US actions in Iraq are being played out in front of a news-hungry audience of millions.

Before Saddam's regime was removed, how Iraqis identified themselves was a focus of heated academic debate. Some experts spoke of an overarching sense of Iraqi nationalism, capable of bridging sectarian and ethnic cleavages in the state, others contended that communal and local identities remained strong, but were cowed into submission by the invidiousness of Saddam's regime. One would expect that the argument would have been resolved once Iraqis had the opportunity to organize themselves free from the bondage of dictatorship. This resolution has not occurred. Instead, as occupying forces faced an increasingly capable insurgency, and political life became dominated by parties/groups representing particular segments of society (e.g. Kurds, Sunni and Shi'i) academic arguments evolved to fit the new developments. For some, the insurgency was representative of a true Iraqi nationalist drive against occupation. For others, it was evidence of a reaction by Sunni Arabs to their perceived disempowerment with the removal of Saddam and the threat of a Shi'i theocracy. The emergence of a strong Kurdish movement and a vociferous Shi'i religious trend was considered as proof of the vibrancy of sectarian and ethnic identity within the state on the one hand, or as an extreme rebound against the chauvinistic policies of Saddam, to be calmed at a later point when common sense would prevail. There is also a prescriptive mechanism to feed into what is already a decidedly complex picture. The US administration, after dealing with a Sunni-Arab-dominated government for decades, and then Iraqi opposition forces in the 1990s (and principally Kurds), in addition to fearing the association of Iraq's Shi'a with those of Iran, had and maintains a natural propensity to view Iraq according to its parts, rather than the sum of them. It should therefore have been of little surprise that one of the first acts of the Americans upon entering Baghdad was to select an Iraqi Governing Council (IGC) according to ethnic and sectarian identity. As with virtually every consociational power-sharing system, it would not take long for IGC members to begin acting according to their local parochial interests, rather than the greater Iraqi national concern.[40]

The empowerment of groups associated with a communal identity is currently the norm within Iraq. As such, it is necessary to investigate the personalities and dynamics of the groups contending power at the present time. These groups are (in no particular order) the Shi'i Arabs, the Sunni Arabs and the Kurds. Of course, many other communal groups exist in Iraq, including Christians and Turkmens to name but two; however, they are not contenders for power in the same way as the former three.[41] The positions of each of these groups are complex, and often display considerable internal differences. Nonetheless, it is possible to identify certain incontrovertible demands.

The Shi'a have emerged in the post-Saddam environment as being the most powerful of all Iraq's communal groups. This should not be surprising. If Iraq was truly democratic, it is highly likely that it would be a Shi'i-dominated state as it is commonly assumed that the Shi'a constitute a numerical majority within the state (at around 60 per cent of the population). While being ethnically Arab (although there exist a significant number of Shi'a Kurds), the Shi'a have been politically marginalized throughout Iraq's history. In addition to being considered heretics by hard-line Sunni clerics, the Shi'a were also feared due to their natural ties with the Shi'a of Iran. Indeed, the policy of marginalization pursued by the Ottomans because of religious reasons (as the Ottomans were Sunnis) was taken up by the British (as they already had dealings with the Sunni), only to be magnified by successive Iraqi regimes and politicized when war with Islamic Iran broke out in 1980.

The Shi'a are represented primarily by religious groups, and most notably influenced by Grand Ayatollah Ali Sistani of Najaf, the most senior *marja'* of Iraq. He maintains his fundamental belief in the separation of clerical and political responsibilities, but in the atmosphere of heightened political aspirations, he is often drawn into making political judgements, most notably enunciating the demand for democratic elections to take place, rather than the selection of prominent individuals as proposed by the United States. Other Shi'i groups and leaders include the Supreme Council for Islamic Revolution in Iraq (SCIRI), led by Sayyid Abd al-Aziz al-Hakim, and al-Da'wa. SCIRI has strong links with the Iranian government, but tends to support the lines taken by Sistani. Al-Da'wa has a much stronger base within Iraqi society and is headed by a collegial leadership. Both SCIRI and al-Da'wa had representatives on the IGC. With the removal of Saddam, many Shi'a have found the quietist approach of Sistani and the association of SCIRI and al-Da'wa with the forces of the occupation distasteful, prompting many younger (and more radical) Shi'a to support more militant (and Iranian-style) groups. Chief among these is the Sadriyyun of Muqtada al-Sadr. With his power base in the Sadr City quarter of Baghdad, Muqtada has managed to carve out an ever-growing niche in Iraqi politics, and his movement is home to the many Shi'a who believe that the time has come to exert their authority over Iraq. As such, Muqtada's political lines are often non-negotiable, and he has been brought into conflict with other Shi'a groups (including SCIRI), and is viewed with trepidation by the United States. A summary of the Shi'a position in Iraq would include:

1   recognition (for now) of Sistani as the pre-eminent figure of authority;
2   a demand that the Shi'a are proportionally represented, thereby ensuring their dominance over institutions of state; and
3   maintaining the territorial integrity of Iraq.

It is this third factor which brings the Shi'a into conflict with the Kurds. As stated previously, the experience of the Shi'a and the Kurds in Iraq has only their suffering in common. Their actual demands are in opposition to each other and inherently non-negotiable. For the Shi'a the issue is about who controls Iraq; for the Kurds it is about whether they should even be 'in' Iraq. For the Iraqi Kurds, the US use of the phrase 'self-determination' for Iraqis was received with a great degree of hope. For decades, the leadership of the Kurds, along with the majority of Kurdish society at large, had longed for a time when a 'Great Power' would return to revisit and correct the state-making process of the early twentieth century when the Kurds were denied statehood and divided between Iraq, Iran, Turkey and Syria.[42] The fact that the world's superpower in the form of the United States had indeed returned to Iraq, driven by what was perceived to be a barely hidden agenda to redraw the map of the Middle East, initially gave the Kurds hope that they would, at last, be granted a homeland, or at least 'something' in Iraq. However, these hopes quickly turned to fears as US policy moved from being seemingly 'pro-Kurdish', to then pursuing a political solution which would see the Kurds kept in their provincial marginalized position in the north of the country.

The Kurds entered the post-Saddam political game as the strongest domestic actor in military terms. Since 1991, they have etched out an autonomous Kurdish region in the north of Iraq which is now home to approximately 4 million people. During this time, the two principal parties of the Kurdistan Democratic Party (KDP) led by Massoud Barzani and the Patriotic Union of Kurdistan (PUK) led by Jalal Talabani have presided over an increasingly efficient and institutionalized state structure, resplendent with a legislature, executive and judiciary.[43] Kurds now speak Kurdish as their first language, with Arabic perhaps coming third to English, and now consider themselves to be Kurdish rather than Iraqi. The baseline requirements for the Kurdish leadership are as follows:

1   to maintain at least the level of autonomy the Kurds currently enjoy (which is considerable) and to augment it with control of Kirkuk;
2   to secure control of oil resources in Kurdish territory (including the major oilfield of Kirkuk); and
3   to control a Kurdish military force, and have the power to block the military deployment of Iraqi forces to the north (which would, in effect, make Iraqi Kurdistan an independent state in all but name).

For the Kurds, this is the most significant moment in their recent history and they are determined to achieve their aims, making their position again inherently non-negotiable.

If anything, the Shi'a and the Sunnis are united in an Arab position against Kurdish demands, as if the Kurds are successful they fear it is the first stage in the Balkanization of Iraq. The Sunnis, as a group, are more difficult to define owing to their current level of disorganization. Since the removal of Saddam, the Sunnis in general have suffered from being associated with his regime, the Ba'ath Party and the atrocities of both. Early US policies of de-Ba'athification and demilitarization affected the Sunni Arabs particularly heavily. This tendency towards victimization was compounded by the fact that they were comparatively poorly represented on the IGC. Although the IGC included six out of twenty-five Sunni Arab members, virtually all of them were selected from exiled returnees, religious groups or tribal formations. The IGC therefore presented two problems for the mainstream Sunni Arab Iraqi nationalists. The first was that, for the first time in the history of Iraq, power no longer resided solely in the hands of a Sunni clique. Second, the Sunni representatives on the IGC enjoyed little, if any, popular support and therefore lacked legitimacy. This perceived disempowerment was arguably responsible for the emergence of a well-armed and highly motivated insurgency, focused in Sunni areas (the now infamous 'Sunni Triangle') against occupying forces, and Iraqis collaborating with them. At this moment in time, it is difficult to identify the Sunni agenda. If history is to be our guide, it is reasonable to presume that

1   the Sunnis fear the dominance of the state by the Shi'a;
2   they demand that the territorial integrity of Iraq should not be threatened by Kurdish autonomy.

However, the Sunnis at present lack a truly representative political force capable of pursuing a popular agenda in post-Saddam Iraq. As such, the danger is that any decisions made in their absence will not be accepted by a significant (and traditionally powerful) proportion of the Iraqi population which will almost certainly enjoy a political resurgence in the future.

The domestic political situation in Iraq is therefore unstable and dangerous. It is difficult to be optimistic about the country's future when faced with the unpalatable fact that the primary political communities (Sunni, Shi'a and Kurds) have adopted non-negotiable positions on their demands for how Iraq should be structured. Indeed, the 'triumvirate of dissonance' which exists with Sunni traditional aspirations and fear of the Shi'a, Kurdish nationalist demands for heightened autonomy, and the Shi'a desire to at last dominate the state would seem to suggest that the future of Iraq is going to be rather traumatic. The direness of the situation is only magnified when the Iraq situation is compared with other examples.

How is democracy created and consolidated?

This is a particularly pertinent question, particularly when states with no previous track record of democracy, such as Iraq, are considered. Speaking in November 2003, President Bush triumphantly proclaimed that 'we have witnessed, in little over a generation, the swiftest advance of freedom in the 2,500 year story of democracy', noting that, in the early 1970s, there were 'about 40 democracies in the world', and, as the twentieth century ended, there were nearly 120 'and I can assure you more are on the way'.[44] Indeed there may be, but optimism regarding the ease with which previously undemocratic states can be 'democratized' in what Samuel P. Huntington was to name 'the third wave of democratization in the modern world' has to face an uncomfortable empirical reality.[45] Of nearly 100 countries considered to be moving towards democracy, fewer than one-fifth are moving in the right direction, and Amitai Etzioni notes that of the eighteen forced regime changes in which US ground troops have been committed, arguably only three deserve the 'democratic' title – Germany, Japan and Italy.[46] Most either regress to former levels of authoritarianism, or are stuck in a grey area where 'liberalization' (a mix of policy and social changes in a non-democratic setting) in various sectors is deceptively championed as proof of 'democratization' (open contestation through free competitive elections over the right to win control of the government).[47] Transitions that are successful tend to be in culturally specific environments such as Central Europe and Latin America and historically have occurred in opposition to external powers rather than under their guidance. Etzioni identifies most nations of Latin America, Asia and the Balkans as evidence of this process in action, with what he terms 'artificial constructions', including India, Yugoslavia, Nigeria and Iraq, as being 'held together only under the thumb of a tyrant'.[48]

Democracy therefore seems to be somewhat difficult to introduce into multi-ethnic–sectarian states emerging from the shadow of authoritarianism even in the best of circumstances. With the IGC constructed according to ethnic and sectarian identity,[49] and with CPA plans going nowhere fast with regard to moving towards 'democratization' compared with 'liberalization', neither empirical evidence nor academic theory augurs well for the emergence and consolidation of democracy in such a socio-politically disparate state. As Patrick Basham observes, 'a foreign power can do little to advance democracy's evolutionary clock beyond the limits imposed by the domestic society's economic and cultural development'.[50] However, a foreign power could do much to set back the progress of democracy in a fragile setting such as Iraq.

Thomas Carothers identifies five core assumptions which define the 'transition' paradigm of successful democratic consolidation necessary for a state to move from dictatorship to consolidated democracy.[51]

1   A country moves away from dictatorship towards democracy.
2   Democratization unfolds in a sequence of stages including an 'opening' (liberalization); the 'breakthrough' (collapse of regime and emergence of new democratic system); 'consolidation' (a slow process in which democratic

forms are transformed into democratic substance through the habituation of society to democratic norms).

3   A belief in the determinative importance of elections.
4   Underlying socio-political conditions will not be major factors in either the onset or the outcome of the transition process.
5   Democratic transitions are built on coherent, functioning states.

Already, it is possible to identify certain problems with applying these assumptions to Iraq. The first assumption, at first sight, appears to be appropriate to Iraq – after all, it is difficult to imagine a situation emerging whereby a Saddam-esque figure comes to power. Or is it? If it were possible to argue that Saddam was an anomaly in the history of the Iraqi state, then perhaps we could be confident in accepting that Iraq must be moving towards democracy. However, if it were accepted that he was, in fact, a product of the political dynamics of the Iraqi state, the appropriateness of this assumption needs to be questioned. In other words, the 'triumvirate of dissonance' as defined previously promotes dictatorship as the most effective mechanism through which to maintain the territorial integrity of Iraq and the subservience of all communal groups through patronage, coercion and fear.

The second assumption outlines the sequence of events a transition should follow. Again, on one level, Iraq can be seen to match the requirements, but problems are apparent if we simply look at the chronology of events. Firstly, the influence of outside powers with particular interests in the removal of the dictatorial regime has rushed the agenda considerably. Secondly, it is questionable whether there has been an emergence of new democratic systems, or newly liberalized ones. The order of events also seems to be inchoate in Iraq, with little liberalization under Saddam, with regime collapse occurring first, and with consolidation of democracy and liberalization arguably being concomitant, rushed and confused.

The third assumption is challenged both by the United States, which seems to be set on promoting selections rather than elections, and the fact that religious groups in Iraq, while calling for elections, may not have democratic development in mind. It is useful to remember that Saddam also held elections, enjoying an immense turnout giving him 99.99 per cent of the vote, yet he used elections to bolster the legitimacy of his dictatorship rather than promoting representative government.

The fourth assumption is obviously flawed for Iraq. Underlying socio-political conditions are arguably pre-eminent factors in both the onset of the transition and its subsequent outcome. The fifth assumption appears to be acceptable, until the Kurdish position is raised. For over a decade, the Kurds have effectively operated autonomously from the rest of Iraq and are now promoting a federal initiative which would see the cohesiveness of Iraq weakened. Larry Diamond notes that 'democracy can be consolidated only when no significant collective actors challenge the legitimacy of democratic institutions or regularly violate its constitutional norms, procedures, and laws. … There must be no "politically significant" antisystem (disloyal) parties or organizations.'[52] The Kurdish movement, with its demands for considerable veto powers within the state, heightened autonomy and the creation of a 'Kurdish national guard' clearly constitute a significant collective actor capable of challenging the legitimacy of future institutions of state.

Even if the concerns of applying Carothers' assumptions regarding the conditions necessary for transition to consolidated democracy are overlooked and we accept US claims that 'democracy' has been established in Iraq,[53] the process of consolidating a democracy established in the aftermath of the collapse of a dictatorship appears to be a rather arduous task, as Juan Linz and Alfred Stepan warn: 'after a democratic transition has been completed, there are still many tasks that need to be accomplished, conditions that must be established, and attitudes and habits that must be cultivated before democracy could be considered consolidated'.[54] For Linz and Stepan, a democracy is consolidated when it has become 'the only game in town'. They judge this from three perspectives:

1   *Behaviourally*, no significant actors attempt to usurp the democratic regime, or secede from the state.
2   *Attitudinally*, a strong majority of the population believe that democratic procedures are the most appropriate way to govern collective life in society.
3   *Constitutionally*, all actors within the state become habituated to the resolution of conflict through laws sanctioned by the democratic process.[55]

In the case of Iraq, it is difficult to argue that any one of the three perspectives has much chance of occurring. The non-negotiable stances of the primary political groups means that it is hard to imagine a democratic regime and procedures emerging which have the support of the majority of the population. There are therefore behavioural problems to overcome, as it is not too extreme to consider that any one of the three major groups may attempt to usurp a regime if dominated (or perceived to be so) by an opposing group, and the Kurdish polity continues to nurture its seed of individualism which could quite easily manifest itself as a secessionist tendency. Attitudinally, there exists serious problems. While democracy is currently banded around Iraq as the panacea capable of curing the trauma caused by years of dictatorship, it is necessary to be brutally realistic about the setting in which this hope is being placed – Iraq and Iraqis have no history of democratic procedures, and it is highly questionable whether the powerful Shi'i leaders are really committed to democracy as an appropriate method to govern collective life. Even in the often-described Kurdish *de facto* state, democracy Kurdish-style is characterized by the continued dominance of two leaders, with little evidence of political decision-making going beyond the political bureaux of the KDP and PUK. Finally, with the endemic instability apparent in post-Saddam Iraq, it is unrealistic to presuppose that, constitutionally, all actors within the state will adopt a non-violent method of resolving conflict – at least in the short and medium term (including several years after any elections). Democracy is therefore far from being 'the only game in town' in Iraq.

Francis Fukuyama develops a similar model of democratic consolidation to that of Linz and Stepan, identifying four levels on which consolidation must occur, but introduces a temporal element which gives a useful structure by which to classify developments in Iraq.[56] Going from the shortest to the longest time-frame, level 1, the most superficial level, involves a normative commitment to the notion of democracy. Level 2 sees democracy consolidated in institutions (consti-tutions, electoral systems, etc.). Level 3 requires the existence of civil society, existing outside the realm of state control. Finally, level 4 is the realm of political culture – family structure, religion, ethnic consciousness. With this model, two issues are apparent. The first is that as we progress from the merely superficial into the realm of habituated action, change becomes slower and more difficult to achieve. As we shall see, the focus of US actions has been almost wholly in the realm of the most superficial levels (1 and 2). The second issue is that democracy cannot be considered fully consolidated until it is rooted in the political culture of the society, and this long-term characteristic is beyond the ability of social engi-neers to produce. Only a stable, liberalized, political environment existing over a considerable period of time would realistically allow the development of civil society and the trickle-down effects of political culture to become features of the Iraqi state. It is unlikely that (1) such an environment will come into being, and (2) that the United States is operating with such a timeframe in mind. Rather than giving cause for optimism, appraisals of the theoretical literature expose the sheer scale of the task confronting the democracy-builders of the new Iraq. How the United States has chosen to recreate Iraq as a 'beacon of democracy' in the Middle East illustrates clearly the problems faced, and the trends emerging for the future.

From Iraqi democratic needs to American democratic needs

It has been said by a variety of commentators that the real battle for the United States would not be the overthrowing of Saddam's regime but its replacement. The speed and efficiency by which the coalition military invaded Iraq and deposed the incumbent regime is only matched by the ineptitude and inconsis-tency by which new authorities have been established, legitimized and empowered. Indeed, consistency of US policy direction in this regard has been sorely lacking, at least from an Iraqi perspective, and has instead been dictated more by the rapidly approaching US presidential elections, and the need to be seen as pursuing a successful policy of transition in Iraq. For the United States, this has effectively meant focusing on the easiest elements of establishing and consolidating a democracy – on normative commitment and institutional arrangements. It has not meant attempting to influence the 'deeper' requirements as identified by Linz and Stepan, and Fukuyama, of civil society promotion and encouraging changes in political culture – both of which would require a consid-erable investment of time and resources. Furthermore, this policy of increasingly focusing on the more superficial aspects of democracy-building has meant that the United States has to work within the historical parameters of the Iraqi state. As such, the United States has refused to acknowledge the inherent structural weaknesses of the state (whether minority governance, Shi'i aspirations or Kurdish distinctiveness), and ignored the fundamental instability that the unresolved legacy of these issues will continue to rouse.

Perhaps it was understandable that the United States went into Iraq totally unprepared for how to manage the post-conflict environment. Prominent political leaders in the United States, led by the neo-conservatives who have an inordinate amount of influence over the US administration, held a particular view as to what would happen in Iraq with Saddam's overthrowing: US forces would be welcomed into the country, democracy would be embraced and the peoples of Iraq would come together in a unified state, enjoying the benefits of a US-style economy, cathartically embracing Israel and being a frontline ally in the US war against terror. Exiled Iraqi political groups, and especially the Iraqi National Congress (INC) of Dr Ahmed Chalabi, played on strong links with the neo-conservatives and fed this belief with timely interjections from dissidents fleeing Iraq, who were themselves expertly cultivated by the INC to encourage the United States in its determination to oust Saddam.[57] The two principal Kurdish parties, similarly, could point to their 'democratic experiment' in Iraqi Kurdistan as evidence of democracy not being an alien concept to Iraqis, and received the adulation of several prominent Republican and Democrat politicians, including Senator John Kerry.[58] Even though the modern history of Iraq would tend to suggest that invading powers have never been made welcome, there was such confidence in the US administration, it seems, that Iraqis would embrace coalition forces, that the level of planning invested into 'regime replacement' was criminally negligible. US policies since Saddam's removal have been inherently reactive, with little evidence of the implementation of a proactive or preconceived plan. For this reason, US actions have morphed over time, often in response to the activities of one of the three major communal groups. Three distinct 'plans' (with a fourth on the way) can be discerned since US forces entered Baghdad and an official end to military operations was declared on 1 May 2003.

Plan A

Retired General Jay Garner was tasked with establishing the Office of Reconstruction and Humanitarian Assistance (OHRA). The role of OHRA was to bring law and order back to Iraq as early as possible. Garner, who established a good working relationship with many of Iraq's communal leaders, sought to maintain as much of the previous state apparatus as possible, including the army, and undertook only a limited 'de-Ba'athification' process of the top two tiers of the party apparatchiks. Garner's approach, while certainly winning converts in Iraq, obviously came into conflict with what was desired in Washington, perhaps due to the lack of progress OHRA made with bringing stability to Baghdad (which was gripped with looting in the immediate aftermath of regime change) and the fear surrounding the emergence of a strong and virulent Shi'i religious identity (which, somewhat surprisingly, took the United States by considerable surprise).[59] Garner, and most of his staff, were unceremoniously recalled to Washington in mid-May.

Plan B

General Garner and the OHRA were replaced by Ambassador L. Paul Bremer III and the Coalition Provisional Authority (CPA) on 12 May 2003. Bremer was tasked with pursuing a much tougher line within Iraq than that pursued by Garner. For the United States, it was essential that the rising tide of militant activity against coalition forces could be labelled as being the actions of a specific group – most notably pro-Saddam militias with support from Islamist organizations associated with Al-Qaeda. As such (and playing to US public opinion more than Iraqi), Bremer outlawed the Ba'ath Party and purged nearly 100,000 people from the newly formed offices of government of ex-Ba'ath Party personnel. He also disbanded the Iraqi Army, putting 400,000 soldiers on the street. Civilian unrest was targeted by US military forces as the United States sought to establish security in Iraq by the barrel of a gun. The result was quite predictable – anti-occupation sentiment was heightened and militant activity increased. Politically, the United States needed desperately to show that a new Iraqi government, staffed by Iraqis rather than by coalition civil servants, was in existence and preparing to take over the administration of Iraq when US forces leave. Many local groups were established, with responsibility to work alongside CPA officials in the administration of localized regions. At the highest level, the CPA selected an Iraqi Governing Council (IGC), constructed according to ethnic and sectarian identity, including many of the exiles who had previously been counselling the US administration.[60]

Three problems haunted the existence of the IGC. First, all of its decisions had to be ratified by the CPA and signed off by Bremer. Secondly, it had no popular legitimacy within Iraq, and the Sunni Arabs felt immediately disempowered as there were no Sunni leaders of any particular standing within the council. Thirdly, IGC members, selected because of their communal identity, would soon act according to that identity, rather than in the interests of greater Iraq. 'Plan B' required the IGC to draft a constitutional law which would prescribe a mechanism by which delegates would be elected to a constitutional convention by 15 December 2003. The Constitution would then have been legitimized by a referendum. Elections would then be held and sovereignty transferred. Worryingly (though somewhat predictably), 'Plan B' never got past stage 1 as the communally minded IGC could not agree on the mechanism by which the constitutional convention would be identified. Grand Ayatollah Ali Sistani, the most senior Shi'i cleric, demanded that delegates be democratically elected – obviously hoping that the Shi'i majority would result in their dominance in this crucial arena. The Kurds, who headed the drafting committee, expected their autonomous demands to be included in the draft and in any structure of convention, and obstructed negotiations when they considered that their views were being ignored. Meanwhile, the Sunnis began to express their own political position via the ever-growing insurgency against occupying forces and IGC institutions. Faced with a deadlock in the IGC and a deteriorating security situation, Bremer scrapped 'Plan B' and introduced 'Plan C'.

Plan C

From being described by Bremer as 'straightforward and realistic' as late as September 2003, it was something of an about face when 'Plan B' was replaced by the much more complex and unrealistic 'Plan C' on 15 November 2003. With the number of US casualties hitting new heights in early November (with forty US troops dying in the first ten days of that month alone) and with political negotiations stalling over deep-rooted ethnic and sectarian aspirations, the United States responded by moving away from the longer-term agenda of nation-building, to the much shorter-term task of state-building, and focused particularly on the establishment of an interim Iraqi government and the transfer of sovereignty. In effect, 'Plan C' represented the retargeting of US efforts onto the more superficial elements of democracy-building – normative commitment and institution-building, rather than to the deeper and more taxing considerations of civil society and political culture.

Plan C required a 'Basic Law' to be drafted by 28 February 2004 which would act as an interim constitution. A Transitional National Assembly (TNA) was then to be formed via a highly complex three-stage selection process. Each of Iraq's eighteen provinces was to select an Organizing Committee of fifteen members appointed by the IGC and approved by the CPA that would then convene a Governorate Selection Caucus (GSC). The GSC would then elect representatives to the TNA by 31 May, assuming full sovereign rights on 30 June. A permanent constitution would then be drawn up, with final elections taking place before 31 December 2005.

In addition to being fiendishly complex, 'Plan C' failed owing to exactly the same reasons that 'Plan B' collapsed – the non-negotiable positions of each of Iraq's leading communal groups failed to find a compromise position. Most notably, Grand Ayatollah Sistani again insisted on the need for the TNA to be democratically elected. This demand developed into a serious stand-off with Bremer, as the United States struggled to come to terms with the fact that the seemingly traditionalist Ayatollah had 'played the democracy card' against the United States, making the occupiers appear to be distinctly undemocratic both to Iraqis and to the international community. In the north, the Kurds stubbornly refused to budge on their autonomous demands, requiring that the Basic Law should define the position of the Kurds in Iraq, and enshrine their autonomous status at least at the level enjoyed in the 1990s, if not more (including control of Kirkuk). Meanwhile, the Sunnis remained distinctly unrepresented in the negotiations as it increasingly appeared that the Shi'a and Kurds were carving up Iraq according to their own interests. The result was, again, predictable. Even though Saddam was captured alive in December 2003, the insurgency against coalition forces and IGC associated groups continued unabated, with several considerable 'victories' being achieved, particularly against nascent Iraqi security organizations.

A new plan

Again faced with deadlock in the IGC, the United States had to react to Iraqi politics, rather than follow a preconceived plan. With the US election campaign starting in the spring of 2004 with the Democrat primaries, the timeframe to deliver success in Iraq was beginning to get perilously tight. With these considerations in mind, the United States turned to the United Nations (UN) to secure a compromise with its fractious Iraqi associates. The UN's Brahimi Report on elections in Iraq gave a certain amount of credence to the US position on the impracticality of holding early elections, but clearly supported the Shi'i determination to have elections at the earliest opportunity. Realizing that the selection of the TNA according to Plan C was never going to happen, the United States moved ahead with the necessity of drafting an interim constitution, and extending the duration of the IGC. Faced with an opportunity to wrestle sovereignty back from the United States, the IGC agreed on certain fundamental issues, but in reality simply froze political negotiations until a later time. The Kurds succeeded in keeping control of their autonomous region (without Kirkuk), and the Shi'a compromised in having Islam as 'a source of legislation', rather than 'the' source. The Sunnis, as usual, remained more noticeable by their absence. The future looks decidedly uncertain. The coalition is proclaiming the interim constitution to be evidence of a successful compromise garnered between the fractious political forces in Iraq. In reality, these political forces are simply waiting for the next round of constitutional discussions after the elections in January 2005 when there will be less of a US-inspired urgency to secure agreement.

Conclusion

For the United States, it now appears to be the case that the removal of Saddam, the recreation of institutions of government and the planning of elections are of themselves considered evidence of democracy emerging within Iraq. Such an interpretation of grand facts has led to the common US-held assumption that daily life for Iraqis must now be considerably improved when compared with life under the authoritarian Saddam. Therefore any US-installed government in Iraq need only measure itself next to the yardstick of Saddam's grievances in order to be presented to the US electorate as at least 'moving towards democracy' – hardly the most testing of scales to be measured against.

In August 2003, the US administration published a document listing the successes of 100 days of progress in Iraq. In it, the United States advertises a ten-point list by which to support its claim that Iraq is being democratized.[61]

1   A 25-member national Governing Council includes three women and Kurdish, Sunni, Christian, Turkmen, and Shi'i representatives. The establishment of this body is a first and important move toward Iraqi self-government.

2   The Governing Council is creating a Preparatory Commission to write a constitution. After a constitution is approved, elections will lead to a fully sovereign Iraqi government.

3   There are municipal councils in all major cities and 85 percent of towns, enabling Iraqis to take responsibility for management of local matters like healthcare, water, and electricity.

4   Provisional councils have been formed in Najaf, Al Anbar, and Basra.

5   The Baghdad City Advisory Council was inaugurated on July 7, 2003. Its 37 members were selected by members of the city's nine district councils, who themselves were selected by Baghdad citizens in 88 neighborhoods throughout the city.

6   Local governance councils are robust in Basra and Umm Qasr, helping to identify areas for immediate humanitarian and reconstruction assistance.

7   The Office of Human Rights and Transitional Justice is working to locate missing persons, investigate, analyze, and exhume mass graves, archive past human rights abuses and promote civic education/public awareness about human rights.

8   To facilitate voluntary resolutions of property claims, the Property Reconciliation Facility is being created.

9   The Coalition is helping fund and train Iraqis wanting to create their own non-governmental organizations. These new NGOs include public policy think tanks and an association of former political prisoners.

10   More than 150 newspapers are now published in Iraq offering Iraqis access to many different kinds of information. Foreign publications, radio, and television broadcasts are also available.

The ten points are highly indicative of the focus being taken in Iraq by the US administration. The majority of the points relate to a primarily institutional (superficial) aspect of democracy-building, with points addressing the deeper aspects of Iraq's political development (civil society and political culture) to be sorely limited. Furthermore, there is an obvious and potentially devastating exclusion: at no point are the structural weaknesses which exist within the construct of the Iraqi state acknowledged. These weaknesses have arguably endowed the state with an unfortunate deterministic proclivity for dictatorship to emerge as the most durable and, in terms of continuity, successful form of government.

Andreas Schedler notes that 'regime transitions ... do not lead inevitably to democratic government. They represent risky journeys from authoritarianism "toward an uncertain something else"'.[62] Even in the most favourable of circumstances, regime change is a decidedly hazardous undertaking and, as we have seen, Iraq seems devoid of the most basic requirements for democracy, whatever viewpoint is taken. Guillermo O'Donnell and Phillippe Schmitter ominously contend that, in transitions from authoritarian rule, 'the unexpected and the possible are as important as the usual and the probable'.[63] In the case of Iraq, the likelihood of the once-deemed probable transition to democracy successfully occurring appears to be slipping into the realms of implausibility. As the Shi'a continue to press for control of the state, the Kurds seek to redress the injustices of nearly a century ago, and the Sunnis struggle to come to terms with their disempowerment, a political solution needs to be found which is based upon consensus, an understanding not to resort to violent means, and compromise – hardly defining features of Iraq's political history. Far from being the 'beacon of democracy' in the Middle East, Iraq now has every potential to become a catalyst for further volatility across an already unstable region.

Notes and references

1 The National Security Strategy of the United States of America, September 2002.
2 J. Kirshner, 'Prevent Defense: Why the Bush Doctrine Will Hurt US Interests', in J. Kirshner, B. Strauss, M. Fanis and M. Evangelista, *Iraq and Beyond: The New US National Security Strategy*, Occasional Paper No. 27, Cornell University Peace Studies Program, January 2003, p. 2.
3 B. Anderson, 'The Champion of Human Rights in the White House', *Independent*, 17 February 2003, p. 15.
4 'President Discusses the Future of Iraq', George W. Bush addressing the American Enterprise Institute, Washington Hilton Hotel, Washington, DC, 26 February 2003. Online. Available HTTP: <http://www.whitehouse.gov/news/releases/2003/02/print/20030226–11.html> (accessed 2 July 2004)
5 L. Anderson and G. Stansfield, *The Future of Iraq: Dictatorship, Democracy or Division?*, New York: Palgrave, 2004, p. 186.
6 'President Bush Discusses Freedom in Iraq and Middle East', remarks by George W. Bush at the twentieth anniversary of the National Endowment for Democracy, US Chamber of Commerce, Washington, DC, 6 November 2003. Online. Available HTTP: <http://www.whitehouse.gov/news/releases/2003/11/print/20031106–2.html> (accessed 2 July 2004).
7 T. Dodge, 'Iraq and the Perils of Regime Change: From International Pariah to a Fulcrum of Regional Instability', in C.P. Hanelt, G. Luciani and F. Neugart (eds), *Regime Change in Iraq: The Transatlantic and Regional Dimensions*, European University Institute: Robert Schuman Centre for Advanced Studies, 2003, p. 66.
8 Analyses which do address this question include D. Byman, 'Constructing a Democratic Iraq', *International Security*, 28: 1, Summer 2003; A. Wimmer, 'Democracy and Ethno-Religious Conflict in Iraq', *Survival*, 45: 4, Winter 2003; L. Anderson and G. Stansfield, *The Future of Iraq: Dictatorship, Democracy or Division?*, New York: Palgrave, 2004, ch. 8.
9 L. Anderson and G. Stansfield, *The Future of Iraq: Dictatorship, Democracy of Division?* New York: Palgrave, 2004, p. 211.
10 A. Wimmer, 'Democracy and Ethno-Religious Conflict in Iraq', *Survival*, 45: 4, Winter 2003, pp. 111–34, reference at p. 111; D. Byman, 'Constructing a Democratic Iraq', *International Security*, 28: 1, Summer 2003, pp. 48–9.
11 A. Hashim, 'The Sunni Insurgency in Iraq', *Middle East Institute Perspective*, 15 August 2003. Online. Available HTTP: <http://www.mideasti.org/articles/doc89.html> (accessed January 2004).
12 Ibid.

13 A. Wimmer, 'Democracy and Ethno-Religious Conflict in Iraq', *Survival*, 45: 4, Winter 2003, pp. 111–34, reference at pp. 111–12; A. Dawisha, 'Iraq: Setbacks, Advances, Prospects', *Journal of Democracy*, 15: 1, January 2004.

14 L. Anderson and G. Stansfield, *The Future of Iraq: Dictatorship, Democracy or Division?*, New York: Palgrave, 2004, pp. 226–32.

15 Ibid.

16 J.J. Linz and A. Stepan, *Problems of Democratic Transition and Consolidation: Southern Europe, South America, and Post-Communist Europe*, Baltimore, MD: Johns Hopkins University Press, 1996; A. Schedler, 'Taking Uncertainty Seriously: The Blurred Boundaries of Democratic Transition and Consolidation', *Democratization*, 8: 4, Winter 2001, pp. 1–22; F. Fukuyama, 'The Primacy of Culture', *Journal of Democracy*, 6: 1, 1995.

17 Sami Zubaida discusses this idea but in different terms: 'The modern Iraqi state at its inception was a "weak" formation, structurally and institutionally "external" to the society over which it was imposed.' S. Zubaida, 'Community, Class and Minorities', in A. Fernea and R. Louis (eds), *The Iraqi Revolution of 1958: The Old Social Classes Revisited*, London: I B Taurus, 1991, p. 207.

18 For a fascinating account of socio-political structure under Ottoman rule, see A. Wimmer, *Nationalist Exclusion and Ethnic Conflict: Shadows of Modernity*, Cambridge: Cambridge University Press, 2002, pp. 157–66.

19 Batatu describes Iraq as being divided into three 'religious zones' of Shi'a, Sunni and Sufi (Kurdish), rather than Shi'a, Sunni and Kurdish. H. Batatu, *The Old Social Classes and the Revolutionary Movements of Iraq*, Princeton, NJ: Princeton University Press, 1978, p. 40. Also see J. Yaphe, 'War and Occupation in Iraq: What Went Right? What Could Go Wrong?', *Middle East Journal*, 57: 3, summer 2003, p. 383.

20 Confidential memorandum of King Faisal I, March 1933, quoted in H. Batatu, *The Old Social Classes and the Revolutionary Movements of Iraq*, Princeton, NJ: Princeton University Press, 1978, pp. 25–6.

21 A. Wimmer, 'Democracy and Ethno-Religious Conflict in Iraq', *Survival*, 45: 4, Winter 2003, pp. 111–34, reference at p. 113.

22 Ibid., reference at p. 114.

23 See T. Dodge, *Inventing Iraq: The Failure of Nation Building and a History Denied*, New York and London: Columbia University Press and Hurst, 2003; L. Anderson and G. Stansfield, *The Future of Iraq: Dictatorship, Democracy or Division?*, New York: Palgrave, 2004, particularly chs 1 and 8.

24 H. Batatu, *The Old Social Classes and the Revolutionary Movements of Iraq*, Princeton, NJ: Princeton University Press, 1978, p. 26.

25 See E. Ghareeb, *The Kurdish Question in Iraq*, New York: Syracuse University Press, 1981, p. ix; S. Zubaida, 'Community, Class and Minorities', in A. Fernea and R. Louis (eds), *The Iraqi Revolution of 1958: The Old Social Classes Revisited*, London: I B Taurus, 1991, pp. 198–9.

26 A. Wimmer, 'Democracy and Ethno-Religious Conflict in Iraq', *Survival*, 45: 4, Winter 2003, pp. 111–34, reference at p. 114.

27 T. Dodge, 'Iraq and the Perils of Regime Change: From International Pariah to a Fulcrum of Regional Instability', 2003, p. 68.

28 Ibid., pp. 68–9, quoting I. al-Khafaji, 'The Myth of Iraqi Exceptionalism', *Middle East Policy*, No. 4, October 2000, p. 68.

29 K. Makiya, *Republic of Fear: The Politics of Modern Iraq*, Updated edition, Berkeley, CA: University of California Press, 1998, pp. 37–8.

30 Extensive original documents illustrating the mechanisms and actions of the Iraqi security services can be found online at the Iraq Research and Documentation Project (IRDP) at: <http://www.fas.harvard.edu/~irdp/ > (accessed 2 July 2004).

31 I. Marashi, 'Iraq's Security and Intelligence Network: A Guide and Analysis', *MERIA Journal*, 6: 3, September 2003, p. 1. Online. Available HTTP: <http://meria.idc.ac.il/journal/2002/issue3/jv6n3a1.html> (accessed 2 July 2004).

Also see K. Makiya, *The Republic of Fear: The Politics of Modern Iraq*, Updated edition, Berkeley, CA: University of California Press, 1998, pp. 37–8; and S. Boyne 'Inside Iraq's Security Network, Part One', *Jane's Intelligence Review*, 9: 7, July 1997 and No. 8, August 1998.

32 I. al-Khafaji, 'A Few Days After: State and Society in a Post-Saddam Iraq', in T. Dodge and S. Simon (eds), *Iraq at the Crossroads: State and Society in the Shadow of Regime Change*, Adelphi Paper 354, International Institute for Strategic Studies (IISS). London: IISS/Oxford University Press, 2003, pp. 77–92.

33 L. Anderson and G. Stansfield, *The Future of Iraq: Dictatorship, Democracy or Division?*, New York: Palgrave, 2004, p. 190.

34 J. Yaphe, 'War and Occupation in Iraq: What Went Right? What Could Go Wrong?', *Middle East Journal*, 57: 3, Summer 2003, p. 381.

35 Ibid.

36 T. Dodge, 'US Intervention and Possible Iraqi Futures', *Survival*, 45: 3, Autumn 2003, pp. 110–12.

37 See G. Stansfield, 'Politics and Governance in the New Iraq: Reconstruction of the New versus Resurrection of the Old', in J. Eyal (ed.), *War in Iraq: Combat and Consequence*, Whitehall Paper No. 59. London: Royal United Services Institute, 2003, pp. 67–83, reference at p. 67.

38 J. Yaphe, 'War and Occupation in Iraq: What Went Right? What Could Go Wrong?', *Middle East Journal*, 57: 3, Summer 2003, pp. 382–3.

39 For a trenchant comparison of the British and US experiences in Iraq, see T. Dodge, *Inventing Iraq: The Failure of Nation Building and a History Denied*, New York: Columbia University Press, 2003. For an analysis of Saddam using certain tribes in his strategy to control the state in the 1990s, see A. Baram, 'Neo-Tribalism in Iraq: Saddam Hussein's Tribal Policies 1991–1999', *International Journal of Middle Eastern Studies*, 29, 2003.

40 For literature on consociational democracy, see A. Lijphart, 'Consociational Democracy', *World Politics*, 21: January, 1969; *Democracy in Plural Societies*, New Haven, CT: Yale University Press, 1977; S. Halpern, 'The Disorderly Universe of Consociational Democracy', *West European Politics*, 9, 1986.

41 S. Zubaida, 'Community, Class and Minorities', in A. Fernea and R. Louis (eds.), *The Iraqi Revolution of 1958: The Old Social Classes Revisited*, London: I B Taurus, 1991, p. 198.

42 See R. Falk, 'The Cruelty of Geopolitics: The Fate of Nation and State in the Middle East', *Millennium*, 20: 3, 1991, pp. 383–93.

43 G. Stansfield, *Iraqi Kurdistan: Political Development and Emergent Democracy*, London: RoutledgeCurzon, 2003.

44 'President Bush Discusses Freedom in Iraq and Middle East', remarks by George W. Bush at the twentieth anniversary of the National Endowment for Democracy, US Chamber of Commerce, Washington, DC, 6 November 2003. President Bush's speech was, in effect, a sequel to the position adopted by the administration of President Reagan in the mid-1980s when US officials referred regularly to 'the world-wide democratic revolution'. T. Carothers, 'The End of the Transition Paradigm', *Journal of Democracy*, 13: 1, 2002, pp. 5–6. Online. Available HTTP: <http://www.whitehouse.gov/news/releases/2003/11/print/20031106–2.html> (accessed 2 July 2004).

45 S.P. Huntington, *The Third Wave: Democratization in the Late Twentieth Century*, Norman, OK: University of Oklahoma Press, 1991.

46 L. Anderson and G. Stansfield, *The Future of Iraq: Dictatorship, Democracy or Division?*, New York: Palgrave, 2004, p. 190, quoting T. Carothers, 'The End of the Transition Paradigm', *Journal of Democracy*, 13: 1, 2002, p. 9. A. Etzioni, 'A Self-Restrained Approach to Nation-Building by Foreign Powers', *International Affairs*, 80: 1, 2004, p. 6,

quoting M. Pei and S. Kasper, 'The "Morning After" Regime Change: Should US Force Democracy Again?', *Christian Science Monitor*, 15 January 2003, p. 9.

47 While the plans for 'democratization' are unclear, with the CPA supporting the notion of selection caucuses rather than direct elections, the plans for economic liberalization are readily apparent. See R. Looney, 'The Neoliberal Model's Planned Role in Iraq's Economic Transition', *Middle East Journal*, 57: 4, Autumn 2003; D. Brumberg, *Liberalization Versus Democracy: Understanding Arab Political Reform*, Middle East Series Working Papers No. 37, Carnegie Endowment for International Peace, May 2003; J.J. Linz and A. Stepan, *Problems of Democratic Transition and Consolidation: Southern Europe, South American, and Post-Communist Europe*, Baltimore, MD: Johns Hopkins University Press, 1996, pp. 3–4.

48 A. Etzioni, 'A Self-Restrained Approach to Nation-Building by Foreign Powers', *International Affairs*, 80: 1, January 2004, p. 5.

49 See A. Dawisha, 'Iraq: Setbacks, Advances, Prospects', *Journal of Democracy*, 15: 1, January 2004, pp. 11–13.

50 P. Basham, 'Democracy in Iraq, Acts I and II', Cato Institute Daily Report, 8 December 2003. Online. Available HTTP: <http://www.cato.org/cgi-bin/scripts/printtech.cgi/dailys/12–08–03.html> (accessed 2 July 2004).

51 T. Carothers, 'The End of the Transition Paradigm', *Journal of Democracy*, 13: 1, 2002, pp. 6–9.

52 L. Diamond, *Developing Democracy: Toward Consolidation*, Baltimore, MD, and London: Johns Hopkins University Press, 1999, p. 66.

53 See The White House, 'Results in Iraq: 100 Days Toward Security and Freedom', in *100 Days of Progress in Iraq*, August 2003. Online. Available HTTP: <http://www.whitehouse.gov/infocus/iraq/introduction.html> (accessed 2 July 2004).

54 J.J. Linz and A. Stepan, *Problems of Democratic Transition and Consolidation: Southern Europe, South America, and Post-Communist Europe*, Baltimore, MD: Johns Hopkins University Press, 1996, p. 5.

55 Ibid., p. 6.

56 F. Fukuyama, 'The Primacy of Culture', *Journal of Democracy*, 6: 1, 1995, p. 7, quoted in L. Anderson and G. Stansfield, *The Future of Iraq: Dictatorship, Democracy or Division?*, New York: Palgrave, 2004, pp. 190–1.

57 While not an admission of such a strategy, the INC leader Dr Ahmed Chalabi made his position clear in a recent interview with the *Daily Telegraph*, in which he remained unrepentant about the possible errors in intelligence forwarded by the INC to the US administration. See *Daily Telegraph*, 'Chalabi stands by faulty intelligence that toppled Saddam's regime', by J. Fairweather and A. La Guardia, 19 February 2004. For an example of such material, see K. Hamza, *Saddam's Bombmaker*, New York: Simon & Schuster, 2002.

58 G. Stansfield, *Iraqi Kurdistan: Political Development and Emergent Democracy*, London: RoutledgeCurzon, 2003, p. 4.

59 For example, Deputy Secretary of State for Defense Paul Wolfowitz, speaking in March 2003, seemed to be oblivious to the importance of the Shi'i holy cities of Najaf and Kerbala when he referred to Islamic holy places only existing in Saudi Arabia. See J. Cole, 'Shi'ite Religious Parties Fill Vacuum in Southern Iraq', *Middle East Report Online*, 22 April 2003.

60 L. Anderson and G. Stansfield, *The Future of Iraq: Dictatorship, Democracy or Division?*, New York: Palgrave, 2004, p. 185.

61 The White House, 'Results in Iraq: 100 Days Toward Security and Freedom', in *100 Days of Progress in Iraq*, August 2003. Online. Available HTTP: <http://www.whitehouse.gov/infocus/iraq/introduction.html> (accessed 2 July 2004).

62 A. Schedler, 'Taking Uncertainty Seriously: The Blurred Boundaries of Democratic Transition and Consolidation', *Democratization*, 8: 4, Winter 2001, pp. 1–22, quote at p. 3, quoting G. O'Donnell and P. Schmitter, *Transitions from Authoritarian Rule: Tentative*

Conclusions about Uncertain Democracies, Baltimore, MD, and London: Johns Hopkins University Press, 1986, pp. 3–5.

63 G. O'Donnell and P. Schmitter, *Transitions from Authoritarian Rule: Tentative Conclusions about Uncertain Democracies*, Baltimore, MD, and London: Johns Hopkins University Press, 1986, pp. 3–5.

10 The democratic transition in Iraq and the discovery of its limitations*

Glen Rangwala

The intense and often violent embroilment of the US-led coalition in the politics of sect and class, of regional ambition and religious authority, within Iraq has served as a powerful and often tragic reminder that radical political change is a disorderly and tortuous process, in which the possibility of failure is ever present. The good intentions underlying the process on the part of political leaders, officials and the wider circle of participants count for much less than one would have hoped, particularly when the overall goals of a very large majority of the relevant political agents are *not* in conflict with one another.

Although real issues of political difference remain, in particular over questions of the extent to which Iraq's regions (and, if so, which regions?) should have autonomous statuses (and, if so, to what degree?), the broad contours of Iraq's future are agreed upon by the members of the coalition, all of Iraq's major political groupings, and the vast majority of the population. Democratization, respect for individual rights and economic development remain key issues for all these parties. And yet, the first year of Iraq's occupation was marked by a high level of uncertainty about the form that the transition would take. Moreover, the prospects for the entrenchment of a stable democratic form of government were by the end of the year very much open to question.

This chapter examines the extent and possibilities of the democratization process from two angles: the electoral process and the creation of a multi-party political system. Both are essential for the establishment of a system of political participation, and there have been positive developments in both spheres. However, the limitations of both aspects of the political transition have been considerable.

The primary reason for these limitations is that Iraq has a weak set of state institutions, and so winning power at the centre has not been the focal point of political contestation since April 2003. In the day-to-day business of the Coalition Provisional Authority (CPA), this is advantageous: political challengers exist only in fragments and are usually in positions of dependence; discrete local agents are easier to deal with than a broad-based national movement, even if it were largely sympathetic. However, the problem of transferring power to a suitable social formation, stable enough to withstand the multiplicity of regional and internal political pressures, remains very real.

The electoral transition

Much of the discussion about Iraq's political transition has focused on the possibility and value of national elections to determine the direction of the country's future. This attention is appropriate; talk of Iraq's democratization without reference to the opportunity for popular and meaningful participation is of limited value. The first year of occupation did not, of course, include national electoral competition. The Bush administration, which had previously voiced its strong concerns at the lack of democratic development in the Arab world, now found itself on the receiving end of large-scale protests in Iraq against its perceived stalling of national elections.

It is possible to trace three interrelated orientations of the Bush administration towards Iraq's future at the commencement of the occupation that could be seen as key tenets in the thinking about the coalition's role in the country. These are the salience of democratization, the exclusion of the old political elite, and economic reforms. Together, these approaches are essentially individuating, in effect if not in design. They would detach the individuals from the interlocking webs of subjugation that existed previously, to ruling party and personal whim, and also from tribe, clan and guild. These detachments are necessary preconditions for the formation of the modern state, and are hastened by its imposition. The market and the political party engaged in competitive elections displace those organizations that are structured around the community or the individual, which can no longer function as centres of authority or exclusive mechanisms for seeking advancement. Equally, the market and the modern party can only function effectively if those partial societies are relegated in standing, and replaced with a single political and economic framework of laws in which all can participate on an equal footing. To achieve this radical break in a political trajectory, in which partial societies are brought under a single administrative apparatus, the ruling authority needs to be in a position of unchallenged dominance, able to act without restriction in the restructuring of the fundamental institutions of society. The coalition would be taking the role of Rousseau's great legislator, who 'dares to undertake the making of a people's institutions' that would take the individual out of the network of personal dependencies – historical aggregations – and into a new relationship of equal dependence upon the laws and mechanisms of the civil state.[1]

The first approach of the coalition leaders was found in the clear motifs of freedom and democracy that have had a central role in their public discourse, throughout the pre-invasion and occupation phases. At the time of the takeover, the democratic transition in Iraq was portrayed as following in straightforward steps. Deputy Secretary of Defense Paul Wolfowitz provided the Senate Armed Services Committee with an account of the transition on the day Baghdad was captured: the Office of Reconstruction and Humanitarian Assistance (ORHA), under retired General Jay Garner, would take care of the population's basic needs through the provision of services. As soon as these services had been restored, their administration would be turned over to an 'Iraqi Interim Authority' (IIA), made up of appointed Iraqis. ORHA would have an advisory role only at this stage. The IIA would draft a new constitution and arrange elections for a new government, which would assume sovereign functions.[2] The democratic transition and the handover of power were thus conceived of as occurring simultaneously, and quickly. Defense Secretary Donald Rumsfeld, backed by Wolfowitz and Secretary of State Colin Powell, put a timeframe for organizing elections for the government 'over some period of months'.[3]

The political process did not remain at the level of projections for future arrangements, but actual preparations began for local elections. Direct elections were held in some districts of Baghdad, such as al-Adhamiyya, on 3 May 2003,[4] and there was the use of 300 local 'delegates' to select the council in Kirkuk on 24 May 2003.[5] Although neither set of elections was untroubled, both resulted in councils able to claim some measure of democratic legitimation. Practical arrangements were made to hold direct council elections in some of the main predominantly Arab cities of Iraq, such as Najaf and Samarra, in June, with US officials involved in initiatives to register voters, prepare ballot boxes and encourage participation. With many Iraqis believing in the prospects for rapid democratization, a large number of political parties were established from April 2003 within the country, advertising their names and slogans prominently throughout Iraq's major cities.

The speed of the projected transition to democracy was considered possible as it was conceived as not requiring the coalition to closely manage or grapple with the political and social forces present within Iraqi society. Instead, the approach towards Iraq was initially presented as being based upon a narrow conception of the problem in Iraqi governance that saw it as lying exclusively in a defective ruling elite: the character of the personnel, and not international or systemic factors, was the locus of difficulty. Iraqi society could only be remade from above, via a state whose leaders held values different from, and antithetical to, those of the *ancien régime*. The individuals under consideration for a role in the IIA were mostly returning exiles and leaders from the northern governorates, who had been ruling the autonomous enclave since 1991. The creation of a 'group of five' exile and Kurdish groups as a contact group for the US military authorities shortly after the Nasiriyya conference of 15 April could be seen as the first step towards creating such a body. There is every indication that the US authorities believed at this stage that a rapid handover of power to an administration led by formerly exiled parties close to the US administration would be possible, and that the subsequent elections would return these groups, as the only organized political forces in the country, to power.

This reliance upon the substitution of members of ruling elites for a transformation of the state's politics also fitted into the established approaches of successive US administrations to democratization. From the 1990s, US-sponsored processes of democratization were not seen as requiring the prior transformation of the non-political institutions of a society. 'All that seemed to be necessary for democratisation was a decision by a country's political elites to move toward democracy and an ability on the part of those elites to fend off the contrary actions of remaining antidemocratic forces.'[6] If the people with the right values of democracy were installed in power, this conception goes, the main political problem of Iraq was solved.

The historical aggregation that served as the greatest obstacle to the formation of the civil state was of course the Ba'ath Party, with its hierarchy of party positions acting as a shadow infrastructure within all of Iraq's official institutions. The idea of 'de-Ba'athification' had been strongly promoted by Iraqi diaspora political groupings close to US decision-makers, most notably by the Iraqi National Congress (INC) of Ahmed Chalabi, which had long argued for an equivalent to the de-Nazification programme carried out by allied forces in post-1945 Germany.[7] According to this conception, not only had the formal party to be removed from power, but its networks had to be dismantled through the removal from positions of authority of personnel linked with it. The argument for de-Ba'athification along the lines of de-Nazification was incorporated into the December 2002 report of the Democratic Principles Working Group of the State Department's Future of Iraq project, partly coordinated by INC member Kanan Makiya, over the objections of a minority of the members of this working group.[8] It was taken up by Donald Rumsfeld on 25 April 2003, and put into effect on 16 May.[9] From its position of unchallenged supremacy, in the wake of the resounding defeat of the Ba'ath regime, the elimination of what had been a central feature of Iraq's political and social sphere for thirty-five years seemed possible.

The approach adopted by the coalition for the restructuring of Iraq's economy and thus its society was also predicated upon an ability to use the dominant position of the occupying power to effect a sharp break in national policy. With a legacy of state-owned enterprises, highly subsidized basic goods as part of the ration, an inflexible wage structure and two unstable currencies operating in different parts of the country, the opportunity for neo-liberal reforms was clearly high. Thus in February 2003, the Treasury Department and the US Agency for International Development produced a 100-page policy blueprint entitled 'Moving the Iraqi economy from recovery to sustainable growth'. Although this document remains confidential, detailed reports on its contents describe its plans for a four-year staged privatization programme, for renovating the banking and tax sector and rapid steps to launch a new currency.[10] In line with these proposals, a large number of sectors of Iraq's economy were opened for foreign investment on 19 September 2003, providing foreign investors with equal rights to Iraqi investors.[11]

As these prior commitments to particular adjustments in the political, economic and administrative structures of Iraq show, the coalition's starting approach was modelled on a specific conception of the good society. However, to label this project as ideologically driven is to mistake the conditions of its formation. A set of priorities had been conceived in the abstract, untainted by the need to engage and compromise with countervailing political forces. This process of conceptualizing the coalition's role in Iraq existed prior to engagement with US political pressures, such as those from corporations seeking to benefit from the invasion and an electorate responsive to news of casualties, and prior to entanglement in the ongoing state of disorder within Iraq's society.

Naturally, the coalition was not in a position of political autonomy from these two sets of pressures. Over the course of the first year of occupation, the costs for the United States of the occupation have been considerable, both in financial and human terms. Furthermore, the run-up to the US presidential elections of November 2004 had taken on considerable weight in the policy-making process. The core international project of the Bush administration was the invasion of Iraq; the prospects of its perceived failure, either through an occupation that appeared interminable and casualty-laden to the US electorate, or through the capturing of power in Iraq of forces hostile to the United States, were grave. Few would argue that the fixing of the date for the formal handover of power on 30 June 2004, and its decoupling from the timetable for Iraqi elections, was entirely unrelated to the US electoral calendar. By the end of 2003, keeping to the handover date was reported to be the one fixed value in the coalition policy-making process.[12]

Nevertheless, developments in the Iraqi political sphere resulted in approaches that stood in tension with the need for a speedy handover. In general, the coalition was in a position of considerable political vulnerability within Iraq, given its status as a foreign occupying power. If a national political challenger to it were to have emerged and won popular legitimacy, the coalition's ability to maintain control would have been highly limited. Thus a considerable part of the coalition's work within Iraq was to prevent the emergence of such a challenger, whilst retaining an approach that was seen to favour political progress, and so undercut any arguments from Iraqis for achieving national self-determination through adopting an antagonistic or uncooperative stance.

These concerns were visible in the process that led to the collapse by May 2003 of plans for the rapid transition from ORHA to an elected Iraqi authority, via the IIA. Firstly, the unanticipated collapse of Iraq's public infrastructure and its urban security led to low levels of legitimacy for the coalition administration. Secondly, after an unproductive set of meetings between coalition officials and representatives of Iraqi parties in April 2003, it became clear that there was little prospect of the previously exiled opposition groups cohering into a single force that took its lead from the coalition. Thus there was no single institution that could act as both a legitimator of and a successor to the coalition, waiting its turn for the coalition to hand over power. Thirdly, the development of indigenous Iraqi political forces that took a more suspicious attitude towards the coalition became apparent. Most notably, Muqtada al-Sadr's movement, arising out of the slums east of Baghdad to take effective control over 2 million perceived malcontents, was a force of unpredictable vigour and prospects: US planners had not even been aware of its existence prior to the invasion. The risk that new and unincorporated political movements could make a bid for power at the centre was sharply felt.

Over the next few months, with the escalation of anti-coalition violence, all three of these factors strengthened in significance. The coalition was unable or unwilling to take over the mechanisms that would usually be associated with the public administration of the modern state, had insufficient personnel and expertise at its disposal, and was largely restricted to engaging with Iraqi society through intermediaries.[13] As a result, the means available to the coalition to generate the authority of the new governing arrangements were very limited. The result has been that the coalition was caught in a classic realist irony: an approach founded upon intentions to remodel a society for the better had become ensnared in strategies to preserve the political authority of the ruling stratum.

The weakness of the institutions of the central state became apparent over the first months of occupation. The collapse of the police force and the fragility of the existing moral order were also instrumental in precipitating a breakdown in personal security. This prevented the re-establishment of the institutions of the state. The deterioration in public order was compounded by the disestablishment of the Iraqi Army on 23 May 2003, putting approximately 400,000 of Iraq's young men out of work,[14] and was exacerbated by delays in engaging the labour force in the processes of state-building. Further, 60 per cent of the adult population was out of work in the aftermath of the invasion. The delays in establishing a national employment programme meant that only 9,100 new jobs were created in the public works sector during the first seven months of occupation, in contrast to the projected figure of 100,000 new workers per quarter.[15] The number employed on new public works jobs had increased to nearly 77,000 by March 2004. Even taking into account the Iraqis newly employed in the security sector, the number of new jobs created in the first eleven months of occupation was at 44.5 per cent of the coalition's initial projections for this time period, according to US Department of Defense statistics.[16]

The significantly reduced level of the workforce, the continuing violence and the parcelling out of contracts to institutions which had no previous engagement with Iraqi society have entailed that basic services have been slowly repaired and subject to limited development. The result has been high levels of political frustration and distrust of the coalition.

The water sector provides an example. The Iraqi institution previously responsible for developing the national infrastructure, the General Company for Water Projects, was disallowed from bidding for water contracts with the CPA owing to pre-invasion US regulations prohibiting the use of Iraqi state-owned enterprises as contractors. Instead, Bechtel National Inc. was awarded the contract for managing the reconstruction of Iraq's water supply system, resulting in excess costs for foreign workers and imports of locally available materials. According to the *Washington Post*, Bechtel 'spent four months studying the General Co. plans, concluded they were adequate, modified them slightly, city officials said, reissued orders for parts from the same supplier, and basically did what was being done before'.[17]

In consequence, water treatment facilities scheduled by the Iraqi company for completion in mid-2003 were not expected to be opened until June 2004. In January 2004, the CPA estimated that the water network was still only working at 65 per cent of its pre-invasion level.[18] Since 40 per cent of all hospitalized children are suffering from gastrointestinal illnesses caused by contaminated water, the issue is clearly one of considerable significance in developing a sense of the effectiveness of governance.

A similar pattern exists in the continuing difficulties of the electricity sector. The destruction and theft of parts of the electricity infrastructure by guerrilla organizations and private individuals has had a significant impact. However, the replacement of the German and Swiss–Swedish companies as suppliers to Iraq's electricity grid with US corporations may have had a role too.[19] The impact has also been highly uneven throughout the country: whilst Basra had round-the-clock electricity in March 2004, the central Iraqi provinces were at considerably lower levels: Salah al-Din at 11 hours per day, Babil at 12 hours, Baghdad at 14 hours. Daily electricity production in central Iraq was at around half the level (1191 MW) it was at prior to the invasion (2300 MW).[20]

The changed perceptions of the US administration in response to the legitimacy crisis in Iraq were caught most clearly in Donald Rumsfeld's famous leaked memorandum on how the coalition faced a 'long, hard slog' in Iraq (and in Afghanistan).[21] Its most clear practical effect was the replacement of ORHA, a body that did not purport to govern Iraq, with the CPA, which solidified through mid-2003 into the structure of a government. Its 'CPA ministries' were organizationally and geographically separate from the 'Iraqi ministries', which played a shadowing role to them, and were subordinate to a quasi-presidential figure, Paul Bremer. The creation of the CPA may not necessarily have represented a sharp break in the approach of the US administration; a number of the policies from the original conception of Iraq's pathway were implemented under its leadership, such as the de-Ba'athification order and the issuing of the foreign investment law. Indeed, CPA officials later protested that both these policies had come from Washington rather than through their own recommendations. Nevertheless, the establishment of a coalition governing presence demonstrates the significance of the search for institutional credibility. An autonomous political dynamic was at work in which the authority of the coalition was open to challenge, with potentially grave repercussions for the international standing of the United States. This repeatedly led to measures that tended to entrench coalition rule in Iraq, sidelining domestic political actors or (more commonly) ensuring their dependence upon the coalition.

In the sphere of the political process, the desire for a handover of power to an Iraqi administration and the need to retain institutional credibility for the CPA institutions had divergent impacts. On the one hand, the existence of an Iraqi agent with popular national legitimacy would facilitate a successful handover of power. Extending the role of Iraqi personnel in administration – 'Iraqification' – and placing them in decision-making positions also lessened the resource and personnel drain upon the United States. Yet given the high levels of expectation created within Iraq by previous coalition discourse on the benefits of democratization, particularly among those excluded previously from the process of governance, there was little prospect of a purely appointed body being accepted as legitimate by a substantial part of Iraq's population.

On the other hand, from the perspective of the coalition, the creation of a rival centre of political power during the interim period would have necessitated some degree of oversight and compromise. An autonomous and legitimate Iraqi political centre would entail continual negotiation over, and challenge to, the coalition presence in and plans for Iraq during the transition and afterwards. This would be highly noticeable in the military sphere, of most immediate consequence to the coalition armed forces: the oversight of coalition military actions by an authoritative Iraqi national institution would almost inevitably lead to their curtailment; significant changes to the counter-insurgency methods of coalition forces would result. The coalition's capacity to hold the monopoly of political authority gives the military the ability to preserve its security as it sees fit, a feature that remains a key requirement of the US armed forces for both political and strategic reasons.

Furthermore, the US administration planned to retain a significant role in Iraq after the formal handover of power, through continuing its leadership of the multinational force based in Iraq, maintaining its control over a significant proportion of Iraq's development funds, and the establishment prior to June 2004 of independent regulatory institutions that would maintain close links with the US authorities. Approximately 4,000 US personnel were kept at its embassy in Baghdad for these purposes.[22] The United States thus needed to manage and balance competing Iraqi political processes in order to maintain its unofficial retention of the levers of state power, particularly given the hostility of a considerable proportion of Iraq's population to a continued role for the coalition military inside Iraq.

The tension between these two factors – the need to build up Iraqi institutions so that there was something to hand power over to, and the need to prevent the emergence of a rival centre to coalition power – can be traced in the political initiatives taken during the first year of occupation. At the time of the creation of the CPA, there was already a sense that the political process was beginning to slip away from the auspices of the coalition, and into routes that were unpredictable. Popular grassroots processes, the very form acknowledged by the coalition as necessary for the spread of a sense and habit of political participation, were thus also a source of anxiety. The first set of major institutions to be affected by the new level of vigilance brought by the CPA was the labour unions. After the ouster of the regime, staff in some state-run workplaces had organized elections for new managers, which in turn resulted in protests from the new military authorities who saw them as a destabilizing force. On 6 July 2003, the CPA issued a public notice, stating that it 'will not recognize the election of Directors, or otherwise allow interference with managerial prerogatives of the Directing Staff of government instrumentalities and enterprises'.[23] Soon after, the local elections scheduled to take place across Iraq were cancelled.[24] Furthermore, few attempts were made to prepare for elections: a preliminary round of discussions on a future Iraqi constitution was allowed to lapse; there were no processes to register voters, train election observers or establish an electoral commission; and no moves were taken to establish regulations on party financing or campaigning. The process of democratization ground to a halt.

At the national level, the prospect of an Iraqi interim government was replaced with a proposal for an 'advisory council', subsequently strengthened after intense criticism from the Iraqi parties to a twenty-five-person 'Iraqi Governing Council' (IGC).[25] Although the IGC was accorded the authority to appoint ministers and issue decrees, its ability to function as a significant political actor was limited. Its major figures, serving within the nine-man rotating presidency, came from antagonistic political factions, and they have not acted in a unified way subsequently. This was demonstrated in how the ministers were selected, with each major participant in the IGC accorded the right to choose one minister, rather than by undertaking a process of selection by collective agreement. Members of the IGC were heavily dependent upon the coalition for their status: their access to the CPA provided many of them with their major political resource, which they could then use for gaining a political constituency. As a result, few within the IGC were willing to risk their good relations with the CPA in order to take a position critical of it. Furthermore, their legitimacy in their national policy-making roles came from their appointment by the CPA, and thus they did not carry the authority to challenge the CPA's decisions in the name of the Iraqi people.

The agreement of 15 November 2003 between the CPA and the IGC decoupled the electoral and the transition timetables, thus preserving the institutional benefits for the CPA of not creating challengers to its authority whilst facilitating a formal handover in time for the US elections. According to this plan, a set of caucuses would select the members of the transitional national assembly that would elect the executive to take over on the handover of power. As these caucuses would be made up of individuals chosen in each governorate by a joint 'organizing committee' of the CPA, the IGC and the local councils, both the process and the individuals selected would remain closely under the management of the CPA. National elections were pushed back to the end of 2005, almost three years after the ouster of the Ba'ath regime.

Nevertheless, as became clear with the large-scale demonstrations over the subsequent month, the November agreement would not result in a government with popular legitimacy. The result of further negotiations was a Transitional Administrative Law (TAL), from 8 March 2004. Owing to its negotiating history, this can be seen as a compromise between the CPA, which favoured a longer delay before national elections, and popular Iraqi sentiment, most closely identified with Ayatollah Ali al-Sistani, which favoured the rapid assumption of power by an elected Iraqi administration. The TAL held out the prospect for national elections more clearly than any previous formal plan. Elections for the transitional legislative authority were required to take place by January 2005, six months after the creation of the appointed Iraqi interim government, although their form was unspecified in the TAL. If the draft constitution were to be approved in a referendum, permanent elections would follow in December 2005.

The tension between the coalition's attempts to preserve a monopoly of authority and the need for institution-building was also found in the development of local political arrangements. With the delays on national political processes in the first year of occupation, the CPA and the governments of coalition states put much emphasis on forming more representative councils at the local level. This took the form of installing leaders perceived to be popular locally, and then, from late 2003 onwards, of diversifying the members of the local councils, as well as expanding the provincial council for each of Iraq's eighteen governorates to forty members, in a process known as 'refreshment'.

Both of these stages of dealing with local councils contained modest successes, although they were far from unproblematic. The mayors installed initially were often removed shortly afterwards. Karbala, for example, went through repeated changes of governors: Ali Kammunah was appointed in early May 2003, only to resign two months later due to allegations of links between a member of his council and a banned party. His replacement, Akram al-Yasiri, was dismissed by the CPA early in 2004, after publicly criticizing the behaviour of US troops. The council underwent a process of refreshment, but a third of those members then resigned when Ayatollah Sistani's representative called the council illegitimate as it was not elected.

Although elections were held in a number of regions, there was little in the way of common procedures. One former senior CPA official referred to this as 'eighteen different arrangements for local government in each of the eighteen governorates'.[26] This lack of common standards inevitably led to a perception that when local elections were held (for example, in Dhi Qar province),[27] it was because the CPA was confident of the success of pro-coalition figures, in contrast to locations in which elections were not held or were cancelled abruptly (as in Basra in mid-February 2004). More commonly, an element of arbitrariness reigned. In Baghdad, for example, the arrangements for local councils and their meeting procedures were copied directly from Colorado, simply because the CPA's senior governance official with responsibility for Baghdad happened to be a former mayor of a Colorado town.[28] The CPA retained the authority to alter the composition of the Baghdad councils at its discretion,[29] and used the refreshment process to remove council members whom the CPA had itself appointed but who were since deemed unsuitable.[30] The CPA also apportioned to itself the role of excluding at its discretion anyone from a position on a local council if it judged that they had, *inter alia*, 'publicly espoused political philosophies or legal doctrines contrary to the domestic order and rule of law being established in Iraq'.[31]

The dependence and marginality of Iraqi political institutions since April 2003 resulted in their low levels of legitimacy within Iraqi society, and limited their abilities to act as autonomous political agents after the formal handover of power. It is not that there was a deliberate attempt to marginalize Iraqi movements in the first year of occupation, but that the existence of a sphere in which Iraqi political agents could come to the fore by seeking and obtaining a status of popular legitimacy was found to be a multiple source of inconvenience for the coalition authorities. Thus what appears to be a systematic attempt to stall the democratic process in Iraq was actually the result of an outside military force grappling with the exigencies of occupation, in which its autonomy in seeking security was threatened by an indigenous political dynamic. The primary countervailing factor that has brought forward the electoral timetable remains closely tied to Shi'i community leaders who believe elections would alter the balance of power within Iraq in their favour. This may well turn out to be a problematic assumption, leaving the democratization process stranded, without political agents with sufficient standing or resources to take it forward.

The embedding of the party system

In the absence of a coalition role in instituting a democratic government, one perspective towards democratization could be that it would develop of its own momentum once minimal political freedoms have been established. Political parties become the forces that maintain popular participation and an ongoing process of political contestation. However, since the commencement of the occupation, this view has been challenged most strongly by those who point to the fissiparous nature of Iraq's politics. One major political interpretation of Iraq's trajectory sees the high degree of power maintained by the political groupings ordered by sect and ethnicity as symptomatic of the salience of particularist identities within Iraq. Remove the oppressive intimidation of the central state, this argument runs, and identities naturally lapse back to primordial sectarian or ethnic allegiances.[32] On this reading, democratization could only result in ethno-nationalist polarization: the battle for votes will descend primarily into calculations of demography rather than assessments of political programmes; and the electoral victor will rule in the name of the largest fragment, rather than that of the country as a whole. Within this archetypal situation of a tyranny of the majority, Tocqueville's description of the three races of America, in which the only alternatives to war are the extermination and brutalization of the minority, looms large.[33]

Within that interpretation of Iraq's path, the struggle for the political future is portrayed as a zero-sum game between the resultant agents. Thus, in the Kurdish region, the Kurdistan Democratic Party (KDP) and the Patriotic Union of Kurdistan (PUK) remain dominant, but within Iraq as a whole they are the representatives of a minority. As fundamentally ethno-nationalist parties (despite their occasional proclamations otherwise), their political interests diverge so radically from the Arabs of Iraq that they will always be pushing for greater autonomy up until either secession or renewed subjugation. In the Shi'i-dominated south as well as in much of the west, the removal of Sunni dominance results in the burgeoning of the Shi'i Islamist parties – the Supreme Council for the Islamic Revolution in Iraq (SCIRI), the Islamic Call Party (Hizb al-Da'wa al-Islamiyya; al-Da'wa for short) and the Sadr II movement, formed through the underground work of junior cleric Muqtada al-Sadr during the closing years of the *ancien régime*. Meanwhile, the displacement of the Sunni Arabs from their Ottoman, mandatory, royalist and post-1963 Iraqi nationalist positions of dominance results in their dissatisfaction with the new political order. To offset the potential for sectarian or ethnic conflict – or, more pessimistically, to stave it off – it is argued that each group must be given just enough to keep it on board: hence the politics of *al-muhassasa* (sectarian apportionment), in which political appointments to the IGC and the Iraqi ministries were made on the basis of estimated proportions of perceived identities within Iraqi society.

There are very real and long-lasting factors that have resulted in the formation and perpetuation of identities based around themes of difference (Kurd against Arab, Shi'a Arab against Sunni Arab) – including the much discussed dominance of the Sunni Arabs within Iraq's polity since its creation. Nevertheless, explanations of current patterns within Iraq's politics that have brought to the fore parties that emphasize purportedly primordialist identities would also need to account for why particularist forms of identification bring loyalty to certain institutional forms, such as political parties. They would also need to contend with a historical reading of Iraq's society in which allegiance to sectarian leaders has been a relatively marginal phenomenon during the past century in comparison with identification with guild, neighbourhood or class, and in which the sect has never functioned as a unified political agent.[34]

To understand the particular salience of the party institutions, their social and patrimonial role within the modern Iraqi state needs to be appreciated. The primary context in which they have operated since April 2003 has been that of a weak central state, in its practical mechanisms, as a seat of authority and as a site of contestation. The centre's weakness has meant that the attempt by political parties to capture the power of the state, the predominant aim of 'normal' politics, has been neither possible given its monopolization by the coalition nor particularly desirable.

In relations with the central authority, the Iraqi political agent was left with the three-way choice: reject the transitional structure of government through political means alone and face marginalization (witness the decline of the royalist party of Sharif Ali, the Constitutional Monarchist Movement, and failure of any of the dozens of indigenous political parties which reject the IGC's claims to legitimacy to make a serious impact); or assert itself through violence and risk elimination through the coalition's response; or allow itself to be co-opted into the new structure of governance. If it took that third course of action, participation was structured solely on the basis of cooperation with the coalition: groups that could demonstrate their relevance to the coalition were in demand, and appointed to positions on the IGC in July 2003. Political positions on issues involving central administration were developed by such groups largely on the basis of the utility of those positions to the coalition, and not in order to contest or rethink policy.

The ineffectiveness of the mechanisms of the state resulted in its marginality: the state was perceived as distant and irrelevant by many Iraqis. Once a representative of each of the major parties had been appointed to a position on the IGC, and had thus also secured the ability to appoint a minister when the Cabinet was established in September 2003, there was little to be obtained through official channels by attempting to secure more of a hold over the central government. National popularity could not result from control over an inefficacious ministry, nor could it be obtained through developing policy proposals on Iraq's future as no forum for their airing existed. The demonstration of abilities in these spheres could not result in the formal transfer of more resources to the party either, as those resources were held by the coalition, which had already fixed the roles of each of the parties for the transitional period. The official paybacks for action at the centre were disproportionately small when compared with the effort necessary.

With the low rewards from bureaucratic politics at the level of central government, parties concentrated their action in two forms: local politics and the role of brokerage. Real politics took place primarily in the locality: this is the arena in which political action has had the chance to be effective. In the aftermath of the invasion, groups strove to capture specific towns or regions in which they could install leading officials and thus hold resources, and obtain recruits through local civil networks. Thus the militia of al-Da'wa, the historic vehicle of Shi'i radicalism, captured Nasiriyya, whilst SCIRI, the more closely Iranian-aligned organization, took possession of Baquba and Kut through its militia, the Badr brigades. Other groupings, some specific to one town, also engaged in attempts to commandeer the local institutions of authority. The result was a set of turf wars. These began on 17 April 2003, when the Sadr II movement drove the Badr brigades out of the eastern suburb of Baghdad then known as Saddam City, to rename it Sadr City. Within days, the armed personnel of this movement – previously unknown outside of Iraq – had established strongholds in Kufa, Najaf and the Shi'a quarter of Samarra. These militias were formalized into Mahdi's Army. Armed confrontations continued to occur between rival militias throughout the subsequent months, with coalition troops rarely intervening, and with the central institutions of the state – including those concerned with human welfare – only intruding erratically into the lives of many Iraqis.[35] This situation was well expressed by the UN mission sent to Iraq in February 2004 to ascertain the possibility of holding elections:

> There are many indications of a growing fragmentation of the political class. Sectarianism is becoming entrenched and inter-communal politics more polarized, all within the context of a political process that remains limited to a few actors, all of varying credibility. This competition among the elite is taking place against a background of massive unemployment, particularly among a large young male population. Many interlocutors also speak of rising disillusionment and anger.[36]

It was on the basis of control over the particular district that some parties sought to create a political base. Other parties that had been created in exile and who now returned alongside coalition forces had also established paramilitary forces: the INC had created the Free Iraqi Forces in coordination with the US Department of Defense, whilst the Iraqi National Accord (INA) maintained a small armed force with the stated purpose of self-defence. The initial tension with the coalition was significant in places. The CPA's Order number 3 (23 May

2003) prohibited the holding of heavy weapons by all except official uniformed military forces; and small arms were prohibited in public, subject to exemptions to groups who would be under coalition supervision. These exemptions were granted only to the militias from the two Kurdish parties, the KDP (with its forces based in the governorates of Irbil and Dahuk) and the PUK (with its militia in Sulaymaniyya governorate and small areas of three other governorates). The coalition made direct attempts to disarm the Badr brigades in particular, with raids on SCIRI offices in al-Jadiriya, Wasit and Kut in June 2003.

The bombing of the Imam Ali Mosque in Najaf on 29 August 2003, in which SCIRI's leader Muhammad Baqr al-Hakim and some eighty others were killed, led to a substantial alteration in policy on the part of the CPA. The assertions from CPA officials that responsibility for security lay with the coalition and not with the party militias no longer seemed convincing: both Iraqi parties and the CPA personnel now talked of a security vacuum. At a press conference a few days later, the tone of Paul Bremer's comments changed: now organized militias would not have a role 'in the long run', but their members would be 'encouraged' to play a role in the CPA's security structures. He confirmed soon after that armed militias within Najaf 'were there with the full authority of the coalition'.[37] Over the coming weeks, party militias were out in force much more openly in Najaf and other areas of southern Iraq, and continued to be subsequently.[38]

By the end of 2003, a three-part structure was created through which party militias were maintained and legitimated. First, there was the legalization of militia activities. CPA Order number 3 was amended in December 2003, so that a group could be authorized to carry weapons, including heavy weapons. The requirement of coalition supervision was removed, allowing militias to operate freely once authorized. Although the TAL in Article 27(b) prohibited 'armed forces and militias not under the command structure' of the central government, it allowed for exceptions 'as provided by federal law'. The Kurdish parties, through the devolution arrangements that were agreed upon for the law, retained the right to keep their armed militias at least until the final constitution is agreed upon. SCIRI for one has argued that it should not have fewer rights than the Kurdish parties with respect to militias, and has pressed for the use of the exemption.[39]

Secondly, unauthorized militias continued to function as nominally civilian organizations engaged in preserving local order. For example, the Badr brigades renamed itself as the Badr organization, and gave itself an explicitly humanitarian mandate although it retained some 10,000 armed personnel. Despite statements from CPA officials that they continued to disapprove of such structures, little if any action was taken forcibly to disband or disarm them. This reflected a perception on the part of many within the CPA that the existing police force would be unable to maintain order in the absence of the militias.[40] There were also repeated allegations that the Badr organization in particular took an active role in attacking individuals associated with the *ancien régime*, and that the coalition at best turned a blind eye towards such activities.[41]

Thirdly, militias retained a significant role through their partial incorporation into the official security apparatus of the new state. The Iraqi Civil Defence Corps, established in September 2003, drew upon the personnel of the militias as well as those of tribally organized armed groupings, and undertook joint operations with coalition troops.[42] The Facilities Protection Service (FPS), established at the same time to guard ministries and government infrastructure, was made up of individuals recruited by and responsible to each participating ministry or governorate. Since individual ministries came under the control of political parties, with members of the IGC dividing up the ministerial posts between their selected officials, militia membership and structures seem to have been preserved through being transferred to the ministry controlled by the relevant party. This would explain why the FPS was severely overstaffed, unlike the other security forces. In January 2004, it had 97,200 members, in contrast to the projected force level of 50,000.[43] A private military company, Erinys Iraq, contracted to guard Iraq's oil facilities, was closely linked to the INC, and recruited heavily from its militia.[44] Thus the new security forces contain shadow networks of faction within them: the boundary between the arms of the state and the activities of political parties is weak.

The strength of the militias rests to some extent upon the aim of defending communities, particularly the Shi'a, that have suffered oppression over the past decades. It was also in response to a heightened sectarian atmosphere, which had descended into inter-communal violence on occasions,[45] that political parties strove to demonstrate their communitarian affiliations. The INC, which had promoted itself in Washington in earlier years as a vehicle for Arab secular thought, sought to align itself with mainstream Shi'i authorities, primarily the Hawza al-Ilmiya, the highest seat of religious learning in Najaf. Ahmed Chalabi publicly consulted with Grand Ayatollah Ali al-Sistani, and voted with the representatives of the Shi'i Islamist parties in the IGC. For example, he refused to sign up to the TAL, in order to hold out for lessening the ability of the Kurdish governorates to veto a final constitution, a position that the INC had itself supported in the past. These actions can be seen as a direct attempt to win legitimacy through accepting a role more in line with communal sentiments.

However, the entrenching of the political party in post-Ba'ath Iraq is not only due to its rhetoric of communitarianism, but also due to a consequence of its ability to provide material forms of resources to its supporters. Most obviously, through the existence of the armed militias, the political institutions are able to provide security and jobs to their supporters. Through capturing the local institutions of government, and either installing leading officials or maintaining a close relationship with governors and council members installed by the CPA, political parties could seek to route resources to themselves and to supportive populations.

The parties with representation in the IGC could also serve as brokers between local populations and the CPA. For example, one significant form of party recruitment took the form of employment brokerage. Employment with the institutions of, and foreign contractors for, the state was much in demand, particularly given that approximately 60 per cent of the adult population was out of work. Perhaps the most straightforward route to priority consideration for employment was to obtain a letter of recommendation (*tazkiyya*) from one of the CPA-aligned parties.[46] According to one report, parties who had cultivated the CPA's trust, presumably through cooperation in local administration and pacification, were more able to act as vetting agents for it; *tazkiyya* from the Shi'i Islamist parties was the most effective of all.[47]

Political sponsorship of this form was particularly important for recruitment to the new security forces, which remained a popular route to employment for many from the disbanded armed forces and intelligence apparatus of the Ba'ath era, despite their frequent targeting by insurgents. The INA was the most successful party in recruiting a new political base from this group, building upon the existing number of its members who were senior officers within Iraq's security apparatus before 1991. It won control over both the IGC's Supreme Security Committee through its long-standing links with the US Central Intelligence Agency, and also the Interior Ministry in the round of negotiations over the apportionment of portfolios. This allowed it to provide employment on a large scale to those who seek advantage through its offices.[48]

Furthermore, former members of the Ba'ath Party often needed to secure the support of the political parties to ensure their reintegration into the labour market. Under the de-Ba'athification order of 16 May 2003, those who had been in the top four ranks of the Ba'ath Party, and Ba'ath Party members of any rank within the top three layers of management, were prohibited from public sector employment, subject to discretionary exemptions. Up to 30,000 individuals, including those who had sought a role in the public sphere and career advancement rather than acting as ideological supporters of the *ancien régime*, were dismissed from their positions as a result.[49] To re-establish a role, the applicant needed first to apply to the CPA. However, responsibility for assessing applications shifted to institutions established by the IGC in November 2003, with the creation of its Higher National Commission for the Eradication of the Ba'ath Party (HNCEBP).[50] This body and its subsidiary institutions gave the appointees of political parties a direct role in choosing which individuals to allow to return to work, and to serve as prospective members of local councils. There was therefore a strong incentive for many Iraqis – particularly from upwardly mobile sectors of society – to become affiliated with one of the political parties within the IGC, primarily the INC, which held the chair of the HNCEBP.

As well as acting as an employment broker in a job-poor environment, it appears that some of the political parties also sought to act as intermediaries for international and Iraqi contractors in their relations with the CPA. Allegations of coalition favouritism to corporations promoted by members of the IGC were widespread after mid-2003. Wider attention focused on a $327 million contract for supplies for the new Iraqi Army that was awarded to a consortium created by a former business partner of Ahmed Chalabi, but that was by no means the only such alleged case.[51] It may well be that parties tried to consolidate their positions by building alliances with supportive corporations. The INC, which held the chair of the IGC's economic and finance committee and which appointed the ministers of finance and trade, was particularly well placed to do so.[52]

As well as the unofficial incorporation of the political parties' networks into the process of governing, the CPA placed some emphasis on recruiting tribal leaders to take part in local government. Some reports have detailed how arms permits, jobs and contracts have gone to tribal sheikhs who accepted a role in assisting with local governance.[53] In the refreshment of local councils, usually fourteen of the forty places went to tribal leaders or clerics.[54] In using purportedly traditionalist forces as intermediary institutions to local populations, the position of the tribal leader – in decline since the latter half of the nineteenth century in Iraq, although resuscitated under British rule and much later by the Ba'ath regime in the 1990s – has been strengthened. As the tribal sheikhs rely upon coalition assistance to retain their positions of significance, their interests remain much in line with the coalition retaining a strong role subsequent to the formal handover. The example of mandatory Iraq, when the large tribal leaders aligned themselves with the British in the 1920s and against any moves by the Hashimite monarchy to take a more independent approach, may be worth bearing in mind.[55] The CPA seems to have adopted a strategy, either by default or by design, of balancing internal political forces within the country so that no Iraqi body has either the leverage or the authority to engage in a critical discourse upon coalition policy without risking alienation from other major institutions within Iraqi society as well as from the coalition itself.

The continued existence of militias and the ability of the political parties and tribal sheikhs to act as brokers with the central government derive from the lack of perceived effectiveness of the official forces of the Iraqi state and the coalition in promoting order and employment, or in adequately penetrating Iraqi society. The resultant form of authority scarcely draws upon Weberian rational–legal modes of state operation, with their orientation towards bureaucratic efficiency, centralism and a rigid distinction between public power and private interests. Instead, with the blurring of the divisions between government, political party, tribe and private business, the form of authority has been much closer to a condition of neo-patrimonialism. Relations of dominance have become structured on the flexible basis of patrons and clients within an administrative system that is formally constituted on a rational–legal model.[56]

Political parties in modern Iraq operate largely as clientelistic networks, rather than as promoters of political programmes. Clientelism is often characterized by the use of ethnic, tribal or sectarian linkages, acting as both the network through which political clients can be acquired and the guarantor of mutual commitments. This appeal to primordial allegiance acts as the 'cement' of economic linkages, providing the stability of relations that the weak institutions of the state are unable to secure. If the modern Iraqi party is to be understood principally in these terms, the prospects for a modern party-based democratic system, in which electors decide between competing parties on the basis of the plausibility of their political programmes, are poor. This point is apt to be missed by those who see the possibility for a successful democratic transition in Iraq in terms of how effectively an appropriate 'political culture' can be created, with the primary task of international institutions conceived of as being the establishment of an Iraqi civil society.[57] The principal problem for democratization is not in the realm of ideas – the ideas that most Iraqis hold about the worthiness or meaning of democracy – but in the role of the political party as a significant social, economic and often military actor within Iraqi society.

Conclusion

If the political parties of the new Iraq have established themselves primarily as channels for their clientele's advancement rather than as originators and promoters of cohesive political programmes, the opportunities for political participation through the party system is limited. The more political competition reduces to vote-buying, the less it centres on deliberation about potential futures.

Such networks seem only to have grown in strength since April 2003; and as the patron–client relationship functions most effectively locally, this has entailed the increased fragmentation of the country. The political parties are unlikely to concede voluntarily the resources they have commandeered in the localities, in return for a comparatively small stake in the weak institutions of central government. This is most clear in the case of the Kurdish parties, which have secured guarantees of their maintenance of autonomy during the transitional period through the TAL. The TAL also secures in place local governments created during the period of formal occupation for the duration of the transition. Any future government will have to resort to coercion in order to assert its centrality for Iraqi politics, or it will remain weak, playing the role of mediator between the different regions rather than devising national strategies for Iraq's political and social development. Neither of these two options appears promising for Iraq's democratic development.

Open electoral contest will inevitably bring with it the possibility of a considerable realignment of political forces along national lines: the Caesarist plebiscitarian element in politics, to revisit Weber, finds its opportunity in the battlefield of elections. This remains a possibility, given the programme for national elections in the TAL. However, the centrifugal forces that played a primary role in Iraq's politics during the first year of occupation diminished the possibility that a strong political centre will prevail at the expense of the regions.

This tipping of power in favour of the local arena may well be recognized as a positive outcome by those who interpret the Ba'ath era as the playing out of the political problems that have arisen from the creation of a unified Iraqi state. But the current strength of local political forces, organized on sectarian or ethnic bases, is not simply the recrudescence of features inherent in Iraqi society. It is at least in part the result of a particular political situation, in which the institutions of the state remain weak and the governing power has sought to disperse authority in order to maintain its unchallenged position. The costs of the diminishment of the national state are high. The negative consequences for democratic development are likely to be severe.

Notes and references

* This chapter has been written as part of a research project with Dr Eric Herring (University of Bristol) and Anne Alexander, funded by the Economic and Social Research Council (RES-000–22–0274). It is based in part on fieldwork undertaken in Iraq in September 2003. The project website is: www.iraqpolicy.org.uk.

1 J.-J. Rousseau, Social Contract, 1762, II.7; most importantly also I.7–8, II.6.

2 'Prepared Statement for the Senate Armed Services Committee: The Future of NATO and Iraq', 10 April 2003; also National Security Advisor Condoleezza Rice, press briefing, 4 April 2003.

3 NBC 'Meet the Press', 13 April 2003; also Colin Powell's interview on NBC News, 11 April 2003.

4 Footage shot by independent film-makers Insider Films, 3 May 2003.

5 UN Office of the Humanitarian Coordinator for Iraq, weekly update, 26 May 2003; J. Sullivan, 'Free Elections Hit Snags in Kirkuk', Knight-Ridder Tribune News, 24 May 2003.

6 Thomas Carothers, 'The End of the Transition Paradigm', *Journal of Democracy*, 13, 2002.

7 For example, Chalabi's speech at the Aspen Institute, Berlin, on 7 March 2002; and A. Chalabi, 'Iraq for the Iraqis', *Wall Street Journal*, 19 February 2003.

8 Democratic Principles Working Group, 'The Transition to Democracy in Iraq', November 2002 as modified on 12 December 2002, pp. 44–5 and 60–3. Objections are recorded on p. 60, n. 67; and more strongly in the earlier draft of 11 December 2002, at p. 62, n. 72.

9 Donald Rumsfeld, Defense Department briefing transcript, 25 April 2003; testimony of Under Secretary of Defense for Policy Douglas Feith to the House of Representatives Committee on International Relations, 15 May 2003; CPA Order no. 1 (16 May 2003).

10 R. Looney, 'The Neoliberal Model's Planned Role in Iraq's Economic Transition', *Middle East Journal*, 57, 2003, p. 570; N. King, 'Bush Officials Draft Broad Plan for Free-market Economy in Iraq', *Wall Street Journal*, 1 May 2003.

11 CPA Order no. 39 (19 September 2003), amended by Order no. 46 (20 December 2003).

12 R. Wright and A. Shadid, 'Changes in US Iraq Plan Explored: Deadline Firm; Other Details are Negotiable', *Washington Post*, 25 January 2004.

13 This was a common theme in many of the project interviews conducted with CPA personnel in September 2003 and subsequently. Also, R. Chandrasekaran, 'Inexperienced Hands Guide Iraq Rebuilding', *Washington Post*, 25 June 2003; C. Clover, 'Unrest Grows over Rebuilding Iraq', *Financial Times*, 25 June 2003.

14 CPA Order no. 2 (23 May 2003). Walter Slocombe, who was responsible for the disbanding of the Iraqi Army, gave his account in 'To Build an Army', *Washington Post*, 5 November 2003.

15 US Department of Defense (DoD) weekly report, 4 November 2003, p. 20.

16 DoD weekly report, 16 March 2004, p. 30.

17 A. Cha, 'Iraqi Experts Tossed with the Water', *Washington Post*, 27 February 2004.

18 DoD weekly report, 12 January 2004, p. 11.

19 Personal communications with CPA and Iraqi sources, August 2003 and subsequently. Also, J. Spinner, 'Lights are Coming on, Slowly, in Iraq', *Washington Post*, 7 February 2004.

20 DoD weekly report, 16 March 2004, pp. 4–5.

21 Memorandum of 16 October 2003, reproduced online at:<http://www.usatoday.com/news/washington/executive/rumsfeld-memo.htm> (accessed 22 March 2004).

22 Article 59(b) of the Transitional Administrative Law; R. Wright, 'US has Big Plans for Embassy in Iraq', *Washington Post*, 2 January 2004; R. Wright, 'US Rushes to Prepare Embassy in Iraq', *Washington Post*, 9 March 2004.

23 CPA Public Notice 2, 'Regarding Organization in the Workplace', 6 June 2003. An example of prior attempts to elect managers was at the South Refineries Co. in Basra, reported by J. Cordahi, 'Iraqi Worker Protests may Further Delay Revival of Oil Output', Bloomberg News, 9 May 2003.

24 D. Rohde, 'US Official Overrules Commanders, Cancels Iraq's First Postwar Election', *New York Times*, 19 June 2003; W. Booth and R. Chandrasekaran, 'Occupation Forces Halt Elections Throughout Iraq', *Washington Post*, 28 June 2003.

25 International Crisis Group, *Governing Iraq*, 25 August 2003, pp. 10–12.

26 Personal communication, March 2004.

27 A. Shadid, 'In Iraqi Towns, Electoral Experiment Finds Some Success', *Washington Post*, 16 February 2004.

28 Denver Regional Council of Governments Regional Report, August 2003, p. 1; K. Rouse, 'Ex-mayor Helps Bring Democracy to Iraqis', *Denver Post*, 7 December 2003.

29 For example, Article 9(1) of the Interim Operating Instructions of the Baghdad councils: the CPA 'may add or change representatives selected to any level of Interim Advisory Council in order to ensure appropriate diversity'. Contained in the Baghdad Citizen Advisory Council Handbook, published by the CPA, Research Triangle Institute and USAID, 3rd edn, 7 November 2003. A different perspective on the development of Baghdad's new councils is A. Dawisha, 'Iraq: Setbacks, Advances, Prospects', *Journal of Democracy*, 15, 2004.

30 'Baghdad Neighborhood Advisory Council Votes in New Members', 9 January 2004. Online. Available HTTP: <http://www.defendamerica.mil/articles/jan2004/a010904d. html> (accessed 22 March 2004).

31 CPA Order no. 62, para. 1(f), 1 March 2004.

32 For example, P. Basham, 'Can Iraq be Democratic?', Cato Institute Policy Analysis No. 505, 5 January 2004, esp. pp. 14–15; more refined, A. Wimmer, 'Democracy and Ethno-religious Conflict in Iraq', *Survival*, 45, 2003, pp. 111–34; and G. Stansfield, 'The Transition to Democracy in Iraq', this volume.

33 A. de Tocqueville, *Democracy in America* (1835–40), I.2.8 and I.2.10.

34 In particular, H. Batatu, *The Old Social Classes and the Revolutionary Movements of Iraq*, Princeton, NJ: Princeton University Press, 1978, esp. pp. 476–80; F. Jabar, *The Shi'ite Movement in Iraq*, London: Saqi, 2003, pp. 63–7.

35 These developments are summarized in J. Cole, 'Shiite Religious Parties Fill Vacuum in Southern Iraq', Middle East Report Online, 22 April 2003; and J. Cole, 'The United States and Shi'ite Religious Factions in Post-Ba'thist Iraq', *Middle East Journal*, 57, 2003, pp. 543–66.

36 United Nations, 'The Political Transition in Iraq: Report of Fact-finding Mission', 23 February 2004, p. 4.

37 Press briefings, 2 September 2003 and 6 September 2003.

38 T. Al-Issawi, 'Previously Banned Militia Patrols Iraqi Holy City, with Coalition's Blessing', Associated Press, 6 September 2003; Congressional Research Service, *Iraq: US Regime Change Efforts and Post-Saddam Governance*, Library of Congress report RL31339, 7 January 2004, p. 12.

39 R. Chandrasekaran, 'Iraq's Shiites Renew Call for Militias', *Washington Post*, 4 March 2004.

40 N. Parker, 'Militias Still Remain Part of Post-Baathist Security Forces', Agence France Presse, 13 March 2004. A similar argument was used by Jalal Talabani, the head of the PUK, to justify the continuation of the peshmerga: 'The Way Forward', *Wall Street Journal*, 20 November 2003.

41 R. Fisk, 'Hooded Men Executing Saddam Officials', *Independent*, 28 December 2003; E. Wong, 'Iraqi Militias Resisting US Pressure to Disband', *New York Times*, 9 February 2004; interview with recently retired middle-ranking US official in Iraq, March 2004.

42 R. Chandrasekaran, 'US to Form Iraqi Paramilitary Force', *Washington Post*, 3 December 2003; International Crisis Group, *Iraq: Building a New Security Structure*, 23 December 2003, pp. 20–1.

43 CPA Order no. 27, s. 2: Organization of the FPS. DoD weekly report, 5 January 2004, p. 16.

44 N. Pelham, 'Rival Former Exile Groups Clash over Security in Iraq', *Financial Times*, 11 December 2003; K. Royce, 'Start-up Company with Connections', *Newsday*, 15 February 2004.

45 N. Blanford, 'The Specter of Sectarian and Ethnic Unrest in Iraq', Middle East Report Online, 7 January 2004.

46 H. Zangana, 'Why Iraqi Women aren't Complaining', *Guardian*, 19 February 2004; interview with Haifa Zangana, 11 March 2004.

47 R. McCarthy, 'How Freedom from Repression has brought Frustration and Fear', *Guardian*, 15 March 2004.

48 D. Priest and R. Wright, 'Iraq Spy Service Planned by US to Stem Attacks', *Washington Post*, 11 December 2003; E. Wong, 'New Iraq Agency to Hunt Rebels', *New York Times*, 31 January 2004. A detailed account of the INA's history is provided by D. Hiro, *Neighbours, Not Friends: Iraq and Iran after the Gulf Wars*, London: Routledge, 2001.

49 Paul Bremer, Defence Department news briefing, 12 June 2003. Ahmed Chalabi gave a figure of 28,000 dismissed in the period up to January 2004: recounted in H. Hendawi, 'Iraq Details Plans to Uproot Ba'athists', Associated Press, 11 January 2004.

50 CPA Memo no. 7 (4 November 2003); Governing Council decree 94 (11 January 2004). The press conference at which Ahmed Chalabi announced the new procedures was covered by Dubai TV (11 January 2004).

51 K. Royce, 'Start-up Company with Connections', *Newsday*, 15 February 2004; also, R. Nordland and M. Hirsh, 'The $87 Billion Money Pit', *Newsweek*, 3 November 2003.

52 Interview with senior official in Iraq, September 2003.

53 C. Clover, 'US Builds up Tribal Rule on Coke, Doughnuts and Power', *Financial Times*, 14 July 2003; G. Packer, 'War after the War: What Washington Doesn't See in Iraq', *New Yorker*, 24 November 2003.

54 Personal communications, February 2004.

55 H. Batatu, *The Old Social Classes and the Revolutionary Movements of Iraq*, Princeton, NJ: Princeton University Press, 1978, esp. pp. 88–92; also, the essays in F. Abdul-Jabar and H. Dawod (eds), *Tribes and Power: Nationalism and Ethnicity in the Middle East*, London: Saqi, 2003, esp. pp. 88–96; more directly, T. Dodge, 'US Intervention and Possible Iraqi Futures', *Survival*, 45, 2003, pp. 103–22.

56 C. Clapham (ed.), *Private Patronage and Public Power: Political Clientelism in the Modern State*, London: Pinter, 1982.

57 This approach has been promoted by Larry Diamond, e.g. in 'Universal Democracy?', *Policy Review*, 119, 2003. Since December 2003, Diamond has been a senior adviser to the CPA in Iraq.

11 Iraq, political reconstruction and liberal theory

John Horton and Yoke-Lian Lee

As other contributors to this volume demonstrate, the post-war political situation in Iraq is complex, confusing and uncertain.[1] It is impossible to predict with any confidence how events will unfold, or what will be their long-term consequences. Clearly, though, the major immediate problem facing both the Iraqis and the occupying powers is the need to establish some kind of political 'normality'; and questions about how to think about what we call 'political reconstruction' lie at the heart of our concerns. We do not, however, directly address the concrete, empirical analysis of any specific institutional proposals. Rather, we seek to explore the relevance to problems of political reconstruction in Iraq of a certain kind of normative political theory. In particular, we examine the work of three contemporary liberal political theorists concerned to articulate the principles of a just political order. These principles, which are of a generally liberal democratic hue, are conceived of as a guide to political practice, in the sense that they set out broad goals for, and constraints on, what counts as a morally legitimate political structure. In undertaking this exercise we aim to draw attention to what we see as the severe limits of normative liberal political theory in contexts such as those of the post-war reconstruction of Iraq. While we raise difficulties that are specific to each of the theorists whose work we discuss, our principal purpose is to explain how the limitations of liberal theory are to be found in certain generic features of this style of normative political theorizing.

It cannot be said that politicians actively involved with Iraq have been desperately seeking out political theorists for their advice, but there is among some of the more thoughtful policy aides, and certainly among some political theorists, the feeling that normative political theory should have a significant contribution to make to discussions about political reconstruction.[2] As briefly indicated in our conclusion, we do believe that there is indeed something that political theorists can contribute; but this is not what normative political theorists typically seek to offer. We are deeply sceptical of the claims by political theorists to any normative expertise that qualifies them to recommend how those engaged in the process of political reconstruction should act – whether this takes the form of advising on the moral acceptability of particular policies, setting long-term political goals or stipulating what conditions a morally legitimate political structure must meet. Generally, we suggest, politicians might be wise to keep normative political theorists at a safe distance.

Before taking our argument further, however, we make a few preliminary points, both to clarify some of the issues we are concerned to explore and to identify others that we are not. Among the most important questions that we do not pursue is that of the legitimacy or justification of the war itself. It is wholly right that these questions should not be forgotten, and that those responsible should be held to account, but the war cannot be undone, and whatever view one has of its legitimacy that cannot determine what should be done now. For instance, it does not follow that if one believes the war to have been wrong, one must therefore believe that the occupying powers should immediately withdraw. Indeed, on some analyses, a rapid withdrawal would only compound the damage of the invasion. This, though, does not mean that justifications for the war can have no bearing on deciding how the occupying powers should act. For example, had 'the weapons of mass destruction' materialized, keeping seriously in play the doctrine of pre-emptive strike as a justification of the war in terms of self-defence, this would not have given rise to much by way of specific expectations about the form of political reconstruction. By contrast, if the principal reason for the war was to remove a tyrant and bring the benefits of freedom and democracy to the Iraqi people, this raises some fairly specific expectations about the kind of political reconstruction that the occupying powers should be undertaking. But we shall not have anything more to say about the relationship between justifications of the war and political reconstruction in what follows.

A little more, though, should be said to clarify what we mean by 'political reconstruction'. Generally, this refers to the project of establishing some 'normal' political structures and processes within Iraq. We are concerned specifically with the relevance to that project of the values manifested in liberal democratic political institutions and practices. While the liberal political theorists with whose work we are concerned rarely use the term 'liberal democracy' themselves, it is not a misleading generic term for the kind of legitimate political structure that they defend. Very roughly, what is meant by it is the kind of political institutions and processes, and the values that inform them, currently to be found in the West, although not only there. In saying this, there is of course no suggestion that the practice of liberal democracy anywhere fully manifests the ideal. In broad terms, liberal democratic government involves an ideal of equality of respect manifest in such practices as a system of equal political and civil rights, a principle of equality of opportunity, universal suffrage, competitive popular elections, freedom of the press, religious toleration, the rule of law, an independent judiciary, an adequate level of public provision of education, health and welfare, and so on. There is no one defining feature, but a range of conditions, most of which have to be met to a reasonable degree most of the time; and the majority, perhaps all, of those features we just mentioned would figure in liberal theories of a morally legitimate political structure.

The one feature of existing liberal democracies that is perhaps particularly problematic is a capitalist economy, and the vast economic inequalities that go with it. There is widespread agreement both that there needs to be some significant sphere of economic activity independent of the state and that the state needs to play a role in controlling and correcting the untrammelled operation of markets, but where the emphasis is placed can vary dramatically. This is particularly relevant to our concerns because 'economic justice' is the issue on which liberal political theorists part company most strikingly from the current practices of liberal democratic states, and most of popular opinion in these societies about such matters. Partly for this reason, but also to keep our enquiry within manageable bounds, we ignore questions of distributive justice. This is in no way to deny the importance of economic issues, either to social justice or as a motive for political action. Nevertheless, we will focus primarily on the political reconstruction of Iraq, interpreted rather narrowly in terms of political institutions and processes.

Normative liberal political theory is marked by considerable internal disagreement on both methodological and substantive issues, although there are also significant points of broad agreement. In order to do justice to this diversity, therefore, we begin by briefly examining separately the work of three leading liberal political theorists: Brian Barry, John Rawls and Will Kymlicka. They do not exhaust the full range of liberal political theory, but are among the most eminent and influential liberal theorists, and all three have set out their ideas at considerable length and have well-developed theories. So, we are not looking at interim or tentative positions, but at some of the most highly elaborated and sophisticated of liberal political theories. It hardly needs pointing out that none of the work that we examine is directly concerned with the problems of political reconstruction in Iraq: it was all written before the events of 9/11, let alone the invasion of Iraq. However, as this work claims some general validity, it seems appropriate to think about its relevance to possible political structures in Iraq where, as one Middle East scholar, Murhaf Joueiati, has bluntly put it: 'there has not been a single day of democracy in its history'.[3]

In such short compass we cannot hope to do full justice either to the three individual theorists whose writings we explore, or to the richness of normative liberal theorizing as a whole: our discussions will inevitably be highly selective. Rather, what we seek to offer is an exemplary or 'symptomatic' reading of this body of work, and in this way we hope that such selectivity will not seriously compromise the general claims that we advance. For, as we will argue, the sources of some of the most fundamental failings are to be found in what normative liberal political theorists share. These have to do with the way in which liberal theory conceives of its task, and especially its parochialism, its lack of an adequate conception of political agency, its excessive moralism, the role of 'idealization' and what we call its 'anti-political' character. We begin by looking at the egalitarian liberalism of Brian Barry.

Brian Barry and egalitarian liberalism

In a number of works over the last decade and a half, Brian Barry has been a formidable and passionate defender of a form of egalitarian liberalism. This combines a strong economic egalitarianism with ideas of personal and political freedom and how they should be legally protected of a fairly traditional, liberal kind. He approvingly invokes J. S. Mill in this latter context, but where he significantly diverges from Mill and many other liberals of an earlier generation is his strong emphasis on economic equality. However, as we previously explained, we are less interested here in questions of distributive justice, and we will focus primarily on his social and political liberalism. While Barry sees himself as building on John Rawls's *A Theory of Justice*, he is highly critical of the direction of Rawls's later work, and still more fiercely critical of Will Kymlicka, even going so far as to charge that 'he is not a liberal'.[4] Barry can, therefore, be seen as occupying a position, at least on social and political matters, which is liberal in a fairly orthodox sense.

Central to Barry's liberalism is the idea of impartiality, modelled by the idea of a hypothetical contract. The basic theoretical device is derived from T. M. Scanlon, who argues that what is crucial in deciding the principles that should regulate a just society is 'whether a principle could reasonably be rejected (for application in our imperfect world) by parties who, in addition to their own personal aims, were motivated by a desire to find principles that others similarly motivated could also accept'.[5] The thought is that, in so far as principles of a just political order are reasonably acceptable to anyone, they are appropriately impartial; hence, justice as impartiality. There are two large, general questions that confront this approach. First, is it the most appropriate way of thinking about the justice of a political order? Secondly, even if it is, are there any substantive principles that are uniquely justifiable in this way? Barry thinks the answer to both questions is 'yes'. We shall look at some of his reasons for answering these questions affirmatively, with a particular eye to how they might bear on the problems of political reconstruction in Iraq, which is not of course a topic that Barry has explicitly in mind.

Why is it that this is the appropriate way to think about the justice of any set of political arrangements? Basically, Barry argues that if we assume people to be free and equal, and to be motivated by a concern to live together on terms acceptable to everyone, this is the only viable strategy. In assuming people to be free and equal we accept that no person's idea of what is the right way to live or what is morally true can legitimately be imposed on anyone else. Let us look for a moment, however, at the apparently innocuous 'agreement motive' as Barry calls it, which is 'the desire to live in a society whose members all freely accept its rules of justice and its major institutions'.[6] Now, when presented in this way the agreement motive may appear pretty undemanding. Surely, it is not asking a lot that people should possess this motive, and that if some people have no such motivation they cannot expect others to want to live with them? However, in this weak form, it is not sufficient to do the work that Barry requires of it. For it will do so

> *Only* if the desire to live together on terms that nobody could reasonably reject overrides all other reasons for action. It is not enough that people merely have it as one reason among others in their motivational set. For, if

some people attach more importance to a feature of their conception of the good than to the desire for reasonable agreement (in Barry's terms) then they will not be sufficiently motivated to give priority to justice as impartiality. These people will have *a* reason for acting as impartial justice requires, but there is nothing in the agreement motive itself which dictates that it must outweigh all other reasons.[7]

What this means is that the agreement motive is really very much more demanding than Barry implies. For instance, it requires that whenever there is a conflict between the principles of 'impartial justice' and a person's fundamental and deeply held moral or religious convictions, priority must *always* be accorded to the principles of impartial justice. To suggest that this is merely a minimal requirement of 'reasonableness' is plausible only if one has already accepted Barry's liberalism, which asserts that the agreement motive must take priority over *everything* else.

It is not difficult to see how this might bear on our understanding of the process of the political reconstruction of Iraq. If Barry were right in his undemanding interpretation of the agreement motive, we might feel confident that at least we have a fairly uncontroversial place to begin thinking about the process. Unfortunately, this is not so: at best such a starting place might be assumed to be acceptable to liberals (although, for other reasons, even that is highly questionable), but it is both an unjustified and unrealistic assumption to make in the context of Iraq.[8] Moreover, if this were not enough, further problems emerge if we turn to the second question, of whether, even if we accept Barry's approach, justice as impartiality is capable of generating a set of reasonably determinate substantive political principles for regulating any society?[9] We argue that it is not.

This is a more difficult issue to do justice to in brief compass, and we do not wish to claim that a procedure of neutralist justification cannot eliminate any potential principles as clearly unacceptable. However, it will be of very modest help if the principles it can successfully eliminate are only those that might justify tyrannies or institutions like slavery, as these are unlikely to figure prominently on the agenda of political reconstruction. Our problem is made harder, however, because Barry has nowhere tried seriously to derive any otherwise controversial political principles from his method. He has many times given examples of principles that he believes *can* be so derived, but that is not the same thing as showing how they actually are so derived. We are still awaiting the next volume of his *magnum opus* in which that task was to be undertaken, several years after it might have been expected to appear, which might suggest that the task is proving more difficult than he anticipated. However, leaving this aside, there are independent reasons for scepticism about his likely success.

We can see why if we look, for example, at one of the principles that he claims would issue from a process of impartial justification: the requirement that 'all religious organizations should face a uniform set of laws',[10] a view he has defended again recently in his vitriolic attack on multiculturalism.[11] However, although this is one possible outcome of a process of impartial justification, there are also other possibilities. Another might be an agreement to compromise or trade-off against each other matters of particular importance to different religions; so legislation might favour one religious group on one issue and another religious group on a different issue. Alternatively, there might be agreement that there could be exemptions from laws on particular grounds that would favour some religions rather than others. Indeed, it may be that even an established religion with, for example, the standing of the Church of England would be acceptable to other religions. For some non-Christians have argued that in the predominantly secular world of the West it is important that religious belief receive public recognition, and it is reasonable that in England the particular religion that should have a special place is the Church of England. Similarly, in Iraq, even non-Muslims might accept that it is reasonable for Islam to have a privileged place in the social and political institutions of the country.

The idea of impartial justification seems to require that a principle must be reasonably acceptable to anyone, but the scope of 'anyone' in Barry's theory is not entirely clear. It seems to mean anyone who *could* be a member of a society either now or at any time in the future. If this expansive reading is correct then there is another question to be asked. This is: why should it matter if the principles of justice are not justifiable to everyone who does or could exist, so long as they are broadly acceptable to those who live under them? There seems no reason to buy into the demanding universalism implied by Barry's interpretation of impartiality. Why, for instance, should one think that the legitimacy of political structures in Iraq must depend upon whether they are justifiable to citizens of the West who will never have to live under them? In short, the demands of impartial justification are both too weak and too strong: too weak in that they cannot justify a single set of reasonably determinate substantive political principles, and too strong in that they set the standards of justification too high.

While we have only scratched the surface of Barry's theory, we believe that we have done enough to show why it would be unwise to look to it for helpful guidance in thinking about political reconstruction in Iraq. Too often Barry seems simply to presuppose the validity of premises that incorporate controversial assumptions, and universalize the local values of contemporary liberalism. Moreover, Barry has not yet shown that the procedure of impartial justification is able to deliver on its promise of justifying a unique set of political principles that cannot be reasonably rejected.

John Rawls and the legitimacy of non-liberal states

John Rawls is the most eminent liberal political theorist of the last fifty years, and some commentators have hailed his *A Theory of Justice* as the most significant work of liberal political theory in the twentieth century. While liberals have mostly received his later work rather more coolly, it has still been enormously influential and generated a huge literature. Clearly, it is not possible for us to enter into the thorny question of how radical a departure his later work is from *A Theory of Justice*, an issue about which there is some disagreement.[12] However, it is worth observing that there does seem to be fairly widespread agreement, and certainly it is our view, that in *Political Liberalism* and other later works there is greater, or at least more explicit, recognition that liberal principles need to be made acceptable to non-liberals. This is obviously important in thinking about the principles that should guide political reconstruction in Iraq, for to expect a wholesale conversion to liberalism among the Iraqi people would be absurd.

Because of this shift in emphasis, and because Barry takes a broadly similar view to the earlier Rawls, we will concentrate on his later work, and in particular on *The Law of Peoples*. This short book represents Rawls's attempt to extend his theory of justice, otherwise designed exclusively for regulating relations within a state, to the international sphere. While, as one would expect, his arguments can be seen to bear importantly on relations between Iraq and other states, that is not our focus. Instead, we want to try to extract from some of what Rawls says about non-liberal, but what he calls 'decent', societies, to see how it might relate to problems of political reconstruction in Iraq. In fairness to Rawls, it should be said that this is not his purpose, but it seems to us nonetheless to be a legitimate enterprise. Indeed, one reason why it is potentially interesting is because Rawls is a rare example of a liberal political theorist who seriously entertains the idea that liberals can accept the legitimacy of some non-liberal states, as a matter not simply of political expediency but also of right. Although, as we shall see, Rawls is ambivalent about the moral status of such states, he does believe that they can properly be regarded as in good standing in the international community of states; not beyond criticism, but certainly to be tolerated. For one of Rawls's main points in embracing this conception of decent, non-liberal states is to distinguish them from 'outlaw states'. The latter are states that systematically violate human rights, and Rawls says of them that 'in grave cases [they] may be subjected to forceful sanctions and even to intervention'.[13]

By decent societies Rawls means 'non-liberal societies whose basic institutions meet certain specified conditions of political right and justice'.[14] In broad terms:

> A decent people must honour the laws of peace; its system of law must be such as to respect human rights and impose duties and obligations on all persons in its territory. Its system of law must follow a common good idea of justice that takes into account what it sees as the fundamental interests of everyone in society. And, finally, there must be a sincere and not unreasonable belief on the part of judges and other officials that the law is indeed guided by a common good idea of justice.[15]

Rawls is noticeably shy about giving real-world instances of decent, non-liberal societies – as he is too of examples of reasonably just constitutional democracies – preferring instead to construct an imaginary example of a decent hierarchical people. However, interestingly from our point of view, the imaginary example he chooses to construct, 'Kazanistan' as he labels it, is of a decent hierarchical Muslim people. Basically, Kazanistan is non-liberal because it is hierarchical and 'does not institute the separation of church and state. Islam is

the favoured religion, and only Muslims can hold the upper positions of political authority and influence the government's main decisions and policies.'[16]
On the other hand, Rawls says that other religions are 'tolerated', and
Kazanistan 'honours and respects human rights, and its basic structure contains
a decent consultation hierarchy, thereby giving a substantial political role to its
members in making political decisions'.[17]

The first thing to say about Rawls's discussion of decent, non-liberal societies
is that it is in some respects a brave attempt by a liberal political theorist to think
about non-liberal forms of political organization that should at least be tolerated
by liberals, and to a degree respected. Not surprisingly many other liberals have
been hostile to this endeavour, and Rawls himself is clear that even the idealized
Kazanistan, unlike the idealized constitutional democracy of his theory of
justice, is not 'perfectly just'.[18] Rather, he defends his approach on the grounds
'that something like Kazanistan is the best we can realistically – and coherently –
hope for', and continues that

> enlightenment about the limits of liberalism recommends trying to conceive
> a reasonably just Law of Peoples that liberal and non-liberal peoples could
> together endorse. The alternative is a fatalistic cynicism which conceives the
> good life solely in terms of power.[19]

However, for all their modesty and moderation, these are in many respects
puzzling remarks that repay attention if we want to elicit some of the difficulties
in Rawls's position.

Let us begin with the seemingly odd reference to 'a fatalistic cynicism which
conceives the good life solely in terms of power', which does not seem to follow
in any very clear way from what has gone before. It is, we suspect, an oblique
reflection of Rawls's low opinion of an American foreign policy, which is long
on the rhetoric of 'freedom and democracy', but too often motivated by its
own geopolitical interests. In this respect it can be understood as displaying a
healthy scepticism towards supposedly 'idealistically' motivated interventions
in the affairs of other states, whether on humanitarian grounds or to support
freedom, democracy or whatever. However, once one begins to introduce
caveats of this kind, which can only appear in the context of Rawls's theorizing as a rather ad hoc concession to political realism, serious difficulties also
start to emerge. In pointing these out it is important to understand that we are
not objecting to greater political realism and contextual sensitivity, but rather
seeking to explain why this gives rise to problems for Rawls. For his style of
theorizing is unreceptive to this kind of intrusion, and once one begins to
introduce the constraints on normative theorizing that this kind of pragmatic
realism brings with it, the nature of the theory becomes unclear and the status
of its conclusions problematic.[20]

There has always been in Rawls's work a 'practical' strain, in the sense that he
has always been concerned that the principles of justice should be 'feasible'.
They must be principles that people could reasonably be expected to endorse,

and must, therefore, take account of the *beliefs* of those for whom the principles are supposed to be valid. Many of Rawls's admirers have tended either to pay relatively little attention to this aspect of his work, or to distance themselves from it. But it was a major point of attack for some of his earliest critics, such as R. M. Hare, who saw him as 'advocating a kind of subjectivism, in the narrowest and most old-fashioned sense'.[21] From the articulation of the method of reflective equilibrium and construction of the original position in *A Theory of Justice* to the idea of an overlapping consensus in his most recent writings, Rawls's arguments have consistently afforded a large place to what seems 'reasonable' to his readers. When we come to consider this in the context of his idea of decent non-liberal societies, however, the problems to which it gives rise are compounded in a way that threatens the very coherence of his theory.

First, we must ask the question of *whose* beliefs it is that are relevant to judgements about the moral standing of decent non-liberal societies. The methodology of reflective equilibrium and the contextual features of Rawls's approach suggest that it should be those who live under them. But when Rawls says that he does not believe that even the idealized model of Kazanistan is 'perfectly just', it is clearly his own beliefs and those of like-minded liberals to which recourse is being made. Obviously, this cannot be presumed to be the view of the citizens of Kazanistan, but nor has Rawls given any reasons, which appeal to their beliefs or to what would be reasonable for them, as to why they should share his view. There is no Archimedean point from which these conflicting judgements can be adjudicated, and we are simply confronted by two distinct perspectives on the justice of such a society, resting on different assumptions and beliefs.

There is, though, a further difficulty. This is that Rawls does not seem to have much of a reason *in terms of his own theory* to explain why liberals *ought*, as a matter of principle, to be tolerant and adopt a policy of non-interference towards Kazanistan or other decent but non-liberal societies. The apparent introduction here of what is 'realistically possible' implies something more like a *modus vivendi*, a conception that he elsewhere unequivocally rejects as having any role in a theory of justice because it will reflect unjustified inequalities of power, and as unstable precisely because it depends on a potentially shifting balance of forces.[22] There is no reason to believe, however, that it would always be impossible to 'encourage' a more liberal constitution in a society like Kazanistan through measures ranging from economic sanctions to military threats. And, if this could be done, what are Rawls's *theoretical* reasons for thinking that it would be wrong? The problem here is that once these practical, and frequently controversial, judgements about what is 'realistic' or feasible enter so centrally, the scope for ad hocery appears to be more or less unlimited. As we have remarked, elements of this problem were at least implicit in Rawls's approach from the start, but in the context of his argument about the moral status of non-liberal but decent hierarchical states they threaten to undermine the whole theory.

How, then, do the preceding arguments bear on the relevance of Rawls's work to problems of political reconstruction of Iraq? The point is not to reject the idea of a decent non-liberal state: quite the reverse. Thinking in terms of a political structure for Iraq that accepted that it would, in some sense, be an 'Islamic state', and so significantly lack certain liberal 'freedoms', but which also tried to protect fundamental human rights, might have a lot to be said for it. But, and this is the crucial point, such an idea lacks any convincing justification in terms of Rawls's own theory. Rather, what such a proposal does is simply assemble some very general ethical desiderata along with political considerations and other practical constraints to try to think constructively about the problems in Iraq. It is to engage in precisely the sort of circumstantial thinking that is not, in any meaningful sense, directed or constrained by a normative *theory*, although of course normative considerations are among those that will play a significant role in such thinking. Although we do not take a view on the question of whether or not aiming to create a decent non-liberal society is the best way forward for Iraq, it does at least seem a credible idea. The problem is that it is not one that is compatible with Rawls's theory.

Will Kymlicka and liberal pluralism

Will Kymlicka explicitly describes himself as one of a number of political theorists who 'have helped to define a new approach to ethnocultural diversity that argues that justice requires the public recognition and accommodation of diversity'.[23] He calls this position 'liberal pluralism', and claims that it differs significantly from 'orthodox liberalism'. The latter holds that 'ethnocultural diversity should be relegated to the private sphere and not publicly supported in the form of minority rights or multiculturalism'.[24] Barry would be a good example of the kind of theorist that he has in mind as an exponent of the orthodox liberal view. Kymlicka's work is especially worthy of attention because he, more than either Barry or Rawls, comes closer to addressing the question with which we are concerned. Indeed, the volume for which he writes the lead chapter, which is our primary source, is directly concerned with the relevance of liberal pluralism to the problems of post-communist political reconstruction in Eastern Europe, having the challengingly bold title, *Can Liberal Pluralism be Exported?* Needless to say, post-communist political reconstruction in Eastern Europe is a vastly different project from post-war political reconstruction in Iraq; but, for all that, Kymlicka's extended essay is the nearest any leading liberal political theorist has come to addressing explicitly this kind of issue in any depth.

One reason why Kymlicka's brand of liberal pluralism might be thought a more promising place to begin than orthodox liberalism is precisely because it starts by accepting that the latter's

> idea of ethnocultural neutrality is simply a myth. Indeed, the claim that liberal democratic states – or 'civic nations' – are ethnoculturally neutral is manifestly false, both historically and conceptually. The religion model, with its strict separation of church and state, is altogether misleading as an account of the relationship between the liberal democratic state and ethnocultural groups.[25]

This is important because although Muslims in Iraq, whether Sunni or Shia, obviously subscribe to the Islamic faith, they also comprise ethnocultural groups in Kymlicka's sense. Acknowledging that ethnocultural neutrality is impossible, therefore, at least accepts that it may not be appropriate, even 'ideally', to try to purge public life in Iraq of all its Islamic features in pursuit of a chimerical 'neutrality'. However, once we move beyond this general point the going starts to get tougher. For Kymlicka's principal concern in acknowledging that no state can be ethnoculturally neutral is not to embed the dominance of any particular culture, but to ensure that, so far as possible, minority cultures are not seriously disadvantaged by the impossibility of ethnocultural neutrality. In short, the thrust of liberal pluralism – what makes it *liberal* pluralism – is the public recognition and protection of ethnocultural minorities, not a belief that because ethnocultural neutrality is an illusion we must accept the hegemony of one particular culture.

Why is the requirement that ethnocultural minorities should receive adequate public recognition likely to give rise to problems? One reason, certainly relevant to the situation in Iraq and acknowledged as a potential problem more generally by Kymlicka, is that this requirement often seems to run counter to the imperatives of nation building. He agrees with Charles Taylor that 'nation-building inescapably privileges members of the majority culture'.[26] However, in part because of the circumstances of Iraq's creation by the decolonializing powers in the area, without too much attention being given to its likely long-term coherence or stability as a political entity, fragmentation and secession are ever-present dangers, especially in the absence of a strong government, and the need for nation building a real and ongoing one, if Iraq is to survive as a single, sovereign state.[27] So, in so far as nation building is perceived as a significant part of political reconstruction, this might appear to put the adequate public recognition of minority cultures under some pressure.

Kymlicka, however, believes that it is possible to distinguish 'liberal nation-building from illiberal nationalism', and highlights nine differences, 'all of which have implications for minority rights'.[28] For obvious reasons, it is impossible for us to explore all of these differences here, but we will look at one of the most important, to indicate of some the difficulties. This is the idea that liberal nation building will

> exhibit a much thinner conception of national identity. In order to make it possible for people from different ethnocultural backgrounds to become full and equal members of the nation, and to allow for the maximum room for individual dissent, the terms for admission are relatively thin – for example learning the language, participating in common public institutions, and perhaps expressing a commitment to the long-term survival of the nation. Joining the nation does not require one to abandon one's surname, or religion, or customs, or recreational practices, etc. …
>
> In non-liberal states, by contrast, acquiring a national identity typically requires a much thicker form of cultural integration, involving not only a common language and public institutions, but also elements of religion, ritual and lifestyle.[29]

As is evident, liberal nation building is a matter of degree; there is a continuum rather than a sharp distinction. Nonetheless the distinction is an important one for Kymlicka, and it plays a crucial role in his account of how nation building and liberal pluralism can be reconciled.

In fairness, Kymlicka is aware that even in post-communist Europe liberal nation building faces serious obstacles, and he also recognizes some 'hard cases', which would no doubt include Iraq, were it part of his remit. Moreover, it is a merit of Kymlicka's approach that he appreciates that ethnocultural conflicts cannot simply be expected to disappear with the enactment of the standard package of individual rights of orthodox liberalism. But this strength can also be a weakness in relation to the normative argument that Kymlicka seeks to advance. For, accepting the importance of ethnocultural identity, one has to accept its importance for dominant ethnocultural groups too, even if these are characterized by the thicker kind of national identity: it is not enough simply to point out that liberal pluralism would find it easier to work with the more pliable material of a thinner form of national identity. In fact, what it shows is how *difficult* it is to grow liberal pluralism where a 'thick' national identity dominates. If ethnocultural identity is as important as Kymlicka clearly takes it to be, those who rightly see their thick national identity as being undermined by the requirements of liberal nation building will justifiably feel threatened. For all his engagement with specific examples in post-communist Europe, and his perceptive critique of orthodox liberalism, Kymlicka is still engaged in a form of pure normative theorizing that pays insufficient regard to the particular historical and political circumstances of the people who are required to embrace the normative principles of liberal pluralism.

So far we have focused more on problems of 'exporting' liberal pluralism rather than its theoretical content. This, too, however, raises difficulties, although we have space to discuss only one of them. It may appear from what has been said about the importance of ethnocultural identity that Kymlicka would at least be sympathetic to the idea that political reconstruction in Iraq should allow a significant place to what might be called, despite the dangers of such shorthand, 'Islamic culture'. This appearance, however, is deceptive. The principal reason culture matters for Kymlicka is because it provides 'a context of choice'.[30] Accordingly, he writes that 'what distinguishes *liberal* tolerance is precisely its commitment to autonomy', and 'we must endorse the traditional liberal belief in personal autonomy'.[31] This might lead one to think, therefore, that cultures that do not place a high value on individual autonomy have little claim to possessing real value. And, indeed, Kymlicka does think it a liberal imperative to try to liberalize 'illiberal' cultures. But, like Rawls, he is also very reluctant to countenance coercive interference. Partly, he fudges the issue by insisting (correctly but not to the point) that 'the liberality of a culture is a matter of degree'.[32] However, he also says that 'as a general rule, liberals should not prevent illiberal nations from maintaining their societal culture',[33] and he is noticeably hostile to any attempts to forcibly liberalize illiberal cultures.

Kymlicka claims that his position is consistent because there are two different questions here: 'The first is the question of *identifying* a defensible liberal theory of minority rights; the second is the question of *imposing* that liberal theory.'[34] But notice that the second question is ambiguous between two interpretations of what is being asked. Is it asking (a) whether it would be *morally legitimate* to impose liberal theory, assuming of course that this could be done at reasonable cost? Or is it asking (b) the *practical* question of whether, in any given situation, it is possible to do this at a reasonable cost? He is quite right to say that a negative answer to (b) need not conflict with his answer to the first question. But it is altogether less clear that the same is true of a negative answer to (a). That is, Kymlicka does not explain what the moral objection is to coercive intervention to seek to 'impose' greater liberalism on a culture, in terms of his own theory of liberal pluralism. Certainly, there may often be practical reasons why this would not have the desired results; but again, as with Rawls, we see how normative theory and practical judgements are run together in a way that makes it quite unclear what is doing the real argumentative work. While this excursus into Kymlicka's theory may seem removed from the problems of Iraq, it has, as we shall argue, taken us closer to understanding some of the generic difficulties inherent in trying to relate normative liberal theorizing to those problems.

The limits of liberal political theory

So far we have examined the work of three leading liberal political theorists with a view to how they might provide normative guidance for the political reconstruction of post-war Iraq. About each we have set out reasons for considerable scepticism, which is not to suggest that their work is therefore without any value. However, that the theories of all three have been found seriously flawed, sometimes in similar ways, might suggest that there is some deeper and more pervasive explanation for this failure, whatever particular weaknesses in their work individually; and this is indeed what we shall argue. We shall offer a number of reasons to support the claim that there are fundamental problems inherent in the project of normative liberal political theory. The upshot is that any such theory is ill-equipped to provide normative guidance in the kind of social and political situation that currently exists in Iraq.

The first reason is that normative liberal political theory necessarily trades on beliefs and assumptions, which may be widely shared in the West, but do not have the same salience for those whose culture and history is very different. Let us explain what we mean by this. Normative political theories cannot be constructed from thin air or out of pure reason. Specific beliefs and assumptions, including particular moral beliefs, provide the indispensable material out of which normative political theories are built. Where there is a significant measure of agreement about the validity and relevance of these assumptions and beliefs, it may be possible to construct a normative theory that articulates political principles that can win widespread assent. Such a theory, while subtly transforming the original material, so that what comes out of the exercise is somewhat different from what went in, remains basically true to the ideas out of which it is constructed. And if, as supposed, the ideas that are used in the construction were originally generally acceptable, it is at least plausible to hope that the resulting principles may also prove acceptable, even to those who might initially be inclined to reject them. The idea that people might be brought to see things differently if they consider the arguments carefully is not hopelessly idealistic, although success is very far from guaranteed, even under the most favourable conditions. Where, however, the materials out of which the theory is constructed are themselves extensively and fiercely contested, it is surely overly optimistic to think that the resulting principles will prove more acceptable. It is, though, not just optimistic but disingenuous, if it is then suggested that those who reject the theory have somehow been given convincing reasons why they should accept it. Only if it can be shown that the original rejection of the beliefs and assumptions from which the theory was constructed is clearly irrational or based on demonstrably false beliefs could such a claim be justified. While no doubt in some instances this can be shown well enough,[35] it is a very demanding requirement to demonstrate that the *only* explanation of why anyone could reject a liberal theory of the legitimacy of a political order is because they hold false beliefs or are guilty of fallacious or irrational reasoning. Indeed, it is to imply a degree of demonstrable validity that liberal political theory simply does not possess.

Although there is some coyness about explicitly acknowledging the implications of this point, the point itself is usually grudgingly conceded somewhere in the small print of liberal political theories.[36] In fairness to Rawls, he is more upfront about this matter in his later writings, where he is explicit that his theory is designed specifically for what he calls 'a constitutional democracy'.[37] This may also explain why Rawls accepts, at least in principle, that some forms of non-liberal polity may also be legitimate, if not really 'just'. However, as we saw in discussing his work earlier, Rawls in fact finds it very difficult to detach himself from his own liberal values. And it is this dependence of normative liberal theories on controversial and disputed beliefs that is especially problematic in a context such as that of Iraq. For some of the assumptions that underlie liberal political theory, for instance about the relationship between religion and politics, and about the meaning of, or weight to be attached to, liberal values such as freedom of speech, personal autonomy, the rights of women and so on, are not widely shared by a number of important political groups in Iraq. Whatever they may claim to the contrary, liberal political theorists have not offered compelling arguments to show that the rejection of liberal values and political structures *must* be mistaken. And in so far as this is the case, the normative claims of liberal political theory lack purchase on those to whom they are supposed to apply.

A second reason is that this style of political theory lacks any adequate conception of political agency. That is, it is essentially 'utopian' in the sense that it sets up supposed goals – models of a just society – but without any realistic or practical idea of how these can be brought about. Of course, liberal political theory cannot be expected to somehow implement itself, and that is not our point. Our objection is that if normative liberal theory is to be genuinely *political*, rather than a more or less sophisticated kind of wishful thinking, it needs to have some idea about how its ideal can be brought into being. And by an idea of how its ideal could be brought into being, we mean more than the banal thought that all it requires is for people to accept the truth of liberal theory and be willing to act on it. At the very least we need some idea of how *that* might be brought about. To think that political agency can be left entirely out of the picture is one of the debilitating 'idealizations' of normative liberal theorizing. Politics is, if anything, a *practical* and *circumstantial* activity; it is about acting in the world as it is. It is fundamentally to misunderstand politics to try neatly to divide it, as normative liberal theorists implicitly do, into means and ends. And it is to compound such misunderstanding if it is then assumed that it is for normative political theorists to decide the ends, while social scientists or politicians determine the best means to achieve these ends. This is to denude politics of its particular character. If we are to think seriously about political reconstruction in Iraq, for instance, we have to think in terms of political possibilities at a particular time and in a particular place, and these comprise both means and ends in a way that construes them as unavoidably entwined.[38] While there is indeed a basis for a division of labour between political theorists and politicians, as we shall suggest later, it is peculiarly sterile to think that this can be adequately conceived in terms of a distinction between means and ends. And once we jettison that then it seems that normative political theorists cannot altogether escape the need for thinking about political agency if they are to engage in normative reflection about *politics*.

Another general failing, closely related to the second, is that normative liberal political theory is in an important sense *anti-political*. Indeed, it is anti-political in two distinct respects. The first, an extension of our preceding argument, is that liberal political theory is excessively moralistic. It treats many of the central features of ordinary political life, not just political agency, as extraneous to its project or entirely subservient to moral principles constructed for a highly 'idealized' world. Thus, for instance, inequalities of power, or the fact that, whether or not they are right to do so, people do not act as liberal principles prescribe, are excluded from normative liberal theory. At best they are consigned to what Rawls calls 'non-ideal theory', which is then usually seen as secondary. Ideal theory is said to have primacy because without an idea of 'a perfectly just basic structure … the desire for change lacks an aim'.[39] But this is simply false. If we think about the situation in Iraq, while some ideas about what would be preferable are of course inevitable, this does not mean that we can have *no* idea of what to do unless we have in our minds some conception of what a perfectly just Iraq would be like. This is highly implausible; and were it true, moreover, would be politically disastrous. For while it is hard enough to find common ground, or even proposals that are grudgingly acceptable to most of the contending groups in Iraq, the position would be truly hopeless if political action depended upon there being a conception of 'a perfectly just Iraq' to guide it. Such a view is not so much a source of direction, without which we are lost, but closer to a counsel of despair.

The second respect in which normative liberal theory is anti-political is to be found in the very conception of an ideally just society itself. As Glen Newey, among others, has persuasively argued, this is because liberal political theory 'aims at deriving philosophically a set of principles, enacted through institutions and procedures, which if implemented would herald the end of politics'.[40] There is a sense in which political theory becomes a surrogate for politics, with fundamental political questions removed from the rough and tumble of political bargaining and negotiation to be settled by liberal political theorists. We are all familiar with complaints to the effect that politics should be 'taken out of' the law, education, the arts or whatever, but liberal political theory seems to carry this not so much to its logical conclusion, as to what one might think is a *reductio*, by seeking to take the politics out of politics. That is, it tries to eliminate the messiness and contingency, the unpredictable interplay of morality, interest and power that is characteristic of political activity. While not unique to contemporary liberal political theory – the tendency goes back at least as far as Plato's desire to institute the rule of 'philosopher–kings' – it remains odd that it should be marked by such contempt for its subject matter that it aims more or less to abolish it. We might indeed prefer a rationally ordered communal life, if there is such thing, but it is precisely this lack that makes politics, rather than mere administration, necessary. In this respect, perhaps, liberal political theory also partakes of the ethos of our age, one in which the public standing of politicians, at least in the West, is extremely low, and in which politics itself, because of its compromises, backroom deals, lack of candour and the tendency to dress up self-interest in the language of high ideals, is often thought to be a rather disreputable activity.

Be that as it may, the upshot is that liberal theorists seem determined to leave as little as possible for political processes to decide. The major constitutional and distributive principles are to be settled by liberal political theory (and in some cases the implementation is to be entrusted almost wholly to the judiciary, who are considered more trustworthy about such matters than either politicians or the populace at large), with politicians left to scrap over less important issues. In any context this does not look too convincing as a theorizing of *politics*, but in the situation of contemporary Iraq, it seems bizarre or even potentially sinister. Potentially sinister because it is all too easy to see how it could be exploited to support some form of neo-colonial administration. If the political fundamentals cannot be entrusted to the Iraqi people themselves or their representatives, because they cannot be relied on to uphold the terms of a suitably liberal constitution, then perhaps the occupying powers or some other external body (the United Nations perhaps) would have to act as the ultimate repository of political authority. We do not suggest that this is something that any contemporary liberal political theorist would explicitly advocate;[41] but it does show that, if one did seek to 'apply' it to the political reconstruction of Iraq, liberal theory might have some unanticipated, and potentially undemocratic, consequences.

Conclusion

If what we have argued is broadly correct, does this mean that political theory can contribute nothing to thinking about the problems of political reconstruction in Iraq? No: what we have argued is that it is at best unhelpful and at worst positively dangerous to look to the kind of normative liberal theorizing examined earlier for moral instruction about what should be done in Iraq, or even for authoritative guidance about what the aims of political reconstruction should be. However, this does not mean that political theory cannot contribute to an *understanding* of some of the problems of political reconstruction. It can shed light, for example, on the complexities of political values and the relations between them; on how conceiving of the problems in one way rather than another may foreclose certain political possibilities that might otherwise be available, or alternatively open up some that would be obscured; on the validity and implications of specific chains of reasoning; and on the conceptual presuppositions and empirical assumptions that underlie various ways of thinking about political questions. It could also offer fresh illumination if political theory became less obsessed by highly idealized theories of justice, and recovered an interest in political judgement, and in political virtues such as prudence, negotiation and compromise. These are largely effaced by the exclusive focus within normative liberal theory on abstract moral principles, and an excessive concern for technical sophistication at the cost of sensitivity to the contingency of political life.

More prosaically, political theorists could devote a good deal more attention to trying to understand Islamic political ideas and practices, and to seeking to engage with them. Such an engagement, if it is genuine, must include at least the possibility that we might have something to learn, and not be treated simply as an opportunity for 'us' to lecture 'them', for instance, on the superiority of liberalism. This kind of engagement is far from easy, and there is certainly no reason at all to think that it must end with a comfortable consensus. Indeed, there are many good reasons for thinking that it will not, but even some improvement in mutual understanding would represent modest enlightenment, and might facilitate more informed and perceptive political interventions, if nothing else.[42] For those who cling to the idea that political theory should be providing instruction in virtue for politicians, the modern analogue of Renaissance handbooks for princes, this will not seem much. But if our argument is sound, however sympathetic one might be to the particular ideals that liberal political theorists seek to defend, this kind of political theory is ill-suited to such ends.

Marx famously wrote in his eleventh thesis on Feuerbach that 'philosophers have only *interpreted* the world in various ways; the point is, to *change* it'.[43] We do not for a moment deny the importance or the desirability of social and political change, but the pursuit of such change inspired by little more than moralism, especially a moralism that represents the local as the universal, is usually a recipe for disaster. Interpretation, or understanding, is not therefore a form of intellectual self-indulgence, utterly irrelevant to 'the real world', but one precondition of informed political action. We suggest that political theorists are likely to have most to contribute when they see the pursuit of understanding as the specific contribution that they can make, rather than seeking to usurp the role of political deliberation and judgement by effectively conceiving of themselves as the legislators for humankind. And if this conclusion seems to be much more about political theory than the problems of political reconstruction in Iraq, it still says something important, if only of a rather general nature, about how *not* to think about those problems.[44]

Notes and references

1   See in particular the chapter by Gareth Stansfield.

2   It is interesting to note the influence on the Bush administration of a number of political advisers taught by students of the late Leo Strauss – the so-called 'Leo-cons'. Strauss was the dominant figure in political theory in the United States in the middle decades of the twentieth century. Although his distinctive approach to political theory means that he does not belong among the theorists with whose work we are here concerned, the strongly conservative character of his influence is perhaps a salutary warning to those who think that an education in political theory will necessarily make for a more liberal policy.

3   K. Nwazota, 'Reconstruction Taskforce Meets in Iraq', posted 04.15.03 on the Internet, *News Hour Extra*. Online. Available HTTP: <http://www.pbs.org/newshour/extra/features/jan-june03/ur_4–15.html> (accessed 10 January 2004).

4   B. Barry, *Culture and Equality*, Cambridge: Polity Press, 2001, p. 33.

5   Scanlon, quoted in B. Barry, *Justice as Impartiality*, Oxford: Oxford University Press, 1995, p. 67.

6   B. Barry, *Justice as Impartiality*, Oxford: Oxford University Press, 1995, p.164.

7   J. Horton, 'The Good, the Bad, and the Impartial', *Utilitas*, 8, 1996, p. 317.

8   This may be an appropriate place to respond briefly to the charge that to suggest that the Iraqi people might not want liberal democracy is patronizing or even racist. On the contrary, our view is that it is presumptuous to claim that everybody *must* want the same form of government, especially if it is that which happens to be prevalent at the present time in the societies of those, like Tony Blair or Condoleezza Rice, who make this charge.

9   We refer to 'reasonably determinate substantive political principles' because such principles need to have sufficient content to be action guiding. A similar argument to this against Barry is set out in more detail in relation to Rawls in J. Horton, 'Rawls, Public Reason and the Limits of Liberal Justification', *Contemporary Political Theory*, 2, 2003.

10   B. Barry, *Justice as Impartiality*, Oxford: Oxford University Press, 1995, p. 164.

11   B. Barry, *Culture and Equality*, Cambridge: Polity Press, 2001.

12   One important aspect of this issue is discussed in J. Horton, 'Rawls, Public Reason and the Limits of Liberal Justification', *Contemporary Political Theory*, 2, 2003, pp. 7–9.

13   J. Rawls, *The Law of Peoples*, Cambridge, MA: Harvard University Press, 1999, p. 81.

14   J. Rawls, *The Law of Peoples*, Cambridge, MA: Harvard University Press, 1999, p. 3.

15   J. Rawls, *The Law of Peoples*, Cambridge, MA: Harvard University Press, 1999, p. 67.

16   J. Rawls, *The Law of Peoples*, Cambridge, MA: Harvard University Press, 1999, p. 75.

17   One might ask, however, whether a society that as a matter of policy permanently excludes part of its citizenry from holding the higher political offices on grounds of religious belief could truly be said to 'honour and respect human rights'. See, J. Rawls, *The Law of Peoples*, Cambridge, MA: Harvard University Press, 1999, p. 66.

18   J. Rawls, *The Law of Peoples*, Cambridge, MA: Harvard University Press, 1999, p. 78.

19   J. Rawls, *The Law of Peoples*, Cambridge, MA: Harvard University Press, 1999, p. 78.

20   As should be clear, neither here nor elsewhere is the term 'realism' being used in the technical sense in which it is employed in international relations theory. In *Justice as Fairness: A Restatement*, Rawls describes his political philosophy as 'realistically utopian'. He then goes on to add: 'Of course, there is a question about how the limits of the practicable are discerned and what the conditions of our social world in fact are; the

problem is that the limits of the possible are not given by the actual, for we can to a greater or lesser extent change political and social institutions, and much else. However, I shall not pursue this deep question here.' Or, it might be added, anywhere else. But, for all that, Rawls's theory necessarily presumes an answer to this question. See, J. Rawls, *Justice as Fairness: A Restatement*, Cambridge, MA: Harvard University Press, 2001, pp. 4–5.

21 R. M. Hare, 'Rawls' Theory of Justice', in N. Daniels (ed.), *Reading Rawls: Critical Studies of 'A Theory of Justice'*, Oxford: Basil Blackwell, 1975, p. 82.

22 J. Rawls, *Justice as Fairness: A Restatement*, Cambridge, MA: Harvard University Press, 2001, pp. 194–5.

23 W. Kymlicka, 'Western Political Theory and Ethnic Relations in Eastern Europe' and 'Reply and Conclusion', in W. Kymlicka and M. Opalski (eds), *Can Liberal Pluralism be Exported? Western Political Theory and Ethnic Relations in Eastern Europe*, Oxford: Oxford University Press, 2001, p. 1.

24 W. Kymlicka, 'Western Political Theory and Ethnic Relations in Eastern Europe' and 'Reply and Conclusion', in W. Kymlicka and M. Opalski (eds), *Can Liberal Pluralism be Exported? Western Political Theory and Ethnic Relations in Eastern Europe*, Oxford: Oxford University Press, 2001, p. 1.

25 W. Kymlicka, 'Western Political Theory and Ethnic Relations in Eastern Europe' and 'Reply and Conclusion', in W. Kymlicka and M. Opalski (eds), *Can Liberal Pluralism be Exported? Western Political Theory and Ethnic Relations in Eastern Europe*, Oxford: Oxford University Press, 2001, p. 16.

26 W. Kymlicka, 'Western Political Theory and Ethnic Relations in Eastern Europe', in W. Kymlicka and M. Opalski (eds), *Can Liberal Pluralism be Exported? Western Political Theory and Ethnic Relations in Eastern Europe*, Oxford: Oxford University Press, 2001, p. 22.

27 It is because of the role of nation building in creating and maintaining a single *political* identity that it is mistaken to say of minority nationalisms and majority nation building that 'the two seem on a par, morally speaking'. See W. Kymlicka, 'Western Political Theory and Ethnic Relations in Eastern Europe', in W. Kymlicka and M. Opalski (eds), *Can Liberal Pluralism be Exported? Western Political Theory and Ethnic Relations in Eastern Europe*, Oxford: Oxford University Press, 2001, p. 27. For a discussion of further problems in Kymlicka's treatment of nation building, as well as a defence of orthodox liberalism, see C. Chambers, 'Nation-building, Neutrality and Ethno-cultural Justice', *Ethnicities*, 3, 2003.

28 W. Kymlicka, 'Western Political Theory and Ethnic Relations in Eastern Europe', in W. Kymlicka and M. Opalski (eds), *Can Liberal Pluralism be Exported? Western Political Theory and Ethnic Relations in Eastern Europe*, Oxford: Oxford University Press, 2001, p. 54.

29 W. Kymlicka, 'Western Political Theory and Ethnic Relations in Eastern Europe', in W. Kymlicka and M. Opalski (eds), *Can Liberal Pluralism be Exported? Western Political Theory and Ethnic Relations in Eastern Europe*, Oxford: Oxford University Press, 2001, p. 55–6.

30 W. Kymlicka, *Multicultural Citizenship*, Oxford: Oxford University Press, 1995, pp. 83–93.

31 W. Kymlicka, *Multicultural Citizenship*, Oxford: Oxford University Press, 1995, pp. 158 and 163.

32 W. Kymlicka, *Multicultural Citizenship*, Oxford: Oxford University Press, 1995, p. 94.

33 W. Kymlicka, *Multicultural Citizenship*, Oxford: Oxford University Press, 1995, pp. 94–5.

34 W. Kymlicka, *Multicultural Citizenship*, Oxford: Oxford University Press, 1995, p. 164.

35 G. Gaus, *Justificatory Liberalism: An Essay on Epistemology and Political Theory*, Oxford: Oxford University Press, 1996.

36 B. Barry, *Theories of Justice*, London: Harvester-Wheatsheaf, 1989, pp. 274–5.

37 Arguably, this limitation was always present in the method of 'reflective equilibrium', as set out in *A Theory of Justice*, although the picture there was muddied by such claims about the original position as 'to see ourselves from the perspective of this position is to see it *sub specie aeternitatis*: it is to regard the human situation not only from all social but also from all temporal points of view'. See J. Rawls, *A Theory of Justice*, Oxford: Oxford University Press, 1971, p. 587.

38 We are not suggesting that it is impossible or necessarily unilluminating sometimes to think about political values independently of practical considerations, but we are claiming that it is a fundamentally flawed way of constructing a *normative political theory* that is supposed to have practical relevance.

39 J. Rawls, *Political Liberalism*, New York: Columbia University Press, 1993, p. 285.

40 G. Newey, *After Politics: The Rejection of Politics in Contemporary Liberal Philosophy*, Basingstoke: Palgrave, 2001, p. 7.

41 Although J. S. Mill defended the idea of an educative empire in broadly similar terms, famously arguing that 'despotism is a legitimate mode of government in dealing with barbarians, provided the end be their improvement and the means justified by actually effecting that end'. See J. S. Mill, *On Liberty*, edited and introduced by G. Himmelfarb, Harmondsworth: Penguin Books, 1974, p. 69. Mill is, perhaps, more consistent in pursuing the implications of his liberal principles than are contemporary liberals who, for understandable reasons, are reluctant to follow him along this path.

42 For some interesting, if in our view rather over-optimistic, reflections on what he calls 'dialogue among civilizations' see F. Dallmayr, *Dialogue among Civilizations: Some Exemplary Voices*, New York: Palgrave Macmillan, 2002.

43 K. Marx, 'Theses on Feuerbach', in L. Easton and K Guddat (eds), *Writings of the young Marx on Philosophy and Society*, New York: Anchor Books, 1967, p. 402.

44 We are grateful to Margaret Canovan, Alex Danchev, Adrian Holmes, John MacMillan and Hidemi Suganami for helpful comments on an earlier draft of this chapter.

12 Afghanistan and Iraq

Failed states, or democracy on hold?

Iftikhar H. Malik

> Because democracy is noble, it is always endangered. Nobility, indeed, is always in danger. Democracy is perishable.[1]

The Anglo-American attack on Afghanistan followed by a similar but more comprehensive and controversial invasion of Iraq may have come about for a variety of reasons, but they nevertheless highlight some unique and variable features of global politics since the 1990s when the erstwhile global bipolarity gave way to a US-led unipolar world. The dissolution of the Soviet bloc may have temporarily signalled 'the end of history' and an ebullient optimism for global peace, democracy and cooperation but the outburst of ethno-regional conflicts and increasing differences between the rich and poor presented a new spectre of instability. The UN, NATO and the EU found themselves confronted with the civil wars of fragmenting 'imperial' states such as Yugoslavia. The Iraqi invasion of Kuwait after an extended and equally taxing Iraq–Iran War, the harrowing Balkan imbroglio, increased tensions in a *de facto* nuclearized subcontinent, volatile civil war in Afghanistan, and ethnic cleansing in Rwanda deflated the growing tide of optimism, engendered by the overthrow of Apartheid and a thaw in Israeli–Arab tensions. The eventual consolidation of the Taliban by co-opting most of the former Mujahideen, a defiant Saddam Hussein and an assertive trans-regional Islamic activism as embodied by groups such as Al-Qaeda seeking sustenance from historic and contemporary grudges against the United States, were initially perceived as mere localist irritants. But such a low-priority image was soon dramatically jolted through the terrorist attacks on New York and Washington in September 2001. The newly established Bush administration, still searching for viable policy measures amidst the signs of neo-isolationism and unilateralism on environmental and other global commitments, took upon itself the responsibility of seeking revenge as well as the 'reordering' of a turbulent world. To many observers, Bush was catapulted into a global role without any personal credentials in that domain nor was he clear on the direction in which he planned to lead the fuming American juggernaut. However, to his supporters, the Republican president was candid, decisive and confident.[2]

The predominant neo-conservative elements within the administration pursued their own plans for a new US-led order especially in the Muslim regions in Asia.[3] A hurt United States with an injured pride and deprived of a rival except, at a stretch, some disgruntled Muslim militants busied itself in building up global alliances for a multi-faceted campaign. However, it is a different matter that, in the process, Washington lost much of global support owing to the overzealous and unilateral nature of its policies. In its so-called retaliatory ventures in West Asia, Tony Blair's support for President Bush remained persistent despite the unprecedented anti-war sentiment and formidable peace movement.[4] The invasions of Afghanistan and Iraq, respectively, happened despite a powerful and vocal global peace movement and seemed to substantiate the Huntingtonian clash of civilizations. Already in the Occupied Territories, Ariel Sharon's inflammatory visit to the Temple Mount on 28 September 2000 had decimated the Oslo Peace Accords, ushering in a bloody new phase of Israeli–Palestinian strife. Concurrently, Moscow, Delhi, Tel Aviv, the Philippines and several other governments across the globe enjoyed Washington's approval in the suppression of the dissenting voices of the Chechens, Kashmiris, Palestinians and the Moros. Chechnya, Kashmir and Kurdistan bore the brunt of the state-led brutalization whereas the diasporic Muslim communities and other intending immigrants and asylum seekers came under a negative spotlight. The North Atlantic region as well as Australia promptly raised barriers against possible refugees, especially from West Asia. Within this global milieu, the mild rebuttals of the cultural clash both by the Western governments and moderate Muslim leaders failed to soothe highly charged sentiments and instead further inflamed a pervasive Muslim anger.

That American military power, duly helped by Britain, demolished the Taliban and the Baathist regime in Iraq, and sought to increase the pressure on Iran and Syria, further exacerbated anti-Americanism across the globe.[5] Anti-Americanism, political Islam and the weakening of the post-colonial state-based order – the three contemporary realities of an uneven world polity – have certainly acquired a new impetus, as has the debate on democracy. This chapter, after a brief overview of the changing ideological climate, identifies the convergence of internal and external forces to explain the decline of states such as Afghanistan and Iraq. It also considers the inadequacies of Western strategies and of nation-building, peace and democracy in these countries.

Ideological shifts: neo-conservatism, Zionism and unilateralism

Contrasted with a rapid regionalization in the North Atlantic regions and South East Asia, the vast Afro-Asian territories have been experiencing political and state fragmentation due to internal schisms exacerbated by external interventions. The internal combustion accrues out of conflicting ethnic and ideological forces whereas border conflicts or invasions provide the external shocks. Theoretically, these two variant trends in the international politics of the region can be interpreted with reference to economic, political and ideological factors.[6] In the post-colonial world, the economic stratification, contested nationhood, elitist control of the state, coupled with a Western hegemonic political–economic dominance, all contribute to the imbalances following the Second World War.[7]

In the Muslim world, critics of US policies towards the Middle East feel that Washington is being dangerously manipulated by a strong pro-Israeli lobby to the detriment of its interests and relationship with the 1.3 billion Muslims across the world. Though Israel was delivered largely through Anglo-American assistance in 1948, Britain's weakening imperial stature and its replacement by the United States coincided with the latter's emergence as the leader and protector of the Western bloc. Concurrently, Zionist lobbying in the United States, cashing in on the traditional lack of proper information on the Muslim affair and benefiting from a pervasive orientalist view of Islam, duly helped by Western guilt over the Holocaust, gathered a new momentum. The US–Israeli bilateralism at the expense of the Arabs was strengthened during the Kennedy era and further during the 1967 Arab–Israeli conflict when President Johnson, faced with travails in Vietnam, chose to ignore the Israeli nuclear programme at Dimona and offered generous assistance to Tel Aviv. Israeli lobbying was helped by an environment in which Arab movements of the period were advocating nationalist and socialist approaches to their political predicaments. Accordingly, Islam was perceived as an ideology of bloodshed with its powerful trajectory of jihad. The Muslim hordes had to be contained by force, since they were inherently anti-democratic and anti-Western. The patronage of corrupt monarchs and khaki dictators facilitated the suppression of the democratic aspirations of the Muslim masses. Consequently, US tax payers have ended up generously financing Israel's steady expansion and occupation at the expense of the Palestinians and the Muslim masses. A new phase of the bilateral US–Israeli relationship has emerged in the post-9/11 period as Sharon's Likud Party oversaw the expansion of settlements in Palestinian lands[8] and an angry United States, helped by Britain, undertook direct and extensive military campaigns against Afghanistan and Iraq simultaneously with pressure on Pakistan, Iran and Syria. Sharon, in this period, successfully 'dissolved the Jewish and the Palestinian public's belief in the possibility of achieving a genuine peaceful solution and any mutual trust'.[9] Even before the 'road map for peace' was announced serious doubts about Israel's real intentions, given its past record and flouting of several UN resolutions, did not bode well.

The growing pressure from the Muslim and Arab world for Palestinian self-determination and a right of return to their own land spawned anti-American and anti-Israeli sentiments where the United States was seen to be the main supporter of an aggressive Israel over and above the legitimate aspirations of the Palestinians. Such Muslim anger was also directed against surrogate Muslim regimes kowtowing to American dictates on the Middle East. Certainly, 9/11 happened at a time when the neo-conservative hold on the US political, military, economic and other vital institutions was already strong. That many neo-conservatives are Zionists and for whom the Muslim world simply means chaos, disorder and violence, leads them to argue that these barren lands have to be fertilized by a Washington-ordained democratization. Islam is viewed by these neo-conservatives as a medieval and non-reformed repressive ideology whose proponents—both in the government and in the opposition—pose the most serious of threats to Western ideals, basically defined as superior Judaic–Christian values. Imam Khomeini, Osama bin Laden, Saddam Hussein, Yassir Arafat or turbaned Taliban look-alikes are the prototype Muslim terrorists who have to be struck down before they can strike civilizational bastions. The diehard Conservatives such as Pat Buchanan have been censuring the United States and the West for lacking vigilance on the issues of immigration, multiculturalism and depopulation. Such scaremongers keep reminding their Western readers of an impending demographic threat from the Muslim world that may eventually overrun Western civilization. To them, time is on the side of 'the Islamic threat' as the Muslim terrorists wait to strike.[10]

The Pentagon under Donald Rumsfeld had become a most powerful centre for pro-Israel and anti-Muslim strategists, who had been trying to capture the key positions for a long time. Their opposition to Bill Clinton also accrued from an ideological divide within the United States with neo-conservatives banded together to see it rule supreme over the 'troubled lands'.[11] Led by the Deputy Secretary of Defense, Paul Wolfowitz, and advised by Richard Perle, the Pentagon gathered like-minded policy-makers to steer US foreign and defence policies in a specific though no less risky direction. Its cornerstone lay in defending Israel and establishing unchallenged US primacy over the vital Muslim regions, disregarding the UN and a critical global public opinion. The Pentagon's Office of Special Plans (OSP) envisaged and implemented schemes for an active US military involvement in changing the West Asian political–strategic contours. Abram Schulsky, Douglas Feith and Elliot Abrams—known for their unequivocal Zionist views—led the OSP at a time when the US Department of Defense has exerted greater influence than the traditionally more cautious State Department in the projection of the neo-conservative agenda. In the powerful troika of Colin Powell, Donald Rumsfeld and Condoleeza Rice, Powell remained the weakest link, though Bush's apologists would like the world to believe that the president is a leader in his own right. Wolfowitz and Perle do not mince words when it comes to a *new* Middle East and in Rumsfeld they have found an ambitious head who, for a long time, had sought implementation of such a forward policy. All of them receive further patronage and official protection from Dick Cheney, the Vice-President. Other than Cheney and Rumsfeld the rest of the leading policy-makers in the Pentagon are staunchly pro-Israel, duly supported by media pundits like William Kristol and Robert Kagan, and through organs such as *The Weekly Standard*, or think tanks including the Project for New American Century, the Hudson Institute and the Center for Middle East Policy. The last is the brainchild of the American–Israeli Public Affairs Committee (AIPAC), one of the most influential and vociferous pro-Israel pressure groups in the United States. Most of these facts are unknown to ordinary Americans and the rest of the world,[12] who are usually warned of a looming threat to US national security from Al-Qaeda or countries such as Iraq, Iran and Syria. Such tainted views when publicized through powerful, obliging media channels like Fox and CNN register ready approval, especially after 9/11. The unsuspecting Americans are vulnerable to specific lobbies and partisan policies emanating from Washington. A global denunciation of Islam, combined with the nationalist and xenophobic elements, duly helps Zionist assaults on Arabs/Muslims and underwrites the support for neo-conservatives in the most powerful country in the world. Most ordinary Americans have very limited access to analytical and unbiased information as the decisions are made by a small power elite representing specific interest groups. Thus, whereas the specific lobbies through their negative agenda preclude a wider participation in decision-making processes within their own countries, it may be equally right to suggest that their discretionary policies under the Bush Doctrine may equally hinder a much publicized democratization of West Asia.

Similarly, in Britain some parliamentarians have been wary of the Zionist influence over the British decision-making processes exerted through powerful politicians, business and the media.[13] The anti-Muslim sentiments since the Rushdie affair and the individual acts of terror since 9/11 have helped such powerful groups to drum up specific attitudes and discriminatory policies. The restrictions on Muslim organizations, internment of several individuals and a constant media trial of Muslim activists are a visible reality in Western Europe. The rolling down of civil liberties and inhuman treatment of the Muslim detainees at Guantanamo Bay and Abu Ghraib Jail, and the trials, fingerprinting and mass deportations across the camps and prisons in the North Atlantic regions, have all been unnerving the democratic forces in these countries. The convergence among the racist outfits refurbishes Islamophobia which eventually helps all those states battling Muslim political defiance in Palestine, Kashmir, Chechnya or elsewhere. The invasions of Afghanistan and Iraq have left a lasting bitter taste everywhere, and not just in West Asia.

Political Islam and the West

The debate on political Islam and its relationship with the West has assumed vital importance. While some may see Islam and the West as two eternally warring communities or civilizations, others may see commonalties in their religio-historical heritage and focus on the wider economic and political disempowerment of the Muslim world—often in collaboration with the Western powers. To Eurocentric scholars such as Bernard Lewis,[14] Islam may have been stuck in a time warp waiting for its long overdue renaissance and reformation, while to others Islam remains the *enemy* per se,[15] despite the fact that *fundamentalism* as a concept originated in the United States almost a century ago and in its current manifestations, including among Muslims, it is mainly typified by purist, strict and literalist interpretations of religious scriptures. Islamic fundamentalism is theological as long as it is confined to the literal expression and practices of the Quran and the Prophetic traditions, but when religion and classical history become the utopian ideal to be implemented at a collective public level, then theology turns into something political—political Islam or Islamism. Though

recourse to political Islam has been a persistent Muslim desire since the overthrow of the early Pious Caliphate in 662 AD, its numerous doctrinal and
territorial expressions are more recent. The current phase of political Islam has
coincided with its encounters with a Europe-led modernity. The earlier Muslim
interaction with the *West* during the Crusades or through Muslim Spain or
subsequently the Ottoman Caliphate was largely based on equality and without
any permeating rancour.[16] However, the colonial dominance of the Muslim
regions by a powerful Western Europe in the post-Napoleonic era is principally
as a resurgent Christendom, developing an intricate, uneven relationship characterized by imperial, political, racial, economic and cultural inequalities. While
Muslim revivalists fought or resisted Western hegemony, some within the new
elites tried to create a synthesis between the Islamic and modernist ethos. Thus
Muslim responses to a complex modernity, itself ridden with several positive and
negative features, further broadened the ideological divide between these two
Muslims groups. The continued challenge of political–economic disempowerment against the backdrop of a dominant West and a greater sense of historical
and cultural loss rekindled the contest between modernists and traditionalists.
Traditionalists, by conviction, felt that the post-independence modernists were
not only corrupt and inefficient but also surrogates for a partisan, immoral and
exploitative West. The attitudes towards the West varied between adulation of its
economic and industrial power to disapproval of its consumerism, disintegration
of family structures and general secularity. In this contest the new elites looked to
London, Paris, Washington, who, just like the former Soviet regime, obliged
through cultivating non-representative regimes that betrayed popular claims and
human rights.

After tasting the systemic ideologies of Arab nationalism, Islamic socialism,
quasi-democracies and khaki dictatorships, the Muslim world began to witness a
resurgence of politico-religious forces, proffering themselves as mouthpieces of
the oppressed. These movements played on hurt pride, romanticization of a
glorious past—long gone but still recoverable—the corruption of ruling elites
and a sustained attack on Western-led modernity. Its emotional and moral
appeal, largely spread through *madrassa* networks, is grounded in an authenticity
due to its local roots. It feeds on the poverty and economic disempowerment of
the Muslim masses. Hence, this new type of political Islam, unlike the official
Islam of the Saudis or other non-representative regimes, is a mass agitation from
below that seeks to redress socio-economic underdevelopment and
political–psychological grudges of the masses across the continents. It equally
contests the official exploitation of Islam and, as seen in several cases varying
from revolutionary Iran to Jamaat-i-Islami of Pakistan or the FIS in Algeria and
Nadwah in Indonesia, uses modernist means and promises egalitarianism to its
adherents. In all its forms and embodiments, it lacks a strong, unifying and trans-
regional leadership or a programmatic alternative, though its proponents
espouse a greater zeal for *Ummah*—the trans-regional Muslim community over
and above class, colour and ethno-national divisions. In other words, despite an
inherent authoritarianism, it promises equality, accountability and representa-

tion—the basic elements of any democratic order. It appeals to the ballot but is also prepared to use arms. In many cases, while posing as anti-hegemonic it itself develops repressive characteristics.

The historical and political bases of political Islam and relations with the West

The contemporary spectre of this political activism, spearheaded by the bearded and turbaned groups and following the two earlier phases of the colonial and post-independence phases, is characterized by a greater self-assertiveness and an all-out strategy to acquire power, no matter through bullet or ballot. This kind of political Islam promises a return to the lost glory, stipulates holistic answers to social–economic stratification, and has a support base comprising mostly the huge underclass of the underprivileged whose unfulfilled basic needs and desires converge with a yearning for a collective revival. Thus, Islam is the healer, panacea and retort to an arrogant West and its partisan surrogates across the Muslim world. This form of political Islam is based on simplicity, shared brotherhood, a devotion to austere lifestyles and is imbued with a Caliphal vision of trans-regional *Ummah*. It combines scripturalist and syncretic visions of the literalists and *sufis*. It is vehemently anti-colonial, anti-elitist and displays an impressive mix of class and creed. Thus, without being trans-regional, it is trans-territorial as it promises a Muslim globalism among the brothers-in-faith.[17] To its proponents, it is a redeemer; to its detractors it is self-immolation; and to superficial observers it is the new enemy or sheer terrorism.[18] Averse to the Huntingtonian frame whereby political Islam is waging a clash of civilizations, it is in fact mainly arrayed against its own ruling hierarchies, though it deeply resents their external backers. Hypothetically, if one removes the fulcrum of ideology from this activism, it is simply a class conflict.

In the elections of 2002 in Pakistan, the religio-political parties captured overwhelming majorities in the two border provinces of the frontier and Balochistan and gained a sizeable presence in the federal Parliament. More than the mainstream politicians, it is these parties which are confronting Pakistan's General Musharraf on domestic and foreign issues. Their ascendance, despite being clipped by his unilateral Legal Framework Order (LFO), was no less astounding to those analysts who, while aware of their street power, simply underrated their electoral potentials. An entire generation of Pakistani political observers, who had expected a peripheral performance by these elements, is now interpreting their salience as just a 'one-off'. This misperception is no different from that of their Indian counterparts who, in the early 1990s, considered the rise of the Bharatiya Janata Party (BJP), espousing a uniformist Hinduized India, and the Ayodhya Mosque/Temple issue merely an aberration with polity soon settling back to its Nehruvian secular moorings.[19] One may differ with the dictum of such religio-political parties, but to write them off merely as the beneficiaries of anti-Americanism or anti-modernity is fallacious. Religion, as witnessed in the former Eastern Europe, the United States, Israel, North Africa, Iran,

Afghanistan, Turkey and now Iraq has refused to coexist as nationalism's junior partner; it is now in the driving seat. The American neo-conservatives, Likud Zionists, BJP's Kar Sevaks and Jihadis are all imbued with a reinvigorated energy and expect to fill the growing authority vacuum in their respective societies, where 'liberals' and modernists are deemed incorrigibly corrupt and hopelessly incompetent.

The rise of religio-political constellations is a global phenomenon and not solely confined to the Muslim world, as the neo-orientalists may like to suggest. Of course, the world of Islam has its enduring politico-economic problems besides the hackneyed views of a static *Sharia* (religious canon), formulated many centuries ago and several after the Prophet, but Islam is certainly the rallying cry for both societal and statist forces. The recourse to Islam—away from the East or West—is as much a retort to external high-handedness as it is an abysmal despondency. For instance, the dogmatic adherence to a rather stultified Kemalism in Turkey maintained by an overpowering military synchronized with a greater sense of humiliation felt by all the Turks (and Kurds!) from scornful European pundits. Half of Cyprus and the former East European countries have all joined the EU whereas Turkey, one of the largest contributors to NATO, stays endlessly sidelined. 'Turkey's values are different from ours', many Europeans including the former French President Valery Giscard d'Estaing have unhesitatingly propounded. Like the Pakistani Supreme Court, the Turkish senior judges, a few years back, outlawed the Islamicist Rifaah Party under the pretext of a sacrosanct Kemalism, which has now rebounded with more public support under a different name. In 2002, the Turks balloted these religio-political elements into power, as the latter espoused a long overdue ideological consensus and autonomous foreign policies and have valiantly resisted US temptations and coercion over Iraq—not a minor decision given the bilateral relationship.

In its single-minded pursuit to invade Iraq without any legal or moral justification, the Anglo-American leadership, by default and also to their deep consternation, has offered the religio-political elements a comeback. If Washington and London fail to find an accommodation with the Shia majority and continue to eliminate Sunni elements in the central and northern regions, Iraq may become another Algeria where the military and France collaborated to thwart the elected religio-political parties. More than 100,000 dead and the country in shambles for an entire decade were the harrowing consequences of resisting the people's verdict. Instead of welcoming an electoral strategy adopted by such forces, their marginalization and suppression only militarizes them further.[20] These are the populist forces of have-nots—a massive underclass of highly politicized and enraged people—and the best way to handle them is through a constructive engagement. Of course, in the Euro-American regions the neo-conservatives are by no means poor, yet they reflect the unfulfilled desires of marginalized clusters.

In the decades of optimism and polarized realism following the Second World War, religion was considered to be less of a unifying force and more of a nuisance in nation-building. Nationalism, despite its racist and fascist undertones in Europe, was perceived by scholars such as Eli Kedourie and Hans Kohn to be a liberationist ideology with a secular elite homogenizing the emerging post-colonial states. 'Modernization', not just to these Jewish liberals but also to sociologists such as Ernest Gellner, Karl Deutsch and Benedict Anderson, after all, was a mundane project where its Western prototypes could hold truth for all.[21] Jinnah, Nehru, Kenyatta, Fanon, Mao, Gandhi, Sukarno and Nkrumah were all modernizing nationalists in their own ways though this generation was soon to give way—in several cases—to the (frequently foreign trained) 'men on horseback,' being welcomed as the new, post-colonial modernizers. Simultaneously, the embryonic mediatory discourse on Islam and modernity as spearheaded by 'moderate' scholar–activists—including Al-Afghani, Abduh, Syed Ahmed, Muhammad Iqbal, Maulana Azad, Fazlur Rahman and Allama Shariati—was marginalized. Instead of activists and intellectuals interfacing across diverse traditions, Muslims were bequeathed to the simplistic and autocratic whims of uniformed harbingers of modernization and development. The role of colonial intermediary was now performed by these khaki bureaucrats, submissive to their Western patrons yet dismissive of the potential of their own peoples.

However, by the 1980s and especially after the dissolution of the Cold War, these modernizers were found seriously lacking in representative and managerial credentials. Despite their serious shortcomings, the Western powers, for their own partisan interests, had steadily used these generals as surrogates—Ayub, Yahya, Pinochet, Numeiri, Saddam, Zia, Suharto, Barre, Ershad, and the list goes on. But the current political mantra of civil society, empowerment and the pre-eminence of democratic universalism further exposes the inherent weakness and inadequacy of these leaders who remain in power due largely to external backing and internal divisions. In some cases, such as General Musharraf of Pakistan, they are expeditiously needed to fight the 'turbaned and bearded hordes', no matter at what cost to the democratic prerogatives in that country.

While the post-colonial world has reasons to be cynical at being used as the guinea pig for all the run-away ideologies and neo-colonial façades, it is equally bewildered at the pre-eminence of 'traditional' conglomerates. In the case of political Islam, while several scholars prefer the model of a *Muslim* state (espousing redefined secular characteristics), Islamicists such as the Ikhawan, Jamaat, Jamiats, Nadwas, the Khomeinities and other Salafiaya groups fervently aspire towards a theocratic *Islamic* state. This kind of intellectual debate urgently needs to find some consensus as otherwise Muslim peoples, while getting out of a simmering pan, may simply fall into a raging fire. Replacing one kind of unilateral oppression with another type of dictatorship, however high-minded it may be, is totally unacceptable. These differing intellectual groups need to focus on the areas of agreement as well as divergences, but in a tolerant and civic manner without rancour and *fatwas*. The new politics of political Islam must offer something tangible and all encompassing rather than add to anarchy and violence. A simplistic view of the Muslim past cannot serve this purpose and is not the basis for a healthy way forward.

Concurrently, the relegation of Islam to a mere dogma is a preoccupation of both Muslims and non-Muslims alike that has led to its reformist capacities and egalitarian character being side-tracked by dismissive obscurants as well as abrasive modernists. Both of these fell into the trap of orientalists, who saw the *East* as mainly inhabited by emotional and half-cultured mobs, whose Westernization was a White Man's burden. The leading contemporary proponent of such a premise is Professor Bernard Lewis at Princeton, to whose Eurocentric outlook Islam remains lost in a medieval time warp earnestly awaiting a renaissance. To Lewis, Islam's regeneration has to come from the West; otherwise its centuries-old crisis intermeshed with a severe inferiority complex remains unbridgeable and prone to terrorist outbursts.[22] This hypothesis has been greatly energized in the West after 9/11, even if scholars such as Edward Said, Albert Hourani, Fred Halliday, John Esposito and Karen Armstrong have been wary of it. While one may find many problems with neo-orientalists such as Lewis, Daniel Pipes, Fouad Ajami, Frank Graham, Pat Roberston, Ann Coulter, Silvio Berlusconi and Oriana Fallaci, it is nevertheless fair to suggest that political Islam has yet to mature into a workable and just order. So far, as forcefully posited by Professor Khalid B. Sayeed, the models of political Islam offered from Saudi Arabia to Ziaist Pakistan, Khomeinite Iran to the Talibanized Afghanistan, have lacked an accommodation with pluralism, a universal empowerment, an egalitarian economic order and a dynamic self-confidence.[23] In all the above cases, it has been a familiar story of repression, unilateralism and intolerance. Millions were mobilized in the name of Islam, *Sharia* and *Nizam-i-Mustafwi* (Prophet Muhammad's system), soon to fall victim to unnecessary and unworthy causes. Muslim masses are not only the victims of violence from the 'outside', but also the sufferers from within. The pervasive Muslim disempowerment is mainly owed to their own leaders, and likewise their internal schisms are due to a suffocating clericalization of this otherwise holistic civilization.

However, this anomalous situation is not to undervalue the role of Islam as a mobilizer and anti-hegemonic force. Muslim literalists and syncretists have been vanguards in the process of Afro-Asian decolonization but the tradition of resistance and sacrifice more often falls victim to waywardness and schisms. Thus, like the modernists, if the Islamists of today are unable to improve radically the quality of life and fail to enthuse and lead their societies to a better, peaceful and prosperous future, their fate will be no different from that of the others. The proponents of political Islam need to trust, protect and celebrate their masses and direct energy and resources to the eradication of poverty and away from militarization and violence. It is only through the people's power and prosperity that political Islam may become a balm instead of a taxing and perplexing ideology. Simultaneously, there is a greater need within the West to understand the plight and pains of the Muslim world and the mundane realities of an unenviable existence. In this respect, the West would be better advised to pursue an unrestrained and honest commitment to democracy, human rights and development over temporary interests such as the extraction of natural resources and arms sales.

The West and Afghanistan and Iraq: democratization or fragmentation?

There is no denying the fact that both Afghanistan and Iraq were being ruled by authoritarian regimes, but externally driven regime change remains an extremely hazardous option. Using terrorism as an excuse and weapons of mass destruction (WMD) as a reason to invade these two countries has exposed the limitations of unilateralist military strategy. Afghanistan under Karzai remains restive and uncertain and the situation in Iraq was at the time of writing highly untenable. Moreover, it reaffirmed the view that ideological and/or geo-economic interests rather than genuine democratic imperatives had geared the Anglo-American decision to attack these two countries. The Taliban had been the beneficiaries of indirect American support as most of them were the former Pushtun Mujahideen, whereas in Iraq, Saddam Hussein had been the recipient of generous assistance in his war against Khomeini's Iran. In particular, the rekindling of the jihad ideology in Afghanistan during the Cold War greatly benefited from Western support.[24] At the same time, serious doubts remain over the extent of the American and British commitment to democracy in Afghanistan and Iraq. While Afghanistan seems to have melted into warlordism, Iraq[25] has been witnessing the upsurge of ethno-religious defiance, by both the Shia and Sunni elements, though the former seem better organized.

Yet the official Western viewpoint is that contemporary Afghanistan is stable and political developments positive. The hated Taliban are scattered and defeated, the Al-Qaeda leadership either has been eliminated or is in a disarray, women are going back to schools in Kabul, ISAF (International Stability Force for Afghanistan) is holding on to Kabul successfully and several thousand US and British troops are involved in a resolute campaign to rid the country's south east from Taliban remnants. Jack Straw's visit to Afghanistan in June 2003, on the heels of a similar high-profile visit by Hamid Karzai to the West, was to reaffirm a continued Western commitment to Afghanistan. Reiterating Tony Blair's earlier pronouncement, Straw declared that Afghanistan will not be forgotten this time around.[26] But relationships based on strategic interests do not promise much for the domestic development of societies. What happens to Pakistan's own constitutional politics, for example, its democratic and judicial institutions, is not of great relevance to the Western backers of General Musharraf.[27] At the most, outside backers may be happy to nudge nuclearized India and Pakistan to stay peaceful and predictable if not totally committed to a resolution of their fifty-six-year-old imbroglio on Kashmir.[28]

The counter view, not just shared by the wider Muslim world but also articulated by vocal pacifists and critics in the West, has been censorious of the high-handedness of the Blair/Bush duo in the post-9/11 years. To them, Afghanistan and its civilian populace have been simply scapegoated to vent Washington's frustrations; Al-Qaeda and the Taliban had been the past beneficiaries of American largesse when Zalmay Khalilzad—the Afghan–American arbiter on Afghanistan and Iraq—had hammered out agreements for the Unocal and others, until the tables were turned on the Taliban. Like the late General

Zia-ul-Haq (d. 1988), the Taliban, the Afghan Mujahideen and more recently the Iraqi Baathists all gradually outlived their usefulness but not before justifying the greatest defence hike in US history. In such a view the West has moved on from Afghanistan except for a reduced military engagement to seek out Osama bin Laden and his close allies. Afghanistan is back to its pre-federation days of tribal demarcations with warlords ruling supreme and competing with one another in corruption, guns and opium. Karzai may stay in power as long as Afghan history does not repeat itself and his luck does not run out. But, plainly, it is difficult to consider a country safe if its own president, despite a well-meaning disposition and natural affability, remains dependent upon Western troops for his own personal security.[29] It is not the re-emergence of the Taliban that poses a serious threat but the recurrence of chaos and widespread socio-economic anarchy—more like Somalia—which begs a serious, persistent and multi-dimensional global engagement in Afghanistan. The paradigm of elimination and co-option, so far pursued by Western troops with a single-minded emphasis on security by eradicating the Pushtun–Taliban elements from the complex power equation in Kabul, may not allow enough optimism.[30]

Thus, Karzai's visit in May 2003 and Jack Straw's subsequent trip to Kabul and Kandahar may have been partly to reassure new allies in the Afghan quagmire but Straw's visit—especially to a battle-prone Kandahar and a session with an uneasy warlord, Gul Agha Sherazi—can be read as principally for Afghan consumption. It is interesting to note that Straw's visit did not follow any debate on Afghanistan nor did it elicit any major news coverage within Britain itself. The reasons for this are most likely that the government's embarrassment over claims about Iraq's WMD made it nervous about drawing attention to an unstable situation in Afghanistan and the failure to capture many leading Al-Qaeda suspects, and its fragile position on a range of international and domestic issues. There was confusion over the question of Britain's place in Europe and sustained criticism of Britain's compliant relationship with Washington. Domestically, the trade unions, a major source of Labour Party funding, had characterized the Cabinet as 'criminals' who were 'putting the boot in' to workers in Britain and abroad.[31] In the same manner, the rural population in England was incensed over Labour's handling of countryside issues. The wider British populace was showing signs of fatigue and disgust over confused foreign policies, a lack of direction in Europe, intermittent news of redundancies and an increased drift over Iraq. To observers like John Pilger, Robert Fisk and George Monbiot, Afghanistan and Iraq were models of disastrous and blundering foreign policy.

Iraq presented a major dilemma to London and Washington at a time when they felt that a swift military conquest, despite adverse world opinion, would pay its own dividends. Once again, the two allies were learning to their bitter realization that demolishing weaker foes may be easy but establishing viable and acceptable political order was most certainly not. The occupying Anglo-American troops in Iraq were confronted with an increasingly coordinated guerrilla resistance combining both Sunnis and Shias with no Karzai-like character available to ensconce in a highly unstable Baghdad. Ahmed Chalabi was already too controversial and stupendously corrupt and faced with the Ayatollahs al-Sistani, al-Sadr and al-Hakim, and the defiant Sunni Baathists, he was too uninspiring and peripheral. Chalabi's Iraqi National Congress, despite support from Dick Cheney and the Pentagon, has been tainted with scandals and shadowy deals with Western intelligence agencies. It was neither fully rooted among the Iraqis back home nor widely respected by critical Iraqi intelligentsia. Chalabi's successors, under the arrangements following the departure of Paul Bremmer on 28 June 2004, amidst the trials of Saddam Hussein and other Baathists, did not reflect any stability within a deeply fractious polity.

Of course, opium, drug trafficking and a continued uncertainty in Afghanistan posed serious concerns to Western planners, but Iraq has clearly become the bigger preoccupation. A solution to the age-old Palestinian–Israeli stalemate, according to them, may help neutralize anti-Western feelings in the Arab world, and, like Somalia, Afghanistan is already being forgotten. After all, in terms of costs and benefits, the country's needs appeared bottomless! Karzai did not have to confront a similar critical intelligentsia and a powerful, anti-Western Arab nationalism but rather a diehard pessimism mingled with anti-Americanism as well as a pervasive sense of alienation among the Pushtuns and Sunnis. Under the circumstances, Afghanistan deserves urgent global, regional and domestic initiatives otherwise the prognosis remains negative. The world must fully reassure the Afghans that this time history will be different and they will not be left to their rent-seeking local chieftains or obscurantist mullahs. They need to be assured that outside forces, especially the United States and Britain, were not just in Afghanistan to add to its tally of the dead, but committed to a new, all-encompassing beginning. These powers must also fully realize that Afghanistan is not a civilizational battleground but an economic wasteland. The UN also needs to reorientate itself to the country at large rather than have officials sitting in Kabul drawing high salaries and writing lengthy reports. The lessons of the 1980s and 1990s of promoting corruption through subservient intermediaries have to be taken onboard in favour of more small-level local schemes based on co-option and self-help.

Regionally, neighbouring countries must stop using Afghanistan as an arena for their own competitive and conflictive interests. A Swiss model of neutrality will be not only in Afghanistan's interests but also in those of West, Central and South Asia. Iran is already preoccupied with the US presence on its two flanks and a restive student populace in Tehran, whereas Pakistan needs to learn some hard lessons to put its own house in order. Its engagement in Afghanistan, despite its own obvious interests, should be geared towards a fair reconstruction of the country and its tormented populace. In the same vein, Central Asia must treat Afghanistan as a mature neighbour rather than a liability. Any opposition to autocratic regimes therein cannot be simply denigrated as an imported fundamentalism.

Internally, Karzai must herald an era of good feeling amongst his peoples through substantive efforts to re-establish inter-tribal consensus on vital national issues. Instead of doling out money to buy individual loyalties, he must offer tangible development schemes to his people. He needs to come out of his self-imposed security shell so as to establish a South-Africa-style Truth and Reconciliation Commission aimed at re-engaging all kinds of Afghans in a cohesive nation-building project. As he observed at St Antony's College in his lecture, Afghans are not factionalists by disposition and history, they are inherently nationalistic; he must now give them a chance to prove that.[32] His sole dependence on the Americans has seriously compromised his own profile but neither should he allow the Northern Alliance, General Rashid Dostam, Sherazi and Ismael Khan a unilateral march over plural prerogatives. If this three-tiered stratagem is ushered into an activist agenda, Afghanistan does have a real chance to re-emerge, otherwise we may see one more chance of rebuilding this tormented country go astray.

The leaders of the impassioned, chest-beating, yet orderly Shia pilgrims that converged in late April 2003 on Karbala soon after the fall of Saddam Hussein's regime resolved to implement political Islam interspersed with democratic ingredients. The speakers also promised to induct a tolerant and non-theocratic version of Islam—mainly to reassure their foreign observers of their distance from the Iranian model of theocracy. While Muslims of various sectarian and ethno-national backgrounds sought a greater sense of pride from the spectacle of elderly and young men and women defying the heat and dust, walking barefoot to celebrate the anniversary of Imam Hussein's death—the Prophet's grandson—the Anglo-American alliance found itself in a quandary. It appeared as if the floodgates of energy and pent-up feelings had been suddenly opened to let in a new-found solidarity among those who had experienced heinous bombings and a total disappearance of civic authority. Instead of fighting fellow Sunnis—the second major Muslim sect—or garlanding the Abram and Challenger tanks, these Iraqi masses represented a new and equally crucial phase of political Islam. Notwithstanding suspicion over Anglo-American motives, the fall of Saddam Hussein was welcomed by these masses wanting to shape their own destiny. The Anglo-American forces have been understandably wary of such a religio-political activity, especially when it seeks sustenance from anti-Western sentiments. They would not allow another Khomeini-style Iraq to raise its head in a crucial area where oil, economy and pro-Israeli considerations have reigned supreme. But this may further aggravate the situation intensifying guerrilla warfare and lead Iraq into a Somalia-like anarchy. However, rather than descending into a typical witch-hunt or a medievalist version of Taliban-style theocracy, the educated Shia clerics may be well placed to offer a unique synthesis of democracy and pluralism, away from violence, unilateralism and coercion. But so far suspicion on all sides abounds, which is neither good for peace nor for democracy.

Yet, where the Anglo-American commanders and bureaucrats were still working out the details of reconstruction, the clerics had already assumed greater local civic responsibilities. It is a different question, however, whether they will attain their political objectives, which may be thwarted by a new era of instability and chaos. Certainly, Islam continues to enthuse, aggregate and mobilize the masses even where food, water, medicines, shelter and electricity may have been absent or when basic civic amenities are non-existent. The spontaneity of people power and their adherence to mutual respect and peaceful coexistence is not a minor feat, though it remained peripheral in many news reports or else has been displayed as a medievalist ritual. Despite widespread scepticism, Iraq may offer a chance to establish a participatory polity 'from below'. But it may also turn into a vast killing field with warring clerics, tribal chieftains and surrogates pitted against one another, ruining their opportunity to rebuild Iraq as a role model for all. Neither theocracy nor dictatorship will take Islamicists anywhere; it is only through democracy, peace and guarantees for pluralism, away from unilateralism and militarism, that political Islam with its historic anti-colonial, anti-hegemonic, anti-racist and anti-violence traditions can come to the rescue of the have-nots. In the same vein, a prolonged occupation that fails to respect Iraq's pluralistic and democratic prerogatives will only further aggravate the situation.

This discussion of historical, domestic and extra-regional factors in the plight of two unstable Muslim countries, Afghanistan and Iraq, highlights formidable challenges towards nation-building. Whereas the issues of security and order need prioritization, a greater global engagement and substantive reassurances through an honest and unfettered politico-economic reconstruction may go a long way to establishing national cohesion and, most of all, allow the democratization of these plural societies. Neither an intolerant version of political Islam nor an interest-centred and partisan approach by Western powers towards the Muslim world will serve democracy and regional security. Likewise, a rash and unilateral military interventionism, however justified, cannot guarantee a stable West Asia. Pre-emptive and brutal military strikes, the use of surrogates from within the developing world and their subsequent abandonment to the forces of decay and disorder in an imperial tradition will make the march towards peace and democracy even more difficult. Like post-war Japan and Germany, Afghanistan and Iraq are the test cases for the Western world and global community. Walking away after playing havoc with their human and natural resources will only intensify 'the clash of fundamentalisms'.[33] Reconstruction, followed by regional cooperation and integration into a just global order, will not only guarantee an enduring democracy in these countries but also reverse the process of fragmentation, so evident in nearly half of the world. A radical change of heart is needed not just in these countries but all around!

Notes and references

1 N. Mailer, *Why Are We at War?*, New York, 2003, pp. 70–1.
2 See B. Woodward, *Bush at War*, New York, 2002, and D. Frum, *The Right Man*, London, 2003; also, J. Moore and W. Slater, *Bush's Brain*, Hoboken, NY, 2003.
3 For further details, see A. Roxburgh, *Preaching of Hate: The Rise of the Far Right*, London, 2002, and N. Klein, *Fences and Windows*, London, 2002; N. Mailer, *Why Are We at War?*, New York, 2003, and N. Chomskly, *9/11*, London, 2002. For a rebuttal, see A. Coulter, *Slander: Liberal Lies about the American Right*, New York, 2002.

4 For an interesting and powerful critique of British foreign policy, see M. Curtis, *Web of Deceit: Britain's Real Role in the World*, London, 2003.

5 Anti-Americanism is not confined to the Muslim regions. Even countries such as Canada, Britain, France, Italy, Germany, Japan, South Korea and Brazil have reflected long-term criticism of the American cultural 'assault'. Various surveys, BBC documentaries and live programmes substantiate the view that since the installation of the Bush administration, anti-Americanism has multiplied. The sympathy for the Untied States found after 9/11 soon evaporated following the destruction of poor countries such as Afghanistan, amidst other factors. See Z. Sardar and M. Davies, *Why Do People Hate America?*, London, 2002; M. Moore, *Stupid White Men*, New York, 2002; A.T. Embree (ed.), *Anti-Americanism in the Third World*, New York, 1983, and E. Ahmad, *Confronting Empire*, London, 2000.

6 See, for example, I. Clarke, *Globalization and Fragmentation: International Relations in the Twentieth Century*, Oxford, 1999.

7 Of course, such a hypothesis is not a new one, as the Marxists, Liberals and New Left have seen global discrepancies in an exploitative relationship between a privileged North and an underprivileged South. Such an argument is being revisited following the unipolar nature of the world and more so with the inauguration of the Bush administration and the rise of neo-conservatives. Analysts all the way from Karl Marx to Antonio Gramsci, Eric Hobsbawm, Andre Frank, Noam Chomsky and several other influential ones have seen the global 'disorder' within a class perspective. An increasingly powerful North, largely dictated by corporate interests and beefed up by the military–industrial complex, seems to determine the class-based divisions across the globe. For a recent study, see J. Pilger, *The New Rulers of the World*, London, 2003. Such critics are wary of globalization but would seek a reorganization of global institutions such as the UN, IMF and the World Back through more egalitarian, democratic and consensual reforms. For instance, G. Monbiot, *The Age of Consent. A Manifesto for a New World Order*, London, 2003. For a rebuttal of the latter by the editor of the *Economist*, see B. Emmott, 'Democratic Revolution', *New Statesman*, 23 June 2003.

8 Several Israeli groups such as Gush Shalom and other liberal elements have been opposed to ethnic cleansing and expulsions. Some British Jews such as Chief Rabbi Jonathan Sacks have been worried about the change in Jewish moral values with violence dominating the public consciousness, but under pressure he was made to withdraw his remarks. He had incensed his Zionist followers by suggesting that all religions basically carried a similar moral ethos and no single religion had any monopoly over goodness. He was made to rephrase his Chapter Three which carried such observations and the first edition (2002) has totally disappeared from the market. See J. Sacks, *The Dignity of Difference: How to Avoid the Clash of Civilisations?* (revised edition), London, 2003. His book was not allowed distribution in Israel though he remains a great friend of Israel. Recently, another Jewish academic has raised serious moral issues over Israeli policies towards Palestinians. See B. Kimmerling, *Politicide: Ariel Sharon's War against Palestinians*, London, 2003. His Zionist critics call him 'Quisling' out of hatred of his views.

9 Quoted in C. Bunting, 'Seeds of the "New Holocaust"?', *Times Higher Education Supplement*, 4 July 2003, p. 17.

10 P.J. Buchannan, *Death of the West*, New York, 2001; and for his columns see: <www.townhall.com/columnists/patbuchanan/pb20020327.shtml> (accessed 6 July 2004).

11 See H. Clinton, *Living History*, New York, 2003, and S. Blumenthal, *The Clinton Wars*, London, 2003; also W. Hutton, 'America is a Harsher Place', *Observer*, 6 July 2003.

12 For further details, see P. Seale, 'A Costly Friendship', *The Nation*, 21 July 2003.

13 See P. Iganski and B. Kosmin (eds), *A New Antisemitism: Debating Judeophobia in 21st Century Britain*, London, 2003.

14 In his recent and populist studies, the US-based British scholar of Islam has rekindled an orientalist discourse positing Islam as a unique case. See his *What Went Wrong? The Clash between Islam and Modernity in the Middle East*, London, 2002, and *Crisis of Islam: Holy War and Unholy Terror*, London, 2003.

15 One may include writers such as D. Pipes, A. Coulter and O. Fallaci whose dramatization of *Islamic Threat* after 9/11 is underrating Islamophobia. See D. Pipes, *Militant Islam Reaches America*, New York, 2001; Coulter, op. cit., and O. Fallaci, *The Rage and the Pride*, New York, 2003.

16 For a comprehensive study of this centuries-long relationship see N. Daniel, *Islam and the West*, Oxford, 2000.

17 For an interesting comparison, see M. Kramer, *The Salience of Islamic Fundamentalism*, London, 1995, and B.R. Barber, *Jihad vs. McWorld*, London, 2003.

18 For a range of diverse interpretations see, for example, T. Carew, *Jihad*, Edinburgh, 2001; G. Kepel, *Jihad: The Trail of Political Islam*, London, 2003; J. Burke, *Al-Qaeda: Casting a Shadow of Terror*, London, 2003, and M.J. Akbar, *The Shadow of Swords*, Delhi, 2002.

19 I have discussed the similarities between the majoritarian version of religio-political identity and the minoritarian secular view elsewhere. I.H. Malik, *Jihad, Hindutva and the Taliban: South Asia at the Crossroads*, Oxford, 2004.

20 Many reports on the rising guerilla warfare in Iraq by reporters such as Robert Fisk have already highlighted this trend where the Anglo-American troops are perceived as occupying forces and not liberators at all. J. Steele, 'Iraqis wait for US troops to leave...', *Guardian*, 5 July 2003. The new head of the Central Command of the US Army, General John Abizaid, in an interview characterized the resistance in Iraq as a 'guerrilla warfare'. Sky TV News Report, 16 July 2003; also, see J. Pilger, 'Bush's Vietnam', *New Statesman*, 23 June 2003.

21 Gellner was an exception in a sense as he saw no clash between Islamic civil society and democracy. See E. Gellner, *Muslim Society*, Cambridge, 1993.

22 Lewis, op. cit.

23 K.B. Sayeed, *Western Dominance and Political Islam: Challenge and Response*, Albany, NY, 1995; K. Armstrong, *Muhammad: A Biography of the Prophet*, London, 1995, and *Islam: A Short History*, London, 2002. Also, F. Halliday, *Islam & the Myth of Confrontation*, London, 1996, and, J.L. Esposito, *The Islamic Threat: Myth or Reality?*, New York, 1993.

24 For details, see A. Rashid, *Jihad: The Rise of Militant Islam in Central Asia*, New Haven, CT, 2003, and *Taliban, Islam, Oil and the New Great Game in Central Asia*, London, 2000; P. Marsden, *The Taliban, War, Religion and the New Order in Afghanistan*, London, 1998.

25 For various perspectives on Iraq, see M. Rai, *War Plan: The Reason against War in Iraq*, London, 2002; J. Green, B. Olshansky and M. Ratner, *Against War in Iraq*, New York, 2003; S.K. Aburish, *Saddam Hussein: The Politics of Revenge*, London, 2000; D. Hiro, *Iraq: A Report from the Inside*, London, 2002; A. Cockburn and P. Cockburn, *Saddam Hussein: An American Obsession*, London, 2002.

26 See the text of his speech in the BBC online report, 2 July 2003. Available HTTP: <www.bbc.co.uk/southasia> (accessed 8 July 2003).

27 For Pakistan's internal developments in post-9/11 months, see O. Bennett-Jones, *Pakistan: Eye of Storm*, London, 2002, and I.H. Malik, 'The Afghanistan Crisis and the Rediscovery of a Frontline State', *Asian Survey*, 42: 1, 2002.

28 The balanced view of the Pakistan–US relationship, especially after General Musharraf's visit to Washington in 2003, highlighted the need for the re-evaluation of priorities and foreign policy trajectories in Islamabad's regional and global policies. See Z. Mustafa, 'Was the Visit a Success?', *Dawn*, 9 July 2003. Online. Available HTTP: <www.dawn.com/opinion> (accessed 8 July 2003).

29 By the summer of 2003, it appeared as if Washington was simultaneously supporting Karzai and several regional warlords through hammering out deals with them. This added to Karzai's own untenable control over these autonomous and rent-seeking

warlords. All the actors in the country were 'hedging their bets'. For a first-hand and detailed view on the contradictory US policies in Afghanistan, see S. Chayes, 'Dangerous Liaisons', *New York Times*, in the *Guardian*, 7 July 2003.

30 For an interesting and well-informed reportage on Karzai, see C. Lamb, 'Afghanistan', *The Sunday Times Magazine*, 29 June 2003.

31 K. Maguire, 'Union Goes to War with Labour. Cabinet Branded "Criminal" on Iraq', *Guardian*, 2 July 2003. Online. Available HTTP: <www.guardian.co.uk> (accessed 7 July 2003).

32 For further details, see I.H. Malik, 'Karzai at Oxford', *The Daily Times*, 8 July 2003. Online. Available HTTP: <www.dailytimes.com.pk< (accessed 9 July 2003).

33 This is in reference to T. Ali's *The Clash of Fundamentalisms*, London, 2002.

13 The Iraq Body Count project

Civil society and the democratic deficit

John Sloboda and Hamit Dardagan

The Iraqis killed by coalition forces probably total between ten and fifteen thousand (it is a disgrace that the coalition forces themselves appear to have no estimate) .... Phrases such as 'We mourn each loss of life. We salute them, and their families for their bravery and sacrifice', apparently referring only to those who have died on the coalition side, are not well judged to moderate the passions these killings arouse.[1]

Introduction: the evolving face of civil dissent

Dissent from the planned invasion and occupation of Iraq has been a global phenomenon on an unprecedented scale. The anti-war marches and demonstrations of 15 February 2003 have no obvious precedent in history. Never have so many ordinary citizens united across all divides of nationality, religion, political and cultural systems, in passionate but non-violent democratic opposition to a war.[2] So impressive were these demonstrations that the *New York Times* was moved to comment on its front page that 'there may still be two superpowers on the planet: the United States and world public opinion'.[3]

At a London Rally of the Stop the War Coalition in January 2003, the former Labour MP Tony Benn characterized the movement as one of 'the people of the world against the leaders of the world'. His rather simplistic catchphrase nonetheless captured an essential and distinctive element of this movement: a popular disillusionment with the normal political process, and a growing belief that political elites play power games over the heads of the needs and aspirations of the people whose interests they are supposed to be representing, heedless of their call.

In modern democracies, elected representatives act according to their consciences and beliefs, and are not constitutionally required to act according to the views or representations of their constituents. Nonetheless, for trust to be maintained in the democratic process there must be some circumstances in which there is a prima facie case for representatives deferring to their constituents. David Beetham has recently proposed five criteria for such deferral.[4]

1   The issue is one of major importance: an issue which people feel is sufficiently important for them to become politically active and mobilize around, through petitions, attending meetings, public marches and demonstrations.

2   The issue should be a national one, in the sense of not representing merely a local or sectional interest.

3   The campaign should involve large numbers, and a wide range of organizations from across the social and political spectrum.

4   The organized mobilization of opinion should be supported by a clear majority in public opinion polls, preferably over time. This condition is necessary to meet the objection that intense minorities should not necessarily be given preference over less intense majorities.

5   The issue in question should have been subject to extensive public debate, in which different aspects and viewpoints have been raised for consideration, so that expressions of public opinion cannot be written off as knee-jerk reactions.

British public opposition to a war on Iraq during late 2002 and early 2003 easily satisfied all of these criteria. Beetham concludes that 'if there was any case in which Government and Parliament should have not only listened to organized public opinion but deferred to it, this was it'. He warns that governments who go against the public will in this way (giving more weight to the views of a foreign president than to their own people) 'intensify the alienation of substantial sections of society from the political process'.

The USA was the prime mover for war against Iraq and had a clear majority of public opinion supporting it.[5] It also has an electorate that as late as January 2004 still believed Saddam Hussein had been directly involved in the events of 11 September 2001.[6] This meant that the public debate was substantially a misinformed one (as it was to a lesser extent in the UK, thanks partly to the government's contributions to public discourse).[7] Even so, organized protest was unprecedented in both countries, with the first-ever sizeable US pre-war demonstrations taking place in parallel with the largest-ever demonstrations in British history.

Opposition to the Vietnam War took years to grow, and only became a potent force after the war had already killed thousands of US soldiers and hundreds of thousands of Vietnamese combatants, as well as a proportion of the 4 million Vietnamese civilians who were killed by the war's end.[8] In contrast, popular opposition to the Iraq War as expressed by mass demonstrations peaked before hostilities commenced, which gave many members of the anti-war movement unprecedented hope. In late 2002 and early 2003, many believed that public opinion had a real chance of halting the war. It is certainly possible to argue that public opposition delayed it by a few months. Under intense domestic pressure, Tony Blair persuaded George W. Bush to give inspections under UN auspices another chance. It is also possible to argue that public opinion was partly responsible for the ability of member states of the UN Security Council to resist the pressure put on them by Washington and London in the weeks and days leading up to the much-vaunted second resolution. This resulted in a much smaller 'coalition of the willing' than the USA had hoped to muster.

Nonetheless, massive principled public dissent was insufficient to derail the long-laid plans of the Bush administration for 'regime change' in Iraq, and the outbreak of war was a heavy blow to those who had campaigned long and hard for its avoidance.[9] The sense of disillusionment and loss of trust was profound in many sectors of society, including, as is now becoming increasingly apparent, senior serving military officers and public servants on both sides of the Atlantic.

Although disillusionment led to disengagement for some, the Iraq War galvanized key elements of dissenting civil society into a re-evaluation of tactics, rather than an abandonment of organized dissent. Western civil society (the press and media, faith communities, politicians and activists, NGOs, lawyers and academics, among others) has managed to maintain a remarkably persistent and effective campaign of attrition directed principally at the administrations of George W Bush and Tony Blair. These administrations have increasingly been forced onto the defensive. Bush's announcement that 'major combat operations in Iraq have ended', made as he stood on the deck of a warship under a banner declaring *MISSION ACCOMPLISHED*, became, in retrospect, the briefest and most fragile moments of triumph for the coalition.

Whereas the most clear manifestation of pre-war dissent was that of traditional oppositional grassroots mass activism (in this case an alliance of the traditional radical political left with the more pacifist peace and anti-nuclear movement, joined in Europe by key Muslim organizations), post-war dissent has been increasingly characterized by a far wider variety of actors and activities, working in a relatively uncoordinated way to expose and challenge a whole variety of weak spots in coalition actions and policies, and operating from a considerably broader spectrum of ideological and political perspectives, with a broader range of techniques and organizational forms. This change seems to mark a shift from 'movement-based' to 'project-based' dissent.

While the relatively diffuse approach of project-based dissent lacks the immediate impact and symbolic unity of mass demonstrations, it has other strengths for the long haul. A broad single-message mass movement is vulnerable to both external attack and internal politicking. Governments and media can undermine such movements by well-targeted attacks on key leaders and concepts. Once a few key leaders are discredited in the public eye, the entire movement can become compromised. A well-crafted riposte can insulate populations against taking key critical arguments of the dissenting minority seriously. For instance, by crudely depicting the anti-war movement and even doubters among its NATO allies as indulging in appeasement, the Bush administration was able (at least during late 2002 and the first half of 2003) to ensure that the majority of the US population never engaged with the detailed critiques which showed that Saddam Hussein posed no threat to the West.[10] Dissenting views from critical minorities, which received hardly any exposure in the mainstream mass media, were unable to counteract the official views, repeatedly and uncritically broadcast by the corporate US media machine. In contrast to this, a dissenting impulse which manifests itself through a range of project-based activities, with differing messages, leaderships, lifespans and outlets, is much less vulnerable to simplistic neutralizing attacks; the failure of one project does not compromise the effectiveness of the remainder.

This chapter tells the story of one such endeavour, the Iraq Body Count project, starting with its philosophical and conceptual underpinnings, and moving on to some key aspects of its operation and effectiveness.

An emerging paradigm: the human security framework

Critical debate in civil society has articulated a variety of perspectives from which to mount challenges on the Iraq War and occupation. These include the legal basis for coalition action, both national and international, examined here by Patrick Thornberry;[11] the evidential basis for the action, including the role of the intelligence services and weapons inspectors, a ferocious debate engaged by Alex Danchev;[12] the effect of the action on international institutions such as the UN, also examined by Patrick Thornberry;[13] the relationship (if any) to the success or otherwise of the 'war on terror', an issue addressed by Richard Falk;[14] and the extent to which the appropriation of Iraq (both its peoples and its resources) can be understood primarily as a means of furthering US economic and geopolitical interests in the region, without reference to the will of the Iraqi people, examined here by Glen Rangwala and Gareth Stansfield.[15]

However, it is possible to argue that there is one issue which, above all others, has motivated and mobilized civil dissent at every stage of the conflict. That issue is the effect of war and its aftermath on the civilian population. People feared a humanitarian disaster,[16] and the urgent need to prevent that disaster fuelled their passion and commitment. In an unpublished survey of attendees at the biggest pre-war London demonstration (13 February 2003), we found that concern for the humanitarian consequences was a major stated reason for attending. One respondent said: 'I did not agree with what was essentially an unprovoked war of aggression which was likely to cause the wholesale slaughter or displacement or large sections of the Iraqi population.' Another said: 'I felt horror at the likely loss of life and injuries caused by bombs and artillery.'

It has been an increasingly recognized feature of modern warfare that civilians are the major casualties of war.[17] Particularly vulnerable to harm and abuse are women and children, who are both 'disproportionately targeted in modern armed conflicts and constitute the majority of its victims', according to the UNHCR.[18] In the light of these developments, informed citizens are increasingly impatient with justifications for war based on abstract slogans such as 'democracy', 'freedom' and 'national security'. They are more concerned with how a proposed war will affect people and the environment in the country that is attacked. They want to know how many people will be killed and injured, and the effect of fighting and bombardment on homes, shops, roads, water and sewage works, electricity supplies and other essential civilian infrastructures.

They want to know the short- and long-term effects on health and sanitation, the risks of starvation, and the number of refugees who may be displaced by the fighting. They want to know what equation can justify the deliberate, and often drastic, worsening of life for people in the country for the sake of some promised 'better life', years or decades later.

It is encouraging that an increasingly educated and informed world population should see things in this way. An immediate and unconditional compassionate response to the death or injury of fellow human beings is the cornerstone of civilization (and a feature of all major world religions and ethical systems). However, the capacity for compassion has often tended to be partial, especially in times of war and the build-up to war. There is a temptation to count the death (or feared death) of our own side (however defined) as more tragic and worthy of note than the death of the other side (however defined). Such bias is still unfortunately an everyday manifestation of the pronouncements of most national leaders and media commentators, as the fifty-two former British diplomats rightly pointed out in the open letter at the head of this chapter.

What is now being made manifest at many levels of civil society is a determined refusal to place *any* human being in the category of 'the other', partly as a result of the spread of anti-racist thinking and policies within contemporary culture. A baby blown to pieces by a bomb is exactly the same tragedy, wherever that baby was born and whoever dropped the bomb. Increasing proportions of national populations are successfully resisting the attempts of their own leaders to demonize and dehumanize other populations, and refusing to accept 'collateral damage' as the expendable civilian cost of some abstract 'noble mission'.

Before the Iraq War, aid agencies, political and religious leaders, as well as political and security commentators, were predicting that war would lead to substantial suffering among the civilian population. A widely quoted prediction[19] was that war in Iraq would result in at least 10,000 civilian deaths. Not only would war cause immediate deaths, but it would create a variety of long-term negative consequences for the people of Iraq, ranging from the destruction of the infrastructure and war-related radiation (from depleted uranium) to psychological trauma, displacement and loss.[20]

Perhaps the most unusual and unexpected reaction to the proposed war was the mobilization of several hundred volunteer 'human shields' prepared to risk their lives on behalf of Iraqi civilians. About seventy remained in Iraq during the bombing and stationed themselves at power plants, water purification plants and other key infrastructure installations. It is a little-reported outcome that none of these installations was bombed by coalition forces so long as the human shields were present.[21] The moral heroism of the human shields cannot be overstated.

The Afghanistan project of Marc W. Herold

The fact that a prospective war on Iraq was being explicitly envisaged by the US administration more than a year in advance of the start of hostilities enabled a much more intensive analysis by non-governmental experts of possible consequences than had been possible, for instance, in the case of the Afghanistan conflict, which was launched less than two months after 9/11. Nonetheless, the Afghanistan War was the stimulus for a ground-breaking initiative which was the single most important precursor of the Iraq Body Count project. This project, a personal initiative of Marc Herold, a Professor of Economics at the University of New Hampshire, came to wide notice through an article in the *Guardian* by Seumas Milne on 20 December 2001.

Writing just three months after the commencement of that war, Milne began by observing: 'The price in blood that has already been paid for America's war against terror is only now starting to become clear' – a price paid by ordinary Afghans, 'who had nothing whatever to do with the atrocities, didn't elect the Taliban theocrats who ruled over them and had no say in the decision to give house room to Bin Laden and his friends'. Noting that the Pentagon had been 'characteristically coy about how many people it believes have died under the missiles it has showered on Afghanistan', Milne noted that the US media had contributed little to understanding the scale of the slaughter. The *Los Angeles Times*, for example, 'only felt able to hazard the guess that "at least dozens of civilians" had been killed'. Yet Marc Herold's systematic and independent study, based on a comprehensive collation of media-reported deaths, had shown that at least 3,767 civilians had been killed by US bombs between 7 October and 10 December 2001 – more even than had been killed on 9/11.

Although champions of the war continued to insist that this slaughter was a world apart from the civilian victims of the attacks on the World Trade Center 'because, in the case of the Afghan civilians, the US did not intend to kill them', Milne argued that 'the moral distinction is far fuzzier, to put it at its most generous'. As Milne wrote:

> The decision to rely heavily on high-altitude air power, target urban infrastructure and repeatedly attack heavily populated towns and villages has reflected a deliberate trade-off of the lives of US pilots and soldiers, not with those of their declared Taliban enemies, but with Afghan civilians. Thousands of innocents have died over the past two months, not mainly as an accidental by-product of the decision to overthrow the Taliban regime, but because of the low value put on Afghan civilian lives by US military planners.
>
> Raids on targets such as the Kajakai Dam power station, Kabul's telephone exchange, the al-Jazeera TV station office, lorries and buses filled with refugees and civilian fuel trucks were not mistakes. Nor were the deaths that they caused. The same goes for the use of anti-personnel cluster bombs in urban areas. But Western public opinion has become increasingly desensitized to what has been done in its name. After US AC-130 gunships strafed the farming village of Chowkar-Karez in October, killing at least ninety-three civilians, a Pentagon official felt able to remark: 'the people there are dead because we wanted them dead', while US Defense Secretary Donald Rumsfeld commented: 'I cannot deal with that particular village.'

Herold's database is still being updated, as is his ongoing critique of the problematic military intervention in that country.[22] The acknowledged and continuing failings of the Afghanistan intervention[23] are not the subject of this chapter, but awareness of them has been a key factor in motivating the current project.

In December 2002 both authors of this chapter independently came to the view that war with Iraq was almost certain to take place. Each contacted Herold with the same question: 'Are you going to extend your methodology to Iraq?' Herold indicated that his work on Afghanistan was far from finished and that he would not be initiating work on Iraq. He urged us to pool our resources to initiate a parallel project.

Some intensive discussions followed, and in January 2003 the Iraq Body Count project was launched. As co-founders we decided to build the project team by recruiting colleagues and friends as volunteers. This allowed the rapid creation of a cohesive team, necessary because we knew it was possible that war could break out at any moment. There was no time to vet potential volunteers who might be unknown to us, and who might complicate and impede the timely implementation of the project. Some twenty individuals offered their time and expertise to the project, and most are still regular contributors to the work.

Key features of the Iraq Body Count project

Extensive information about the project and its methodology is publicly available on the Iraq Body Count (IBC) website.[24] It has a number of key features.

1   **Data are derived from web-published news media reports.** The project gathers and collates published information, and includes non-combatant civilian deaths in its count when they have been reported by at least two reputable press and media sources. It does not undertake primary research, but extracts data from previously published reports into a standard format, adjusting total deaths each time a new incident is added to the database. The validity and reliability of the data rest on the professionalism of the publishing agencies, and the wide range of sources consulted. Current sources can be inspected on the online database.
2   **Data entries incorporate variations in reporting.** Most variations are due to the placement of quoted eyewitnesses and other primary sources in relation to an incident: for instance, a hospital doctor will almost certainly have a greater overview of an incident's toll of casualties than a bystander. Where there are irreconcilable reports of equal weight the database entry takes the form of a minimum and a maximum range incorporating this variation in numbers.
3   **Data 'tagging' is employed to avoid double entries.** A standardized system of indicators to 'flag' incidents – Date, Time, Place, Targets, Weapons, etc. – is used to distinguish between entries and avoid double-counting errors. Here, too, the 'Min–Max' system may be used whenever

intractable uncertainties remain: an entry of 0 in the Min column (to allow for the possibility that a death already exists in the database) and 1 in the Max column (to allow for the possibility that it has not yet been recorded by IBC).

4   **Data extraction is reviewed and confirmed by at least two independent verifiers.** Before publication, the proposed entry to the database is checked and where necessary commented upon by at least two further members of the project team. Often this serves mainly to catch simple human errors but in the case of complex incidents the analysis and review process may take days or even weeks, and involve the entire team until an agreed analysis is reached. All such conferences are conducted electronically and remain visible to the team for ongoing reference and as a permanent archive of the work.

5   **Data are continually updated and collected for processing.** Since January 2003, media sources have been scanned several times a day. This is necessary because news disappears rapidly from subscription-free wires and websites, commonly within a week or thirty days. Just as important, the news of the day (particularly if it is sensational) can completely obscure the many 'small' news items on which much of the IBC count is based, making these much more difficult to retrieve. Only daily scanning can guarantee the maximum 'harvest' of stories. Generally, far more stories are gathered than are used.

6   **Data are disseminated beyond the IBC website itself.** Not only are the latest data published on the project website as soon as they are processed and verified, but the updating cumulative totals and selected details are available in the form of a dynamic 'webcounter' that can be downloaded and easily displayed on any other web page. At the peak of interest in the war there were 19,000 websites worldwide using the counter, vastly extending the project's audience and impact.

7   **Accuracy is always favoured over speed.** Whilst wishing to publish data as soon as a reliable count can be extracted, the project is not, in itself, attempting to be first with the news. The larger and more complex an incident is, the more time it may take to publish a responsible and defensible figure. This is not solely a matter of project team size and resources. For instance, very early-breaking news and eyewitness accounts rarely provide a complete picture. People injured in an attack may die later from their injuries. Controversial or well-known incidents are often revisited by journalists who may revise pertinent details with information from better-placed sources.

8   **Project personnel are exclusively independent citizens of the UK and the USA.** The Iraq invasion and occupation, and its resulting loss of life, derives primarily from the decisions of George W. Bush and his principal ally Tony Blair. We feel it is our duty as British and American citizens to document the consequences, because these momentous decisions were – nominally – taken on our behalf, and funded by our taxes. No other popu-

lace has a greater responsibility to the Iraqi victims of the war than the electorates of our two countries. The IBC project's material costs have been
funded solely by donations from supportive individuals (also mostly from the
USA and UK). IBC is unaffiliated to any other organization. The project is
independent of any external influence and is therefore a true reflection of
the concerns of those who have been working within it.

9 **All media-reported civilian deaths are included in the count if
they can be shown to be a direct consequence of the invasion
and occupation of Iraq.** This includes civilian deaths from coalition
bombardment and gunfire, but also from weapons fired by the Iraqi regime
in attempting to defend itself. It also includes deaths of civilians due to
attacks by various anti-occupation forces or in possible inter-ethnic conflicts,
as well those killed in other manifestations of the general breakdown in civil
security in post-invasion Iraq, including rampant lawlessness and violent
crime.

10 **We avoid excessively legalistic or moralistic formulations and
adopt a predominantly 'causal' perspective in distinguishing
between combatant and non-combatant civilian deaths.** The war
and occupation-related deaths of children, women (apart from a very few
exceptions) and elderly Iraqis, and of foreign journalists and humanitarian
aid workers, are automatically included in our database after undergoing the
filtering processes outlined above. Iraqi civilian males described as
bystanders, passers-by or uninvolved in initiating deadly violence against
occupying troops are also automatically added to our count.

Automatically excluded from the count are reported deaths among
members of the Iraqi Army when this still functioned as a fighting force, or
of any irregular militias who fought alongside it. In the post-war occupation
phase, when assessing the status of Iraqi males of military age killed while
reportedly exchanging fire with occupation troops, the test for us is this:
*Could these Iraqis reasonably have expected themselves or others in the immediate circum-
stances to survive had they not resorted to deadly force? If the answer is yes, we consider
them to have died as combatants, not civilians.* This formulation parallels the
requirement under international humanitarian law for occupying powers
only to resort to deadly force 'when strictly unavoidable in order to protect
life'.[25] The issue for us is not one of moral responsibility (which resides overwhelmingly with political leaders), but of causality – that is, whether these
deaths were a *necessary* outcome of the war and occupation, or if they could
have been avoided had the individuals concerned not taken upon themselves
the additional danger of initiating mortal combat with occupation forces.

Thus civilian Iraqis who died after initiating deadly violence while
facing no direct or immediate threat to themselves or others are considered
by IBC to have adopted combatant status, while those who were forced to
use arms in order to protect life are not considered combatants, and retain
their civilian status for the purposes of our count. An example of the former
would be Iraqis who set ambushes for routine military patrols or convoys; an

example of the latter, a man who uses the family rifle in an attempt to repel an attack by occupation troops.

Also excluded from our count are foreign civilian (or semi-civilian 'security') workers under the employ of the CPA or its commercial sub-contractors. These violent deaths are also not a *necessary* result of the war and occupation, because the individuals concerned could have survived its dangers by simply staying out of war-torn Iraq. Nor can the desire for material gain, particularly when it is the predominant motivating factor, be compared with recognized humanitarian imperatives which bring foreigners into war zones, such as the provision of emergency relief or crucial news-gathering.

The power of the World Wide Web

A project such as IBC would not have been possible even five years ago. What has made it possible is the development and ubiquity of the World Wide Web. Five factors have been crucial. Firstly, almost every news and media organization of repute publishes its stories on freely available websites or newswires available through the Web, albeit in most cases for a limited time only. Secondly, powerful free search engines (in particular Google News) allow sophisticated keyword-based searches to be conducted across the entire contents of the Web. This allows exhaustive scrutiny of reports of civilian casualties. Thirdly, anyone with access to the Web can cheaply set up a website which is accessible worldwide on a continuous basis. Fourthly, the predominant language for web-based news and media organizations is English, and so the work does not require multilingual expertise. Fifthly, the proportion of the populations of the USA and UK who have direct access to the Web and make daily use of it is constantly rising. Therefore, by publishing on the Web, we reach more individuals than any other medium allows, except perhaps primetime network TV.

Further factors which have assisted this particular project include the use of email and web-based bulletin boards as the primary medium for internal team communication and archiving of data. This has made the geographical location of the members of the project team irrelevant. Additionally, menu-driven software means that updating the site can be accomplished by individuals with no expertise in HTML or web authoring. All that is required to be an effective project member is the ability and free time systematically to analyse and extract data from press and media reports.

Difficulties encountered and obstacles to be overcome

Despite the immense opportunities afforded by the Web, the project has had to overcome a number of difficulties. Some purely technical challenges were solved by the creative input of sympathetic and committed individuals with specialized computing expertise. A more *intrinsic* difficulty and limitation is that IBC relies entirely on secondary sources. More specifically, our reliance on news reports means that if a death is missed by the media then it cannot appear in our database. The database contains many entries of single deaths, and it is to their credit that the major media do not neglect such individual human tragedies. But our experience confirms the suspicion that many deaths go unreported for one reason or another, because whenever journalists have consulted local sources who gather relevant statistics (such as official coroners or hospitals) we have discovered that far more deaths attributable to the war and occupation had occurred than had been directly reported by journalists. Indeed, a significant proportion of IBC's tally is derived from reports of this nature, albeit usually delayed until such cumulative statistics come to light.[26]

We believe that a mixture of dedicated primary and secondary research would help to overcome this limitation and provide a much more comprehensive (and therefore accurate) picture of a war's toll on civilian lives.

The significant *extrinsic* difficulties have been of a political and conceptual character. There have been direct attacks on our own work, both theoretical and psychological. Over and above these there are the difficulties associated with the refusal of the US and UK governments (or indeed any official agency) to engage seriously with the issue of civilian casualties, despite massive public concern, and substantial press and media attention.

Objections to our 'one-sidedness'

There have been a number of different ways in which the work of IBC has been 'tested' by public reaction, much of it rather hostile, particularly from the USA. There are four main accusations: our count is not 'balanced' by deaths attributable to Saddam Hussein; our perceived political bias and lack of experience in the field; our apparent overreliance on Iraqi Ministry of Information sources during the initial war phase; and our failure to include military deaths in our count.

The most frequent condemnation of our work, as expressed in countless emails, is that we do not include civilian deaths caused by Saddam Hussein in Iraq up to March 2003. We are therefore 'anti-American' and 'pro-Saddam'.

These complainants are generally split into three groups. There are those who focus on the huge numbers of people killed by Saddam prior to 1991, regardless of whether they died in wars as soldiers or were civilians murdered in the crushing of internal dissent. There are those who point to the civilians and especially the children killed as a result of sanctions from 1991 to 2003, now 'saved' as a result of the sanctions being lifted after the war. And there are those who ask us to take into account deaths that Saddam would have caused had he remained in power, and insist that there has already been a 'net gain' in human lives thanks to his forcible removal.

These may all be answered quite directly. Saddam's mass graves are in no way negated by ours, which are simply additional to his.[27] The UN sanctions did not require a war in order to be lifted.[28] And neither before nor after the war was any evidence offered to suggest that Saddam would slaughter Iraqis, or anyone else, in the hundreds let alone the thousands during 2003–4, despite much rhetoric to the contrary.[29]

An indirect but more fundamental answer would point to the one issue these objections miss, namely that the historical and social worth of a project like IBC is not dependent upon extraneous factors, such as whether a war is of 'noble purpose' or has full UN Security Council approval. Its first duty is to that portion of humanity which is harmed or killed by it, regardless of whether this is in the interests of others. Even if all the claims of the Iraq War's proponents were entirely justified, there would still be a need to record and honour the dead, and to assess and understand the extent of suffering caused by the war.

A different basis for the claim of 'one-sidedness' has been made on the grounds of our personal politics, and/or our lack of authority/experience in the work. The members of the project team, all of whose names and vitae appear on the iraqbodycount.net website, make no attempt to apologize for, or hide, the fact that we have all been passionately opposed to the war and occupation since it was first envisaged. Critics of our work have taken our opposition to the war to argue that our results must therefore be biased. Our most effective defence against these charges is complete transparency about our methods and our sources, published in full on the website, and with documentary backup available to any serious enquirer. If our methodology is transparent and public, then our political views are irrelevant. Any third party can assess the data for him- or herself.

Authority and expertise, we feel, is earned through the consistency and accuracy of the work. In the initial weeks of the operation of the project we fully understood that observers had a right to be sceptical of our work. A number of similar projects were started at around the same time (see the editorial of June 2003)[30] and not all deserved serious attention. By consistent and accurate work, day by day, over a period of a year, the project has now become 'the source of record' on civilian deaths. Particularly since the passing of the 10,000 mark on our maximum in February 2004, our figures tend to be cited without comment or criticism (and very often without acknowledging the source) as the best available estimate.[31] At the time of writing, it is in fact the only comprehensive estimate in existence.

During the 'war phase' from 19 March to 9 April 2003, an important source of data for our count was the official releases from the Iraqi Ministry of Information. These releases gave very precise information about numbers of civilians killed by coalition forces in a format usable to IBC (the reports bore the incident 'identifiers' referred to above). The fact that these casualty figures were reported by numerous Western press and media outlets made them clear candidates for inclusion in our count; this became an early, if short-lived, criticism of our work.

Soon after the war, it was discovered that wherever independent verification was possible the Iraqi government's figures (which had apparently been communicated to it by hospitals) were either entirely accurate, or underestimates of the true picture.[32] By the end of summer 2003, almost all the Iraqi figures were confirmed by, and incorporated in, reports from other independent sources, and at the time of writing no more than 130 deaths in our total count rely entirely on these original Iraqi reports.

We have no hesitation in rejecting criticisms that we do not count coalition military deaths. Although all deaths are tragic and require recording, there are numerous other agencies and organizations which devote resources to this task. These include official US agencies (the Pentagon) as well as independent analysts such as 'Coalition Casualty Count'.[33] Those wishing for an accurate coalition count have many sources to choose from (and we link to these from our own site).

Iraqi military deaths require a more considered response. In many ways, Iraqi soldiers can also be considered true victims of the war that led to Saddam's rout. Many, if not most, were unwilling conscripts, some little more than boys, badly trained and badly led.[34] A comprehensive tally of Iraqi military deaths would be of inestimable humanitarian value. However, there exists almost no published data which would help us understand fully what happened to Iraqi soldiers in the period 19 March to 1 May 2003.[35] They cannot be included in the count because there is no reliable data on which to construct such a count.

A notable aspect of our experience, most intense during the first months of our project, was the massive hate campaign mounted against our work from the USA. This took the form of thousands of abusive and threatening emails flooding our inboxes, almost all from US destinations. These included vile racist statements about Iraqis, accompanied by the wish that many more Iraqis would die, and that we would join them. We soon discovered that many of the messages we received had identical or almost identical wording. This is most consistent with the notion that many opponents of our work were being encouraged and resourced for their campaign in an organized way. This was not just a set of random isolated comments, but an organized attempt to sabotage the project through demoralizing and distracting its personnel. The systematic attempt to wear down people by constant psychological abuse is a form of psychological terrorism used by the US military (among others) and given the name PSYOPS. In the run-up to the Iraq War, US and UK warplanes dropped millions of threatening leaflets on the Iraqi population, and broadcast similar messages on specially targeted radio programmes.[36]

The attacks on IBC personnel were deeply stressful, and our strategy for handling them was to channel them all to two members of the team, both US nationals, who dealt with them as best they could, and protected the rest of the team from exposure to them. Although this allowed the project to move forward unhindered, the psychological cost to the two people involved was heavy. Fortunately abusive attacks on the project dropped off significantly after 1 May 2003, and now arrive at a much lower rate.

Coalition resistance to estimating civilian casualties

A far more serious threat to the goal of establishing an authoritative record of civilian deaths than anything mentioned so far has been the almost complete silence of the US and UK administrations on the matter.

The Labour MP Llew Smith sent a detailed set of written questions to the UK government asking if it would: examine reports of Iraqi deaths from eyewitness correspondents embedded with the military in the invasion of Iraq; request the Coalition Provisional Authority to make a survey of deaths reported in hospitals in Iraq, from 19 March to 1 May 2003, arising from military conflict; and make the estimating of Iraqi military deaths part of the aim of interrogation of Iraqi military commanders in custody. The government's reply stated:

> Any loss of life, particularly civilian, is deeply regrettable, but in a military operation the size of Operation Telic it is also unavoidable. Through very strict rules of engagement, the use of precision munitions and the tactical methods employed to liberate Iraq's major cities, we are satisfied that the coalition did everything possible to avoid unnecessary casualties. We do not, therefore, propose to undertake a formal review of Iraqi casualties sustained from 19 March to 1 May.

Smith's comment on this reply:

> Surely this is both an inhumane and unacceptable position. As at least part of our aid to post-war Iraq must be targeted at assistance to families left without breadwinners who have been killed or seriously injured by the invasion, then our planners are going to have to calculate the numbers of families left destitute by their loss.[37]

A thorough analysis and critique of US and UK positions and statements is provided in the IBC editorial dated 7 February 2004.[38] All of the statements on record are deeply flawed. It is notable that statements about the matter have been left entirely to relatively junior military spokespersons, or second-level government representatives. No one close to George Bush or Tony Blair has ever gone on record with a clear and comprehensive statement of the official position. The importance of this silence on Iraqi civilian suffering cannot be overestimated. In a widely published letter, fifty-two former senior diplomats of the UK government have branded it 'a disgrace', and have pointed out yet again how self-defeating the coalition posture is.[39]

Iraqis are of course the first victims of the silence and the indifference which accompanies it. They are unlikely to be the last.

An assessment

If one takes the ending or reduction in the daily loss of Iraqi lives as a yardstick of success, then the IBC project may be judged a failure to date. More civilians were killed in the months of March and April 2004 than were killed in the previous six months. However, there are other criteria by which one might judge the project more favourably:

1   **Increased awareness and firmer knowledge among the general public, advocates and legislators about the civilian cost of the war and occupation.** At the height of the war, in March–April 2003, the IBC website was receiving over 150,000 visits per day worldwide. At the time of writing it receives around 10–20,000 daily visits. The daily total has rarely dropped beneath 5,000.

   The success of the Google search engine is largely due to its objective system of ranking websites not by their total visitor numbers but according to their 'overall importance' as sources of information as indicated by the number of *secondary* websites that link to them, combined with the importance ranking of those secondary websites, and so on.[40] Today typing only the word 'civilian' into Google brings up Iraq Body Count as the top-ranked website, as does 'count'; the word 'Iraq' currently puts IBC in third place. More focused searches similarly bring IBC to the fore.

   IBC's updated totals are now routinely cited by major media outlets and press agencies including Reuters, the *Guardian*, the *Independent*, the BBC, and others, including in the US press.[41] In April 2004 the *Independent* devoted an entire broadsheet page to an item-by-item list of civilian deaths taken directly from the IBC database.[42] IBC figures have been used in other important published assessments of the human costs of the war and occupation by respected human rights agencies and NGOs.[43] Our output has also been a tool for public representatives and advocates of Iraqi compensation to make their case, including in debates by UK parliamentary representatives,[44] and an open letter to the US president from the presidential candidate Ralph Nader.[45]

2   **Increased likelihood of body counts being a primary civil response to any future war.** It is our belief that Herold's Afghanistan project and our Iraq project have so firmly established the feasibility and necessity of such 'watchdog' projects in the consciousness of dissenting civil society that such body counts will be an inevitable consequence of future wars involving the USA and the UK. Our methodology and experience shows that the work can be done well by any group of committed volunteers anywhere in the world at negligible cost. The knowledge that such counts will inevitably accompany military interventions and be widely reported may act as a restraining influence on governments, and may encourage official bodies or longer-established NGOs to take earlier initiatives in this field, including combined or complementary primary and secondary research efforts.

3   **Helped maintain sustained and effective critical dissent against the past and current actions and policies of the USA and the UK in Iraq.** Whatever the temporary peaks and troughs in public attention, or political and humanitarian response, the IBC project has maintained a persistent daily drip-feed of consciousness-raising through its constantly updated website and web counters. The site has not been offline for a single second since the first bomb was dropped, and it has thus been constantly

available to activists, reporters, critics and researchers, worldwide, no matter what else was going on politically or militarily.

On the other hand, IBC has been able to mount or contribute to time-limited initiatives in response to specific occurrences, as for example the series of editorials on its website, and articles published elsewhere. A well-developed 'rapid-response' press and media wing has allowed appropriate IBC perspectives to be inserted into the debate on whatever topic the developing situation throws up.

It would be optimistic to believe that IBC is about to render itself, and projects like it, obsolete. A commitment from an international body such as the UN or the Red Cross always to undertake such assessments in future might be an outcome which would incline the activists to hand over the work to the professionals. However, the realists among us believe that no powerful aggressor nation will ever willingly submit to an external agency monitoring the behaviour of its own military. A promise by the Swiss government to undertake a body count in March 2003 was withdrawn just one day later for reasons that are still unclear.[46] And when a civilian casualty count was undertaken by US census bureau worker Beth Daponte months after the end of the first Gulf War, she was fired for producing statistics 'unhelpful' to the White House.[47]

It is likely that body counts will remain a task for the dissenting civilian population for the foreseeable future. So long as such counts are undertaken with the methodological rigour and transparency that we have shown is possible, then this need not be the serious disadvantage it might seem.

Notes and references

1 'A Letter from 52 Former Senior British Diplomats to Tony Blair', *Guardian*, 27 April 2004; reprinted in *New York Review of Books*, 27 May 2004.
2 J. Vidal, 'Global marches ... are thought to have attracted more than 15 million people in 75 countries on February 15', *Guardian*, 4 March 2003.
3 P. Tyler, 'A New Power In the Streets', *New York Times*, 17 February 2003.
4 D. Beetham, 'Political Participation, Mass Protest and Representative Democracy', *Parliamentary Affairs*, 56, 2003, pp. 597–609.
5 ABC News poll, 5–9 March 2003 (65 per cent for, 30 per cent opposed to taking military action to force Saddam Hussein from power). Online. Available HTTP: <http://www.pollingreport.com> (accessed 10 May 2004).
6 *Newsweek* poll conducted by Princeton Survey Research Associates, 29–30 January 2004. But this had reversed by April: see CBS News/*New York Times* poll, 23–27 April 2004, ibid.
7 P. Wintour, 'Straw Rounds on Campbell – PM's Press Chief made "Complete Horlicks" of Iraq Dossier', *Guardian*, 25 June 2003.
8 *Wikipedia, the Free Encyclopedia*, 'Vietnam War – Casualties': 'Vietnam released figures on 3 April 1995 that a total of one million Vietnamese combatants and four million civilians were killed in the war. The accuracy of these figures has generally not been challenged.' Online. Available HTTP: <http://en.wikipedia.org/wiki/Vietnam_War> (accessed 10 May 2004).
9 An analysis of some of these frustrations as manifested in the USA can be found in R. Kaiser, 'There's a Reason Why There Hasn't Been Much of a Fight', *Washington Post*, 16 February 2003.

10 J. Dickerson, 'The president warns NATO that failure to confront Saddam equals appeasement': 'Failure to confront Saddam would be to appease aggression–although he didn't use that supercharged word from Europe's initial failure to confront Hitler, it was in the air, as he appealed to the continent's history of wrestling with totalitarian regimes.' *Time*, 21 November 2002.

11 Public Interest Lawyers (http://www.publicinterestlawyers.co.uk) are one of several legal organizations that have been collating evidence on both the legality of the war and potential war crimes committed by the US and UK governments.

12 An early demolition of the evidential basis for the existence of WMD was made in S. Ritter and W. Rivers Pitt, *War on Iraq*, New York: Context Books, 2002.

13 S. Zunes, 'The Bush Administration's Attacks on the United Nations', 13 February 2003,. Online. Available HTTP: <http://www.commondreams.org/views03/0213–05.htm> (accessed 10 May 2004).

14 Oxford Research Group is one of many NGOs analysing the effects of the Iraq War on the progress of the War on Terror. See P. Rogers, 'The War on Terror: Winning or Losing?', ORG Briefing Paper, 2003. Online. Available HTTP: <http://www. oxfordresearchgroup.org.uk> (accessed 10 May 2004).

15 A good example is the powerful 'Statement on Iraq' by the World Council of Churches, 2 September 2003. Online. Available HTTP: <http://www.pcusa.org/ oga/newsstories/wcc-iraq.pdf> (accessed 10 May 2004).

16 J. Preston, '500,000 at Peril in Iraq War, UN Reports', *New York Times*, 9 January 2003. 'As many as 500,000 people in Iraq could suffer injuries and require medical treatment if the United States and its allies launch a war there, according to a confidential United Nations contingency planning report.'

17 C. Ahlstrum, *Casualties of Conflict*: 'In the later decades of this century the proportion of civilian victims has been rising steadily: in World War II it was two thirds, and by the end of the 1980s it was almost 90 per cent.' Cited in *UNICEF: Children in War*, 1996. Online. Available HTTP: <http://www.unicef.org/sowc96/1cinwar.htm> (accessed 10 May 2004).

18 UNHCR, 'Report of the Secretary-General on Women, Peace and Security', 16 October 2002. Online. Available HTTP: <http://ods-dds-ny.un.org/doc/UNDOC/ GEN/N02/634/68/PDF/N0263468.pdf> (accessed 10 May 2004).

19 P. Rogers, 'Iraq: Consequences of a War', ORG Briefing Paper, 2002. Online. Available HTTP: <http://www.oxfordresearchgroup.org.uk> (accessed 10 May 2004).

20 Medact, 'Collateral Damage: the health and environmental costs of war on Iraq', November 2002. Online. Available HTTP: <http://www.medact.org/tbx/pages/ sub.cfm?id=556> (accessed 10 May 2004).

21 Online. Available HTTP: <http://www.humanshields.org/index.htm> (accessed 10 May 2004).

22 Online. Available HTTP: <http://pubpages.unh.edu/~mwherold/> (accessed 10 May 2004).

23 T. Deen, 'Afghanistan Starting to Look Like Iraq', 6 May 2004. Online. Available HTTP: <http://www.antiwar.com/ips/deen.php?articleid=2488> (accessed 10 May 2004).

24 Online. Available HTTP: <http://www.iraqbodycount.net/background.htm> (accessed 10 May 2004).

25 UNHCR, 'Basic Principles on the Use of Force and Firearms by Law Enforcement Officials', 1990. Online. Available HTTP: <http://www.unhchr.ch/html/menu3/ b/h_comp43.htm> (accessed 10 May 2004).

See also Human Rights Watch, 'The War in Iraq and International Humanitarian Law – Frequently Asked Questions on Occupation': 'May an occupying power issue "shoot on sight" orders to soldiers or police in order to stop looters or otherwise maintain security?', 16 May 2003. Online. Available HTTP: <http://www.hrw.org/ campaigns/iraq/ihlfaqoccupation.htm> (accessed 10 May 2004).

26 IBC Press Release, 'Over 1,500 violent civilian deaths in occupied Baghdad', 23 September 2003. Online. Available HTTP: <http://www.iraqbodycount.net/press.htm#pr5> (accessed 10 May 2004).

27 To elaborate briefly on these points: if Saddam's mass graves, and the victims they hold, deserve to be recorded, then why not our mass graves and our victims? There is no contradiction in wishing for both to be known. We record the latter because no-one else is doing so. This is not the case for Saddam's victims: see 'USAID Documents the Horrors of Iraq's Mass Graves in a New Publication and Film', 17 March 2004. Online. Available HTTP: <http://www.usaid.gov/press/releases/2004/pr040317.html> (accessed 10 May 2004).

28 The primary responsibility for the deadly effect of sanctions rested with those who imposed them on Iraq, not Saddam, even if he exacerbated their effect. If the goal was to reduce the suffering they caused, sanctions could have been lifted or substantially modified years ago – instead of being enforced so harshly they became 'genocidal in their impact', in the words of the UN's Human Rights Coordinator for Iraq, Denis Halliday, who resigned over the issue, as did his successor, Hans von Sponek. This story remains hugely under-reported to this day, according to 'Burying Genocide – The UN "Oil For Food" Programme', *Media Lens Alert*, 23 April 2004. Online. Available HTTP: <http://www.medialens.org/alerts/2004/040423_Burying_Genocide.HTM> (accessed 10 May 2004).

29 Tony Blair himself stated on the eve of the war that '[Saddam Hussein] will be responsible for many, many more deaths even in one year than we will be in any conflict', but offered no grounds for this declaration. House of Commons Debates, 19 March 2003. Online. Available HTTP: <http://www.parliament.the-stationery-office.co.uk/pa/cm200203/cmhansrd/vo030319/debtext/30319-03.htm> (accessed 10 May 2004).

    The best predictions available at the time of Blair's statement would have been based on extrapolations from Amnesty International's annual human rights monitoring reports, which showed that judicial and extra-judicial executions by the Iraqi regime numbered in the 'hundreds' up until 2000 and in the 'scores' in 2001 and 2002. Online. Available HTTP: <http://web.amnesty.org/web/ar2001.nsf/webmepcountries/IRAQ> (accessed 10 May 2004). <http://web.amnesty.org/web/ar2002.nsf/mde/iraq?Open> (accessed 10 May 2004). <http://web.amnesty.org/report2003/irq-summary-eng> (accessed 10 May 2004).

    In a comprehensive debunking of any 'post-facto' justifications for the war, Human Rights Watch simply concluded: 'In sum, the invasion of Iraq failed to meet the test for a humanitarian intervention.' K. Roth, 'War in Iraq: Not a Humanitarian Intervention', Human Rights Watch, January 2004. Online. Available HTTP: <http://hrw.org/wr2k4/3.htm#_Toc58744952> (accessed 10 May 2004).

30 Online. Available HTTP: <http://www.iraqbodycount.net/editorial_june1203.htm> (accessed 10 May 2004).

31 L. Tayler, 'Civilians under Attack', *Newsday*, 27 March 2004: 'The number of Western civilian deaths pale in comparison with the 584 US troops, 96 from other coalition nations, and an estimated 10,631 Iraqis – scores of them US-trained Iraqi police – who've been killed since the war began.' (A rare instance of an unattributed, exact IBC number. More common are unattributed estimates: '9,000 to 11,000' etc.)

32 N. Price, 'Iraqi Civilian Deaths', *Atlanta Journal Constitution*, 10 June 2003: 'Iraq's dying government did try to track civilian casualties, and appeared to have done so accurately for as long as its communications withstood the bombing.'

33 The Coalition Casualty Count is at <http://lunaville.org/warcasualties/Summary.aspx>. Its principal researcher, Patricia Kneisler, has told us that Iraq Body Count inspired her own, slightly later, project.

34 L. Harding, 'The Choice for Iraq's Rag-tag Army: Be Killed by the US or by Saddam', *Guardian*, 8 February 2003.

35 F. Biedermann, 'What happened to Iraq's army? Nobody knows how many thousands of Iraqi soldiers were killed – and the U.S. doesn't seem eager to let reporters find out', *Salon*, 22 April 2003.

36 H. Friedman, 'Psychological Operations in Iraq: No-Fly Zone Warning Leaflets to Iraq, 2002–2003', 20 March 2003. Online. Available HTTP: <http://psywar.org/noflyzone.php> (accessed 10 May 2004).

37 L Smith MP, letter to *Independent*, 18 September 2003.

38 Online. Available HTTP: <http://www.iraqbodycount.net/editorial_feb0704.htm> (accessed 10 May 2004).

39 British diplomats letter.

40 Online. Available HTTP: <http://www.google.com/corporate/tech.html> (accessed 10 May 2004).

41 A list of over 150 press references to IBC and its work can be found at <http://www.iraqbodycount.net/coverage.php>.

42 'After the Fall: One Year's Civilian Death Toll', *Independent*, 9 April 2004.

43 Examples include the health charity Medact, 'Continuing Collateral Damage: The Health and Environmental Costs of War on Iraq', 11 November 2003; Amnesty International, 'Iraq – One Year On the Human Rights Situation Remains Dire', 18 March 2004; Institute for Public Policy Research (IPPR) and Friedrich Ebert Stiftung, 'Promoting Effective States', January 2004. IPPR, 'Human Rights and Global Responsibility', mirrors a long-standing IBC demand: 'The UK Government should … record and publish the number of people killed because of coalition military action in Iraq, and consider the introduction of a structured system of compensation for the dependants of those killed'.

44 Jeremy Corbyn MP, 9 September 2003. Online. Available HTTP: <http://www.parliament.the-stationery-office.co.uk/pa/cm200203/cmhansrd/vo030909/debtext/30909–19.htm> (accessed 10 May 2004). Lord Rea, 28 January 2004. Online. Available HTTP: <http://www.parliament.the-stationery-office.co.uk/pa/ld199900/ldhansrd/pdvn/lds04/text/40128–12.htm> (accessed 10 May 2004). Alice Mahon MP, 25 March 2004. Online. Available HTTP: <http://www.parliament.the-stationery-office.co.uk/pa/cm200304/cmhansrd/cm040325/debtext/40325–25.htm> (accessed 10 May 2004).

45 R. Nader, 'Creating Blowbacks and Backlashes', 15 May 2004. Online. Available HTTP: <http://www.antiwar.com/rep/nader.php?articleid=2580> (accessed 10 May 2004).

46 A. Nelson, Billi Bierling, 'Foreign Ministry Abandons Iraq Victims' List', *Swissinfo*, 31 March 2003.

47 'Toting the Casualties of War – Beth Osborne Daponte Talks about How Her Estimates of Iraq's Gulf War Dead Got Her in Deep Trouble with the White House', *Businessweek*, 6 February 2003.

14 Story development

Or, Walter Mitty the Undefeated*

Alex Danchev

The fall of Baghdad, the toppling of Saddam and his statuary, and the declared end of 'major combat operations' in Iraq permitted the resumption and intensification of hostilities on the home front. In Britain, three official inquiries were soon under way. Two of them were parliamentary. The Foreign Affairs Committee inquired into 'The Decision to go to War in Iraq', reporting in July 2003. The Intelligence and Security Committee inquired into 'Iraqi Weapons of Mass Destruction – Intelligence and Assessments', reporting in September 2003. The third and most consequential was quasi-judicial, or rather post-judicial, for not only did Lord Hutton retire as a Lord of Appeal in Ordinary (a Law Lord) before the publication of his report in January 2004, but the proceedings of his inquiry into 'the circumstances surrounding the death of Dr David Kelly' contrived to render obsolete the proceedings of all previous judicial inquiries, whilst at the same time exposing and overshadowing the amateurish efforts of the muddling parliamentarians.[1] After Hutton, in the wake of another preemptive announcement from Washington, there came a surprise fourth: an inquiry into 'the gathering, evaluation and use of intelligence on WMD', led by Lord Butler, patterned on a similar US Commission, and precipitated by the shocking declaration from the resigning head of the Iraq Survey Group that there appeared to be no WMD to survey – prompting one sardonic commentator to observe, 'it's like me holding an inquiry into why my fridge is empty'.[2]

Inquiries are a continuation of politics by other means, as Clausewitz might have said. In the nature of the case, these inquiries were more political than most. They were steeped in high politics, and played for high stakes. Hutton in particular held the fate of the prime minister in his hands, as the prime minister himself effectively acknowledged. Variously directed and separately prosecuted, they had some family resemblance, as to characters and plot, and a cumulative demonstration effect. In terms of democratic accountability they functioned as a kind of overseers' chorus, stage left. Wittingly and unwittingly, one inquiry shed light on another – a welcome seasoning of the democratic stew. Sometimes they took it upon themselves to address each other, rhetorically, engaging in something like apostrophe, to say nothing of aspersion. The Foreign Affairs Committee recommended that the Intelligence and Security Committee should be reconstituted. The Intelligence and Security Committee passed comment on the Foreign Affairs Committee's conclusions, rather in the manner of a school report; 'could do better' was the inescapable inference.[3] Even before Hutton had spoken, the Liaison Committee of the House of Commons decided to review the working of select committees in the light of his inquiry – a potentially significant move – as the Hutton Report coolly noted.[4]

Regardless of their status or provenance, each according to its means addressed fundamentally the same matter. W. J. M. Mackenzie's marvellous 'translation' of the Plowden Report on the control of public expenditure applies with equal force to all four: 'It turns out that the real problem is about the nature of government in general, and of the British Government in particular. This is what we are discussing, but of course we have to wrap it up in Mandarin prose.'[5] In other words, they rendered an account to the nation of the way in which the responsibilities of government were discharged, to adopt the terms of reference for the Franks Inquiry into the events leading up to the Argentine invasion of the Falkland Islands in 1982, often invoked as precedent or exemplar, first for Hutton, and then for Butler.[6] Inquiries, therefore, are expressions of democratic politics – symptoms – and also investigations of fitness for purpose – tests – at once probe and gauge. The reports that issue out of them are the fables of our age, narratives in which things irrational and sometimes inanimate are made to act and speak with human interests and passions, for the purpose of moral instruction; tales in literary form, not necessarily probable in their incidents, intended to improve.[7] The fabulist must needs be a modern Merlin. The hopes vested in a Franks or a Hutton are impossibly high: for the wisdom of a seer, the moral clarity of a demigod. Such paragons are hard to find. Franks was at bottom a moral philosopher, which only added to his aura. He had also lived the life.[8] Hutton had the office (Lord of Appeal sounds just right for the part) but not the compass. Unwise in the ways of the world, the judge may not be the best judge of the nation's privy councils.

First into the lists was the Foreign Affairs Committee (FAC), one of the departmental select committees, 'appointed by the House of Commons to examine the expenditure, administration and policies of the Foreign and Commonwealth Office and its associated public bodies', chaired by Donald Anderson, a Labour loyalist.[9] The FAC's inquiry was a shambles, and its report little more than a confession of ignorance. That was not entirely the FAC's fault, though it surely did not help itself. It rushed the job – no one could get to the bottom of all this in a bare four weeks, including several days spent taking evidence. It was bound and gagged by party loyalties, most particularly by its invariable practice of voting, paragraph by paragraph, on every point of contention. Above all, the FAC was tractable to a fault. When it came to the questioning or arraigning of witnesses, the FAC did as it was told. 'Allegations of politically inspired meddling cannot credibly be established,' the committee concluded, rather nebulously, of the intelligence on Iraq's weapons of mass destruction.[10] Politically inspired meddling is precisely what scuppered the FAC.

To fulfil its remit the FAC depends upon the cooperation of its target, the Foreign and Commonwealth Office, and, especially in this instance, certain elements of the Cabinet Office. It functions, in effect, by grace and favour of the government. In the forbidden realm of national security, where need to know trumps right to know, parliamentary scrutiny of the executive is a charade. Donald Anderson and his merry men set themselves the right question, but the FAC proved utterly incapable of answering it. Operationally, it was hamstrung from the start. In the matter of the decision to go to war in Iraq, the government paid it no heed. The sirs of the secret state contemptuously ignored it. All it got for its pains was five hours of the Foreign Secretary's time; 'limited extracts' from a single intelligence assessment, read to it in private session like a bedtime story; and a flea in the ear from the over-mighty Alastair Campbell. Understandably frustrated, the FAC complained loud and long of this treatment in its report:

> We are strongly of the view that we were entitled to a greater degree of cooperation from the Government on access to witnesses and to intelligence material. Our Chairman wrote to the Prime Minister (requesting his attendance and that of Alastair Campbell [his Director of Communications and Strategy]); the Cabinet Office Intelligence Coordinator [Sir David Omand]; the Chairman of the Joint Intelligence Committee [John Scarlett]; the Chief of Defence Intelligence [Air Marshal Sir Joe French]; the Head of the Secret Intelligence Service [Sir Richard Dearlove]; and the Director of GCHQ [Dr David Pepper]. None of them replied. It was the Foreign Secretary [Jack Straw] who informed us that they would not appear. The Chairman wrote a further letter to Alastair Campbell and after an initial refusal he agreed to appear. We asked for direct access to Joint Intelligence Committee (JIC) assessments and to relevant FCO papers. That was refused, although some extracts were read to us in private session.
>
> In contrast, the Prime Minister has repeatedly said in the House [of Commons] that he will cooperate with a parallel inquiry by the statutory Intelligence and Security Committee (ISC). This is hardly surprising, since [the ISC] was appointed by and reports to him, and it meets entirely in private. The Foreign Affairs Committee, on the other hand, was appointed by and reports to the House of Commons, and we meet almost entirely in public. We believe that our inquiry is the more credible of the two, and that it would have been in the Government's best interests to have given full cooperation.[11]

The FAC was also used. With a calculating display of righteous indignation, Alastair Campbell hijacked their hearings to pursue his vendetta against the BBC in general and the correspondent Andrew Gilligan in particular – a classic sideshow – browbeating the committee into concluding, prematurely, 'that on the basis of the evidence available to us Alastair Campbell did not exert or seek to exert improper influence on the drafting of the September dossier [*Iraq's Weapons of Mass Destruction: The Assessment of the British Government*]'. That verdict was reached only by means of the chairman's casting vote, after deadlock on a non-committal amendment.[12] It is thought to have been influenced by the last-minute intervention of Nicholas Soames, a former Conservative minister, who met the head of the Secret Intelligence Service to hear for himself whether 'improper influence' had been exerted. He then issued a statement to the Press Association to the effect that he had been assured that it was entirely untrue to say that the government had in any way interfered with the flow of secret intelligence (which was not quite the point at issue). Soames's intervention was inspired by the selfsame Alastair Campbell.

After it had reported the committee was tossed a bone. The MPs were given the chance to question the government scientist and weapons inspector David Kelly, now under suspicion as the fount and origin of the main assault on the citadel of Tony Blair's self-belief – and the belief system of the Blairite apparat – that the intelligence on Iraq's WMD had been 'sexed up', in the jargon, which is to say that the case for war had been deliberately oversold. If this charge could be upheld, the Iraq War of 2003 was not a good war, as advertised, but a bad one; indeed, it was a war of the worst kind, a war of false pretences. The warmongers were at best disingenuous and at worst mendacious. WMD were weapons of mass distraction, as the prime minister told British troops, after the battle, in a Freudian slip of the tongue. The case made was a conscious misrepresentation. Nuclear, biological and chemical weapons were lumped together as a threat. Readiness to launch in forty-five minutes was hyped as a fact. Long-range delivery was accepted as a given. Conflation, exaggeration and obfuscation served to ratchet up the pressure for pre-emption. Sceptics had their motives impugned and their character traduced. The French were not the only cheese-eating surrender monkeys of old Europe. Thomas Friedman, the Bart Simpson of the *New York Times*, opined:

> I have no illusions that if the Bush team had only embraced Kyoto the French wouldn't still be trying to obstruct the Americans in Iraq. The French are the French. But unfortunately now the Germans are the French, the Koreans are the French, and many Brits are becoming French.[13]

On the streets, dissentient masses marched into oblivion. Overdosed with dossiers, the public was debated into silence, as the sociologist Richard Sennett said.[14] Misrepresentation bred 'misinterpretation', to borrow Sir Richard Dearlove's expression, for example over what exactly could be made ready in forty-five minutes (battlefield munitions, if anything, as the Hutton Inquiry served to reveal).[15] The misinterpretations went studiously uncorrected. 'War is sell.'[16]

The moral and political reckoning could not be evaded. For those most deeply implicated, the reckoning was severe. For the missionary intervener, 'master of the pulpit philippic and courtroom defence', it was piercing through and through.[17] Tony Blair is famously a pretty straight sort of guy. He says so himself. If Margaret Thatcher's political persona was constructed on the premise 'I am right', it has been argued, Tony Blair's is constructed on the premise 'I am good.' Dan Keohane analyses that formation elsewhere in this book. Being good means blazing sincerity and breast-beating annunciation. The rhetorical keynote is honest belief ('I honestly believe ...'): *frank-seeming*, as Alan Bennett has remarked. *Time* magazine's correspondent at the Hutton Inquiry made a similar observation. 'In two and a half hours of apparently frank testimony – always thoughtful and reasoned, passionate when passion was called for – Blair gave a masterful performance.'[18]

Sexing-up threw frank-seeming into confusion. The sedulously promoted self-image was shot. Honest belief began to look as frazzled as the man himself. People who believe themselves to be the incarnation of good have a distorted view of the world, Tzvetan Todorov has argued.[19] A new image gained currency, subtly subversive, imprinted in the photographer Rankin's eerie portraits of Blair as Billy Bob Thornton in a Coen brothers' *film noir*, and abetted by a heart scare: a frame of fallibility, at root moral. Ominously, *Newsweek* used the Rankin portraits as the backdrop to a cover feature on 'The Twilight of Tony Blair'.[20] The word was out. 'We look in vain for this man's convictions, beyond a negative version of Ecclesiastes with victory the prize for the strong', in Edward Pearce's blood-curdling exegesis. 'Blair is about power shallowly perceived and public show shimmeringly done, right down to the dreadful sincerity.'[21] The message carried. The prime minister was crooked timber – not Blair but Bliar, as the cover of the *Economist* and the placards of the demonstrators alike proclaimed. 'If he told you the time,' said a man queuing to get into the Hutton Inquiry, 'you'd check your watch.'[22]

Sexing-up was the nub of the story purveyed by Andrew Gilligan, to which Tony Blair and his alter ego Alastair Campbell took such visceral exception. It found an echo in quarters usually as silent as the grave. Hans Blix, the tight-lipped chief UN weapons inspector (terminated with prejudice by the Anglo-American crusaders) mentioned nothing so indelicate, but did venture to suggest 'over-interpreting'.[23] The interpreters themselves were restive. Giving evidence to the Hutton Inquiry, Dr Brian Jones, the former head of the nuclear, biological and chemical weapons section of the Defence Intelligence Analysis Staff, testified to professional concerns about 'a tendency ... to over-egg certain assessments' and professional suspicions of 'the spin merchants of this administration' – strong language from that clam-like conclave.[24] Jones subsequently put on record a meticulous statement of his disquiet, at once a demonstration of the intelligencer's art and a remarkable exposé. The secret world had spoken out.[25]

Speaking out caught on. Most extraordinarily, former chairpersons of the Joint Intelligence Committee, a cadre not given to riotous display, began openly to examine the gravamen of the charge. Their utterance offered no crumb of comfort to the government. 'Fishmongers sell fish; warmongers sell war,' Sir Rodric Braithwaite concluded a trenchant summary.

> Both may sincerely believe in their product. The Prime Minister surely acted in the best of faith. But it does look as though he seriously oversold his wares. The final judgement will be delivered not by the mandarins, the

judges, or the politicians. It will be delivered by the consumer – the British public.[26]

Dame Pauline Neville-Jones mused spaciously on the puzzling lack of evidence of WMD in Iraq three months after the fall of the regime. 'If you tell people you are going to war because there is an imminent threat to national security, and then in the aftermath nothing is found, it opens up a credibility gap of a kind which is dangerous in a democracy.'[27] Sir Paul Lever reflected on professional custom and practice. 'The language of JIC assessment is carefully chosen,' he pronounced carefully. 'The JIC spends a good deal of time agonizing over whether a particular phrase carries the right message.'[28] The message of these interventions was clear. Custom and practice had been overborne. A net assessment is not a clarion call. The shrill certainties of the Assessment of the British Government did not comport with the syntactical prudence of the British tradition, 'the judgements often hedged about with the subjunctives and conditionals of cautious prophecy', as Sir Percy Cradock has it.[29] 'Could' and 'may' mutated, Frankenstein-fashion, into 'can' and 'will'. That which was 'probable' or 'on balance likely' succumbed to absolute conviction. The analysis of intelligence is a fine art, and the assessments in which it finds expression are fine-tuned. Analysts have a Derrida-like devotion to the text. Semantics are a matter of life and death. Professional concerns about the government's dossier were in the first instance concerns about the drafting – about language – 'but language is the means by which we communicate the assessment so they were about the assessment', as Dr Jones tutored Lord Hutton.

What Brian Jones called the translation of probability into certainty is what Andrew Gilligan called sexing-up. The agent of that process was Alastair Campbell, the vulgarizer, his master's voice. The instrument was John Scarlett, Chairman of the Joint Intelligence Committee, the translator-in-chief. One of the strengths of the British system is that the JIC is a collegial enterprise. If there was an intelligence failure – if there were no WMD in the first place – then that was a collective failure, and the JIC (and the analysts, and the agencies) must hang together. With the passage of time it has become clear that there was such a failure, and that it was not confined to Britain. 'We were almost all wrong,' confessed the CIA's former chief weapons inspector in Iraq in January 2004.[30] That is worrying; ostensibly, it is what impelled the governments most immediately concerned (Britain, Australia, Israel) to follow the American lead and establish more inquiries, several months after the war, focusing directly, but secretly, on intelligence. Even more worrying, however, is the exploitation of that sparse and inadequate product – the vamping, the cherry-picking, the stovepiping, the cutting and pasting and plagiarizing that became a kind of force-feeding.[31] Sexing-up was not simply a failure – a failure of government – it was a disgrace. The taint of moral turpitude is what gave the story its political combustibility. As the Jacobeans knew, the relationship of ruler and intelligencer is full of dramatic potential. To focus on the shortcomings of the latter is to write a revenger's tragedy. Inquiring into intelligence may be politically convenient, especially in a presidential election year, but it is tantamount to shifting the blame. 'It's slime and defend,' as one Republican Party aide put it. The scurry of self-exculpation was one of the hallmarks of the Hutton proceedings: unedifying, but entertaining; and continued in camera, it is rumoured, before the noble Lord Butler.

The modern interface, centring on the chairman of the JIC, has vexed inquirers for decades.[32] In the Blair era it is a study in anomaly and co-optation. Appointed by the prime minister, the chairman reports to the Cabinet Office Intelligence Coordinator, who is a member of the committee; in this wonderland world, the chairman is outranked by several members of his committee. Ironically, unlike his predecessors, John Scarlett was a professional (a former SIS station chief in Moscow). Still it seems he did not keep his distance. 'Ideally, intelligence and policy should be close but distinct,' Percy Cradock writes sagely. 'The best arrangement is … separate but adjoining rooms, with communicating doors and thin partition walls, as in cheap hotels.'[33] This chairman was caught in the wrong room. Whatever his motives, he did Alastair Campbell's bidding. Scarlett's much-vaunted 'ownership' of the dossier was a sham (or a blind). He did not own the document in any meaningful sense. He merely looked after it for Campbell and his crew of information warriors. One of that eager-beaver brigade was christened 'Director of Story Development' by the Permanent Under-Secretary of the Foreign Office.[34] The sobriquet perfectly encapsulated the mentality of those at the heart of the project – and also, perhaps, the attitude of the less *engagé* in Whitehall.

How it worked emerged more fully in the course of the Hutton Inquiry. An early draft: 'Iraq's military forces maintain the capability to use chemical and biological weapons, with command, control and logistical arrangements in place. The Iraqi military may be able to deploy these weapons within 45 minutes of a decision to do so.' Among Campbell's 'drafting points' for Scarlett: ' "may" is weaker than in the [executive] summary'. The published version: 'Iraq has a usable chemical and biological weapons capability … which has included recent production of chemical and biological agents. … The Iraqi military is able to deploy these weapons within 45 minutes of a decision to do so.' Despite Campbell's modest disclaimer, story development did not stop there. The Prime Minister's Chief of Staff: 'Alastair – what will be the headline in the *Standard* on the day of publication? What do we want it to be?' The banner headline in the London *Evening Standard* on 24 September 2002: 45 MINUTES FROM ATTACK.[35] Nuance is a nuisance to the salesman.

The pattern traceable in Britain was replicated elsewhere among the belligerents, especially in the United States and in Australia. Intelligence was used or abused tendentiously to legitimate a certain worldview and to support a certain course of action. In Hans Blix's characterization – a parable of his own predicament – 'the witches exist; you are appointed to deal with these witches; testing whether there are witches is only a dilution of the witch hunt'.[36] This deformation was institutionalized and internationalized, as for example in the Office of Special Plans in the US Department of Defense (a sort of in-house alternative assessments staff), and in the clandestine dissemination operation of Operation Rockingham, a British intelligence cell. Some of the initiatives were so crude as to be self-defeating. The British government's plagiarized confection, *Iraq – its infrastructure of concealment, deception and intimidation*, the so-called 'dodgy dossier' of February 2003, is a case in point. Some were laughable. An academic acquaintance of the editor of the literary magazine *Granta*, a Middle East specialist, was asked by an intelligence agency in Washington if he would care to write a paper which would answer their question, 'Why Arabs Lie.'[37] Others were more sophisticated. The intimidation of intelligence staff by policy-makers in all of these countries has yet to be fully explored – pressurizing them to produce the required material, bypassing them if they proved unwilling or unable to do so, vilifying them if they rebelled or talked out of turn. Such practices raise serious questions about the character and conduct of the national security state *in extremis*. Politicization is a dirty word, but it may not be an inappropriate one.

This is evidently a matter of unusual delicacy. The inquiries to date do not do it justice. Strictly speaking it was outside Hutton's remit. Nevertheless he succeeded in exposing it as an issue, almost in spite of himself, an achievement perhaps too much taken for granted in retrospect. His report musters a good deal of incendiary material, but his treatment of it is disappointingly partial. It finds him at his most tortuous and least convincing, adrift in a sea of sub-clauses and speculation:

As the dossier was one to be presented to, and read by, Parliament and the public, and was not an intelligence assessment to be considered only by the Government, I do not consider that it was improper for Mr Scarlett and the JIC to take into account suggestions as to drafting made by 10 Downing Street and to adopt those suggestions if they were consistent with the intelligence available to the JIC. However, I consider that the possibility cannot be completely ruled out that the desire of the Prime Minister to have a dossier which, whilst consistent with the available intelligence, was as strong as possible in relation to the threat posed by Saddam Hussein's WMD, may have subconsciously influenced Mr Scarlett and the other members of the JIC to make the wording of the dossier somewhat stronger than it would have been if it had been contained in a normal JIC assessment. Although this possibility cannot be completely ruled out, I am satisfied that Mr Scarlett, the other members of the JIC, and the members of the assessment staff engaged in the drafting of the dossier were concerned to ensure that the contents of the dossier were consistent with the intelligence available to the JIC.

The term 'sexed-up' is a slang expression, the meaning of which lacks clarity in the context of the discussion of the dossier. It is capable of two different meanings. It could mean that the dossier was embellished with items of intelligence known or believed to be false or unreliable to make the case against Saddam Hussein stronger, or it could mean that whilst the intelligence contained in the dossier was believed to be reliable, the dossier was drafted in such a way as to make the case against Saddam Hussein as strong as the intelligence contained in it permitted. If the term is used in this latter sense, then because of the drafting suggestions made by 10 Downing Street for the purpose of making a strong case against Saddam Hussein, it could be said that the government 'sexed-up' the dossier. However, in the context of the broadcasts in which the 'sexing-up' allegation was reported and having regard to the other allegations reported in those broadcasts I consider that the allegation was unfounded as it would have been understood by those who heard the broadcasts to mean that the dossier had been embellished with intelligence known or believed to be false or unreliable, which was not the case.[38]

Hutton's definitions of sexing-up had the advantage or disadvantage of following the prime minister's construction of the allegation. They clearly did not exhaust the possibilities; nor did they foreclose the debate. His speculation about 'subconscious influence' invited ridicule and duly received it.[39] Curiously enough, speculation about the unconscious was prefigured in the report of an Australian Parliamentary Joint Committee, *Intelligence on Iraq's Weapons of Mass Destruction*, completed in December 2003, shortly before the Hutton Report, but published a few weeks after it. Australia, like Britain, had been divided by the war. John Howard, like Tony Blair, had stood shoulder to shoulder with George W. Bush. 'Howard's war', like Blair's, was a driven affair, deeply unpopular, and deeply suspect among many government officials.[40] In this context the committee sought to discover whether 'overt pressure [was] brought to bear on the intelligence agencies to provide assessments to suit a war policy or whether the pressure of a "policy running strong" created a mind set, an unconscious skewing of judgements towards a known end' (issues further complicated in the Australian case by an acknowledged dependence on Anglo-American intelligence, another potential source of pressure). Its report is careful to return an open verdict; but the drift of its conclusion is plain enough:

The Committee notes the assurances of both the ONA [Office of National Assessment, waggishly rendered Office of Nodding Agreement] and DIO [Defence Intelligence Organization] on the question of their objectivity and independence. It accepts their declarations that there was no overt pressure from Government to change assessments. The Committee has received no evidence that political pressure was applied to the agencies. However, the Committee is aware that a fine distinction might often be made between 'being relevant to the policy issues of concern to the Government' [ONA's formulation] and catering to the policy concerns of the Government. Changes did occur in the nature and tone of some assessments. The sudden variation in ONA's assessments between 12 and 13 September 2002 is difficult to explain. ... It is so sudden a change in judgement that it appears ONA, at least unconsciously, might have been responding to 'policy running strong'. The compilation was made at the request of the Department of

Foreign Affairs and was intended to be the basis of Ministers' speeches. However, DIO comments 'that the final product was not formally cleared by the contributing agencies'.[41]

In Britain, the charge of sexing-up placed the onus of responsibility firmly where it belonged: with the policy-makers. Tony Blair's attack dog Alastair sniffed the air and smelled a scandal. He, who routinely dismissed unwelcome news stories as 'bollocks', 'complete bollocks' and 'bollocks on stilts', reacted very differently to this one.[42] He wrote in his diary of a firestorm developing. The image is significant. Not only is it suggestive of the way the story caught and spread (and slow-burns still). It is even more revealing of the way in which it engulfed No. 10 and the Cabinet Office, eating away at the very fabric of the social contract, as Tony Blair and his accomplices struggled desperately to regain control. 'It was grim,' Campbell recorded, 'it was grim for me, grim for TB and there is this huge stuff about trust.'[43] The Prime Minister's Foreign Policy Adviser, Sir David Manning, referred squeamishly to the 'strong feelings' washing round the inner circle. 'It was seen as a pretty direct attack on the integrity of the Prime Minister and officials at No. 10 that they would try to persuade the Chairman of the JIC to massage or revise his conclusions, his recommendations, for political advantage.' For Manning it was also an attack on the processes of government.

> I did not see it, myself, as a row between two particular individuals [Campbell v. Gilligan], or between No. 10 and a particular part of the media. I saw it as something where it was important that we tried to restore elements of trust which had been challenged by this very direct assault on the integrity of people and of process.[44]

For Tony Blair it was personal. An interview with the *Observer* in July 2003 produced a telling outburst:

Observer: Do you agree with Alastair that the BBC has lied over the claims that it made?

Blair: Well, it is untrue, that statement [Gilligan's report] is untrue. The idea that I or anyone else in my position frankly would start altering intelligence evidence, or saying to the intelligence services 'I am going to insert this' is absurd. Now look, what we are saying is something very simple, for about three or four weeks this has been run at me as a charge, and there couldn't be a more serious charge, that I ordered our troops into conflict on the basis of intelligence evidence that I falsified. You could not make a more serious charge against a Prime Minister. The charge happens to be wrong. I think everyone accepts that the charge is wrong.

O: But they are still standing by their story.

B: I am astonished, if they are saying it is still accurate, on what basis are they saying that?

O: They are saying it is a credible source.

B: Well, whether they had a source or not, only they know. But the claim
         that the source was making, if that was the claim that they were
         making, was not true, and that has been said by myself, by the Foreign
         Secretary, by the heads of the Joint Intelligence Committee and the
         intelligence services.

O: What do you think of the BBC's reporting on this issue?

B: There will be various reports that come out and we will make
         comments then.

O: But you must have a view. As you say, they continue to report on it,
         that surely raises big questions about the credibility of the BBC.

B: The issue surely is this, that if people make a claim and it turns out to
         be wrong, they should accept it is wrong.

O: And apologize?

B: Well I am not getting into that – look, as far as I am concerned, the
         issue of what the BBC has done, I take it as about as serious an attack
         on my integrity [as] there could possibly be, and the charge is untrue
         and I hope that they will accept that. I think they should accept it.
         That is all I am going to say.[45]

For a brief moment the emergence of 'the source' seemed to be good news
for the government, or at any rate good news management. David Kelly was
indubitably an expert, with stronger ties to the secret world than he or others
let on, but he was not of that world, strictly, as had been bruited about by the
BBC.[46] In fact it was difficult to establish exactly which world he did inhabit,
so many reporting lines and email accounts and identities and desks did he
have, in the United Nations, in the Foreign Office, in Counter-Proliferation,
in Defence Intelligence. Fortunately, from No. 10's point of view, he had not
been centrally involved in the compilation of the government's much-
punished dossiers, though he was only too well aware of the drive for
compelling new material, and ideally placed to offer his own assessment of
the claims made for Iraq's chemical and biological warfare capability.
Evidently, he had a conscience, and there was something on it, as yet
unknown. In the apparatchiks' book, David Kelly was unsound – and expendable – but he gave every appearance of being a man of measure. For an
embattled government his public identification was a standing reproach to the
BBC. It was also a propaganda coup against the weasel tendency, the
doubting Thomases, and the conspiracy theorists. Parading him in front of
the FAC would serve to underline the point. Schooled in safe topics – witness
and committee alike were warned off 'tricky areas' such as the wider issue of
Iraqi WMD and the preparation of the dossier – he might even be induced to
repudiate Andrew Gilligan and squash the story.[47] In official circles there
were high hopes of David Kelly. Months later, redacted entries from Alastair
Campbell's diary were imparted to the Hutton Inquiry, with electrifying
effect. They told an intriguing tale:

Spoke to [Geoff] Hoon [Secretary of State for Defence] who said that a man had come forward who felt he was possibly Gilligan's source ... and was being interviewed today. GH said his initial instinct was to throw the book at him, but in fact there was a case for trying to get some sort of plea bargain. Says that he'd come forward and he was saying yes to speak[ing] to AG [Andrew Gilligan], yes he said intel[ligence] went in late [into the September dossier], but he never said the other stuff. It was double-edged but GH and I agreed it would fuck Gilligan if that was his source.[48]

Campbell, his capo, and their mafia, elected and unelected, wished for nothing more than the source to become the stool pigeon.

Hopes were dupes. After several days of softening up in the precincts of the Ministry of Defence – including what John Scarlett was pleased to call 'a proper security-style interview'[49] – Kelly was bear-led into the ring by his MoD minders. The FAC had its day, televised for the occasion. The tone was set by the attention-seeking Andrew Mackinlay: 'I reckon you are chaff; you have been thrown up to divert our probing. Have you ever felt like a fall guy? You have been set up, have you not?'[50] Kelly squirmed and stonewalled. He gave little away – less than Alastair Campbell would have wished – but this was a very public humiliation. Even worse (but unnoticed at the time), he was ambushed by a well-informed question from David Chidgey about his dealings with yet another journalist, Susan Watts.

Kelly was a true arcanist. He felt a responsibility for the public understanding of the scientific mysteries in which he dealt. That was part of his job; yet it seems he was indiscreet. The line between briefer and leaker is a fine one. Kelly had talked too freely of his professional concerns. 'Something seems to happen to people when they meet a journalist,' Janet Malcolm has observed, 'and what happens is exactly the opposite of what one would expect. One would think that extreme wariness and caution would be the order of the day, but in fact childish trust and impetuosity are far more common.'[51] So it was, perhaps, with the wary Dr Kelly. His employers waved penalties and procedures at him, but an experienced weapons inspector is not so easily intimidated. He had his pride. He did not make a clean breast of it to his evasive line manager, Bryan Wells, Director of Counter-Proliferation and Arms Control in the Ministry of Defence; he never would. The security-style interview failed to achieve its purpose. The circus in Committee Room 15 with the FAC was an ordeal without a purgation, at once sordid game and damp squib. Kelly had been fingered, and he knew it. He knew also that he was the author of his own fate – fate loomed large in his Baha'i faith. His innermost feelings are impossible to gauge. This garrulous figment of other people's imaginations was a closed book: closed and locked like an old-fashioned diary, even with his own family. He told a friend he had been totally thrown by David Chidgey's question. He told his wife he felt physically sick. Did he have the stomach-churning sense of letting someone down – himself, perhaps – or of being found out?

He is facing death but not yet dying
and when asked what he is thinking about he replies:
Nothing; of nothing: leave thy idle questions.
I am i'th'way to study a long silence:
To prate were idle. I remember nothing.
There's nothing of so infinite vexation
As man's own thoughts.[52]

David Chidgey had been primed by none other than Andrew Gilligan. The tables had been turned. Reprehensibly, the reporter had shopped his source. Campbell and Hoon were destined to be disappointed. Their ruse had misfired. It did not fuck Gilligan. It fucked Kelly instead.

The next day the unhappy source appeared before the Intelligence and Security Committee. This was a more civilized grilling.[53] As the FAC complained, the ISC always meets in private. It is a recent creation, established under the Intelligence Services Act of 1994 'to examine the expenditure, administration and policy' of the three intelligence and security agencies: the Security Service (MI5), the Secret Intelligence Service (MI6) and the Government Communications Headquarters (GCHQ).[54] Chaired by Ann Taylor, another Labour loyalist, it reports directly to the prime minister and through him to Parliament, by the publication of its reports. Its members are notified under the Official Secrets Act, as they say, and therefore operate within 'the ring of secrecy'; unlike other parliamentary committees, or their comparators in other Parliaments, they are privy to highly classified material, including complete assessments and the raw intelligence behind them. As a quid pro quo, in consultation with the committee, the prime minister excludes any parts of its reports 'prejudicial to the continuing discharge of the functions' of the agencies. These suppressions are indicated by three asterisks, as if blasphemous. In certain passages of the ISC's annual reports the effect is to reduce the content to gibberish, but occasionally it borders on the comic. In the course of his interrogation David Kelly was asked to give a fuller picture of the intelligence he saw. His reply begins: 'Certainly. I see the intelligence reporting concerned with Iraq and ***, with regard to chemical and biological weapons, that arrives in the Proliferation and Arms Control Secretariat [of the MoD].'[55] To date, the committee says, no material has been excluded without its consent. Nonetheless, the reports are rather too full of *** for many people's liking. When it comes to democratic accountability, this is not entirely reassuring. The ISC is far from being the prime minister's creature, but its investigatory muscle is weak. Moreover, it cannot comprehend intelligence performance as a whole: confining its remit to the agencies serves to exclude other parts of the machine, the Joint Intelligence Committee and the Defence Intelligence Staff, for example, not to mention the Cabinet Office Intelligence Coordinator. It may be that in practice the committee strays beyond (at the prime minister's pleasure), but its formal remit makes nonsense of its function.

As for its business with Dr Kelly, the committee concluded robustly that 'the dossier was not "sexed up" by Alastair Campbell or anyone else'.[56] At the same time the committee excelled itself in pointing up significant examples of misleading presentation – of misrepresentation – all of them tending to inflate the threat.

> The 45 minutes claim, included four times, was always likely to attract attention because it was an arresting detail that the public had not seen before. As the 45 minutes claim was new to its readers, the context of the intelligence and any assessment needed to be explained. The fact that it was assessed to refer to battlefield chemical and biological munitions and their movement on the battlefield, not to any other form of chemical or biological attack, should have been highlighted in the dossier. The omission of the context and assessment allowed speculation as to its exact meaning. This was unhelpful to an understanding of this issue.[57]

Much the same applied to the claims made about Saddam's continued production of chemical and biological weapons, and about his capacity to launch a strategic nuclear strike (or indeed any kind of nuclear strike).[58] By then, it seems, robustness had given out. The ISC drew no conclusions from the pattern of misrepresentation it had discerned.

The following afternoon, 17 July 2003, David Kelly committed suicide.

In death as in life he was smeared, persistently, by everyone from the Permanent Under-Secretary of the Ministry of Defence to the Prime Minister's Official Spokesman. Complaisant Cabinet ministers joined in with a will. Jack Straw put it about that he was 'too junior' to be of much use. (The two men had been contemporaries at the University of Leeds. 'Straw will not remember me,' commented Kelly drily, 'because I was not a political animal.') Geoff Hoon let fall the opinion that he was 'no martyr', and that in days of yore his indiscretions would have incurred a rather stiffer penalty. The imputation of treachery, if not treason, was hard to miss. According to Sir Kevin Tebbit, he was 'rather eccentric' and 'a bit weird' (this accompanied by a knowing circular movement of the finger to the head, indicative of the deranged).[59] According to Tom Kelly, he was 'a Walter Mitty-style fantasist'.[60] *Pace* Hutton, there appears to have been a concerted attempt to undermine his credibility by painting him as dreamy, or loopy, or both: an unreliable source, manifestly, who had difficulty telling truth from fiction. Truth is a difficult concept, as one of Tebbit's mandarin predecessors informed another inquiry. Kelly had deviated from the official version. For that he was denounced and excommunicated by 'the ever-present evangelists of the mores of the moment'.[61] Hans Blix had a similar experience. Brian Jones was given a milder form of the same treatment. In each case it was a put-up job. In Kelly's case the suggestion of unreliability was nothing more than scurrilous fabrication. James Thurber, however, was a humorist of uncommon prescience. His original conceit, 'The Secret Life of Walter Mitty' (1939), may be more apropos than we think:

'I've been looking all over this hotel for you,' said Mrs Mitty. 'Why do you have to hide in this old chair? How did you expect me to find you?' 'Things close in,' said Walter Mitty vaguely. 'What?' Mrs Mitty said. 'Did you get the what's-its-name? The puppy biscuit? What's in that box?' 'Overshoes,' said Mitty. 'Couldn't you have put them on in the store?' 'I was thinking,' said Walter Mitty. 'Does it ever occur to you that I am sometimes thinking?' She looked at him. 'I'm going to take your temperature when I get you home,' she said.

They went out through the revolving doors that made a faintly derisive whistling sound when you pushed them. It was two blocks to the parking lot. At the drugstore on the corner she said, 'Wait here for me. I forgot something. I won't be a minute.' She was more than a minute. Walter Mitty lighted a cigarette. It began to rain, rain with sleet in it. He stood up against the wall of the drugstore, smoking. … He put his shoulders back and his heels together. 'To hell with the handkerchief,' said Walter Mitty scornfully. He took one last drag on his cigarette and snapped it away. Then, with that faint, fleeting smile playing about his lips, he faced the firing squad; erect and motionless, proud and disdainful, Walter Mitty the Undefeated, inscrutable to the last.[62]

David Kelly's death transformed the political landscape. John Sloboda writes elsewhere in this book about Iraq Body Count, the tally of civilian deaths in that faraway country, the collateral damage too often discounted in the Western calculus of war. Closer to home, it was as if a British Body Count of one was of greater consequence than an Iraq Body Count of 11,000. Seen from the bunker in Downing Street, the government's 'game of chicken' with the BBC had claimed its first victim. No more was heard of that corrosive pastime (a coinage of the ineffable Official Spokesman). A shaken prime minister immediately announced an inquiry – into the death not the war – and in the same breath an inquirer: Brian Hutton, a former Lord Chief Justice of Northern Ireland; a trial judge, practised in defining and deciding, with a nose for rascality of the criminal rather than the official variety; a habitual clarifier, of narrowing inclination, conventional cast of mind, above-political aspect, and what one shrewd acquaintance dubs pedestrian integrity. A pre-emptive war had been followed by a pre-emptive inquiry, with tightly drawn terms of reference, a premium on expedition, and the safest pair of hands that Tony Blair's old friend Charlie Falconer could find, in sole charge.[63]

Hutton had the distinction of disappointing first one constituency, then another, making history in the process. The Hutton Inquiry was an event. (Conducted with great dignity, as the Kelly family acknowledged.) It had everything, even a body. As well as an inquiry, it was an inquest, an identity parade, a scandal sheet, a courtroom drama, a piece of grand guignol, a soap opera – 'not the daily diet of froth; not turning serious politics into soap opera, debasing it, turning it into an endless who knew what, when, as if politicians simply competed on villainy', ran some prime ministerial rhetoric at the time, affording a glimpse of the nameless bitterness in the breast of the wounded politician.[64] 'The most eloquent message concerns the Blair Government,' wrote Hugo Young in one of his last, coruscating columns:

> It must be right at all times. Above all, the integrity of the leader can never be challenged. He never did hype up the intelligence. He didn't take Britain to war on any other than the stated terms. Any suggestion of half-truth, or disguised intention, or concealed Bushite promises is the most disgraceful imaginable charge that deserves a state response that knows no limit. That's how a sideshow came to take over national life. Now it seems to have taken a wretched, guiltless man's life with it. Such is the dynamic that can be unleashed by a leader who believes his own reputation to be the core value his country must defend.[65]

Here was the gauge of democratic politics. 'The Kelly tragedy is a pimple on the hide of a bigger elephant,' as Young put it, indelicately.

> The British political class is in deep crisis. Its promises are not trusted, its words are not believed. The people who are meant to be our leaders no longer get any real purchase on the public mind. … The political class needs rescuing from a predicament that poisons the life of the entire country.[66]

The huge stuff about trust swirled around every war leader in the Western world, not least the self-proclaimed 'War President' of the United States.

The inquiry began to take shape in the mind's eye. The element of theatre was impossible to ignore. The judge himself was a figure out of central casting, *circa* 1950. For Alan Bennett, Hutton had the look of the actor Bernard Archard, 'who specialized in policemen of the middle rank who played things by the book'.[67] No sooner had he finished taking evidence than *Justifying War: Scenes from the Hutton Inquiry* opened at the Tricycle Theatre in London, the dialogue fashioned from the transcripts.[68] To the surprise of the uninitiated, it was gripping. *Justifying War* was filmed and shown on TV. It was not the only televised reconstruction.[69] The leading man may or may not have missed his calling, but his inquiry was in its way a very post-modern phenomenon: serial reproduction, media saturation, multiple Hutton.

It was a drama in four acts. Act one was the evidence-taking: 24 days' worth, over 900,000 words of transcript, from anyone who was anyone (and even someone who was no one, known only as Mr A), plus some 800 documents comprising more than 10,000 pages of evidence, right down to the personal emails. All of this material was published without delay on the inquiry's website: a triumph of technology and democracy.[70] It constituted the biggest cache of contemporaneous documentation on the inner workings of government ever disgorged – so soon that it was hardly yet classified, so sensitive that in normal circumstances it might never have seen the light of day. Many of the documents, especially the personal emails, proved highly embarrassing to their perpetrators.

The nature of government was exposed, in all its horrible fascination, as if turning over a stone. Did Hutton himself grasp the significance of what he had caused to be revealed? He admitted afterwards that he had not realized what an impact the website would have.[71] In this sense, the inquiry exceeded both his brief and his expectations. It took on a momentum of its own. It had unintended consequences. Hutton and his sponsors made an alarming discovery. The safe pair of hands was not so safe after all. In more ways than one, the politics of the process eluded him.

To some observers it was meat and drink. Anthony Sampson, at work on the latest edition of his *Anatomy of Britain*, was reminded of the Watergate tapes. 'You had this glimpse of the intensity, and almost the vulgarity, of power.' For Sampson, the war against the BBC was similarly cancerous. 'The atmosphere of vendetta was very creepy. This obsession with revenge was distorting the whole system.'[72] From elsewhere in the audience there were gasps of amazement. 'Not only is government conducted more informally than we had imagined – all coffee mugs, sofas, shirtsleeves and malice,' marvelled Alan Watkins. 'What is more surprising is that this very lack of formality is preserved by technology rather than destroyed by it. What is more surprising still is that Lord Hutton has been able to find out about it.'[73]

Act two had overtones of Samuel Beckett. It consisted entirely of waiting for Hutton, the invisible saviour, who had withdrawn to write his report – an opportunity to regain control. For four months the tension mounted. The Conservative Party attempted a number of pre-emptive strikes of their own, including a dossier, *Compendium of Sourced Material and Key Facts*, which of course 'in no way seeks to prejudice the inquiry'.[74] The bookmaker William Hill offered odds of 20:1 on Tony Blair resigning on or before 31 January 2004. Discreet arrangements were made to provide counselling for civil servants subject to criticism. Elaborate precautions were taken to prevent leaks. Six parties represented at the inquiry were given copies of the report twenty-four hours before publication: the government, the BBC, the journalists Andrew Gilligan and Susan Watts, the Kelly family, and the Speaker's counsel, because it touched on parliamentary procedure. All parties were required to declare in writing where their copies would be kept, and to sign an undertaking not to reveal the contents in advance of publication. Hutton had learned from his predecessors.[75] The report went under armed guard to unknown printers, unknown even to the security services, it was said, since they too had an interest to declare. In spite of all, the headlines were leaked, ignominiously, to the *Sun*.[76] It did not augur well for the denouement.

Act three was short and sweet. The Hutton Report was published, digested and regurgitated in disbelief.[77] Seldom has a saviour fallen so swiftly. Hutton had resolved his main task into an adjudication between the government and the BBC, apparently conceived as an even-handed 'finding of fact', but received as absolution for the one and mortification for the other.[78] Not only did he find in favour of the government, his own arguments were premised on the government's contentions. Thus there was no dishonourable or underhand or duplicitous strategy by the Government covertly to leak Dr Kelly's name to the media. ... I consider that in the midst of a major controversy relating to Mr Gilligan's broadcasts which had contained very grave allegations against the integrity of the Government and fearing that Dr Kelly's name as the source for those broadcasts would be disclosed by the media at any time, the Government's main concern was that it would be charged with a serious cover up if it did not reveal that a civil servant had come forward.[79]

The MoD's slipshod staff care was subject to minor criticism, mitigated by the fact that, 'because of his intensely private nature, Dr Kelly was not an easy man to help or to whom to give advice'.[80] The victim himself, it seemed, might be blamed for contributory negligence. The BBC's practices and procedures were severely dealt with. As a document the report was a toilsome assemblage, bulky with testimony, full of rigmarole and repetition. As a narrative it was almost incoherent. As a morality tale it was a bad joke.

Act four followed without intermission. The BBC was convulsed. The chairman resigned. The director-general resigned. After some prevarication, Andrew Gilligan resigned. Internal inquiries bred internal strife. Bad feeling lingered for many months; and in the news division, according to some, a certain editorial timorousness. For the world's finest public broadcasting corporation, the Hutton Report was a calamity. Hutton was said to be aghast at what he had wrought.

The government was first of all relieved, then pleased, then disconcerted. Elation surged and faded like an electric current. Complete vindication curdled overnight. Alastair Campbell crowed; Tony Blair did not. The government had won 12–0, as the papers said, but it was a Pyrrhic victory. In the political marketplace, Hutton's judgment was strangely weightless. To the dismay of its author, the *Report of the Inquiry into the Circumstances Surrounding the Death of Dr David Kelly* was written off as a whitewash. The findings were dismissed, more in sorrow than in anger. There was a good deal of disappointment, and in many quarters an almost personal sense of betrayal. Expectations had been raised that were not fulfilled. The report belied the inquiry. The last act was a let-down. The long-awaited fable of fables was neither enchanting nor believable. It failed in many respects, but in this above all: it failed to achieve closure. The people still sought reassurance. Lurking suspicions remained. Trust and credibility were unappeased. Hutton begat Butler. The caravan rolled on.

A lesson from the master:

Once upon a time there was a bird sanctuary in which hundreds of Baltimore orioles lived happily together. The refuge consisted of a forest entirely surrounded by a high wire fence. When it was put up, a pack of foxes who lived nearby protested that it was an arbitrary and unnatural boundary. However, they did nothing about it at the time because they were interested in civilizing the geese and ducks on the neighbouring farms.

When all the geese and ducks had been civilized, and there was nothing left to eat, the foxes once more turned their attention to the bird sanctuary. Their leader announced that there had once been foxes in the sanctuary but that they had been driven out. He proclaimed that Baltimore orioles belonged in Baltimore. He said, furthermore, that the orioles in the sanctuary were a continuous menace to the peace of the world. The other animals cautioned the foxes not to disturb the birds in their sanctuary.

So the foxes attacked the sanctuary one night and tore down the fence that surrounded it. The orioles rushed out and were instantly killed and eaten by the foxes.

The next day the leader of the foxes, a fox from whom God was receiving daily guidance, got up on the rostrum and addressed the other foxes. His message was simple and sublime. 'You see before you,' he said, 'another Lincoln. We have liberated all those birds!'

Moral: Government of the orioles, by the foxes, and for the foxes, must perish from the earth.[81]

Notes and references

* I am grateful to Rodric Braithwaite, Michael Herman, Ibrahim al-Marashi, Pauline Neville-Jones, Gary Samore, and a number of others who wish to remain anonymous, for their willingness to discuss these matters; to Diane Birch and Jonathan Lewis at Nottingham, for guidance on Lord Hutton's legal form; to fellow contributors at Keele, for comments on the work in progress; and to John MacMillan, inspirer of this project.

1 Hutton retired early, as planned, on 11 January 2004, two weeks before the publication of his report; he had announced his intention to stand down before receiving this extraordinary last commission.

2 A. Pearson, 'We Are All Labour's Scorned Lovers …', *Evening Standard*, 4 February 2004.

3 Cmnd. 5972, Intelligence and Security Committee, *Iraqi Weapons of Mass Destruction – Intelligence and Assessments*, London: TSO, 2003 [hereafter ISC Report], Annex B. Conclusion 28 is the ISC's rejoinder to reconstitution.

4 HC247, *Report of the Inquiry into the Circumstances Surrounding the Death of Dr David Kelly CMG*, London: TSO, 2004 [hereafter Hutton Report], para. 461.

5 W. J. M. Mackenzie, 'The Plowden Report: A Translation' [1963], reprinted in R. Rose (ed.), *Policy Making in Britain*, London: Macmillan, 1969, p. 274. The original was Cmnd. 1432, *Control of Public Expenditure*, London: HMSO, 1961.

6 A. Danchev, 'Introduction', *The Franks Report*, London: Pimlico, 1992, originally Cmnd. 8787, *The Falkland Islands Review*, London: HMSO, 1982.

7 These definitions follow *The Chambers Dictionary*, with only a little licence.

8 See A. Danchev, *Oliver Franks*, Oxford: Clarendon, 1993.

9 HC 813-I, Foreign Affairs Committee, *The Decision to go to War in Iraq*, Vol. I, Report and Formal Minutes, London: TSO, 3 July 2003 [hereafter FAC Report], preliminary matter.

10 FAC Report, para. 86.

11 FAC Report, paras 6–7.

12 FAC Report, para. 84; Formal Minutes, p. 98. The Conservative members, together with the Liberal Democrat and the maverick Andrew Mackinlay, favoured the non-committal amendment proposed by John Maples ('we are neither equipped nor willing to arbitrate that dispute'); the Labour members favoured the verdict quoted, exonerating Alastair Campbell. The committee split again, after the fact, on the issue

of writing to Campbell for an explanation of 'inconsistencies' in his evidence to them – painfully evident in the fuller disclosure to the Hutton Inquiry – deciding against on the chairman's casting vote. *Independent*, 19 March 2004.

13 Quoted in A. Danchev, 'Greeks and Romans: Anglo-American Relations after 9/11', *RUSI Journal*, 148, 2003, p. 19.

14 R. Sennett, 'Mistaken on trust', *Guardian*, 12 July 2003.

15 According to the Chairman of the JIC, 'battlefield mortar shells or small calibre weaponry, quite different from missiles'. Hutton evidence, 26 August 2003.

16 A coinage of S. Rampton and J. Stauber, *Weapons of Mass Deception*, New York: Penguin, 2003.

17 Hugo Young's phrase. *Observer*, 28 September 2003.

18 Bennett diary, 29 May 2003, in *London Review of Books*, 8 January 2004; J. Chu, 'Winning the Battle, Losing the War', *Time*, 8 September 2003.

19 T. Todorov, trans D. Bellos, *Hope and Memory*, London: Atlantic, 2003.

20 S. Mcguire, 'The Final Chapter', *Newsweek*, 29 September 2003.

21 Letter to the *London Review of Books*, 8 May 2003.

22 Quoted in J. Cassidy, 'The David Kelly Affair', *New Yorker*, 8 December 2003.

23 BBC1 'Breakfast with Frost', 8 February 2004. See H. Blix, *Disarming Iraq: the Search for Weapons of Mass Destruction*, London: Bloomsbury, 2004.

24 Hutton evidence, 3 September 2003; Hutton Report, paras 186–94.

25 B. Jones, 'There was a Lack of Substantive Evidence …', *Independent*, 4 February 2004. See also the follow-up interview, *Independent*, 10 February 2004. Clearly, the experience was a deeply troubling one. Jones has remained a careful and sceptical observer of the nature of government ever since. See, e.g., 'I've Finally Made up my Mind about Iraq', *Independent*, 24 April 2004.

26 Letter to the *Financial Times*, 10 July 2003. See also his speech to the Royal Institute of International Affairs, 'Defending British Spies: The Uses and Abuses of Intelligence', 5 December 2003. Braithwaite was Chair of the JIC in 1992–3.

27 BBC News 24 'Hardtalk', 4 July 2003; *Independent on Sunday*, 6 July 2003. Cf. her evidence to the FAC: minutes, 18 June 2003, Q360–79. Neville-Jones was Chair in 1993–4. During the period in question she was also a governor of the BBC, the arch enemy.

28 Interview on Channel 4 'Dispatches', 23 January 2004. Lever was Chair in 1994–6.

29 P. Cradock, *Know Your Enemy*, London: Murray, 2002, p. 2. Cradock was Chair in 1985–92.

30 'David Kay at Senate hearing', 28 January 2004. Online. Available HTTP: <http://www.cnn.com/2004/US/01/28/kay.transcript> (accessed 3 February 2004). Kay's unbeatable credentials gave his testimony special resonance: he was a former hawk, he had supported the war, and he had led the Iraq Survey Group for seven fruitless months before drawing his own conclusions and tendering his resignation. For further pointed comment see B. Jones, 'Why John Scarlett is the Wrong Man for the Job', *Independent*, 8 May 2004; T. Powers, 'The Failure', *New York Review of Books*, 29 April 2004.

31 The pioneering work in this murky area has been done by that one-man inquiry, Seymour Hersh, e.g. 'The Stovepipe', *New Yorker*, 27 October 2003. See also T. Powers, 'The Vanishing Case for War', *New York Review of Books*, 4 December 2003.

32 See Franks Report, para. 319. Cf. M. Herman, 'Threat Assessments and the Legitimation of Policy?', *Intelligence and National Security*, 18, 2003, pp. 174–8.

33 Cradock, *Know Your Enemy*, p. 297.

34 Sir Michael Jay on Paul Hamill, whose electronic fingerprints were found all over the 'dodgy dossier' of February 2003. Afterwards Hamill was quietly removed from Whitehall and sent to Baghdad as a press officer for the embattled Coalition Provisional Authority. Poetic justice, perhaps. *Independent*, 25 June 2003; *Mail on Sunday*, 3 August 2003.

35 *Iraq's Weapons of Mass Destruction*, p. 17 (cf. executive summary, para. 6); Campbell to

Scarlett, 17 September 2002; Powell to Campbell, 19 September 2002; *Evening Standard*, 24 September 2002. The process can be followed in the Hutton Report, paras 198–215.

36 *Guardian*, 6 March 2004.

37 I. Jack, 'Introduction', *Granta*, No. 84, 2003, p. 7.

38 Hutton Report, para. 228. Cf. para. 220, which elaborates a little on the reporting. Transcripts of Andrew Gilligan's (and Gavin Hewitt's) original broadcasts appear in paras 32–3 and appendix 2.

39 He had invoked the unconscious before. In 1981, presiding at a trial of a British soldier who drove into a group of people in Londonderry and killed two of them, Hutton advised the jury 'to consider whether you think that perhaps unconsciously some of the witnesses … had a tendency somewhat to strengthen their evidence against the army'. Here the possibility is plainly not ruled out but in. Hutton went on to suggest that the driving, while reckless, might not have been unreasonable given the rioting going on at the time. The soldier was acquitted. See D. Morrison, 'My Report on Lord Hutton', *Guardian*, 3 February 2004.

40 See A. Broinowski, *Howard's War*, Melbourne: Scribe, 2003. Probably the best-known case of the dissident official is Andrew Wilkie, who resigned in protest from the Office of National Assessments just before the war, but there are others. Jane Errey, a former adviser to the Chief Defence Scientist, went on leave the day after the war began and was sacked a year later, allegedly because of her refusal to comply with the Department of Defence's line on WMD. Wilkie was vilified in similar but stronger terms to Kelly ('unstable, unreliable, flaky and irrational'). Unlike Kelly, he gave as good as he got. ('The government lied every time. It skewed, misrepresented, used selectively and fabricated the Iraq story.') He was interviewed by the FAC: evidence, 19 June 2003 (Q570–9).

41 Parliamentary Joint Committee on ASIO, ASIS and DSD, *Intelligence on Iraq's Weapons of Mass Destruction*, Canberra: Commonwealth of Australia, 2004, paras 3.32 and 3.38. 'Policy running strong' was an expression of W. B. Pritchett, former Secretary to the Department of Defence, in a submission to the committee.

42 Cassidy, 'Kelly Affair'.

43 Campbell diary, 1 June 2003, in *Guardian*, 20 August 2003.

44 Hutton evidence, 18 August 2003.

45 *Observer*, 6 July 2003. Online. Available HTTP: <http://observer.guardian.co.uk/Print/0,3858,4706903,00.html> (accessed 8 July 2003). See also the follow-up, *Observer*, 25 January 2004.

46 Kelly's résumé of his access and contacts, in evidence to the ISC, is in the Hutton Report, para. 112.

47 Hoon to Anderson, 11 July 2003, in *Guardian*, 22 August 2003.

48 Campbell diary, 4 July 2003, Hutton Report, para. 305.

49 Scarlett to Omand, 7 July 2003, Hutton Report, para. 58.

50 FAC evidence, 15 July 2003, Hutton Report, para. 103.

51 J. Malcolm, *The Journalist and the Murderer*, London: Granta, 2004, p. 32. In this instance, Kelly was keen to talk to Gilligan about his (Gilligan's) recent visit to Iraq.

52 J. Webster, *The White Devil* [1612], in J. Webster and J. Ford, *Selected Plays*, London: Dent, 1984, p. 91. I owe this reference to Christopher Ricks, who quoted some of it, unattributed, and to Sarah Grochala, who identified it for me.

53 To assist the Hutton Inquiry, the ISC passed on a redacted transcript of Kelly's evidence, together with extracts of Campbell's and Omand's, in a form suitable for publication. ISC Report, para. 23. Some of this can be found in the Hutton Report. See para. 112.

54 The statutory position is summarized in the preliminary matter of the ISC Report. The government also publishes formal responses to the committee's reports. See Cmnd. 6118, *Government Response to the Intelligence and Security Committee Report on Iraqi*

Weapons of Mass Destruction – Intelligence and Assessments, London: TSO, 2004, which comments on all of the conclusions highlighted here.

55 Hutton Report, para. 112.

56 ISC Report, para. 108.

57 ISC Report, para. 112.

58 ISC Report, paras 110 and 111.

59 Robbins to Sambrook, 17 July 2003, in *Guardian*, 14 October 2003. Tebbit said his words 'were not intended as a smear'. According to Campbell, he also called Kelly 'a bit of a show-off'. Campbell diary, 7 July 2003, in *Independent*, 23 September 2003.

60 *Independent*, 4 August 2003. Cf. Hutton Report, paras 380–1, 462–3.

61 P. Roth, *The Human Stain*, London: Vintage, 2001, p. 315.

62 J. Thurber, 'The Secret Life of Walter Mitty', *The Thurber Carnival*, New York: Harper, 1945, p. 51.

63 As Secretary of State for Constitutional Affairs, Falconer formally commissioned the inquiry. He also appointed its secretary, Lee Hughes, a senior civil servant from his own department. Hutton Report, paras 1 and 2.

64 Speech by the Prime Minister to the Labour Party Conference, 30 September 2003. Online. Available HTTP: <http://www.labour.org.uk/print.php?page_name=tbbournemouth> (accessed 7 October 2003).

65 H. Young, 'Kelly didn't Stand a Chance against the Frenzy of No. 10', 19 July 2003, reprinted in *Supping with the Devils*, London: Atlantic, 2004, pp. 309–10.

66 H. Young, 'If Politicians Want Power, They Must Give Some Away', *Guardian*, 22 July 2003. Cf. R. McKibbin, 'How to Put the Politics Back into Labour', *London Review of Books*, 7 August 2003.

67 Bennett diary, 2 February 2004, in *London Review of Books*, 19 February 2004.

68 R. Norton-Taylor (ed.), *Justifying War*, London: Oberon, 2003.

69 Notably BBC1, Panorama, 'A Fight to the Death', 21 January 2004.

70 The official site is: <http://www.the-hutton-inquiry.org.uk>. A guide to relevant Internet sites is included in the *Guardian*'s vade mecum, *The Hutton Inquiry and its Impact*, London: Politico's, 2004.

71 Hutton appeared before the Public Administration Committee of the House of Commons some three months after the publication of his report. *Guardian*, 14 May 2004.

72 B. Tonkin, 'Britain's Heart of Darkness', *Independent*, 23 April 2004. See A. Sampson, *Who Runs This Place?*, London: Murray, 2004.

73 A. Watkins, 'An Inquiry that Need Never have Happened', *Independent on Sunday*, 25 January 2004.

74 *The Hutton Inquiry: Compendium of Sourced Material and Key Facts*, 8 January 2004. Online. Available HTTP: <http://www.conservative-party.org.uk> (accessed 19 January 2004).

75 Both Franks and Scott had encountered serious difficulties with leaks and pre-publication spin. *Franks Report*, introduction, p. xv; R. Norton-Taylor, M. Lloyd and S. Cook, *Knee Deep in Dishonour*, London: Gollancz, 1996, pp. 27–35.

76 T. Kavanagh, 'Hutton: The Verdict', *Sun*, 28 January 2004.

77 A sample of early reviews: C. Gearty, 'A Misreading of the Law', *London Review of Books*, 19 February 2004; B. Urquhart, 'Hidden Truths', *New York Review of Books*, 25 March 2004; M. Zander, 'It's the Way You Tell Them', *Law Gazette*, 20 February 2004.

78 Hutton's expectations of his own report were leaked, after the fact, to the *Guardian*, 4 March 2004. His subsequent reflections on the inquiry, before the Public Administration Committee, tended only to reinforce the impression that he was unable or unwilling to grasp the political import of all he surveyed.

79 Hutton Report, para. 427.

80 Hutton Report, para. 439.

81 Thurber, 'The birds and the foxes', *Thurber Carnival*, p. 245.

Index